Doing Teacher-R

BOLD VISIONS IN EDUCATIONAL RESEARCH

Series Editors

Kenneth Tobin
The Graduate Center, City University of New York, USA

Joe Kincheloe
McGill University, Montreal, Canada

Editorial Board

Heinz Sunker, *Universität Wuppertal, Germany*
Peter McLaren, *University of California at Los Angeles, USA*
Kiwan Sung, *Woosong University, South Korea*
Angela Calabrese Barton, *Teachers College, New York, USA*
Margery Osborne, *Centre for Research on Pedagogy and Practice Nanyang Technical University, Singapore*
Wolff-Michael Roth, *University of Victoria, Canada*

Scope
Bold Visions in Educational Research is international in scope and includes books from two areas: *teaching and learning to teach* and *research methods in education*. Each area contains multi-authored handbooks of approximately 200,000 words and monographs (authored and edited collections) of approximately 130,000 words. All books are scholarly, written to engage specified readers and catalyze changes in policies and practices.

Defining characteristics of books in the series are their explicit uses of theory and associated methodologies to address important problems. We invite books from across a theoretical and methodological spectrum from scholars employing quantitative, statistical, experimental, ethnographic, semiotic, hermeneutic, historical, ethnomethodological, phenomenological, case studies, action, cultural studies, content analysis, rhetorical, deconstructive, critical, literary, aesthetic and other research methods.

Books on *teaching and learning to teach* focus on any of the curriculum areas (e.g., literacy, science, mathematics, social science), in and out of school settings, and points along the age continuum (pre K to adult). The purpose of books on *research methods in education* is **not** to present generalized and abstract procedures but to show how research is undertaken, highlighting the particulars that pertain to a study. Each book brings to the foreground those details that must be considered at every step on the way to doing a good study. The goal is **not** to show how generalizable methods are but to present rich descriptions to show how research is enacted. The books focus on methodology, within a context of substantive results so that methods, theory, and the processes leading to empirical analyses and outcomes are juxtaposed. In this way method is not reified, but is explored within well-described contexts and the emergent research outcomes. Three illustrative examples of books are those that allow proponents of particular perspectives to interact and debate, comprehensive handbooks where leading scholars explore particular genres of inquiry in detail, and introductory texts to particular educational research methods/issues of interest. to novice researchers.

Doing Teacher-Research
A Handbook for Perplexed Practitioners

Wolff-Michael Roth

Applied Cognitive Science, University of Victoria, Canada

SENSE PUBLISHERS
ROTTERDAM / TAIPEI

A C.I.P. record for this book is available from the Library of Congress.

Paperback ISBN   978-90-8790-061-8
Hardback ISBN   978-90-8790-062-5

Published by: Sense Publishers,
P.O. Box 21858, 3001 AW
Rotterdam, The Netherlands

Printed on acid-free paper

All Rights Reserved © 2007 Sense Publishers

No part of this work may be reproduced, stored in a retrieval system, or transmitted in any form or by any means, electronic, mechanical, photocopying, microfilming, recording or otherwise, without written permission from the Publisher, with the exception of any material supplied specifically for the purpose of being entered and executed on a computer system, for exclusive use by the purchaser of the work.

CONTENTS

Preface	vii
Glossary	xiii
INTRODUCTION: Getting Started as Teacher-Researcher	1
1 Investigating Student Learning during Collaborative Concept Mapping	13
2 Investigating Student Views on Collaborative Concept Mapping	51
3 Investigating how Students Learn in and Through Open Inquiry	89
4 Combining Quantitative and Qualitative Information: Teacher-Researchers Collaborate Investigating a Community of Practice	131
5 Analyzing Discourse: Text and Speech, Content and Interactions	177
6 Analyzing Conversations and Levels of Analysis: Learning With Information Technology	231
EPILOGUE: So What? What? and What For?: Criteria for Judging the Adequacy of Teacher-Research	263
References	271
Index	275
About the Author	279

PREFACE

Over the past two decades, an increasing number of teachers have enrolled in graduate school to obtain M.Ed., MA, or PhD degrees. Many of them have shown interest in conducting research within their schools and classrooms. There are also teachers who want to research what happens in their classroom without currently being enrolled in some program—I recently gave a plenary address at a conference in Singapore and noted a large number of teacher-researchers, which my hosts attributed to the encouragements on the part of the government. The literature on teachers and teaching has identified the need for teachers to be researchers. Yet all these calls for teachers to be researchers by and large are unrealized in teacher practice on the whole; and few teacher education programs institute the idea of the teacher as researcher as a regular feature of teacher training (the teacher education program at the University of Pennsylvania while Ken Tobin was its director has been an exception). As a professor teaching research design as well as qualitative and quantitative inquiry courses, I have come to realize that most of these teachers have the intention of doing research but find themselves in situations of not knowing where and how to begin, which topics to investigate, how to go about these investigations, which data sources to assemble, how to construct data, and what to do with your analyses—writing them up or using them to change their own classroom practices. It is not surprising then if many or most teachers engage in research only reluctantly and if they do so, perhaps, with some trepidation; others drag their feet for years, never getting to the point where they can submit their completed thesis that reports what they have done and learned. Many teachers are troubled by uncertainties due to the apparently complex and unexplained matters of research; they may be confused, baffled, bewildered, or confounded. In a word, they are *perplexed*. This precisely is the point where this book comes in: it is written for the perplexed teacher practitioner who, for one or the other reason, wants or has to enact research generally or one research study in particular. My tenor throughout this book is: there is little you have to lose. *Just do it!* As practicing classroom teacher you are in a position of strength because you know the situation to be researched so well, better probably than most university-based researcher ever could know your classroom situation. But caution! This strength also is a weakness: Because you are at school and in your classroom like a fish in the water, you may no longer recognize it as such. This, too, is the topic of this book: How does one make teacher-research as solid as it can be, drawing on its strength and keeping in check its weaknesses.

My own research as a teacher began while I was teaching physics full time and concurrently serving as a department head of science. (Actually, I had one course release to be able to accomplish my duties as a department head.) I had taken this position after a disappointing year at Indiana University, where I was trying to become a professor but where my senior colleagues told me that I was insufficiently talented to make it through the tenure barrier; they told me that I did not have what it takes to be a researcher let alone what it takes to be a good researcher. This only repeated a pattern that had made me quite insecure about my own abilities ever since I had entered high school. My parents used to ask me how I would ever be able to complete high school given the problems I appeared to having learning. Similarly, when I did my master's degree, the program advisor said that he only gives me two semesters in the program for physics teachers before I would drop out; and, when I spitefully decided to do a research degree, my professors seemed to indicate after I was successful that I did not have enough ideas to do a PhD. In any case, I remember that I rejected any idea of doing doctoral studies because I felt I was not inventive or innovative enough to do an advanced graduate degree. When my experienced colleagues at Indiana University articulated themselves negatively about me having what it takes to be a researcher, I decided to return to my roots, doing what I know to do best: teaching science. I was confident that I knew how to be a good teacher and I knew that I always have had good relationships with students. I never again wanted to hear about research and publications, and I was determined never to return to academic pursuits. During my first year in my new position, I began to ask questions about what students were doing while I did not watch them in their student-centered tasks. In fact, I realized that students spent most of the time on their own: even in the small classes I taught—e.g., 20 students or less—a 60-minute period amounted to less than 3 minutes per person. So I thought that it would be good to carry out some investigations to find out what students were doing while working on the tasks that we had negotiated or that they had decided to do. I spoke to my school administrators and they were excited about the idea of improving teaching through research. Re-energized about the prospects to do some research, I contacted the education faculties at five universities located within an hour's drive of our school. But there appeared to exist no interest in doing research concerning teaching and learning nor in having preservice teachers do their practicums at my school. I therefore launched into teacher-research all on my own.

For me, doing research in my own classroom and in those of my fellow teachers constituted a major turning point: a reorientation from using statistics to seek general patterns underlying learning to doing interpretive research to find out how best to attend to the needs of individual students and student groups. During the two years prior to my stint in Indiana, I completed a PhD degree at the University of Southern Mississippi, Hattiesburg. Given that I had obtained a Master's of science degree in physics before, it perhaps was not surprising that I also obtained a statistics minor as part of my doctoral studies and then studied correlations between cognitive variables (aural and visual short term memory), on the one hand, and learning variables (learning rates, developmental levels), on the other hand. As I returned to the classroom, however, I found that although quite interesting and playful, none of the information I could get from the statistical analyses was helping me to address the needs of individual students. In fact, the mediation of learning by these special needs is treated as error variance in statistical models: I came to understand that what my statistical models treated as noise was the very phenomenon of interest to me, a teacher who had to figure out the best ways of helping individual students to learn.

So I bought a video camera and started to record students both in and out-of class working on a variety of tasks. At night, I studied the tapes I had recorded during the day and, when I thought to have discovered something that interfered with student learning, changed the ways in which I set up the lessons often beginning with the next day. I continued recording students to see whether changes in the learning environment were bringing about the desired facilitation and whether change continued until students were learning at what I felt to be the limits of their capabilities. For example, when I realized that my physics students struggled with finding the trends in the data they collected, that is, how to find the best curve that fits through a set of data points, I introduced them to a statistics program that they could use to identify such curves and also provided them with an algorithm they could use in the context of a mathematical modeling program. (Most science students learn this technique near the end of their undergraduate programs, and social science students learn them only in statistics courses during graduate studies.) Only later did I find out that I had begun to be a teacher-researcher; and I got better at it over the course of the years conducting study after study on teaching and learning in my classrooms. To guide my interpretations of the data source materials I collected, I mostly read research articles attempting to see how the authors I read were linking interpretations and conclusions to the specific data they had presented; and I tried to understand how the authors of the articles selected particular data from the various data sources that they had accumulated in the course of their empirical work.

Although I had not intended so initially, I began to write up what I learned in a more formal way. Taking some published qualitative studies of teaching and learning as my models I wrote several reports based on the research I describe in this book. (In this, Ken Tobin was my "hero," and I pegged his articles against the wall behind my desk so that I could closely follow his patterns of writing to report my own research.) It turned out that all of this work was accepted for publication in highly ranked journals of science education—and this at a time when many university professors complained that it was difficult to get qualitative research published in these journals. After a few years of successfully publishing the research from my classrooms, and finding it difficult to put up with what I felt to be an oppressive school administration, I decided to try one more time the life in academia. This time it turned out to be a positive move—I have been at the university ever since. But I continued to do much of my research in classrooms where I shared the responsibility of teaching with resident teachers of the schools that hosted my research team.

For me, the progression from asking questions to buying a camera, recording students, and making sense of the recordings appeared to be straightforward. I had done what I recommended two pages earlier: I just did it, likely with all the naiveté that comes with such an approach. If any one of the universities that I contacted had reacted to my request for doing collaborative studies in our classrooms, my life may have unfolded differently. When I subsequently taught research design and quantitative and qualitative research methods, it became evident to me that designing research in one's own classroom is not so straightforward after all. This book is intended for teachers who, like the graduate students in my research courses, are perplexed with respect to the idea of doing research. Such perplexed practitioners I want to provide with an easily understandable narrative about the concrete praxis of doing research in their classrooms or in those of their teacher peers teaching next door in the same hallway or somewhere else in the same school. The fundamental idea underlying this book is to provide an easily accessible but nevertheless intellectually honest text that allows teachers to increase their agency with respect to research and to better understanding their praxis and the events in their classrooms.

In the preparation of this text about how to do research in one's own classroom, I draw on my experience of doing teacher research while being a high school teacher and department head. I use six concrete research studies that I conducted alone or with peers to describe the salient parts of any study including: what topic to study; issues of ethics and permissions from students, school, and parents; how and what data source materials to collect; how to structure these materials into resources that support arguments; how to construct data from the materials gathered; how to derive claims; and how to write a report/research study. Although I was teaching physics at the time, only one of the case studies explicitly focuses on experimenting in science; the other case studies are situated in contexts that can also be found in other domains, such as history, mathematics, social study, or drama education. I chose to organize this book according to the cases in the context of which I "teach" how to do research, because I believe that the context provides the details necessary for understanding why and how I make decisions, and what I would do differently today. I know that this is the major problem students of research method have: they do not understand how the general descriptions found in methods and methodology textbooks are related to the practical situations they face in their classrooms. Using a case-based approach, I am able to provide context that allows readers to tie my methods choices to situations that they likely are familiar with (though particulars will always differ).

1. I use an easily accessible style, with few references.
2. There are many (photo-) graphical materials, images, and copies of actual materials to provide concrete detail of all aspects of doing research in your own classroom or those of fellow teachers.
3. There is a glossary featuring all terms that may be less familiar to my readers.
4. There are grey-grounded inserts to highlight specific ideas associated with the current text.
5. A detailed index allows readers to find pertinent items throughout the book.
6. I provide critical commentary on the methods used based on the hindsight I have today after having conducted another 15 years of research.

PREFACE

In summary then, this text is intended for (beginning) perplexed practitioners, that is, teachers in training at the undergraduate and graduate levels, practicing teachers interested in conducting research both pursuing and not pursuing a higher degree, and gradate students and professors of education. It is addressed to all those teachers who study in countries where methods and design courses do not necessarily exist—e.g., the educators in some countries come through faculties where they hardly ever get to take a course on methods and design. The book will therefore appeal to a broad, international audience and is written at a level that allows easy access to issues all too often, and unjustifiably deemed to be esoteric.

* * *

In the course of becoming a researcher and theoretician, I have learned that works such as this book cannot be understood if we merely (try to) look into an individual brain case, in this case mine. Rather, such works are the outcome of social and material processes realized in concrete way by individuals; but these works do get associated with the name of an individual or small group of individuals. Here I want to express my gratitude to two individuals in particular who are part of my network that made this book possible: Ken Tobin and Sylvie Boutonné. Since 1990, the former has been a tremendous supporter, mentor, and friend without whom "Wolff-Michael Roth" as he is known today would not exist. His assistance and encouragement allowed me to take sometimes less-trodden paths and to engage in research that has challenged the status quo of the field. Sylvie, who for a period of four years conducted classroom research with me, has been a supportive partner for the past 14 years, providing me with the space and the emotional support that sustained scholarship appears to require. Thanks to Ken and Sylvie, this book has not remained an idea but come to be realized concretely in a relatively short period of time.

Victoria, Canada
January 2007

GLOSSARY

Any item in the text of an entry that is written in small capitals is itself an entry.

ANONYMITY In respect to human research ethics, this concept means that the identity of a research participant is entirely unknown, including to the researcher. This concept frequently is confused with CONFIDENTIALITY.

ASSERTION It is useful to articulate a research claim or pattern in the form of a full sentence or two, which assert(s) something about the DATA SOURCES at hand. Such assertions can then be tested in the complete set of evidentiary materials as to the extent of its validity. Researchers should focus on finding evidence that *disconfirm* an assertion as much as on finding all instances that are consistent with the assertion. An assertion functions like a hypothesis about patterns in the materials at hand.

CAUSE–EFFECT RELATIONS To determine whether one thing is the cause of another, experimental studies are required—in many disciplines, only double blind studies (neither participant nor experimenter know who receives treatment) are accepted as evidence for cause–effect relationships. Thus, to determine whether a teaching technique *causes* higher achievement, a laboratory experiment normally is required that keeps constant all factors but the technique.

CONFIDENTIALITY Pertaining to human research ethics, this concept refers to the fact that the identity of a research participant is known to a limited number of individuals who are held not to reveal any information about participants including their participation. For example, a researcher who interviews a participant knows about the participation of this individual. This concept frequently is confused with ANONYMITY.

CONFIRMATORY ETHNOGRAPHY I used this term to denote an ethnographic study that seeks to test the extent to which THICK DESCRIPTIONS and GROUNDED THEORY are TRANSFERABLE from a previous setting studied to another.

CONVERSATION ANALYSIS (CA) is a research PRACTICE that focuses on the turn-by-turn unfolding of human interaction (see chapter 6). In classical conversation analysis (CA), only talk was analyzed. Many applied CA studies now also include gestures, body positions, and prosody as materials to be analyzed.

CORRELATION A correlational relationship type simply indicates that the variations in two variables are associated positively or negatively. For example, the heights of persons tend to be correlated with their weights; the scores on intelligence tests tend to be correlated with school achievements. Correlations tell us nothing about causes, as other variables could have intervened or as the correlation has not causal underpinning (see CAUSE–EFFECT).

COVARIATION A term used to denote that the variation of one variable is related to a variation of another. Covariation may be CORRELATIONAL in nature or of a CAUSE–EFFECT type.

DATA Whatever bits and pieces are taken from a DATA SOURCE in support of some claim is a piece of data. Sometimes a sentence quoted from an interview serves as data, at other times it is a longer quotation; a piece of data also may consist of some student work in its entirety, such as a concept map. Data frequently is confused with DATA SOURCE (MATERIAL).

DATA SOURCE Whatever a researcher collects—e.g., written tests, videotapes, audiotaped interviews, and transcriptions constitute sources—constitutes a source of DATA.

DEPENDABILITY The extent to which the inquiry process is stable or consistent over time. This concept corresponds to that of RELIABILITY used in statistical research.

DESIGN EXPERIMENT a form of research that is tightly integrated with educational PRACTICE, often also drawing on experimental design and statistics in concert with interpretive methods of research.

DISCOURSE In the literature, this term is used in various ways. Sometimes, its sense is that of spoken language; at other times, its sense is that of all forms of written and spoken language, even including other representational forms such as diagrams, photographs, maps, and so on.

DISCOURSE ANALYSIS (DA) Depending on the sense in which DISCOURSE is taken, the analysis of discourse focuses on language use in spoken conversation or written media. When DISCOURSE is understood to include all representational forms that are used in a culture, then diagrams, photographs, film, and other media are also objects of analysis. See also DISCOURSE.

DISCURSIVE DEVICE When an individual has made contradictory statements based on two incompatible INTERPRETIVE REPERTOIRES, he or she may draw on some discursive device to explain how the contradiction can be resolved.

ECOLOGICAL VALIDITY The ecological validity of a study concerns the extent to which something observed under one type of conditions, for example, students doing a task after school when no other students are around, are representative of observations made of the same kind of task under different conditions, for example, students doing concept maps in class.

EPISTEMOLOGY refers to the theory or science of human knowledge and its methods or grounds. The term is distinct from but often discussed in the context of ONTOLOGY, a term denoting the bits and pieces a person or group perceives in a situation.

GLOSSARY

ETHNOGRAPHY literally means *writing* (Gr. graphein) *the people* (Gr. ethnos). The term may refer to a field of inquiry or to a research method. The field concerns itself with the scientific description of nations or races of men, with their customs, habits, and points of difference.

GENERALIZABILITY A term used in research employing statistics to articulate the extent to which the research results of a study can be said to be valid in a much larger group of people than the one that actually participated. In some (e.g., dialectical) approaches, the general is taken to be a concrete rather than an idealized general, always concretely realized in the specific observation at hand. In interpretive research, the equivalent term is TRANSFERABILITY.

GROUNDED THEORY refers to the results of an analytic process striving to represent THICK DESCRIPTIONS, that is, largely textual materials into a more parsimonious, often diagrammatic form (see chapter 5). A grounded theory only stands for the evidentiary materials available—whether it has relevance to any other situation is an empirical matter.

IDEOLOGY a way of seeing and understanding (an aspect of) the world that is taken as the normal, unquestioned state of affairs. A typical American ideology would be that surrounding the primacy of the individual and the fact that everyone can have success in American society. Ideologies are dangerous not only because they hide discrimination and injustices but also because those negatively affected often contribute to sustaining them. For example, working class students often take the same jobs their parents had unwittingly reproducing the injustices of a class society.

INTERACTION ANALYSIS is an analytic PRACTICE in which a group of researchers meet to collaboratively analyze a videotape owned by one of them. The videotapes generally show interactions. The intent of interaction analysis is to generate many different ideas about how to understand the recorded events.

INTERPRETIVE REPERTOIRE is a term used in DISCOURSE ANALYSIS to refer to particular forms of *discourse* taken to be unassailable for the moment. Participants can draw on these forms of DISCOURSE in supporting more contentious claims they make. When the same person draws on two incompatible interpretive repertoires, they may, if the situation requires, draw on some DISCURSIVE DEVICE to explain the contradiction away.

METHOD denotes the patterned way in which you arrive at making particular claims in a research study. This, therefore, is the term teacher-researchers should use, if at all, as the heading of the section in which they describe how they arrived at the results of their study. The term is often confused with METHODOLOGY.

METHODOLOGY is the science of method. Thus, in a strong sense only books in which different METHODS are discussed as well as their relative benefits constitutes a book on methodology. The term frequently is confused with METHOD.

MOMENT The smallest element that can be understood independently is taken to be the UNIT OF ANALYSIS. It may turn out that units of analysis have internal structures. But rather than thinking of these structures as elements we have to think of them as moments, which are smaller than elements—i.e., UNIT OF ANALYSIS—but cannot stand on their own. For example, in dialectical theories of culture, *structure* and *agency* form a pair of irreducible moments, each being constitutive of the other so that none can be used to define or theorize the other.

NEGATIVE CASE ANALYSIS can be thought of as the interpretive researcher's equivalent to experimental design. The THICK DESCRIPTION of a case or cases that do(es) not support a research claim or ASSERTION articulate(s) the conditions that mediate(s) the applicability of an interpretive concept or construct.

ONTOLOGY is the *science* (Gr. logos) of *being* (Gr. on). The term is used to refer to all those things that make up a particular situation for the people. That is, the term refers to the way we cut up the world into different pieces relevant to our actions. In the problem solving and cognitive science literature, ONTOLOGY is used to denote all those pieces of material and knowledge relevant to the problem at hand or all those categories that make up a computerized database. A checklist, too, establishes an ONTOLOGY, as it specifies precisely what there is to take account of; items that do not get captured in the checklist do not exist for the purposes of the checklist users (e.g., institutions). The term is distinct from EPISTEMOLOGY, which denotes the science concerned with how and what we know.

OPEN CODING usually occurs at the beginning of an analysis, where researchers read the data sources highlighting, underlining, and commenting upon anything that they find interesting even though they may not yet know. There is no structure yet available so that researchers can attempt to take a new look and perspective on a situation of interest. It is a way of establishing what there is, that is, the ONTOLOGY.

PRACTICE is the term used to denote a patterned action; thus, describing what someone does as OPEN CODING is describing a research PRACTICE. The term is distinct from PRAXIS.

PRAXIS is the term used to refer to the situated experience itself; thus, when I am doing what is denoted by the term OPEN CODING, then I am engaged in praxis. The term needs to be distinguished from PRACTICE.

PROGRESSIVE SUBJECTIVITY refers to the process by means of which researchers monitor and record their developing construction of patterns and understanding in the research site.

QUALITATIVE RESEARCH The term is often used to denote research that is based on the interpretation of data sources such as videotapes or transcribed interviews. The distinction of research into qualitative and QUANTITATIVE RESEARCH is not very useful, as one can do largely interpretive research but still use numbers to represent one's results.

QUANTITATIVE RESEARCH The term is often used to denote research that uses statistics to make inferences to extend research findings to populations of which the studied group is thought to be a small sample. See also QUALITATIVE RESEARCH.

REFLEXIVITY The term is used when an entity—an observation, a statement, a fact—about something else refers to itself. For example, researchers implement reflexivity when they not only claim that knowledge is socially constructed but also make explicit that this is the case for their own knowledge claims.

RELIABILITY refers to the extent to which an instrument—questionnaire, measure of intelligence, classroom environment scale—measures what it was designed to measure. A variety of indicators exist, including internal consistency, test-retest reliability, and interrater reliability.

SPEECH ACT THEORY attempts to explain real, ordinary conversation by making salient that speech simultaneously (a) is a physical event (utterance, *locution*), (b) is a form of action (illocution) to which intents can be ascribed, and (c) has effects (perlocution). A speech act can be understood only through the coincident analysis of all three functions, which inherently means going beyond the individual speaker.

THICK DESCRIPTION is a term that refers to the ETHNOGRAPHIC practice of providing detailed accounts of what happened in the situation of interest. The accounts are sufficiently detailed so that readers get a feel for what it means to be in the situation although they have not been there. This book, in a sense, constitutes a thick description of teacher-research as realized by one practitioner.

TRACER The term refers to some researcher-defined entity used to focus the collection of material evidence or to focus data analysis. For example, "water quality" might be used as a tracer, which means that the researcher investigating a community collects anything and everything her or she comes across relating to the term. This might involve collecting all newspaper articles in which the term appears, attending town hall meetings in which water quality issues are discussed, or following a consultant advising stream stewards on next steps in a creek improvement project.

TRANSFERABILITY In experimental research, which makes use of statistics, the concept of GENERALIZABILITY is used to discuss the extent to which the patterns in the data sources describe patterns of situations not included in the collection of material evidence. In interpretive research, the equivalent concept is *transferability*, which is the extent to which patterns identified in one situation are useful for understanding another situation. Transferability is an empirical matter rather than something that can be established a priori.

TRIANGULATION   Some researchers assume that the phenomena they attempt to understand, for example, human beliefs or knowledge, exist independent of the form of inquiry. In this case, different forms of inquiry or instruments can be used to assess the same phenomenon. Like geometers, they may use multiple instruments to eliminate the uncertainties and unreliability of any individual instrument. Triangulation is not an option when the researcher works with a theoretical framework in which actions are understood as being mediated by a variety of setting aspects. In this case, different perspectives or different materials lead us to different rather than the same understanding, meaning, and sense.

UNIT OF ANALYSIS refers to the smallest unit ("atom") that an entity under investigation can be reduced to. When the individual participant is the unit of analysis, researchers assume that (the results of) actions can be understood just by looking at the individual; social phenomena are understood as the sum total of all individuals contributing to the event. For example, many researchers assume that an interview can be reduced to what the interviewee says plus what the interviewer says. A different unit of analysis is chosen when a researcher assumes that a conversation (its transcription) cannot be attributed to the independent contributions of individuals—in which case the researcher cannot attribute a particular belief to the interviewee but can only make assertions about belief talk. Within a unit, smaller structures may be identified. These are referred to as MOMENTs. However, moments cannot stand on their own, because they always are determined by and determine other moments.

INTRODUCTION

GETTING STARTED AS TEACHER-RESEARCHER

There is no doubt about the fact that teachers who research their own practice are and become better practitioners. But how does one do research as a teacher? This book is for those perplexed by this question. Once teachers have decided that they want to do research, a second question poses itself: How does one get started doing research as a teacher? Given that you, the reader, have picked up this book means that you already have at least some interest in the topic and that you may consider doing research in your own classroom or, together with a colleague, in his or her classroom. For many individuals, being enrolled in a M.Ed. or MA in education program means *having to do* a project or a thesis, which generally requires graduate students to investigate something of their interest or something that leads to the generation of knowledge that interests others in the research community. Some individuals come to be interested in, and want to find out more about, teacher-research while they are enrolled in a teacher preparation program that emphasizes the idea that teachers as professionals *ought to be* interested in improving their own practices and therefore do research. For still others, as it has been in my own case, the interest in research may begin with the interest of becoming a better teacher. I was not so much thinking about doing research that meets the approval of other researchers and some research community. Rather, I was using teaching techniques that I had been reading about but which did not appear to work in my own classrooms. One of these techniques was *concept mapping*—some also call the technique *mind mapping*, yet others use the term *semantic networking*. I present the research I conducted in chapter 1, but, to get us started into this introduction, I articulate here just enough about what has happened.

In 1985, while teaching in a small Newfoundland community, I had bought a little book entitled *Learning How to Learn* (Novak & Gowin, 1984). I had been experimenting with a variety of student-directed laboratory inquiries but noticed that the students were not learning as much as I wanted them to. When I saw the book, I realized that my students might need to reflect more on their own understanding rather than just design and conduct their research. The authors of *Learning How to Learn* proposed two types of mapping: (a) concepts and (b) experiments that were to help students to think about their thinking. In the process of mapping, students are to learn how to learn. The technique I was particularly interested in was concept mapping because I saw in it a way of getting students to think about those concepts that the curriculum prescribed. I had already practiced something like it when I started teaching—at which point I had not taken teacher preparation courses—to organize my ideas about how all the concepts in my eighth- and ninth-grade courses related, how to find out how these concepts were connected, and what possibilities there were for sequentially ordering the different units

INTRODUCTION

throughout the year. In *Learning How to Learn* I had found specific instructions to teach the technique to students of all ages so that they could use concept mapping for their own benefit.

The technique asks students to write the concept words on pieces of paper (sometimes I already prepared those labels for them) and then to order them hierarchically. Once the concepts are ordered from most general to least general (most specific), students draw pencil lines between them and write one or more words on each line that connects two concept words. As proposed by the authors of the little book, I had my students do these mapping exercises individually. When they did so in class, I could see how difficult they found this type of activity. Although I tried the technique with my students repeatedly and over several years, it turned out not to be as useful as I hoped it to be.

Then, in 1989, I had the idea of putting students into groups and to ask them to produce, in the course of a 60-minute period, maps containing between 20 and 30 terms. I also had the idea of using a camera to record them so that I could subsequently view the tapes to better understand how students were going about the task, what their main difficulties were, where any hang-ups interfered with their learning, and so forth. To test the approach, I first asked a number of students whether they would do a concept map after school, in the science laboratory. When I figured out how to set up the camera, what camera angles to chose, and so on, I began to extend my investigations into the normal classroom situation. Whenever I did a concept mapping exercise, I recorded one group of students. But because I was teaching five classes—three eleventh-grade and two twelfth-grade physics courses—I was able to record many tapes that I subsequently watched and analyzed. In this way, the topic of my first teacher-researcher investigation had arisen from the difficulties I saw my students having and from my interest in devising strategies that would help them to learn how to learn using concept maps. The questions I had arose with the topic: How do students produce a concept collectively? What do individual students retain after having participated in a collaborative session? How do students settle differences? I later learned that asking the right question frequently is more difficult than it had been for me when I started my teacher research.

FINDING A (THE) TOPIC, RESEARCH QUESTION

In the course of teaching research methods courses for the past 15 years and having assisted my faculty colleagues in designing studies for which they sought funding from federal agencies, I have come to understand that asking the right kind of questions is not as apparent as it looks. Here I understand a *right* question to be one that usefully directs the research I design and conduct. Many teachers find it easy to define some general area of interest, like finding out more about how students actually make a concept map or how students actually design an experiment, set up the equipment, collect data, and then interpret the results, and write a report. But defining an area of interest does not yet constitute a research question: how you frame the question that actually drives what kind of research you conduct. That formulating the question in a particular way is not self-evident can be seen from the following: In my courses and in my grant support workshops, it usually takes about one hour during which a student or colleague may present the area of interest and frame an initial question. Then all other participants including myself attempt to clarify what the presenter *really* wants to find out.

What a researcher *really* wants to find out is not always clear. In one of the workshop it turns out that someone has decided a priori to do some statistical work to better understand the enrollment of new mothers in a school-based educational support network. Yet the question she asks, "How does an educational support network help new mothers to cope with the stresses of motherhood?," is not suited to do a study in which statistical comparisons and correlations are conducted. Because it is a process question, the appropriate answers are more likely obtained by conducting interviews with the new mothers who enroll. One of the problems of doing statistical comparative work lies in the fact that the new mothers would not enroll at the same point in time; and this leads to major problem for *generalization* using statistics because the process requires everything other than the treatment and control (support network, no support network) to be equal. (Unfortunately, my colleague abandoned this interesting and important study because she had received statistical training but felt uncomfortable doing the kind of interpretive research that her interest, as articulated in her questions, required.)

A teacher who asks the question "Does the teaching technique I developed lead to higher achievement?" implicitly sets up a study in which a cause–effect relationship is to be evaluated. But as the comparative adjective "higher" suggests, there is something to which the teaching technique is to be compared. Simply contrasting the grades students received prior to my new teaching technique to the grades the students received this year does not constitute a valid answer, because there are many other reasons why the grades may be higher, lower, or unchanged. A comparison requires a comparison group that can be considered the same in all aspects other than the treatment, i.e., treatment versus control. Thus, the students in the treatment group (the new teaching technique) have to compared to another, similar group of students taught in a different way but at the same time, in the same material, under the same conditions (e.g., mornings or afternoons), and so on.

> **Cause–Effect Relationships** cannot be established based on correlations—though this is common to medical research, where doctors investigate, for example, what healthy people have been eating and then suggest that the red wine they drink is the cause of a lower incidence of coronary heart disease. To be able to state that one thing is the cause of another, a controlled experiment has to be conducted.

A teacher who asks a question such as "How do students learn when they do their own experiments?" or "How do students write a collaborative essay?" implicitly sets up a learning process study. This teacher will have to collect materials that allow him or her to find out what students do from the moment they begin a task to the moment that they complete it. For example, a study attempting to answer the question "How do students collaboratively construct a concept map?" likely uses a video camera to record students construct concept maps from the moment they

INTRODUCTION

read the instructions to the moment they complete the transcription onto a sheet of paper (see chapter 1). As I found out in the course of my work, asking students afterward what they have done in the process of concept mapping and how they have arrived at the end result provides very different information—not in the least because after-the-fact accounts of what someone has done (as available from an interview) tend to differ from what they really have done (as available on the tape). This difference between what someone does and what the same person afterward says he or she has done shows has been observed not only among students of all ages but also among all sorts of practitioners including very educated and highly successful scientists.

> **"Quantitative" Versus "Qualitative" Research** Do not allow yourself to fall into the trap of the false dichotomy: Don't begin your teacher research by choosing an approach and then finding a problem. You would be like the people to whom the entire world consists of nails just because the only tool they have is a hammer. They hammer even where it would be more appropriate to glue or to use a screw.

The questions we chose to answer in research are the single most important aspect of doing research. So the upshot of all the preceding is that the questions we ask drive the studies we design. Some individuals begin by saying, "I want to do a quantitative study" or "I am doing a qualitative study." But this is the wrong approach, because all you are doing is define the means of producing data sources and data. What you really need is a question. Once you have a well-framed question, the design follows almost automatically, especially if the question implies the context in which the study is to be conducted. The process of clarifying the research question is facilitated when you discuss what you want to do with someone else, a fellow teacher, a professor, or a peer group. Sometimes people (graduate students) think that it is easier to do an interpretive study—perhaps believing that they do not have to study statistics; others feel that doing a statistical study is easier. As in many other situations, there is a little bit of truth in both. Once the design of an experimental study that investigates some cause–effect relationship has been done, it is rather easy to process the information collected—in my own dissertation it took me all but two days of analysis, including the data snooping that had not been planned beforehand. Interpretive studies may not require as much a priori planning, but it is much harder and longer to make sense of what most likely are tremendous amounts of data materials—one of my teacher-researcher investigations produced 3,500 typewritten interview and classroom transcripts, essays, and other written artifacts. Just reading these materials, let alone making sense of it, will take weeks (see chapter 5).

Not all questions require research. *Basic information* questions seek information often conveyed in textbooks or encyclopedias. These questions do not require research but have answers that can be looked up. *Wonderment* questions reflect curiosity, puzzlement, and skepticism. *Covariation* questions are those most often asked in the natural sciences because they link two or more variables in causal or correlational manner and thus advance the understanding of complex phenomena. Even wonderment and covariation questions already may have been answered, at least within some contexts. So a good starting point would be to try and find out whether there has been research in the areas and concerning the questions in which you are interested. If there is, you do not have to engage in the research yourself—you already get all the answers by reading relevant texts. This is true whether a teacher-researcher project is just for ourselves and our local context, whether we do research to satisfy the requirements for obtaining a degree, or whether we are interested in writing up our findings for publication in some journal. Given the amount of effort that goes into designing a study, finding and enlisting participants, collecting data sources, transcribing and interpreting data sources, doing a research study when the answer/s to the question/s posed already exist does not make much sense. Knowing about existing studies actually may help us define the particularities of our own situation, allowing us to sharpen the research question to focus on what is *not yet known* and thereby making a particular study useful (for others as for ourselves).

TEACHER-RESEARCH AND ETHICS

At the time I conducted the teacher-research presented in this book, I was not affiliated with a university; nor was I enrolled in a graduate program where I was to do a research project in partial fulfillment of the degree requirements. Furthermore, in the beginning of the 1990s when I conducted my studies the ethics requirements were not as stringent (in Canada, the US) as they are today. For example, many institutional research ethics boards (IRBs) pay more attention to the potential abuses of the power differential associated with the different institutional positions of teachers and students or administrators and teachers. Teacher-researchers actually need to get their projects approved in two institutional instances, their school board and school, on the one hand, and at the university where they are fulfilling degree requirements, on the other hand. Although teachers may normally conduct research—such as I have done as described in this book—there are additional concerns when the purpose of research is other than quality improvement in their classes or their schools. Thus, without adequate provisions, students may feel coerced into participating or participate because they *believe* they gain favors, better grades, and so forth. But teachers also have stated or unstated codes of ethics, which may be more stringent than those that are employed by university IRBs. Thus, at my university, a special committee was struck to produce recommendations for teacher-researcher studies. These recommendations are available at URL: http://www.research.uvic.ca/ethics/action_research_guidelines.pdf. I believe that these guidelines provide you with a sense of the attendant issues although you may live elsewhere in the world.

The report, of which I was one of the co-authors, recognizes that although teacher-researchers may conduct practice as usual (e.g., classroom instruction), for which they do not need IRB approval, they must follow IRB procedures to collect and use the data sources generated during their practice (e.g., samples of students' work, student interviews, pictures or videos, professional journal notes, etc.) for explicit research purposes. This is so because in such situations, data source mate-

INTRODUCTION

rials collected in the course of regular professional practice are used both for the purposes of professional practice (e.g., for formative and summative evaluation) *and* research. When there is such a dual use of data from regular professional practice, IRB approval has to be obtained for the research component and consent must be sought from participants (and if applicable, their guardians) to use the data for research purposes. If instruction is changed for research purposes, then this has to be stated explicitly and provisions have to be made for those students who chose not to participate in the research.

> **Keep Separate** the normal components of your teaching from those aspects you require students or colleagues to do for the purposes of the research study. You do not have to get your normal practices approved, but your IRB wants to know about the extra work participants in your study have to do above and beyond their normal involvement in the school.

When teacher-researchers conduct investigations in their classroom, they are in a *power-over* situation with respect to students, where *power over* denotes the power differential between a teacher-researcher and his or her students. Similar situations exist in administrator–teacher, department head–teacher, or friendship relationships. The nature of such relationships is thought to mediate the potential research participant's ability to give *free* and *uncoerced* consent. If you ask your spouse, sibling, or child, then they are likely to participate in your study; the danger is that they do so because of the family relations to you, whereas they might say no to someone else wanting to do an identical study. To be ethical, teacher-researchers must ensure that consent is given freely and voluntarily.

Some ways thought to mitigate power-over relationships listed in the document that we produced at my university include:

1. Inclusion of participants in the study only after there is no longer a power over relationship (e.g., end of school year or term);
2. Exclusion from the participant pool of individuals with whom the teacher-researcher has a power-over relationship;
3. Declaration of the power-over situation in recruitment and informed consent materials;
4. Description in the recruitment and informed consent materials of the safeguards that are used to prevent inducement, pressure, and coercion during participation.

Some of the ways in which teacher-researchers can prevent inducement include the following practices (usually made explicit in the consent form):

1. Asking another person who does not have a power-over relationship to potential participants (i.e., not the principal) to undertake the recruitment and consent processes (e.g., explains study, provides information letter and collects signed consent form); the third-party is usually the designated person that participants may contact if they wish to withdraw from the study;
2. Assuring participants that they have the right to refuse to participate and that they can withdraw their information from the research at any time without consequences or penalty of any kind;

3. Acknowledging that the researcher is aware that potential participants may feel pressure to agree to their (or their child's) participation because the researcher is in a position of power;
4. Assuring participants that their participation or non-participation will have no effect on outcomes (e.g., grades) nor on their relationship with the researcher or professional setting;
5. Explaining that there is no disadvantage in not consenting (e.g., all students will be taught the lesson);
6. Informing participants that if they have concerns about their rights or treatment in connection with the research project, they can contact a person in the university hierarchy (usually, the Vice-President Research);
7. Using a neutral tone in the recruitment and consent materials to diminish pressure on potential participants to participate (i.e., no emotional appeal or expression of how important the project is to the practitioner-researcher);

Important to the ethical conduct of research is the implementation of a process of seeking consent *in an ongoing manner*. For example, students may not want to participate on a particular day; provisions then have to be made so that they can opt out without feeling that they will be penalized or punished for their decision. I ask my research participants in each and every situation (day, lesson) whether they are fine with participating, being recorded, doing an interview, and so on. I let them know each time that it is okay if they said no and that it is their right to say no.

> **Anonymity** means that nobody in the entire world knows who participates in a research project; **confidentiality** means that those few who know about a person's participation will not reveal this knowledge.

Two further issues of great importance in any research are *anonymity* and *confidentiality*, two terms often confused with one another. *Anonymity* means that neither the researcher nor anyone else knows who the participants in the research are. This would be the case, for example, if students or colleagues were to be asked to fill out unmarked questionnaires to be submitted in some box or by mail. Unless everyone in the sample submitted the questionnaire, in which it would be known that all individuals to whom the mailing went out had participated, it is impossible to distinguish participants from non-participants. *Confidentiality* means that the researcher or someone else knows that a person has participated in the research but assures that his or her knowledge will not be divulged to others.

At my university, students under the age of 13 normally require parent or guardian consent to participate in a study. In addition to including recruitment and consent information for parents or guardians, it is also important to provide age-appropriate recruitment and consent information for children. For students under the age of seven, a simple verbal script is recommended for explaining the research, including who the researcher is and what the children are being asked to consent to. It is also recommended to ask the parent or guardian to talk with their child about the research and ensure that their child understands that he or she can freely choose to allow the researcher to use their work or not. Students between the ages of 13 and 16 are able to provide their own consent but teacher-researchers usually inform the parents or guardians. This can be done, for example, by sending

INTRODUCTION

home an information letter. Some school districts require parental or guardian consent for all students younger than 19 at the time of the research. In such cases, the policy of the school district is binding.

DON'T WORRY: JUST DO IT!

Some readers, as many of the graduate students and teacher-researchers who have attended my graduate courses on research design or research method, are overly worried about "doing it right," "immediately getting the answers," or "knowing whether they are on the right track." If you were in a situation where you could see an experienced and successful researcher at work, as do the graduate students who are part of my research team, you would see that there are a lot of false starts, wavering, stumbles, impasses, renunciations, and reconfigurations. Having spent much of the last twenty years analyzing data and writing articles and books, I still do not just sit down and, within a few hours, have some results that I then write up over the period of a few days. I tend to spend many hours of transcribing, reading, annotating, elaborating, and explicating data source materials before I get to know the data sources so well that I can begin to structure and make sense of them. I work so much with the data sources that they become second nature to me. The main point is to just do whatever one is able to do at the moment and to keep a detailed trail of activities and records. Throughout this book I point out how this strategy allowed me to learn both about the phenomena of interest and doing the research.

MY SCHOOL AND CLASSROOM CONTEXT

The different types of teacher-researcher studies described in this book all derive from my time at Appleby College, a private college preparatory school, which, during my three years there changed from a boys-only to a co-educational institution. I was working fulltime, which means that as the department head I was teaching five courses, each meeting for three one-hour periods per week; and I had one course release to be able to pursue my duties as department head. The regular load therefore engaged teachers in 18 of the 27 scheduled periods per week. In addition, I participated in the compulsory sports and extracurricular activities on three afternoons and had dorm duty once every six days, which lasted from 7 to 11 P.M. The studies that constitute the context for the methods I describe in this book can be thought of as *design experiments*. Design experiments are investigations that follow, document, and analyze complex interventions in actual classrooms. In addition, the results of the research are fed back into the classroom—unlike in experimental studies where nothing can be changed until the experiment is completed. Design experiments therefore are highly adaptive, which also requires that the researchers produce detailed documentation about what was done, what and when something was changed, and how events in the classroom unfolded (differently) following a change in the design. Normally, outside researchers conduct design experiments and enroll classroom teachers in their efforts. My research was different as I also was a fulltime teacher.

School Context

Appleby College has much in common with traditional British private schools: there are compulsory (for students and teachers) extracurricular activities and after school sports. Its operating budget was to a considerable extent covered by tuition fees. As a consequence, the administration viewed schooling as a business enterprise in which the demands of the customers (students and their parents) determined the services provided. High tuition fees, a business mentality (parents and students are customers), traditional values, and parent demand for back-to-the-basics approach created an atmosphere within which economic considerations sometimes outweighed educational decisions by teachers. This situation, a collapsing job market for teachers in the province, the non-existence of a union, and a contractual situation according to which a teacher could be released on short notice gave rise to a sense of insecurity among teachers. As a consequence, in a four-year period five teachers were fired either because of parent pressures or because of differences with the administration. Not surprisingly, many teachers adapted making their classrooms teacher-centered, focusing on algorithmic problem solving, and concentrating on getting students the grades needed to assure them acceptance in the colleges and universities of their choice. Most science teachers felt less constrained and continued to explore alternatives to traditional, textbook-oriented approaches that were common, for example, in the mathematics classes.

Students

There was a cap on class size. In fourth through tenth grade, there generally were 22 students per class. In the junior and senior years, classes were considerably smaller and varied from year to year. In the physics courses were I conducted most of my teacher-researcher studies, the class size ranged from 12 to 20 students. On the basis of my previous public school teaching experience, I estimate that the students in this school represented all but the bottom 25 percent in achievement levels of the student population in the surrounding public schools. Up to one-third of the eighth-grade students left the school each year, transferring into the public school system. In the upper classes remained those who eventually enrolled—without necessarily succeeding—in a variety of colleges and universities. About 5 percent of the students in each relevant subject area also completed college-credit-earning advanced placement courses, which were available as after-school study opportunities. Typically, the students in the junior year had chosen physics not because of an interest in the subject per se. Rather, sometimes encouraged by their parents, sometimes on their own, they chose the subject to keep their career choices open; one of the basic requirements of the nearby universities for getting into premedical studies was the completion of two high school physics courses. Because such a requirement did not exist for biology, the ratio of junior year physics to junior year biol-

INTRODUCTION

ogy students was about three or four to one, uncharacteristically high for most high schools in the North America.

Structure of My Courses

My teaching always had differed from the way my peers approached instruction in science. I therefore provide a brief description of how I organized it, in this way contextualizing what I did and how I organized in my teacher-research. Physics, like all other subjects, was allotted 360 minutes in a two-week cycle. During the first two years of my tenure, these 360 minutes were divided into nine 40-minute periods; during the final year, however, there were six 60-minute periods.

The students spent most of that time in my class on individual research projects for which they framed their own focus questions (see chapter 3). They spent the remainder of the time on presenting and discussing their findings as part of whole-class sessions. In these discussions, the students could share what they learned with their peers; and in presenting their work they learned more about their topic as they tried to explain, elaborate, and justify what they had done. I generally did not lecture but, upon student requests, would gather those interested in a particular topic or word problem in a corner of the classroom and would talk them through the issues that they had or I would respond to their questions. These mini-lectures therefore were provided on an as-needed basis (as defined by students) and the students could choose whether to participate or not.

Every now and then I presented a short demonstration to introduce students to new equipment, computer programs, or data analysis techniques. Frequently, these demonstrations arose from my evaluation of what students might need at the moment. For example, I showed students how they could use a statistical software package to put curves through the data points they had collected in their experiments. Thus, whenever I thought that the entire class would benefit from something an individual student group had requested, I introduced it to other students as well.

I regularly organized discussions of topics such as "objectivity in science," "quantity and patterns," "physics and language," or "the nature of knowledge," especially after the students had read some chapter or article on a topic. There were also regular sessions during which students worked together on concept maps (see chapters 1 and 2) in which they incorporated the key terms from their last experiment, or from a textbook chapter that served as a referent for their current experiments.

Open-Door Policy

The physics laboratory came to be a place for learning and working: it was open to anyone and everyone as long as those who came did not interfere with the learning and work of others. The classroom was always accessible to anybody who wanted to work there, even if there was a physics class going on. The doors were open: visitors, teachers, and students (from other than the scheduled physics course and even non-physics students) freely entered. There was only one main rule: do not interfere with the activities of the currently scheduled class. Some of the visitors merely watched whereas others participated in the on-going activities, asked students questions, or did their own work. Some science and mathematics teachers, for example, came to use the computers, to interact with the students, or to observe my class as part of the on-going staff development I had organized. Students from non-scheduled courses came to use the computers to print out their results, to do an analysis, or to write their reports.

The classroom was open until I left my office, sometimes in the wee-hours of the morning. I generally prepared the lessons of the following day, graded assignments and tests, and, frequently and extensively, did something related to my teacher-research such as transcribing videotapes or analyzing the data sources I had accumulated. Both physics and non-physics students regularly came to the physics laboratory to work and study in the evenings. During my third year at the school, the administration, feeling that students were spending too many hours in the physics laboratory, had the teacher doing library supervision lock the laboratory at 10 P.M., that is, at the same time that the library was closed.

CHAPTER 1

INVESTIGATING STUDENT LEARNING DURING COLLABORATIVE CONCEPT MAPPING

Teachers do what they do in their classrooms based on their experiences, including those that they had as students, during teacher training, and while practicing. We teachers do not generally ask *why* some technique works but, as other practitioners, adopt what appears to be working well. For example, most teachers have included lectures in their toolbox without actually asking whether giving lectures leads to learning or whether requiring students to read and discuss certain texts and topics would not lead to deeper understandings. Based on my own experience of having learned best in the laboratory while doing my Master's degree in physics and having enjoyed work the most and having started teaching in the far north of Canada without previously receiving a teaching certificate, I rarely ever lectured in my teaching career. But as most of my teaching peers, I picked up new strategies in workshops or from reading books. Yet I never asked the *how* and *why* questions: How do students learn when they do this or that task? Why do students not learn under certain conditions? How do students deal with problems that they encounter while working on assignments? I never asked, that is, never until the Summer of 1990, when, while teaching a summer course in physics for elementary teachers at the University of Victoria, I happened to pick up several books featuring ethnographic studies of scientists at work, mathematics in the everyday world, and cultural studies of children doing school tasks. At this point it occurred to me that I could use a video camera to find out more about *what* students were doing and talking while they were engaged in the different types of tasks that I used as part of my teaching. One of these types of tasks that I regularly used asked students to organize the 20 or 30 concept words of an entire unit into a hierarchically organized *concept map* (e.g., Figure 1.1).

CONCEPT MAPPING TASK

In all of my classes doing collaborative concept mapping, I went about the same way setting students up. Each group received a stack of paper slips, about 2 by 3 inch in size. On each of these slips I printed one of the concepts that I wanted them to map. In some cases, when students were more experienced, they either added their own concepts on empty snippets provided or identified all of the concepts themselves. During my years at Appleby College, the part during which students arranged the concepts on the slips and discussed linkages and hierarchies lasted about 35 to 40 minutes. At this stage I usually encouraged students to begin copying their concept arrangements onto the 14-by-17-inch sheets and to begin making and naming the links that they had arrived at. The students spent the final twenty

CHAPTER 1

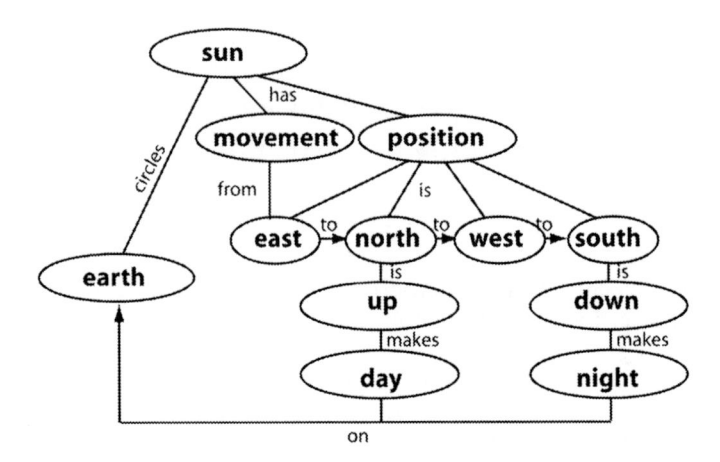

Figure 1.1. In the concept mapping task, students order concepts from the most inclusive (general) ones on top to least inclusive (general) ones on the bottom and then label the links such that propositions (concept–link–concept) representing knowledge are produced.

minutes of the class transferring the concept arrangement onto large sheets of paper, drawing links between concept words, and writing the linking words to form propositions. Even during this phase, my students talked in animated fashion, they argued and they discussed. Toward the end of the class, the students often had to rush to complete the assignment prior to the end of the period. Figure 1.1 provides a sample concept map representing the explanation a study participant provided about the reasons for having day and night and how the differences between day and night are related to the movements of sun and earth. Figure 1.2 shows a group of students who have been asked to map about 30 concepts in the process of transcribing the map onto the large sheet of paper, where they also produced lines and linking words. The end result of one such task collected as part of my study can be found in Figure 1.3.

The students in the participating physics classes usually worked together in groups of three or four. Each group began the concept mapping activity by grouping the concepts (see the paper snippets on the table [Figure 1.2]). In many student groups, two, three, and even four individuals simultaneously moved the paper snippets with concept words marked on them, talking as much to themselves as they did to others. Through this process, they arrived at the first rough classifications of concepts into groups and hierarchies. Then they went into further detail with their outline, pushing concepts back and forth, trying hierarchical ordering, arranging, and re-arranging. New local arrangements (e.g., the way the terms "position," "east," and "north" are related hierarchically [Figure1.1]) forced them to regroup the concepts from other subgroups. Shifts around one concept often required shifts around others. Because the concepts were on movable paper snippets, these frequent changes in the arrangement were done easily; much more easily than if the students immediately had tried to draw their concept maps on paper.

Figure 1.2. Conducting a concept mapping session with one group of students allowed me to figure out how to use a camera, at what distance from the students to set it up, how high to place it above the ground on the tripod, and so on.

The discussions always were very animated as the students negotiated and defended their individual positions with the purpose of arriving at the required single final map for each group. In some groups, even with the preliminary ordering, students made a sketch to see a preliminary map with links before they committed to a final version of the concept map.

One of the important distinctions I ask teacher-researchers to make during all stages of their work is between their curriculum and their research. I have found that others—university research ethics committees, professors, or school board officials—better understand what you attempt to do if you can clearly describe what you normally do. Then, making a clear separation, you explain on which aspects of your normal activity you intend to research. This allows you to clearly distinguish between data sources that are *naturally produced* and materials you intend to collect for the express *purposes of the research*. These latter materials might require student to do extra work; and others, especially those responsible for making decisions, including students and their parents who give their consent, need to know what is required of them.

Normal Tasks Versus Research-driven Tasks Everyone concerned will want to be clear about which tasks research participants *normally* would be required to accomplish and which tasks are required only because of research participation. This is important to know because you may have to make special previsions for those who decide not to participate in your study.

GETTING STARTED

I had used such maps from the very beginning of my teaching career to see how the concepts in some unit I was teaching connected and how I would structure the

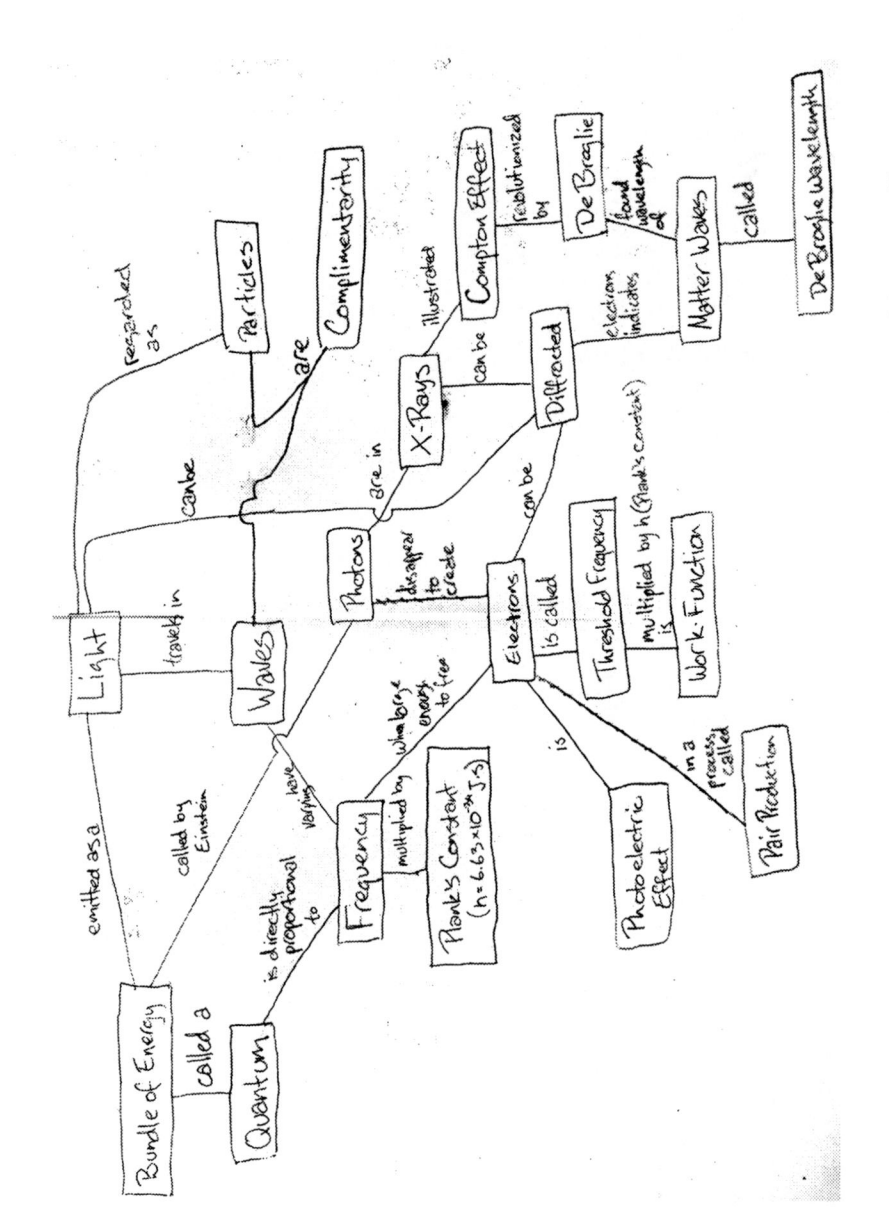

1.3. This concept map is a transcription of the one students had created on their laboratory table.

course over the year. It was only half a decade later that I came across *Learning How to Learn* (Novak & Gowin, 1984), which presented concept mapping as a strategy for helping students not only to learn the specific concepts of some unit but also to learn how to learn. I used the strategy for several years, but was not overly satisfied with the results—in part because even I was struggling constructing maps despite my deep familiarity in the subject area. After having read about the social nature of everyday knowing and learning, I decided to give concept mapping another try, but, this time, to put students into groups to allow them to learn by thinking together through the relationships between the different concept words. I asked myself questions such as "How do students learn concepts when they construct concept maps collectively?" "If knowledge is constructed collectively, what if anything do students pick up into their individual knowledge?" "Do students retain what they have produced together over longer periods of time?"

My first impulse was to check the existing literature. I found out that the existing studies of concept mapping focused on their construction and use by individuals; I also found that many studies were conducted using experimental designs, that is, studies in which two or more teaching methods were compared. There were also studies suggesting that concept mapping led to the reduction of anxiety levels in male and female students; and there was at least one study claiming that more meaningful learning was attained when students collaborate on producing the maps. That is, after perusing the literature I knew that although concept mapping has been shown to help students in meaningful learning, particularly when done as a collaborative activity, little has been done to understand the microprocesses during the task itself, that is, the minute-to-minute actions that ultimately lead to the finished products I got to see in the end. However, I was thinking that to be able to improve how students go about the task I had to know more about these microprocesses that constitute concept mapping as an unfolding event and the final concept maps as its product. I decided to conduct a teacher-researcher study designed to investigate concept mapping as a means of assessing the quality of student understanding from two perspectives: the analysis of the process of constructing meaning and the analysis of the products resulting from this process. But, in part because I was not experienced, in part because I wanted to figure out beforehand how to set up the camera and other aspects of such a research project, I decided to do some pilot work.

> **Look Up the Literature** Before you begin a study, check through the literature in your field whether there are studies that have investigated the same or similar phenomena that you are after. If there are answers to your questions, you do not have to do all the work a teacher-researcher study requires. Just go to the library or use Google to look up existing information.

DOING A PILOT

Doing a pilot is always a good way to start a project, because it allows you to become familiar with some of the contingencies that any project faces however well you have planned it. I, for example, knew I had to figure out how to operate the

CHAPTER 1

camera, at what distance to set it up to get the best information, how high I could possibly set it on the tripod above the ground, and so on. There were many things I did not know at the time and which I had to figure out before conducting any formal study. I therefore invited a group of students to do a concept map after school and used this opportunity to figure out how and where in the classroom to record (Figure 1.2). In this pilot study, I did everything in the way I would normally do to set up the task in my classroom. Thus, students received an envelope with two-by-three-inch paper snippets on which the concept words were printed just as they would in their classroom. (I used the paper cutter to do entire class sets in a few minutes.) I hung around without actually getting involved or assisting students just making sure they knew I was there if they really needed me.

When I watched my first videotape, I noticed that it was sometimes difficult to know what students were talking about. I could see them move a concept word but, because of the camera position, could not see what was printed on the snippet (e.g., Figure 1.2). Thus, it was impossible to know the sense they marked out in the following exchange unless I found out what was printed on the cards that they pointed to while talking:

```
01   Ma:   this goes down here, this goes out here, this part
02   Ra:   but they have to be at different levels, they have to
            go here and then
03   Mi:   no, these can be related
```

It should be immediately apparent to the reader that without knowing what the words "this," "this part," "they," and "these" were pointing to I could not know the sense of their communication unless I was keeping track of each bit of paper over time. (I later learned that linguists refer to these terms as *shifters* or *indexicals*.) I was asking myself whether it would be possible to mount the camera differently, but, as can be gauged from Figure 1.2, the size differences between the paper snippets and the maps as a whole precluded me from seeing the writing. I could have zoomed in periodically, but, whereas this might have been feasible for the pilot session, it would not have been feasible for recording during regular lessons where I could not operate the camera. I rapidly found out during the lessons that the recording had to run on its own, because as a teacher I first and foremost was responsible to my students; and there was hardly a minute that I had for thinking about things other than interacting with them.

To find out more about concept mapping, I wanted to do this pilot study with my senior physics students one year, and then do a full scale study during the next. Despite these intentions, it turned out that my pilot itself yielded so many insights that I ended up publishing the results of some of them. Normally, though, pilot studies are to find out about how to conduct a study, to learn about the contingencies that possibly and actually emerge, to evolve ways of dealing with contingencies, to understand the nature of the data sources, to learn how to improve upon the quality of the materials in the data sources, and so on.

PILOT STUDY DESIGN

Ultimately ten students enrolled in my senior year physics course participated in the study more extensively, as I videotaped them and their groups; from the other students I only had the group maps that they handed in at the end of the mapping sessions and the results on their tests and exams. I wanted the ten students on the videotape to represent a cross section of the course. So using their year-end marks, I selected four students within one standard deviation below the mean, four students within one standard deviation above the mean. Two students had marks between one and two standard deviation above the mean. All students had taken my junior-year introductory physics course during which they regularly employed and became familiar with concept maps. In all of my junior and senior year courses, students used concept maps at the end of units to summarize the main ideas.

For starters, I videotaped a total of seven concept mapping sessions, each lasting from 45 to 60 minutes. Five of these sessions were scheduled out of regular class time and included the videotape from my pilot. During these sessions, the students also did not have access to other resources for looking up terms; I did this in part to constrain them to discuss their differences rather than to quickly look up a word in their textbook or encyclopedia and settle on a given definition. I videotaped two sessions during regular classes. In this way, I was able to ascertain the *ecological validity* of what I was doing. Ecological validity is concerned with answers to the question: "Is thought and action observed in one context [here the out-of-class session] representative of that displayed by people in their natural context [here the regular class]?" Two groups came for two sessions spaced by a two-week interval; one group came once at the time of the other two groups' second session.

	95
	90
	83
	87
	76
Mean =	**86.2**
SD =	**7.2**
=AVERAGE(B3:B7)	
=STDEV(B3:B7)	

Mean and **Standard Deviation** constitute ways of describing a group of people, marks, and so on. Today's spreadsheets allow you to calculate these values using functions, such as in this case where the mean and standard deviation of the first five figures (grades) has been calculated. The standard deviation is a measure of how broad your distribution is; it also provides you with information about how close around the mean you find 68% (± 1 SD) and 95% (±2 SD) of the population.

As part of this study I wanted to find out how the collaborative sessions influenced the way in which individuals organized their concepts. So I decided to collect information allowing me to answer this question as well. One week after, all students in the class were required to make individual concept maps as part of a test on the unit, which, in this instance, focused on concepts from the topic of light as a wave phenomenon. As part of the final examination five weeks after the first test, all students constructed a second individual map. As I knew that some students used concept maps to study, I asked two of them for the maps that they had

CHAPTER 1

used to study for the exams. In addition to the videotapes and the transcripts I made, I collected as data sources the following artifacts: (a) the concept maps produced during the sessions; (b) the concept maps produced individually during both test situations (test, final exam); (c) the concept maps produced by all other groups during the two regular class periods; and (d) the concept maps which two students had used to study the unit on the quantum character of light.

CONCEPTUAL UNDERPINNINGS

The students concept mapped in groups of three, a regular arrangement for collaborative work in this physics course. Three students working together on a task that either of them could do on his or her own (though in a different way) are faced with the problem communicating with each other. In the interest of collaboration, each student makes available to other participants his or her thoughts: about the nature of the next move, how much progress has been made, how much remains to be done, the rationale for making one over another, and so forth. In this way, the participants provide each other with a sense of the task's status, and they provide the teacher-researcher with that same sense as well. An artifact of such collaboration—e.g., a videotape and the transcript that goes with it—therefore, is a *naturally generated protocol*; it is a much better account of what happens than asking participants after the fact. First, it contains all the framing and resolution of problematic junctures rather than the ones participants remember after the fact—even if they write about the events soon after they have occurred, as I did during the second year of the study (see chapter 2). Such natural protocols of collaborative work are evidence for the individual reasoning of participants and they give researchers windows onto the processes of how the participants attribute meaning to the context and how participants make evident and persuade each other that the events and activities in which they are involved are consistent and coherent.

> **Natural Protocols** Videotapes and transcripts are natural protocols documenting how people make sense in situations. This is so because co-participants make available knowledge and reasoning to each other to be able to resolve issues jointly. And they make this knowledge available to the teacher-researcher as well. To understand what is going on all the researcher has to have are the same cultural competencies that the interlocutors have.

MAKING VIDEO RECORDINGS

At the time, I had no experience using a camera. Getting used to operating one was an important goal of my pilot study. Even more important, while I did this study, I found out that I could not think as a researcher and as a teacher simultaneously. While I recorded students after school, the situation was easy—not much different from what I do today that I am a full-time researcher. But in class, I wanted and had to be available to all students—this ultimately was my job. Any research— even if conducted for the sole purpose of improving my teaching and the learning environment—had and has to take second place. Thus, everything had to work smoothly and on its own. Under these conditions, some of my questions were about where in the classroom to put the camera, or perhaps more precisely, where to place the students whom I recorded so that I could operate the camera in a way that it did not interfere in normal classroom procedures. Being unfamiliar with recording, I had to do some actual recordings and then, by inspecting the tapes *in the light of my specific purposes*, figure out whether the shots are sufficient and how they might be improved.

When I did my afternoon recordings, there was lots of room; I also recorded a number of sessions in the prep room, where there were no windows. I only realized subsequently, that these were ideal conditions for at least two reasons. First, the light came from above and did not change the automatic brightness adjustment of the camera (Figure 1.2). When I later recorded in the classroom, the configuration of electrical outlets, laboratory tables, and other equipment was such that I had decided to shoot towards the windows (Figure 1.4); I also thought that in this way I would pick up less of the other sounds in the classroom and thereby would decrease the "noise." Little did I know about the way cameras adjust their aperture to the light from the window making it nearly impossible to see the faces of the persons sitting in the more sparsely lit room. If there are trees in front of the window or the windows are directed north and it is a cloudy day, the light problems are lessened. A pilot study allows you to find out about all of these contingencies that you do not or cannot know beforehand.

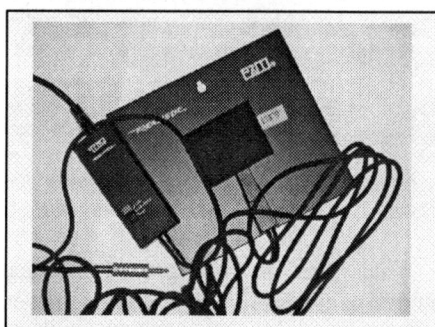

PZM Flat table microphones, which have a dome-shaped sensitivity, are excellent for picking up talk—but they are equally excellent in picking up any background noise, including paper rustling and especially any contact with the table on which they rest. Attention—do not forget to switch the microphone's power on and off!

The second and even more important aspect of recording—one that is inherently problematic under most classroom situation—is sound: If we teacher-researchers do not get the sound, there is little we know about how the participants construe sense for one another, what they find to be the problematic issues at hand, and how they resolve them. *Good sound is* the *key issue of all video recording!* When I video-recorded after school, and especially when I recorded in the prep room, there were no other sources of sound that would have made it difficult to hear what students were saying. Initially, I therefore did not even think about alternatives to the built-in microphone. I found out in the pilot stage that when there were other students in the room working on their own tasks, then the background noise to the sound of interest increased—somewhat proportional to the number of students and groups. The more students in the room, the more background noise there will be, and the more difficult it will be to transcribe the talk of interest.

CHAPTER 1

Figure 1.4. Using a camera in a regular classroom is subject to multiple constraints and has to take into account noise levels and how to minimize them.

Somewhere on the Internet, I read that there is little that is worse than the built-in microphones of video cameras. I never did compare cameras and always bought rather high-end types; it is perhaps for this reason that my problems were not as bad as those that some other (teacher-) researchers have come to face. When I started to do research as a teacher, I did not know or think about cameras; but since then, I have tried many different ways to improve the sound without finding an ideal solution. The built-in microphones of video cameras are somewhat directional; and some manufacturers sell highly directional microphones that can be attached to the camera. The disadvantage is that the camera needs to be moved back from the recorded scene to optimize the image, and this also means that other students likely are sitting somewhere near the cardioid-shaped field covered by the directional microphone.

The camera microphone turned out to pick up too much background conversation, which, because I was interested in the talk of the group recorded, actually constituted noise. I therefore began using a rather simple table microphone, which improved the sound quality, though it never reduced the noise to zero. Later I used external microphones known under their brand name of *PZM*. These are microphones that have a metal plate as their backing (see insert). When placed on the table or desk near the students, they pick up the talk and even whispers. But because they are designed to resonate with the material on which they are placed and because of their dome-shaped pick up characteristics, PZM microphones may worsen the sound quality. I also tried lapel microphones but found that they only pick up well the person they are attached to but other students, especially if they do not speak with sufficient intensity, become inaudible even if only centimeters away. I ultimately ended up using table microphones because they constituted the best among non-optimal solutions. More recently, I found that digital cameras record in stereo; because I use headphones for transcribing the tapes stereophonic sound tends to help locating speakers in space and improve audibility. The table microphones I know, however, record in the mono mode. I therefore have shifted to using the camera microphone; when I do not teach and actually operate the camera, then I may use an additional directional microphone.

An important lesson I learned about using cameras is this: whenever there are cables, someone will walk into and tear down anything connected to them. When I started recording in my classrooms, I had to record with the camera plugged into an electrical outlet, because I often taped two or three lessons in a row. Unless the camera is positioned on a tripod right next to the outlet, the power cord may become a snare. In one case, a student actually brought down tripod and camera as he got hooked. When using a table microphone wired into the camera, the danger of someone getting hooked increases.

UNIT OF ANALYSIS

My study was concerned with processes and achievements. The achievements were *trans*actional, which means that the contributions of individual students could not be understood independently from the group processes; and yet, the group processes are realized through the individual productions. Using the term *inter*action allows me to think about students as independent beings each of whom contributes something specific; the total would then be the sum of individual production. The term *trans*action, on the other hand, is used when the different parts of a collective entity cannot be thought independently. Those familiar with ecology already are familiar with the difference I am in the process of pointing out here. Thus, a niche cannot be thought independently of the organisms occupying it; niche and its inhabitants mutually define and presuppose each other. On the other hand, thinking in terms of *inter*action would allow us to think of the niche as a box into which one or the other occupant might fit; or we might think that the occupant changes to fit into the pre-given box. But in many situations, this is not a good way of thinking because of the mutual and irreducible influences both the situation and occupants have on each other. The same is the case when we think about teacher–student relations: who is teaching and who is learning is a transactional issue, as all participants mutually adjust to the behaviors of all others. Teachers not only learn to teach but they also learn the subject matter—one of my graduate-level chemistry professors was quite right when he said that after 20 years of teaching he felt to know the material well enough to really begin teaching it. In my effort to assess the interactions and learning of the participants, I found that the individual was not the most useful unit of analysis for many situations. Thus, I adopted the perspective that transactions and learning are inherently connected to the context. That is, transactions and learning are connected to the environment, tools, and other resources, in such a way that they cannot be understood without reference to them. This is why in many cases I could not attribute some achievement to a specific individual, but had to think about it as the result of a transaction of three *moments*: the individual, the social, and the physical environment. A *moment* here is understood as something (e.g., a structure) that can be identified but which does not exist

CHAPTER 1

in, of, and *for itself*: it stands in a constitutive relation with other moments that have to be accounted for.

Researchers have suggested various units of analysis for the analysis of social units. Among these were *activity* or *event*, socially assembled *situations* or *cultural practices*, *task-within practices* or *work task*, and *work sequences, networks*, or *techniques of argument*. For the present investigation, I followed some study that I had read during the summer of 1990 suggesting that the task was the most appropriate unit. To reiterate, the task was to represent concepts in a hierarchical configuration and to produce linkages that would turn the map into a network of propositions (statements). Cognitive tasks, however, cannot be identified independently from their social context, because they are always social constructions. Any transformation of the social organization of the actors, whether these are changes in group composition or changes to individual work, transforms the nature of the task. To deal with this changing nature of tasks, I made use of a *tracer*, which is some form of device that allows me to follow knowledge from the way it was used and produced in collaborative work to the way the same knowledge would show up in individual work.

TRACER

My records show that the idea of a tracer and its use arose from my thinking about how to analyze the concept maps for their structure and how this structure changed over time. My research note written at the moment I was conducting the study (while analyzing students' work on a concept map involving the terms crest, trough, interference, node, and anti-node) reads:

> Is the [concept map] structure due to one student? Check Mark, Ralf, Miles.
>
> It would appear obvious that crest, trough, interference, node, anti-node were somehow connected. It seems as if in many, crest and trough are not connected to the other concepts. Follow this lead for analysis through the various concept maps.
>
> Use of a tracer. In the present case, the tracer would be a particular set of concepts. The analysis would look for the history and final product of this relationship. (Research note 91/06/24)

This research memo shows that at the time I wanted to look for the origin and history of the structure in the maps and that I was interested in a particular set of concepts that I thought should be connected and that other concepts from the unit (crest, trough) were not connected in the maps of most students. There are three instructions to myself: (a) check in the records of three students, which would provide me with some initial information; (b) follow this thought of a set of connected concepts through various maps; and (c) use a tracer, which I then define. It is precisely this note that is at the origin of this aspect of my research and the notion of *tracer* as something that allows me to "trace" a concept configuration through time and different records.

The concept maps students produced both in class and after school resulted from collaborative work. When I later tested students individually, a third setting, the context had changed sufficiently that the task may no longer have been the same— an important issue that is little addressed in many educational research studies. For example, in the collaborative setting, the three students of a group had each other as a resource, the teacher, and the concept labels that they could see and manipulate without actually thinking about them (putting them in a situation like the one we find ourselves in opening a door, where we do not have to think "turn the knob" to actually get the door opened). When my students worked on concept maps during regular class time, they had additional resources available. For example, they could go to a neighboring table and ask their peers; or they could take out a textbook to see if they could find something to settle a difference; or they could take any one of the textual resources that I had assembled to make for a little classroom library (a variety of old and new textbooks, encyclopedias, and dictionaries).

During the testing situations, however, none of these resources were available. To find out what happened during individual testing to the collaborative achievement, experimented with the use of a tracer. The idea of a tracer is not very difficult to understand using the following analogy. For example, the police use finger prints as tracers to see whether a person has been present in one or more locations; and anthropologists use a particular form of carbon (C-14) as a tracer to identify the time an object was used. From these analogies it should be clear now that a tracer is some bit of knowledge, procedure, set of actions, talk, or written symbol that allows me to follow knowledge through various settings or contexts. I therefore used a set of concepts as a tracer to see what knowledge is present in different situation. In the present case, because I could not assume that the overall maps would maintain any sort of consistency across participants during the two tests, I decided to trace the configuration of a subset of concepts. To select specific concepts I studied the transcripts for recognizable clusters of concepts, which was also under considerable debate during the sessions. I conjectured that the debate literally might leave traces in students, mediating the way in which they would be mapping when asked to construct maps individually on some later occasion.

These considerations, the analysis of the transcripts, and the inspection of all concept maps on light as a wave phenomenon led me to select the configuration of the concepts light, phase, interference, reflection, air wedge, diffraction, and double slit/grating as the tracer.

For each group session, I produced a tracer map (e.g., Figure 1.5a). On a sheet of $8\leq$ by 11 inch, I did the same for each student on the test (e.g., Figure 1.5b) and on the exam (e.g., Figure 1.5c), placing the two maps side by side. From top to the bottom of the sheet, I could therefore see the tracers of all three students in comparison and from left to right I could see how the student had done on the test and exam compared to what he had done with his peer during the group session. To this sheet containing the tracers each student had produced, I taped the one or two maps that they had done in groups. For each student I also noted on the sheet my rating of the test and examination concept maps as like or slightly modified with respect to the group map (+), moderately modified (0), or strongly modified (-). As

CHAPTER 1

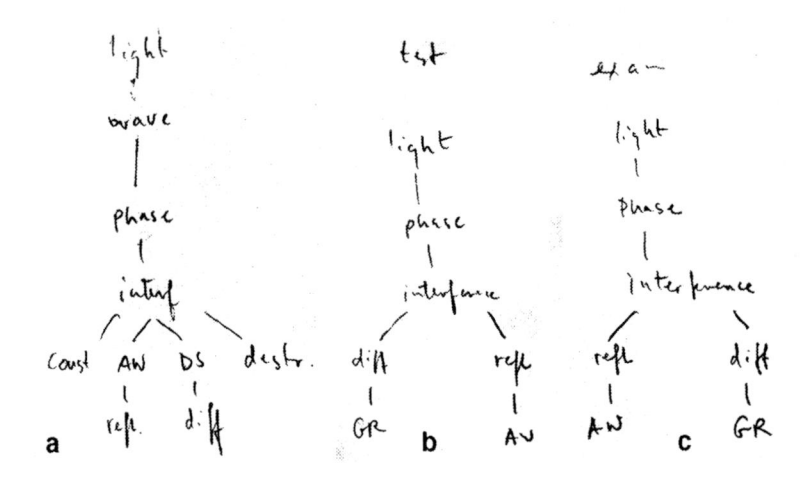

Figure 1.5. To be able to follow achievement across situations, I chose a small number of concepts and then studied how they were related on different occasions. The configuration of the concepts became my tracer. *a. The concept arrangement one group produced. b. The tracer configuration one student produced on a test one week after the group session. c. The tracer configuration of the same student five weeks later on the final exam.*

I did have no other measures, I had to make them up. I reserved "+" for those tracers that were identical or had only one term or link that differed. I used "0" for instances where there were two or three differences (position, link) with the original group tracer; and I assessed an individual tracer configuration as "-" when the changes were more substantial. I also noted the grade that each student had obtained on the final exam part covering the unit as a measure of how well he had understood the concepts.

INDIVIDUAL ACHIEVEMENT

One of my main interests in conducting this study was to find out how collaborative tasks in my classrooms related to what students knew when tested individually. Although I am quite doubtful about the usefulness of such testing and questions, having come to see scientists struggle when presented with the simplest of tasks from undergraduate textbooks in their own field, at that time I wanted to be able to make a good argument for doing group work. In part, researchers and teachers argued (and still do) that if students have to know their stuff individually, it makes little sense to have them work in groups. Some even say that putting students in groups interferes with the learning of the better students and thereby holds them back. I decided to use concept maps on my tests as a legitimate form of the assessment process. At the same time, I considered the concept map task on a test to have some *ecological validity* as a measure of learning from concept mapping, because it is a highly similar rather than a different type of task—the differences being the level of access to other resources, including peers. Figure 1.6 shows the

INVESTIGATING COLLABORATIVE CONCEPT MAPPING

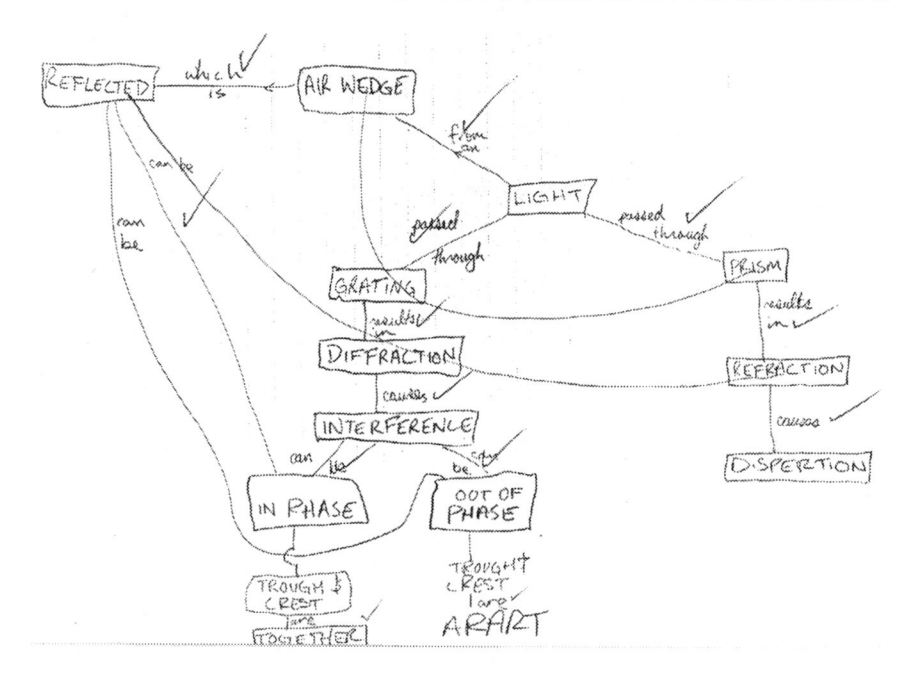

Figure 1.6. I used the concept map Nico produced on his final exam to evaluate the impact of collaborative concept mapping on individual performance.

concept map one student, Nico, produced on his final examination; the check marks indicate correct links.

The comparison of the concept maps done during the tests with those done during the collaborative sessions showed variations for some students in both global and local arrangements of concepts, while others showed only little variation. The results with respect to the variation of the tracers are presented in Table 1.1. The table shows that one week after the last concept mapping session focusing on light as a wave phenomenon, seven students used configurations almost identically to that of their respective groups. But the work of others on the test featured quite dramatic changes from their group work. For example, Paul and Ed, both from the same group, showed entirely different organizations, globally as well as locally. On the other hand, Nico, the third student in the group and in terms of achievement in this physics course between the other two, showed a remarkable consistency over both individual testing situations. (I come back to discuss his performance in more detail below.) Six weeks after the last session, five students showed identical maps or only minor modifications (+); two students' maps showed moderate modifications (0); while Peter's and Ed's maps still showed drastic modification from the original without any improvement (-).

Two of the students, Ralf and Miles, produced individual concept maps virtually identical to the original group map, both in terms of local as in global arrangement. However, the analysis of their maps showed a difference in one link that had al-

27

CHAPTER 1

Table 1.1. Degree of similarity between tracer configurations in collectively constructed group maps and the maps students constructed individually during test and exam

Tracer	Number of Tracers	
	1 week	6 weeks
Identical or slight modification	7	5
Moderate modification	0	2
Drastic modification	2	2

ready appeared during their discussion and had been heavily debated. Ralf had held that for interference to occur, the sources of the waves must be out of phase. Miles on the other hand had argued that the two sources must be in phase. This issue had been repeatedly addressed during their session, and the group had finally decided that the sources (waves) must be initially in phase, then out of phase for interference to occur. However, their individually constructed maps showed that neither of the two had accommodated the other's view and the maps expressed their views from before the discussion. This indicates the resilience of students' ways of talking to instruction, although here instruction was in the form of a peer discussion during which the students had to make explicit their understanding and where the flaws in their argumentation could be detected.

I was interested in whether quantitative comparisons between the two tests would confirm or disconfirm my qualitative observations. To do this, I needed some form of measure on the basis of which I could compare the maps. I was thinking about counting the total number of correct links as a measure; but I also noted that there were incorrect links. I then thought that a more valid measure of achievement would be to subtract the number of incorrect links from the number of valid links. I do not remember precisely why I went about the process in this way and had not written a research note about it. It is likely that I read a research paper about doing the counts in this way; but one can possibly argue about which way to go. In my records, there are several notes pointing to papers Jo Novak, one of the authors of *Learning How to Learn*, had written with respect to assessing the quality of concept maps. These papers and the book are likely influences for my choice in coding.

When I did the comparison, I found that the small qualitative variations between the first and the second test were also apparent in our quantitative comparisons. The mean number of links for all students participating in the study rose from 11.5 to 12.9. I used a statistical program available for my computer at the time (a program my high school students also used), but today's spreadsheets can do the required calculations (see sidebar on next page). From a statistical point of view, the difference between the two means is significant—which statisticians express in terms of Student's t and the associated p-value. In my case, the results were $t(9) = 2.49$, $p < .05$. Here the real point of interest is the p-value, as it tells me that the possibility that the difference from the first to the second test has arisen by chance is less than 5 percent. In other words, if the experiment were to be repeated with the same kind of students, similar differences would have been observed in all likelihood. But let us take a look at the educational significance. Although statistically different, the magnitude of the effect actually was small. The average increase per student between the two tests was 1.4 links. The high consistency between both performances—as shown in Table 1.1—was also confirmed by the quantitative analysis: Those students who did well or poorly on the first test, did likewise on the second test ($r = .94$, $p < .0001$). Here, the *r*-value simply is a number indicating the degree of relationship, where $r = 1.0$ would be a perfect relationship and $r = 0.0$ is no relationship at all. (To find *r* for the two sets of numbers in the sidebar example, the formula "=PEARSON(A2:A6,B2:B6)" would be entered into a cell; the result has to be compared with the critical *r* values under the entries for 4 degrees of freedom.) The *p*-value again indicates the degree to which the correlation has arisen by chance—here, $p < .0001$ means that this chance is less than 1 in 10,000.

Most propositions that the students had ended up with in their map had been intensely discussed, negotiated, or collaboratively constructed. This led me to believe that the students' understandings were far from identical. Through the sessions, the participants had negotiated global and local hierarchies between the concepts. The foregoing results indicate that the conceptual relationships developed collaboratively were stable in more than half of the participants, even over a six-week period. I thought that I may have here one of the contributing elements to the effectiveness of concept mapping in helping students to develop a better understanding of both individual propositions and an overall organization of the conceptual framework of a topic. On the other hand, Paul and Ed did not seem to benefit from the collaborative concept mapping, at least in terms of being able to appropriate from the collaborative experience. At this point, I had no evidence to answer the question whether the concept mapping activity, the collaboration, or both in combination failed to assist the two in achieving what the other participants did.

	A	B	C
1	X	Y	
2	1	1	
3	2	3	
4	2	3	
5	4	5	
6	6	7	
7			
8	3	3.8	0.016
9			4.00

A dependent *t*-test performed for 5 fictitious students each producing 2 scores. To do this calculation, I use the spreadsheet Excel. The mean of the first variables are calculated entering "=AVERAGE(A2:A6)" into A8, resulting in the value 3; a similar operation yields the mean of the scores in column B. "=TTEST(A2:A6,B2:B6,2,1)" entered into cell C8 results in $p = .016$. Entering "=TINV(C8,4)" into cell C9 yields $t = 4.00$.

An interesting question to me was how Nico was able to turn the collaborative mapping session into a successful learning experience. Although Nico had suggested during the mapping session to use light as a central concept, from which all concepts were to emanate ("I think light and waves are the most important, they are the most general . . . make them both the center."), his individual maps were clearly hierarchical and ordered around the tracer. He not only maintained the structure of the original tracer, but also was able to improve on it. Consequently, he

CHAPTER 1

used this tracer to anchor his whole map, thus constructing successful global and local hierarchical orderings of the concepts. For comparison purposes I included in my report Ed's tracer configuration produced during the six-week delayed test. It was apparent that his tracer configuration had little similarity with that of the two collaborative sessions. The figure also showed that four of his linkages were invalid, more so than for any other participant.

In the foregoing, readers see how I have come to a first answer through my research. I gained a better understanding of the relationship between group work, how group work affected individuals, and how stable individual learning was over time. In part, my analyses had to be qualitative; in part, I felt that the quantitative data allowed me to make claims that I would not have been able to make otherwise. The most crucial aspect of the study thus far was that I could support my arguments about group work in discussions with school administration and parents alike. Most students benefited tremendously. In subsequent studies I needed to find out what to do with students who thus far were not benefiting.

TRANSCRIBING

To find out more about learning than is possible from the products of student work, I needed to analyze the students' talk. After watching my first videotape, I knew I had to transcribe it, for as soon as I was searching for something that I had already seen I no longer could find it (easily) and had to scan forward and backward on the tape. From the beginning of my teacher-research, therefore, I completely transcribed each tape. Today, the ease with which tapes can be digitized leads some of my students to think that they can do without doing full transcripts; they attempt to find what they are looking for by rapidly scanning backward and forward in the digitized recording. But as soon as I ask a question about the prevalence of some phenomenon, they are stymied and find it would have been better to have a transcript. Thus, one of my graduate students this year went on for months trying to analyze his tapes and, in the end, resigned to transcribing them. He had spent many times the hours on his analysis that he would have needed had he immediately and completely transcribed them.

When I began to do teacher research about 15 years ago, I did not type very well and so hand-wrote the first version (Figure 1.7). I did not even have a remote control and operated the VCR directly with the left hand while transcribing what students were saying with the other hand. Whenever I wanted to make a comment concerning an observation or an analytic note, I used a differently colored pen (red) and, separating it from the transcript further by indenting considerably, I wrote whatever had come to my mind. For example, the excerpt depicted in Figure 1.7 includes the note "words lost in exchange as both try to 'dominate' discourse by raising voice." I had indicated the extend to which two speakers overlap by using brackets across the two turns and entered in parentheses codes (e.g., "ds," "aw," and "3 w iA") that denoted the concept label the student was pointing toward when the talk itself did not reveal it. The figure also shows that certain terms in the transcript have been highlighted (e.g., "interference" and "constructive"); and there

INVESTIGATING COLLABORATIVE CONCEPT MAPPING

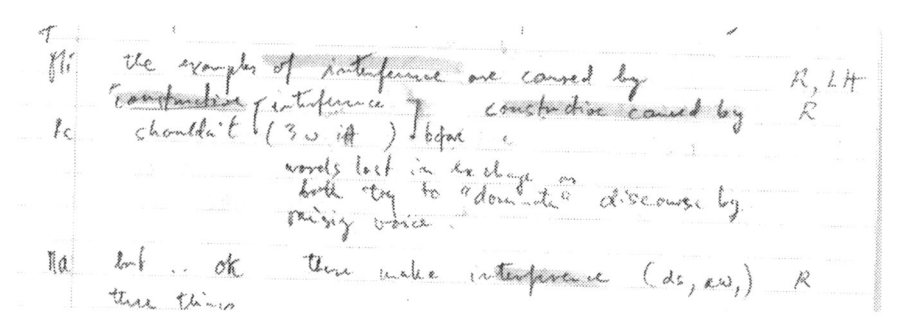

Figure 1.7. In my early work, I first transcribed in hand writing. Commentaries (originally in red color) are indented, key terms highlighted (blue), and codes on the right margin. The disadvantage of handwriting is that it cannot be easily searched.

are the codes "R" (for "indeterminate *R*elation") and "LH" (for "*L*ocal *H*ierarchy") on the right-hand margin. These have been added later while I was interpreting the transcript prior to rendering the transcripts into typewritten form; I return below to the coding used in this study.

These handwritten transcripts constituted my first material for analysis. In subsequent studies, I immediately typed the transcripts, adding comments as I went along; I sometimes even opened a second file where I typed interpretations that came to me in the process of transcribing. Electronic transcripts and comments are preferable, as they can be searched easily for content using the search function of modern-day word-processing programs. Ethnographers and sociologists often suggest that learning from an investigations means breaking the gaze and looking at familiar events in new ways. When the material is in textual form, the format itself may constitute a boundary to our seeing and hearing what has been said. Because there is no inherently right way of transcribing, arranging the text in a different way actually may assist in the process of interpretation and in the identification of patterns. As part of my analytic process, I learned a lot about this when I began to play with the layout; and playing with different layout options is much easier when the text already exists in electronic rather than in handwritten format. For this reason, in subsequent studies that I conducted as a teacher, I immediately produced a transcript on the computer.

After typing out the transcript, I created different copies, one of which produced the text as a narrow, four-inch band on the left side of the page leaving the right side for comments and diagrams (Figure 1.8). For example, to explore how utterances ultimately came to result in concept map structures, I diagrammed all statements (those that lent themselves to being diagrammed in this way) as partial maps. My sense was that this would then allow me to construct relationships between the concept map resulting from a session and the different utterances students made in the process constructing it.

In this study on concept mapping, I was interested in finding out how the ultimate map emerged that students had constructed. I thought that in the course of their transactions, the students might have articulated relations between concept

CHAPTER 1

	going downward, this is going down, that's one, that's another theory, and that is under quantum
Rand:	But quantum is part of the wave. Quantum is the part that/ its the end/ no no
Kevin:	Yeah, its different, there is a wave theory
Mick:	(In the background) ?? don't worry about it
Kevin:	Electron is a particle and not a quantum
Rand:	No, there is a wave theory and particle theory but, but thats onlyt one transm,itted by waves. Quantum says that a wave has not continuousband of energy.
Mick:	Yeah, this should come in fron because of those,/ are also discovered first
Kevin:	An this is
Mick:	No remember, we screwed that up the last time the wave goes on top

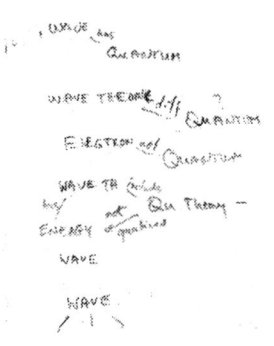

Figure 1.8. After I had typed out the transcripts, I created a version that only covered the left half of the page allowing for notes and diagrams on the right-hand side.

words. Thus, I wondered whether I would be able to see fragments of the ultimate map emerge. Would some way of relating a concept stabilize or continue to change in the productive process? Because the ultimate product was a visual representation—i.e., a map as in Figure 1.1—I thought that it might be useful to produce a version of each transcript in which all suitable utterances were "transcribed" into visual representation, a fragment of a concept map (see diagrams next to text in Figure 1.8). More so, because I was interested in finding out how the group work related to the maps individuals produced at some later stage—i.e., on tests and examinations—I thought it might be useful to "pull out" the individual contributions they had made during their negotiations so that I could simultaneously see how the partial maps produced by students in the sequential give-and-take related to what individual students produced in the course of a session.

Figure 1.9 presents a small part of one of the resulting double transcripts. In the left-most column, I produced a textual form of the transcript. I then drew four columns, one for each of the three students in the group and one for myself, the teacher (not represented here). Wherever possible, I then translated statements into a visual representation, a partial concept map. Readers easily recognize that scanning downward in a column allows the analyst to see the conceptual relations that an individual stated, and moving from line to line allows understanding how individual statements relate to one another. To produce this representation, I created a table with five columns in a text file with landscape format. I drew the concept maps in a graphics program (MacDraw at the time) and pasted them into the corresponding cell. Once I had produced the protocol for an entire session, I created a printout and then taped the individual pages to produce a roll—or two partial rolls when the transcript was too long. To be able to take both close-up and distant views, I hung the transcript onto a wall. Stepping forward and backward then provided me with different perspectives onto the transcript—from farther away, more global visual aspects become salient, whereas close-ups tended to bring out microscopic features of the interactions. In subsequent studies focusing on other topics, I continued using the tabular format but arranged the text according to speaker (Fig-

			Ralf	Miles	Ken
1.	Ralf:	What is quantum?	QUANTUM?		
2.	Ken:	What quantum means, are light is a particle instead of waves			QUANTUM LIGHT isn't / is WAVE PARTICLE
3.	Ralf:	But that is quanta			
4.	Ken:	Yeah, its like this			
5.	Ralf:	And its quanta, its the singular form			
6.	Ken:	Yes I see what you mean, wave and quantum are an instant			
7.	Ralf:	Quantum is part of a wave and then, photon, photon and quantum is the same thing	WAVE — has — QUANTUM - is - PHOTON		
8.	Ken:	They are the same, non no, I am saying if we are going downward, this is going down, that's one, that's another theory, and that [photon] is under quantum			LIGHT is / is QUANTUM WAVE is PHOTON
9.	Ralf:	But quantum is part of the wave. Quantum is the part that/ its the end/ no no	WAVE — has part — QUANTUM		

Figure 1.9. Being interested in the evolution of concepts, I turned propositions, where possible, into mini concept maps.

CHAPTER 1

Ralf	Miles	Ken
What is quantum?		
		What quantum means, are light is a particle instead o waves
But that is quanta		
		Yea, it is like this
And its quant, it's the singular form		
		Yes I see what you mean, wave and quantum are an instant
Quantum is part of a wave and then, photon, photon and quantum is the same thing		
		They are the same, no, no, I am saying if we are going downward, this is going down, that's one, that's another theory, and that is under quantum
But quantum is part of the wave. Quantum is the part that, it's the end, no, no		
		Yea, its different, there is wave theory
	((in the background)) ?? don't worry about it.	

Figure 1.10. To get a better sense of the relation between individual and group, I often put transcripts into a tabular format, which makes individual contributions stand out more than a "linear" transcription.

ure 1.10). This, too, provides the double perspective relating transactions to patterns in individual utterances over time.

However the transcript is produced, it should provide opportunities for using a variety of colors to highlight and link different parts, use specific colors to make salient patterns, and to write comments. I found it useful—and still do—to step back from the transcript, to walk around it to get a different, second, and even a third look. This distancing helps in the analysis, to see what is familiar in new ways.

CONSTRUCTING ANALYTIC NOTES

The time it takes to do an analysis depends on the type of research one does. For example, for my PhD, I had stated several hypotheses about the expected relationship between various measures of (auditory, visual) short-term memory, on the one hand, and several learning- and development-related measures, on the other. Once

I had collected the data sources, I entered them into the computer. In two 16-hour sessions, I not only did the analyses but also all the data snooping I wanted to do to identify any possible patterns that I had not predicted. That is, it only took me two long days to get my analyses done. On the other hand, when I interpret textual data in a research area that is totally or relatively new, I have to generate patterns and codes before I can check whether these patterns are consistent within and across students in my database as a whole. Before I actually come to write a report, I often spend weeks if not months going through the data sources to generate possible patterns and testing them in other parts of the database. To aid in the production of patterns, I produce *analytic notes*, in which I record anything that comes to my mind while going through the materials. I also include quotes from texts I have read, comments as to the degree of similarity and difference between what others have written and what I can see in my materials.

When the transcript exists in electronic form, I either comment directly in it by making some space and using a marker such as "COMMENT:" to visually mark the place that I have added additional text. More frequently, though, I copy relevant transcript parts into the note file containing my research memos, which I save in a special folder (directory) containing research notes (memos) using the date in its name. Thus, an excerpt from a research note while conducting the study on collaborative concept mapping could be found on my hard drive under the file name 09/28 Data I in a nested data structure of this type:

Concept II > Data > 09/28 Data I

Organizing analytic notes in this way comes with the advantage that one can track the evolution of one's own understanding, a phenomenon that is denoted by the term *progressive subjectivity* (Guba & Lincoln, 1989). In Figure 1.11, I present one of the many notes I wrote while going over-and-over again through the materials. In this instance, excerpts from the database are surrounded by analytic text, which, as it continues to grow, may one day be suitable for inclusion in a report, thesis, or journal article.

I am often asked to be more specific about *how* to do the analysis, but each time, and despite many years of experience in analyzing and teaching, I cannot say more than "try." The gap between a description of what to do while analyzing and actually doing an analysis is the same as the one existing between a recipe and what you do in the kitchen. When you closely observe yourself while following a recipe or while following any other set of instructions, you may notice that you discover the relevance of an instruction only after having done the process described. My taking you through my thinking during a research project is precisely at the origin of writing this text on research method differently than most books on the topic are written. In this book, the method is described and explicated with the concrete materials collected in research projects and the decision-making underlying many of the problems that emerged as I went along. It is in this way that I provide readers with the possibility of experiencing analysis vicariously—an experience that my own students actually get during our many analytic meetings. But because one remembers only what one has done before, you still have to *do* analysis to learn it.

CHAPTER 1

> **An example of a long utterance**
> "We can take this [concept card] right out of here and say 'light is a transverse wave', and don't bother with it here, because it's a waste of time."
>
> **Fragmented discourse**
> N: Light
> E: Light
> N: Light is, may be a wave, or as a wave?
> E: Is a wave, go put that.
> K: Light
> N: Has a wave
> E: Sort of
> N: I am trying
> K: Light is in the form of waves
> N: No yeah
> K: No matter what
> N: Light is a wave/ what I sort of/ so we really should have
>
> In this discourse, available to the listener is only what the also available for recording on audio- and/or videotape. However, there is no reason to assume that this is all the participants think about the problem they are having, or that these are all the propositions that the participants test. Rather, those that they propose are those that they are willing to have tested in the public forum of the group. Others that potentially exist are never tested, and are unavailable for the group construction of meaning, although it is not unavailable for the construction of meaning by the individual, as he or she appropriates form the group work, that is, as these individuals construct their own meaning from what is available to all of them as joint constructs.
>
> **Joint construct**, however, should not mean that meaning is necessarily shared. There could still be differences in the understanding of the individuals, although they had constructed the conversational object in collaboration. In many situations, however, participants are dealing as if they shared the meaning; they take the shared meaning as granted. They constructed taken-to-be-shared meaning.

Figure 1.11. In this excerpt from an analytic note, certain terms are bold-faced because they appear to point towards patterns prevalent in the materials.

Although I generally find it easy to get into the mood of interpreting materials even if they originated in someone else's project—even my graduate students who have been working for years wonder about how I do it—I know from observing them struggle initially that getting into the groove takes some time. But would you expect otherwise? Cooking, skateboarding, gardening, and everything else we do in life takes some time until we hit the groove. So the best advice I can give is this: Write, write, and write . . . until you have nothing more to say; on the next day, you write, write, and write . . . until you have nothing more to say; and on the next day, you do the same. Then, at the end of a week of writing everything that comes to your mind while staring at a transcript or some other piece of material, you go back and read what you have written in the course of the week.

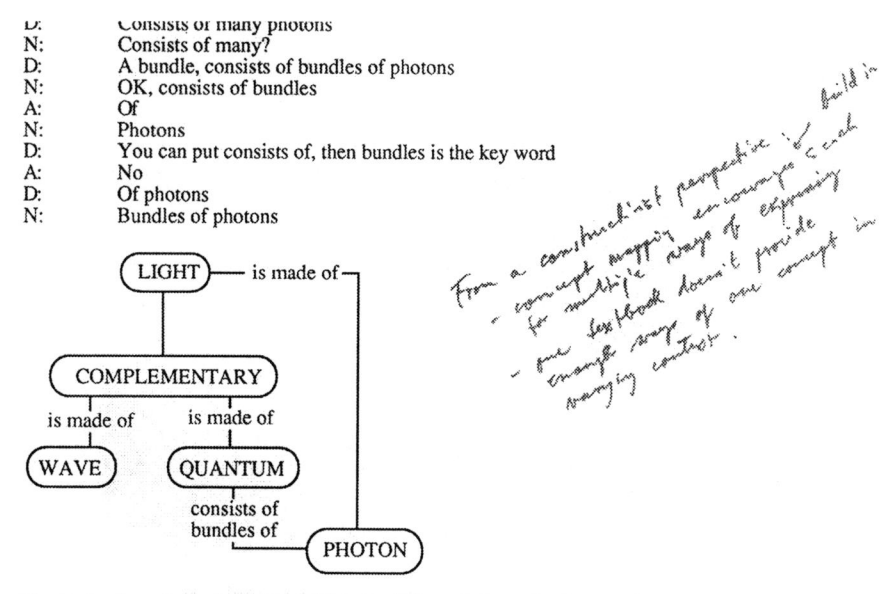

D: Consists of many photons
N: Consists of many?
D: A bundle, consists of bundles of photons
N: OK, consists of bundles
A: Of
N: Photons
D: You can put consists of, then bundles is the key word
A: No
D: Of photons
N: Bundles of photons

```
        ┌─────────┐
        │  LIGHT  │──── is made of ──┐
        └────┬────┘                  │
             │                       │
    ┌────────────────┐               │
    │  COMPLEMENTARY │               │
    └────────────────┘               │
    is made of   is made of          │
    ┌──────┐   ┌─────────┐           │
    │ WAVE │   │ QUANTUM │           │
    └──────┘   └─────────┘           │
               consists of           │
               bundles of            │
                      └──┌────────┐──┘
                         │ PHOTON │
                         └────────┘
```

From a constructivist perspective I seek to build in...
- concept mapping encourages ways of expressing
- the textbook doesn't provide for multiple
enough ways of one concept in
varying contexts.

The textbook probably doesn't provide enough formulations. Students try here a number of different ones. Students really try many formulations until they find one which seems to

Figure 1.12. I print out my analytic notes and then, as a way of learning from my learning, read and comment upon them.

While you go back over your analytic notes, have another memo file open in which you record every pattern in your own writing that comes to your mind. For example, you might find that you use certain terms or concepts repeatedly and in the context of different pieces of material. This then points you to patterns that appear to be more prevalent and constitute more than singular cases. You may wish to go through printed versions of your notes and write any comments on them—which is something I have frequently done and continue to do (Figure 1.12); in this instance, the comment I added pertained to two implications from my research from a constructivist perspective, the value of expressing content in multiple ways and the limitation of using only one textbook. Or you might write comments and information on sticky notes when you have an idea and subsequently attach them to the appropriate page in your printed analytic files. Nowadays, I do a lot using a professional version of Adobe Acrobat, which allows me to highlight text and add notes electronically. In this way, I have all the color possibilities that I have with highlighter and pen, but I use less paper and have all my materials in more portable form. I can share the files with colleagues around the world, who can add their own comments, lines, and highlights. Acrobat automatically keeps track who entered a note so that we never loose who wrote or said what.

Reading articles and books related to the topic you have chosen to research provides seeds for your reflective activity. I always found that reading what others have written stimulates my thinking and sharpens my gaze. For example, in one of my research notes on this collaborative concept mapping project, I entered the following comments:

> Reference to Bloom, 1991:
> knowledge and meaning undergo constant change as new information, connections, and perceptions are taken in and influenced by various contextual factors.
> 24. Concept mapping as an instance of collaborative construction of text? Compare to Wells, Chang, & Maher, 1990. Does the concept mapping combine the effects of reading and writing? Reflection and talking?

In this research memo, I made reference to two texts I had read—I both entered the complete reference in the note itself and in a special file where I continue to keep all references I ever used. I continually update the file named "BIBLIO" followed by the most recent date that I entered a reference yielding a filename such that today, November 16, 2006 it reads "BIBLIO061117.doc." In this particular memo reproduced here, the idea that emerged in reference to the first author (i.e., Bloom) pertains to the changing nature of knowledge and meaning in the course of student–student discussions. I also noted the hypothesis—to be tested subsequently in the remainder of the materials—that perceptions changed. In this way, that is, by keeping notes about my emerging ideas and the context of their emergence, I keep track of the process of making sense in the course of my teacher-researcher project. This process leads to the establishment of its credibility.

The second part of the note is actually numbered, because it is connected to a series of questions (see below) I was establishing for guiding my search for patterns. The note also makes reference to an article where the researchers had studied the collaborative construction of text. This topic was not directly related to my topic, collaborative concept mapping, but it did have a link in the collaborative production of something at least in part textual—each proposition in the form of concept-link-concept constitutes a basic textual element. I then posed some questions that came to my mind at the moment, and to which I would be able to return once I was stepping a bit back. Or I could return to these questions with the express intent to find an answer to them.

> **References and Bibliography** It is a good strategy to create a reference or bibliography file in which you note everything you read. You will, in this way, never have a problem of finding a reference when you need it in something you write.

Yet another way of getting into the groove and finding first patterns is to look at some piece of material with others, colleagues or fellow graduate students. They may note something you have not seen, but which you could pursue once you are on your own again. My graduate students regularly meet in this way to generate ideas and to hear others talk about their data. So that they do not have to take notes, we videotape such meetings. The person whose materials are discussed takes the tape as a reference, going back over it to note those aspects that appear to be salient.

COLLECTIVE ACHIEVEMENT

One of my major goals in this teacher-researcher study concerning concept mapping was to find out about the relation between doing tasks in collaborative groups and subsequent performance on tests. The answers were particularly important to me teaching in a private school that prepared students for pursuing tertiary studies. The attitude in the families that were able to send their children to the school was one of "We paid for the education of our child, not for him [her] to help others!" In my conversations with parents, it always helped me to have good supportive evidence for what the teachers in my department and I were doing. My teacher-researcher activities provided me with the sort of evidence I needed when a particularly insistent parent thought he or she knew more about education than we, the science teachers. Among others, I wanted to know more about the difference between a successful and a less successful group.

For this purpose, I defined success in terms of individual appropriation from the collaborative experience. In one successful group, all students transferred their group results into the individual test situation one week after their session, two of them transferred even into the second test, delayed by six weeks; at that time, the third students' tracer showed moderate alterations. In the unsuccessful group, the maps of two students did not show the group tracer either after one or after six weeks; on the other hand, the third student (Nico) did transfer and even improve over the group results. I was thinking that these differences might have their origin in the way the group construction process unfolded.

But how does one go about checking transcripts for differences given that each is highly contingent, emerging from the unpredictable give and take between the students? I was thinking about the number and length of the statement students made in the group. I was also thinking that the type of statements related to the hierarchy might have something to do with it. I knew that there probably were other possible ways in which groups might differ, but I began by pursuing these two.

> **Analytic Notes** Although you might think that you will remember your thinking and decision-making processes, my experience is that after some time you tend to forget. Therefore, it is helpful to record everything you do and the reasons you make this or that decision.

First, I went through my transcripts and measured the length of the statements students produced (in the form of word counts) and then entered the counts in a statistical program to find out average length, standard deviation, and distribution of lengths. I then wrote the following research memo.

> The sentence length was determined from the protocols. Most often, the sentence length was equal to the length of the utterance. Sometimes, however, long utterances were treated as a collection of sentences when the context indicated a shift in the thought of the speaker. The sentence length of 5.3 words is even shorter than the 7 words for informal speech, the 17–25 for formal speech Chafe (1982), or the 9 words reported for the sentence length of users of a natural language interface with computers

CHAPTER 1

> (Guindon, 1991). A distribution of the sentence lengths is presented in Figure 1 [not presented here]$_{WMR}$. A rather broad distribution is apparent with a mode at 5 words per sentence. When the utterances were counted, the mean sentence length increased to 6.0.

This analysis supported the comment I had made about the fragmented nature of student discourse (Figure 1.10) but it did not lead me much further. There were no differences between the groups and the length of the utterances was highly context dependent. Not surprisingly, I never included this analysis in any reports and it never became part of an article submitted for publication. The analysis also showed that I was reading the linguistics literature concerning the length of the sentences people use in a variety of contexts. This teaches us that some analyses do not lead any further and have to be abandoned. In fact, as part of the research that is the background for chapter 3, I framed a concept *blind alley* to denote those cases where students do not find the results in their experiments that they were looking for. Our social science research methods, too, do not provide us with any assured way of predicting whether an analysis will or will not yield useful results. There never is a way of knowing beforehand whether an analysis will reap fruit or not.

The second analysis I conducted concerned the frequency with which different types of utterances related to the hierarchy of the concept map occurred. To do this, I came up with the following four categories: (a) phrases that make reference to the *global hierarchy* of the concepts, GH, such as "Light is the most inclusive and should be on the top"; (b) phrases referring to a *local hierarchy*, LH, such as "Phase goes above interference"; (c) phrases that simply expressed *proximity*, P, such as "Crest goes with wave"; and (d) phrases that expressed a clear *relationship*, R, such as "A node is a point of destructive interference." I then coded all instances in all transcripts I had made in terms of these four codes. An example of codes entered in the transcript can be seen in Figure 1.7.

One of the next questions I asked was "How can I compare the different groups on the basis of these codes?" When it was its time to be considered, I was thinking that I could compare, for example, the student groups based on the total number of phrases in each category; or I could establish a relative frequency, where the measure of instances in each group is relative to the total number of phrases coded; or still, I could represent the temporal frequencies of codes, which would allow me to generate hypotheses about success in terms of the moments (beginning, middle, end of session) when the different categories peak or peter out. I explored all these options, one at a time, and then wrote the following analytic memo. The codes RMM and PEM refer to the successful and unsuccessful group, respectively.

> The transcripts of the sessions showed that during the first ten minutes, the successful group had more than twice as many propositions formulated than the unsuccessful group. After that, RMM formulated about 50 percent more phrases than PEN.
>
> The figure [only one of the two graphs is reproduced here]$_{WMR}$ illustrates how the four categories were distributed over time. In both cases, a majority of the initial phrases pertained to the groups "proximity" and

"global hierarchy," indicating that the groups where concerned with the overall ordering of the concepts into groups and the groups relative to each other. We have to keep in mind, however, that over the first 10 minutes, RMM had 11 GH, but PEM had only 6 GH phrases. While the proportion of relationship expressing phrases shows a similar pattern, there are significant differences in the use of phrases referring to the local hierarchy. PEN had used only one LH-phrase over the first 12 minutes, while RMM showed a consistent concern for local hierarchies.

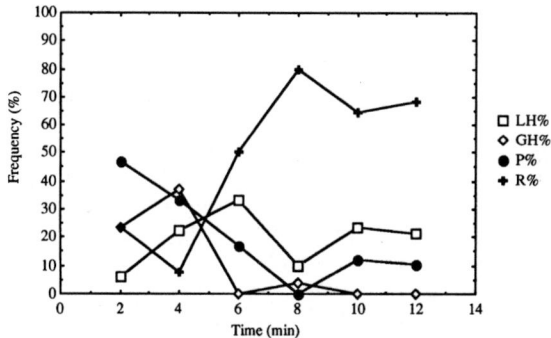

On the other hand, the less successful group exceeded the more successful group in the relative frequency of phrases that merely expressed proximity. These differences could also be seen from their concept maps. Other than the tracer, no hierarchical relationship could be discerned from PEN's map. Rather, the concepts of light and wave were surrounded by star-like emanating propositions. On the other hand, RMM's map was highly structured with a discernible global hierarchy, and many local, hierarchical relationships.

When the concept maps of RMM and PEN produced during the sessions were compared, striking differences became apparent both in terms of the number of linkages produced and in the hierarchical organization. During their first session, PEN produced 29 links, out of which 25 (4) were valid (invalid). A link was judged valid if the associated proposition was acceptable within the language of standard (canonical) physics. During their second session, they again produced 29 links, all of which were valid. RMM, on the other hand, produced 36 (1) links during the session that was on the same day as PEN's second session. The third group increased their linkages from 25 (4) to 36 (1) valid (invalid). RMM's concept map was highly structured, with definite hierarchies within local clusters of concepts, and between local clusters, that is at a global scale. For example, RMM developed local hierarchies for interference and for dispersion phenomena. However, equivalent concepts such as double slit and air wedge versus prism (i.e. devices that bring about interference versus dispersion phenomena) or diffraction and reflection versus refraction (processes caused by these devices) still appeared at the same level in the

CHAPTER 1

overall map. This organization gave the map a highly structured overall look. On the other hand, PEN's maps showed little global organization; the only apparent local hierarchy was that around the tracer concepts and was not without flaws. Concepts seemed to be connected with little regard of structure, in a more or less haphazard way. The concept maps between the two extremes frequently exhibited well-developed local hierarchies with little comparison between the local clusters of concepts. I am thus seeing a definite relationship between the concern for hierarchy, as expressed by the number of phrases pertaining to this issue, and the organization of the resulting product. It is also apparent that the less successful group's comments pertaining to global organization such as "Light is the most important" does not lead to any hierarchical ordering.

It is immediately evident that to produce this research note, I had to have gone through the transcripts and had to have coded them. This process itself takes a considerable amount of time, and sometimes even requires the refinement of one's coding system. It is a good practice to record the doubts one has and to produce a list of the ambiguous cases that not easily lend themselves to be coded one way or another. If there are such doubts, the reasons for categorizing a statement this or that way also should be recorded. Readers can see from the note that it is written for myself. For example, toward the end of the note I had written, "I am thus seeing a definite relationship between the concern for hierarchy . . .," which clearly was for myself rather than for someone else. I have learned to appreciate such writing, because I do not worry about others' opinions about my work. I always write for myself first and then take my writing as a source from which I copy or that I transform parts of it when I write for an audience. In this way, I am never afraid to write something down, because the notes and memos exclusively are for my personal use.

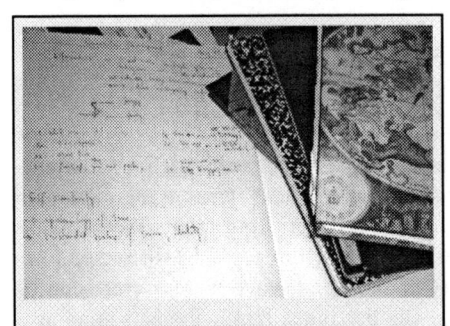

Memos, Notebooks Throughout my career as a researcher, I have found it helpful to have notebooks for recording anything and everything in a quick way. Because all entries are dated, I simultaneously establish an audit trail and the possibility to document progressive subjectivity. I like to work in multiple modes—drawings, diagrams, words—so that it is easier form e to use an old-fashioned notebook and pencil.

QUESTIONS FOR DIRECTING ANALYSIS

How does one drive the analysis along? How does one conduct a productive analysis? *Writing* questions that one subsequently answers is a good way of moving an analysis ahead. One of my personal goals for this study was to find out more about my students' learning processes. To direct my search for patterns in the materials I

42

collected, I began writing a list of questions, which I expanded as I went along. In many instances, I simply noted the new questions that emerged in the daily analytic notes I kept (e.g., the note on p. 37 has a question numbered "24"). These questions—other than the big ones that I address in the introduction—are intended to focus my gaze on the data source materials and to drive the analysis of the particular entities and processes I am looking for. Most of these questions cannot be answered in a simple manner but require extended analysis. For example, in one of the first analytic notes concerning this study, I wrote 34 questions and made many additional comments that directed my attention in a similar way. The following excerpt features the first ten of these questions:

Some questions to be resolved:
1. How is intersubjectivity achieved?
2. How do students arrive ascertain that their meanings are the same?
3. Is there evidence for the co-construction of meaning?
4. Is there evidence for the reciprocal completion of sentences?
5. Is there evidence for the negotiating meaning in a small group?
6. Are there changes in the formulation/expression of one student's ideas? Several students?
7. Is there evidence that one student dominates the discourse? That "weaker" students contribute equally to the discourse?
8. How do students arrive at consensus? Do they arrive at consensus?
9. Are there misconceptions on which the students settle? Why do they settle on these?
10. What resources do students have at their hands? How do they use them? Possible resources are books, peers, time, teacher . . .

Some of these questions possibly were the results of my readings at the time; others might have arisen while I was wondering about what was happening in the student groups, which I had little idea about because, as the teacher, I was going from group to group. Watching the tapes was the first time that I had a chance to see a group go from the beginning to the end. I found out later from other teachers who watched tapes with me that they shared my own amazement. Teachers generally are surprised about what their students are able to do when they take the time trying to understand what students *actually* do while engaging with the tasks.

LEARNING PROCESSES

In my analyses, three major processes emerged that students used to arrive at suitable propositions. Students mediated propositions verbally and non-verbally, they took adversarial positions and appealed to authority, and they formed temporary alliances based on presumed expertise. Both product and process hold promise but also show some limitations. I found out on the positive side that the process of mapping concepts leads to sustained discourse on the topic and improved the declarative knowledge of several students both in terms of the hierarchical organization and "local" configuration of the concepts. In contrast, concept mapping also

CHAPTER 1

led unintended and scientifically incorrect notions become ingrained or left them unchallenged. In the following, I focus on how I found out about the process students used to construct on the spot new links. In this, I found a pattern that was at the intersection of several questions with which I had started my investigation, including questions #3 and #8 in the preceding list

From the literature I knew that within- and across-topic linkages are among the hardest things to establish for textbook-oriented students. I was wondering whether there were occasions in my video recordings where students discussed or came up with novel linkages. To find an answer, I had to do a number of things. First, I had to find out whether there was evidence on my classroom tapes—shot for other purposes—of certain concepts that have been linked into statements. I could do this rapid check in other materials, because I was transcribing continuously and could rapidly check; once I worked electronically, such searches were even more rapid. (Today, the *Spotlight* feature of my Macintosh OS 10.4 system rapidly searches all types of files for the occurrence of specified features.) Second, I had to check the main textbook students were using for all the ways in which it linked the concepts under investigation it. Third, I had to identify stretches in the transcript that were leading to a new set of linked concepts or in which students discussed linkages during concept mapping that did not exist in the other materials. It is immediately evident that this analysis required me to bring different materials to convergence because I needed to be familiar with all three sources (other lessons, book, concept mapping) simultaneously.

My interest was peaked when I read the following stretch of transcript, in which I subsequently underlined the different ways in which the three students attempted to link the same pair of concepts. I copied the transcript into file named "11/16 help document" and then wrote an initial note based on what came to my mind.

Ralf: Diffraction <u>affects</u> matter waves
Miles: Yeah, because they do diffract
Ken: Frequency <u>can alter</u> matter waves, it just means that matter waves can diffract. Just put, like, <u>can alter</u> or <u>affects</u>, which ever one you feel.
Ralf: Matter waves can, <u>can</u> diffract
Miles: Put like, <u>can</u>
Ralf: <u>Undergoes</u>
Miles: You aren't going/ undergo
Ralf: Give me another word
Miles: We gave you about six
Ralf: Matter waves <u>can</u> diffraction?
Miles: OK, just go, <u>undergo</u>
Ken: He says, I said that, I said diffraction <u>affects</u>, or

In this episode, the three are trying to establish a link between matter waves and diffraction. In their textbook, these two concepts had never been explicitly linked in one proposition or sentence:

Textbook
a. For electrons, the matter waves can be approximately the same as the wavelength of some X-rays.
b. A beam of electrons can be diffracted
c. Electrons passed through a thin metal foil, and the diffraction pattern was approximately the same as that for X-rays
d. Particles exhibit wavelike properties.

Part of the students' task is to establish links that are meaningful to them, that is, links that they can express in their own language. However, these links should at the same time be compatible with those of canonical science. Part of the difficult task during concept mapping is to establish such links using linking words of their own, which means that they have to connect concepts in new ways, but which are under the constraints of the field.

The textbooks only provide a limited way of presenting possible linkages, possible expressions with the concepts involved. Even a teacher cannot do much more than what a textbook can do. Ultimately, the students have to try on their own, and with corrective feedback, establish their own way of talking about the different themes within a science. Corrective feedback can come from both peers and teacher. This analysis also gives us a hint to the usefulness of using more than one textbook. Because different authors will use different propositions, the students will increase the number of possible connections they encountered, and which they then find admissible to be used.

> **Analysis and Free Writing** Think about your initial analyses in terms of free writing. Take a piece of transcript, copy it into a special file, and then write as much as you possibly can about the transcript. Then do the same with another piece of transcript, which you select based on a sense that it might be interesting. This process attunes you to your materials; and it is likely that you can use what you write in the reports and manuscripts you prepare from your teacher-research.

This also gives some sort of notion about the difficulties students face with tests, where they might find new connections between concepts that they had not thought of or encountered before. Doing problems form multiple textbooks increases the number of admissible formulations, usages of the concepts of a thematic.

Afterward, I checked all other materials whether there were similar or contradictory situations and, based on this search, came to the conclusion that I was observing a general pattern. Thus, in this situation, the three students tried here five different formulations (due to, can affect, can alter, can, & undergoes) for linking the words "matter," "wave," and "diffraction/diffract." They stopped only after they had found that link on which they could all agree, one that "sounded right." In such cases, the teacher's input would be of importance to provide the feedback necessary to assist students in the construction of propositions, thus knowledge compati-

CHAPTER 1

ble with that of canonical (standard) science. Textbooks and teachers can never provide all possible propositions. Besides, no matter how many formulations there are and how explicit they are, students will always have to construct their own ways of expressing the relationship between pairs of concepts. Thus, while it is very important that students have the opportunities provided by collaborative concept mapping that allow them to construct new propositions in their own words, it is also important that appropriate feedback mechanisms are present which prevent inappropriate propositions to be constructed. In the first instance, such feedback is provided through the activity structure itself in that peers can criticize and question a proposition. Or students can ask for classification, explanation, and justification. Then, the teacher (and to a limited extend the textbook) serves as a second instance for feedback.

In the present case, the students' textbook never explicitly linked the two concepts matter wave and diffraction in one proposition or sentence. Through my analysis of the textbook, I found out that it brings together the wave-like properties of matter and diffraction in the following four ways: (a) "for electrons, the matter waves can be approximately the same as the wavelength of some X-rays"; (b) "a beam of electrons can be diffracted"; (c) "electrons passed through a thin metal foil, and the diffraction pattern was approximately the same as that for X-rays"; and (d) "particles exhibit wave-like properties." Then, the textbook only provided a limited way of presenting possible linkages or possible expressions with the concepts involved. This allowed me to conclude that the students had to try on their own, and with corrective feedback, establish their own way of talking about the different themes within a science. In many cases, such corrective feedback came from both peers and me, the teacher. My present analysis also gave me an indication about the usefulness of using more than one textbook. Because different authors use different propositions—i.e., join concepts in different ways for making statements—the students would increase, so I thought, the number of possible connections they encountered, and which they then find admissible to be used.

> **Objectivity and Quality** Some people think that interpretive research cannot be "objective." In fact, in many ways it is more objective than other research *if* you capture the process of your research on paper. Then, every claim you make, every concept you construct, and every piece of knowledge you arrive at can be traced back to the original data sources. The entire process therefore can be exhibited, becomes public, and can be *audited*. Establishing an *audit trail* is an important aspect of the quality of interpretive research.

As a result of these analyses, I concluded that concept mapping provided for occasions where the students had to construct propositions that they have never seen or heard before. But in such a case, they have no way of deciding whether this sentence lies within the language of standard science or outside—putting them much in the same situation as the mathematician Kurt Gödel, who found that even the most formal of formal languages allows statements that lie outside of the formal system and therefore cannot be evaluated concerning their truth value. My teaching also provided for occasions where students had to construe patterns of relationships among concepts that were widely separated in time or place, relationships that had been only slightly emphasized by the teacher or textbook, if at all. Concept mapping, thus, gave students practice in constructing novel relationships, an important part in learning to speak the language of science, and, from a social constructivist stand point, in understanding the subject.

I then thought about what the students' task really was: In concept mapping, the students are asked to establish links that are meaningful to them, that is, links that they can express in their own language, for their own purposes, and for which they have a sense that they are making sense or, alternatively stated, that *it* all makes sense. However, these links should at the same time be compatible with those that my course was to teach them. Part of the difficult task during concept mapping was to establish such propositions where students used their own linking words, which meant that they had to connect concepts in new ways, but which were under the constraints of the field, here of physics. I realized that my students were faced with similar difficulties on tests, where they might have to construct new connections between concepts that they had not thought of or encountered before. Doing problems from multiple textbooks would increase the number of correct formulations and usages of the concepts of a thematic. For this reason, the participating students already were asked to select problems from at least one other textbook. This feature of concept mapping to reveal student difficulties in establishing meaningful links is also one of its powers as a tool in uncovering conceptual problems. I realized that these conceptual problems, once brought into the open, could be subjected to criticism and become topics of the discussion.

QUALITY AND AUDIT

The reader may have already asked how it is possible for me to recall events that have happened more than 15 years ago; some may suggest that I must be an orderly person. Now, neither is my memory exceptional nor am I particularly good in ordering things around myself—seeing my offices, you might be tempted to exclaim, "What a mess!" However, the secret may be that I have always put everything down in writing and kept both handwritten and electronic records. In part I have done this because I have felt that I needed to write stuff down so that it acquired a concrete quality of material stuff with which I could engage; just talking about something never allowed me to articulate my thoughts and rarely ever allowed me to learn. It is when I attempted to articulate myself precisely that all the snags in my thinking have become apparent, open to critique, and possible to revise. Thus, for me *writing (drawing) has been and still is the same as thinking*.

In the process of writing and keeping dates on each sheet or file, I established a set of records that now can be used to track my published articles right back to the original sources, including the videotapes that I have stored as well. I only later became aware of the idea that such records support the *confirmability* of my research, a criterion that is somewhat similar to the conventional notion of objectivity (Guba & Lincoln, 1989). Because I annotated files, and generated new files and text based on previous files and text, the entire logic underlying my research can be inspected. Much like in a fiscal audit, an auditor could go through my records and

CHAPTER 1

confirm what I have done—though in this kind of research this is a rare event indeed. Such an event would constitute a *dependability audit*.

The records I constructed and left behind allow others or me to monitor the process by means of which my understandings, concepts, and claims have come about over time. This process is generally referred to as *progressive subjectivity*, and allows a teacher-researcher to check the various ways in which prior and new knowledge mediate what he or she learns in and through doing a study. Monitoring one's subjectivity is particularly important for teacher-researchers for at least two reasons. On the one hand, we teacher-researchers are so familiar with the context of our research that we are like the proverbial fish that never recognizes the water allowing it to swim and live in the first place. This familiarity with the context comes with advantages that other researchers have to work hard to achieve to make their research credible: *prolonged engagement* and *persistent observation*. It is self-evident that we teacher-researchers have had substantial involvement in the site of our research, which helps us overcome the problems outside researchers would face, including misinformation, distortion, and so on. Prolonged engagement has allowed us to make persistent observations, which exists especially when we have collected a lot of material that we can use in making sense after the fact of what has happened.

> **Ideology** The basis underlying our common sense normally remains hidden, like the water remains hidden to the proverbial fish. This hidden basis of assumptions and ideas constitutes an *ideology*. Because there are hidden assumptions, ideologies are dangerous for researchers generally but for teacher-researchers especially. To avoid getting trapped in our ideologies, we need to engage in radical doubt with respect to our thinking: "Why do I think this or that?" (content) and "Why do I think this way?" (process) are questions that we continually need to ask ourselves.

On the other hand, our own preconceptions about knowing and learning may actually lead us away from understanding what is happening on the videotapes, because these preconceptions work like filters or distorting lenses. This possibility of falling prey to our own prior ideas requires us to be especially watchful, to be critical both of our constructs and of the way in which we construct new concepts. This is especially important because of a general human tendency to have a *confirmation bias* and to take insufficiently into account all information that would contradict our current ways of understanding. It is only by *radically doubting* ourselves that we teacher-researchers will sufficiently take control over confirmation bias and reification of received ways of understanding and explaining events. For example, a common way of teachers to look at students is in terms of their "ability," where ability itself is a product of schooling rather than something determined independently. Thus, "good students" tend to do well, and we continuously see good students do well. But going about teacher-research in this way only confirms past and possibly inappropriate understandings rather than fulfilling the promise and raison d'être of teacher-research. Why would we go through the labor of doing teacher-research if we were not ready to learn something new, that is, question and ultimately throw overboard what we have known before?

WHAT I LEARNED FROM THIS STUDY

I concluded this teacher-researcher investigation with specific recommendations for the use of concept maps in the classroom. These include continued instruction in establishing proper hierarchies and in cross-linking to increase the quality of the concept maps' structure and the number of high quality links. Then, instruction should facilitate students' attempts to reflect on the nature of the relationships expressed in their maps. And finally, specific roles could be assigned to individual students to improve the overall quality of the process of constructing the map and thus, of the final product.

Although concept mapping structured the student–student and student–teacher transactions in important ways, it also fostered transactions that were not favorable to the development of complex expressions. On the positive side, (a) concept mapping provided for a framework within which students engaged in sustained discourse over periods of an hour length; (b) the fixed set of concepts delimited the content of the discourse; and (c) the students not only linked individual pairs of concepts, but also built a map of a thematic territory. Thus, I learned that concept mapping provided a structure that scaffolded the ways in which students learned the language patterns of science and with it, construct scientific knowledge. These language patterns are learned much in the same way that we learn our own native language, namely in implicit ways, by hearing, speaking, being corrected, but mostly by shaping our speech to conform to what we hear around us.

In doing this study, I established the usefulness of concept mapping as a tool for engaging students in sustained science discourse. Such discourse is of considerable importance in the establishment of a classroom culture that reflects the kind of scientific practices that I wanted to foster in my classrooms. I was able to see that students externalized their conceptual framework regarding the concepts of interest. Thus, I learned that the concept map is a valuable evaluation tool for me and for other classroom teachers as well (e.g., the teachers in my department used concept maps for this purpose). They can use both the process and the final products of concept mapping to examine the quality of student understanding. Using concept maps as an evaluation tool for process and product also permitted me to identify potential dangers in collaborative concept mapping. Students may perpetuate alternative views or construct scientifically incorrect knowledge. In order to facilitate the collaborative construction of concept maps, I drew the following instructional consequences. First, there should be specific instruction to foster students' abilities in the three modes of discourse we identified. Second, students may need instruction for establishing hierarchies and seeking cross-links between local hierarchies. Third, I should support students' efforts for understanding the special significance of general concepts and principles and how they organize the knowledge in the scientific field; and I should support students' efforts in establishing the relationships between the various levels of abstraction in the hierarchy of concepts. Fourth, there should be specific instruction urging students to reflect at the end of the mapping session on the nature of the hierarchical relationships between the concepts. And finally, the within-group transactions could be more structured by assigning specific roles to each individual. For example, members in each group could be assigned specific responsibilities for checking the correctness of propositional linkages, the validity of the concept hierarchy, and the cross-links between different parts of the hierarchy.

I ultimately wrote up some of what I learned in the form of research articles because a number of acquaintances in academia suggested that this work would be of great interest to science educators. Because I was not sure of myself and also because I felt that reviewers and editors might charge me with subjectivism, I linked up with a university-based researcher in the US, Anita Roychoudhury, with whom I discussed what I was doing, who raised questions and critique, and who thereby became a *disinterested peer* with whom I could debrief every step of the process. *Peer debriefing* is but another method for increasing the credibility of a study. Readers interested in what we ultimately published may want to look up some of the articles I wrote (e.g., Roth & Roychoudhury, 1992, 1993). Based on my work with concept maps, I also wrote up some other articles, for example, for elementary and middle school teachers concerned with providing means for their students to learn about learning and with alternative means for assessment. Peer debriefing is an important device in any research, and my graduate students regularly practice it with their respective work even when I am not present.

CHAPTER 2

INVESTIGATING STUDENT VIEWS ON COLLABORATIVE CONCEPT MAPPING

In chapter 1, I describe how I got started doing the research on concept mapping, which had the purpose of finding out *what* students were learning and *how* they were learning science when completing concept maps in collaborative groups. I was particularly interested in designing a research method that would allow me to show how the achievements students made in groups came to be embodied in their own personal practices of concept mapping one and six weeks after the original sessions. In the course of doing this project, which I had viewed as a pilot study preceding more in-depth research on this form of engaging students in my classes, I also came to have new questions that I dutifully recorded in my research memos. These new questions took over and became more important and interesting to me than the ones I had started out with and originally planned. Thus, one of the main new questions I had was about the new roles and possibilities that emerge for teachers and students when collaborative concept mapping becomes an important dimension of their course. A second main question became for me how students were viewing this aspect of their learning environment. I thought that the answers to these two questions would provide me with important information about how to redesign the teaching–learning environment my courses provided, in addition to other changes I might make as a result of finding out more about the process of constructing the maps. The central finding from the initial pilot study was that students do learn and remember what they have learned for a considerable amount of time.

During the summer months preceding the new school year, I planned to build a research agenda around the collaborative concept-mapping task. This research would have as its main driving questions those concerning student–teacher transactions and student views of the task, including questions about how they experienced the process of arriving at a jointly constructed map and how they felt they had learned physics in and through their engagement with this task. In this chapter, I describe how I went about doing this research in my own classroom.

FRAMING THE RESEARCH QUESTIONS: CONCEPT MAP AS CONSCRIPTION AND INSCRIPTION DEVICE

Teacher-researcher investigations do not emerge from a vacuum, just as those studies others design, for example, university-based researchers. What I learned during the first two studies concerning processes and products of learning during collaborative concept mapping (see chapter 1) mediated the new questions I was beginning to ask. Although I initially had thought to investigate questions concerning

CHAPTER 2

individual and collective learning—processes and products—my interests shifted and I began wanting to know more about ongoing teacher evaluation and students' own experiences. Following the pilot study, and reflecting on the role of concept mapping as a process and the material concept map as its result, my thinking about the nature of concept maps and concept mapping was in the process of evolving. Rather than rigidly sticking to the research questions I had originally framed, I allowed this evolving thinking and understanding about what was happening when I assigned this task. An understanding of the nature of research as an evolutionary process framed my teacher-researcher studies as they unfolded.

Evolving Thinking About Concept Mapping

As a result of the pilot study, the method for which I describe in chapter 1, I had come to the conclusion that concept maps are tools for social thinking—in contrast to individual thinking. Because they are constructed in collaboration, the emerging design of the maps serve as a means of organizing the task, the task environment, the ways of talking in which students engage to construct the design, and the final concept map. This organization is achieved, because the map's emerging structure is part of a common problem space in a double sense. First, this problem space permits students in a group to work simultaneously on the same task—frequently this simultaneous engagement is expressed in the concurrent talk and movement of concept words on paper. Second, the emerging map design also provides for a common conceptual space in which the participants can refer to objects by means of words, drawings, or gestures. The participants' individual involvement is indicated by their attention to the objects and the other participants of this space. Thus, a concept map can be thought of as a *conscription device*, that is, a medium that brings together different individuals to work on a common task *together*. It therefore serves as a form of social glue, forming a new cohesive unit rather an assembly of independent bodies. A conscription device enlists the participation of those who would employ it, since users must engage in the generation, editing, and correction of the device during its construction. The concept map is also an *inscription (device)*, that is, a form of keeping a permanent (written) record of the students' work. Inscriptions stand for that which the students take as shared: a representation of their understanding of the concepts involved and a representation of the structural relationships between, and the meanings of, the concepts of their common task.

This way of thinking about collaborative concept mapping allowed me to link the task to evaluation. When I think of the concept map as an inscription, that is, as a product of students' engagement, then it is something that I can assess. These maps, so I was thinking at the time, allow me to evaluate the students' understanding in an after-the-fact fashion. Feedback and intervention to help students in reconstructing their ideas—so that they become compatible with the stated science curriculum—have to await future lessons. However, when I think about concept maps as conscription devices that engage students and constrain them to articulate talk about scientific concepts, then the concept maps are tools for and terrains of social thinking: I now can conceptualize evaluation as dynamic and ongoing.

One of the struggles I was experiencing at the time concerned the relationship between individual and collective. I clearly had shifted to analyze group efforts from a collective perspective, taking the conversation as my new unit. It made sense to me. It took many years thereafter, however, to understand how to think about education from a collective perspective, which is not easy given that the whole enterprise of schooling is based on the individual and on the societal sorting mechanism it fulfills to get some individuals into the upper class with access to much cultural and economic capital and to keep other individuals in the working classes with minimum and decrepit financial and other resources barely allowing them to make do. I continued to do my research despite the fact that I continued for years struggling with the question about schooling and the collective.

Research Questions: New Teacher Perspectives

The purpose of one follow-up study that I designed was to use the conceptualization of the concept map as a conscription and inscription device and to apply it to concept mapping sessions. I wanted to investigate its potential to serve as a tool and terrain during teacher–student transactions. Working on the task, students articulate understandings, which the teacher can evaluate; and I wanted to investigate the role or roles that I played while engaged in conversations with the students, for example, those concerning evaluation. Furthermore, I wanted to find out about the relationship between assessment and intervention that would lead to changes in the way students talked about the concepts. I considered what I was doing to be an effort in finding a research and development method for bringing about student-centered learning environments. I thought that I was ideally placed to do this kind of investigation because my research and development work took place in the very setting in which this learning environment was to function. This method, I thought, should supersede the older, pipeline models by means of which educational research traditionally had informed school practice.

Research Questions: Student Perspectives

In the course of the year, especially because I already asked students to reflect on their concept mapping activities—as well as on other activities—I decided to devote considerable effort to finding out how the students in my eleventh-grade physics course viewed the concept mapping task and everything that surrounded it, including the writing of reflections. I was interested in finding out more about students' perspectives on the structure of collaborative concept mapping, for example, how students viewed and experienced having to justify, elaborate, and explain the claims they were making during their discussions. The research questions that guided my inquiry included "What understanding do students have of concept maps?," "From the students' point of view, how does collaborative concept mapping help in learning?," and "From the students' point of view, what are the bene-

CHAPTER 2

fits of reflecting on the experience of collaborative concept mapping?" I knew that these questions would lead me into new and uncharted territory. To ascertain a sufficient degree of fidelity to what I was learning from the study, I needed to engage students—one of and possibly *the* most important group of stakeholders in educational practice—in the process of learning about their views and learning. Thus, a secondary purpose of my project was to provide me with a sense for the viability of engaging students in the authentication of research.

RESEARCH DESIGN

In all my classes, students engaged in concept mapping—both to articulate the theory that underscored the experiments that they designed and conducted (see chapter 3) and to summarize all salient concepts at the end of an entire unit (e.g., concerning motion, electricity, optics, or heat). In the two investigations of concept mapping, the methods of which I describe in this chapter, I focused on the junior-year physics course, which meant, I had shifted from the original group involved, the senior year physics classes, to a new target population. There were 48 students enrolled in the junior-year physics course during the school year when I conducted the study; these students were split into three sections. In the course of the year, I planned ten major collaborative concept-mapping sessions in each section.

In each class, I decided to videotape one group over the entirety of the year, which was made possible because groupings tended to remain constant. This would give me three (one per section) one-hour tapes per session, and therefore, given that there were ten sessions, a total of 30 hours of recorded concept mapping discussions. In addition to the videotapes I would collect (a) the concept maps produced by all groups during each session, (b) the individually produced concept maps during formal tests, and (c) the individual concept maps that students produced during and following their readings. In part, my pilot study already had primed me concerning this decision: another reason for conducting a pilot, because it gives us teacher-researchers a better handle on the studies we ultimately conduct without having to worry about getting "everything" possible during the one and only time a study is under way. I am convinced that without some pilot work, investigations never turn out as good as they possibly could in a given context with given participants.

Because I wanted to find out how students experienced the process of concept mapping generally and what they felt they had learned, I asked that each student write and submit a reflection immediately following each collaborative concept mapping session to be submitted during the next class. I planned to have students write an essay on collaborative concept mapping later in the year and to conduct interviews with selected students. More so, I expected each student to address in his or her writing what was most salient. (During that year, the school had become co-educational so that there were five female students among the 48 that made up the three sections of junior-year physics.) However, this would not allow me to ascertain how representative a particular view was for all students taking junior year physics. I therefore planned constructing a survey in which I would use student statements together with a Likert-type scale the degree to which they shared the view expressed by one of their peers.

A Likert-type item involves some statement—e.g., "By making concept maps as a group, we learn a lot from each other"—and then provides a number of choices for participants to agree or disagree. From the literature I knew that a five-point scale is the most frequently used; such a scale forces participants to respond by indicating strong disagreement, disagreement, neutral, agreement, and strong agreement with the statement. A typical item would then be presented as follows, requesting students to circle the answer that best represented their position.

By making concept maps as a group,
we learn a lot from each other   SD   D   N   A   SA

Likert-type instruments frequently are used to *measure* something, for example, how students viewed their classroom learning environments; the *Constructivist Learning Environment Scale* (CLES), in its various instantiations over time, is a typical instrument designed to measure the degree to which students' perceptions of their learning environment matches with constructivist ideals (Taylor & Fraser, 1991). In the construction of such instruments, researchers write statements that they believe measure students' perspectives. Thus, CLES consists of four groups of seven Likert-type items that students are asked to rate their preferences for, among others, the *autonomy* of learning that they experience. A typical item intended to measure the degree of autonomy is the statement "In this class, I decide how much time to spend on an activity." To decrease the measurement error, the researchers who developed CLES originally produced seven statements for each trait to be measured. Also, for the evaluation of the results, researchers who want to measure use numerical scores, for example, from 1 to 5 in lieu of the letters, assuming that the underlying scale from strongly disagree to strongly agree is more or less linear.

My own approach differed from the normal usage of Likert-type items because I was not interested in developing an instrument to measure student perceptions in general, that is, comparable to those found in other classes at my school, in Canada, or around the world—in the way researchers have done it, including myself, using CLES. Nor did I want to make comparisons between different groups of students or use the instrument results in some other statistical work, so that I did not really need numerical scores instead of the categorical responses (e.g., agree, disagree, neutral). Rather, I was interested in better understanding the degree to which *these* students—and these students only—agreed with each other's statements. I wanted to understand *this* group of students rather than (private school) students *in general*. In the course of the year, I had the idea that I

Likert-type Scale In the 1930s, Rensis Likert developed instruments for *measuring* attitudes. These instruments consisted of series of declarative statements. Participants were asked to indicate the degree to which they agree or disagree. There usually were six to 30 items in a scale, some worded in positive direction, others in negative direction. Because responses tend to be *normally distributed* (i.e., bell curve), these scales lend themselves to be used in statistical comparisons between groups.

could check on the prevalence of certain student reactions to the course. I wrote a research memo to the effect of constructing a Likert-type survey (see below). I therefore constructed items by extracting statements from students' reflective essays about concept mapping. I wanted to cover both negative and positive experiences (as these would be used on other Likert-type scales), and really all the aspects that students addressed in their writing.

Finally, I wanted to ask a small group of students to read what sense I had gotten from their input and debrief with them in small groups after they had provided me with their feedback. These debriefing sessions, I wanted to record, too. At that time, it was rather innovative to involve students directly in research, for example, asking them to work through a research report and ask them about the degree to which they find that it reflects their views. Finally throughout the project I intended to keep my own research memos to preserve my teacher-research process to the extent possible.

PROGRESSIVE SUBJECTIVITY AND RADICAL DOUBT

The *preconstructed*, notes Pierre Bourdieu (1992), is everywhere. This means that we see not so much what there is to see but more what we have come to see in the course of our past experiences. That is, our past experiences mediate our *dispositions* for seeing social situations in particular ways. A particularly striking example that I recurrently observed is how teachers assess a short video-clip that I use during my research courses. Invariantly, there is someone who talks about the "exclusionary behavior" on the part of three students currently involved in building a tower from drinking straws and needles and a fourth student asking them what they were doing. But exclusion is not at all the case in this particular instance, because the same, so-called "excluded" student subsequently worked with one of the three others; and he did so in a highly productive manner. That is, our dispositions that rapidly make it possible for us to assess a situation, therefore allowing us to be as effective as we are without having to reflect, also lead us to make inappropriate assessments because we accommodate everything we see to

Dispositions allow us to rapidly understand situations without having to think and interpret. They develop in the course of our experience in the material and social world and correspond to sedimented social knowledge. But this preconstructed is dangerous, because it makes us see a group of student in a particular way without requiring us to ask ourselves whether there are other ways of understanding the situation. As researchers, we have to break this gaze; and perhaps as teachers, we have to do so too to do better justice to students.

familiar patterns rather than construct new and more appropriate ones. This is what Bourdieu denotes by the term *preconstructed*—the world we see is a familiar one even when situations are new and unfamiliar. The converse of these dispositions therefore is that everything looks familiar, and novice researchers wonder what special there is to see in the data sources that they have collected. That is, because we have been socialized so well, we feel like the proverbial fish in the water, no longer seeing what makes social action so special and possible in the first place.

Engaging in research without knowing how our common ways of seeing the world mediate what we are perceiving and doing means that we no longer *know* in explicit ways what we are perceiving and doing—some learning scientists talk about the *tacit nature of knowing*. That is, our ways of knowing normally are hidden from view and therefore invisible. If we do not question ourselves and our ways of seeing, we merely record during our research what we already know implicitly rather than opening up ourselves to new learning, which occurs in and through the process of research. To prevent this reification of existing ways of seeing our classrooms, we teacher-researchers need to take special care and do something that allows us to be on the alert—even break with received ways of seeing and experiencing our everyday classrooms. The mere fact of being on the alert is important; however, it hardly suffices. To institute a form of *radical doubt*, an important instrument is the recording of the individual and social history of the problems that we investigate. We must be able, as I suggest in the previous chapter, to articulate the progressive constitution of our own understanding—both the one invoked when I design a study and the one that comes about in the course of the study.

> **Radical Doubt** means that we have to engage in certain practices that break our habits of seeing and understanding the events in our classrooms. Otherwise we tend to retain ideological perspectives on the events that we set out to understand better by conducting research.

To address this important issue of learning from my teacher-researcher investigations, I keep notes from the moment I start a study—sometimes even from before, as new ideas about doing research often arise from something else I have thought or done. The excerpt from my notes reproduced in Figure 2.1 shows that I thought all categories that had been developed in the first and second study (chapter 1) also applied to the present work, especially to the teacher–student transactions. However, in the first line following the title "possible categories," I noted that as a teacher I was asking students for justification and elaboration. In fact, it turns out that in this aspect, there was a considerable difference between what students were doing and how I related to them. This turned out to become a major aspect of my redesign of the task. The comparison between patterns of teacher–student and student–student transactions would show to me that I asked for justifications, explanations, and elaborations, whereas students frequently engaged in head-budding arguments without holding each other accountable for the grounds on which they favored one concept configuration over another one. Their conversations seemed to lead nowhere as they simply opposed one opinion to another without asking or providing others for justifications or explanations.

CHAPTER 2

I subsequently arranged for a whole-class session in which I modeled how students could hold each other accountable for taking one or another position on the topic at hand by asking for justifications, explanations, and elaborations. While walking about the classroom during a concept-mapping exercise, I encouraged and further modeled the use of one of these three terms. In the evenings following these sessions, I watched the videotapes in respect to this redesign to monitor whether the intervention was changing how students related to one another when I was not standing next to a group. I also included items concerning the introduction of the justification-explanation-elaboration device on the survey. All of these data were to provide me with information concerning the hunch (presupposition) that these particular terms, when used during discussions, would allow students to engage more deeply in the conceptual issues of the topic that they were mapping and learning (about).

LEARNING ABOUT LEARNING: THE DATA SOURCES

Asking students to reflect on something they have done, to me, is a legitimate aspect of any course because I strongly believe that it allows them to learn about learning. Rather than merely attempting to come to grips with the new forms of disciplinary language and doing well on tests, writing reflections and essays en-

---

Possible categories
Teacher asking for justification, elaboration
- engaging students in discourse with feedback possibilities
- extending what students know into new area, vertical teaching for advanced
- diagnosing using the map to begin questions, students use map to recapitulate
- identifying and remediating misconceptions
- offering alternative framework for discussion
- teacher keeping track of time, timing for activities
- justification "forces"/encourages reflection
- pointing out discrepancies/ contradictions asking for elaborations. The concept map design provides a trail, a semi-permanent record that can be used by the teacher to begin questioning.
- concept map as conscription device engages students in extended discourse. This allows teacher to "listen in." If there seem to be no problems, he can go on to the next group. If there are, he can intervene. This intervention may take a number of different forms. Discourse, or rather teacher-student interaction can be structured around the concept map, but can also be structured around other resources that facilitate the negotiation of meaning such as drawings.
- all the categories identified in the first concept mapping study for students are applicable to teacher–student discourse, at least those with respect to negotiation of meaning. Particularly with respect to the resources used to negotiate meaning. Key among them the use of drawings and gestures. Instantiation of situations such as potential energy by holding up object, or jumping up on table, and down.

Figure 2.1. Beginning of a research note designed to capture the nature of my thought and my preconceptions at the beginning of the study.

courages students to articulate themselves about their own engagement and learning needs within a course. I have engaged in learning-about-learning and learning-to-learn strategies many years before actually doing research on this aspect of my teaching, probably when I first used concept mapping and vee mapping in 1985; but I did begin even earlier, for example, in a course on personal development that I taught in the small Labrador village of St. Paul's River during the first two years of my teaching career. What students wrote on their assignments for me, the teacher, also was immediately usable for research purposes, as students wrote everything using the computer, making the files available to me in electronic form. Beginning with my teaching computer science in 1983, I have never accepted assignments from high school students other than in typewritten form. For this reason, all reflections and essays I collected from my Appleby students already existed in usable (typewritten, electronic) form.

As a teacher-researcher, it is important to me that I keep separate in my mind the two activities I am engaged in although they go on simultaneously: teaching and researching. It is important for me to keep them separate, because I want to be able to explain to others what my regular classroom practices are. This also allows me to explain whether students produce something, like a reflection or an essay, is part of the regular course or whether students produce them for the purposes of my research. Teacher-researchers will find that making this distinction is going to clarify what they are doing to members of a university-based research ethics committee; the members of these committees will better understand what is happening during a teacher-researcher investigation, in particular, which of the activities are part of the normal routines and which ones are done only because of the research. Many or most members of these committees do not have (much) experience with teacher-research—and even less have experience doing it themselves—and often believe that teachers coerce their students into participation.

In fact, if the teacher-research uses nothing other than artifacts students naturally produce during a course, the investigation largely is a *quality improvement study* rather than a research study. In this case, my university ethics committee often makes a difference. A quality improvement or assurance study gets a waver or passes rapidly, even when it is done for the purpose of a graduate student's partial fulfillment for receiving his or her degree, whereas the evaluation of a normal teacher-research study may take considerably longer and be more arduous especially because of the potential *power-over* issues that arise.

The *power-over* issue is a thorny one for many research ethics committees and not an easy one to resolve. Whereas university-based committees do not worry about teachers doing research in their classrooms generally, they do get concerned when a graduate student or professor also does teacher-research in his or her classes *for the purpose of getting a degree* or *for the purpose of writing an article*. It is the difference that makes a real difference: the purposes of doing a teacher-researcher study as part of regular professional development versus doing it while a person is enrolled in a graduate degree program where the purpose of the study is other than professional development and quality improvement.

CHAPTER 2

PLANNING AND REPORTING MY INVESTIGATION

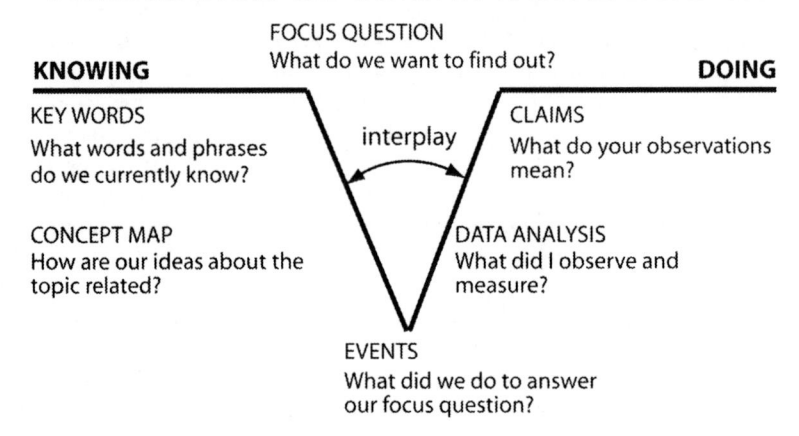

```
                    FOCUS QUESTION
                    What do we want to find out?
   KNOWING                                              DOING
   ─────────────────────────────────────────────────────────
   KEY WORDS           \         /   CLAIMS
   What words and phrases  interplay  What do your observations
   do we currently know?  ←—————→    mean?

   CONCEPT MAP              \  /    DATA ANALYSIS
   How are our ideas about the \/    What did I observe and
   topic related?                    measure?

                          EVENTS
                          What did we do to answer
                          our focus question?
```

Figure 2.2. The vee map is useful for learners and researchers of all ages to engage in inquiry and to learn from their own learning.

In my own situation, I had discussed what I wanted to do with my school administration. Both the head and assistant head of school took the position that our school was a leader in its field; and, to keep its cutting edge, research was encouraged to improve teaching and learning. Thus, several teachers and administrators engaged in research while I was at the school; and all fed back what they learned into the practices enacted at our school. All but my own studies also led to graduate degrees that the teachers pursued at nearby universities.

Reflections

The idea has been around for a while that reflection on an action allows us to understand the action better and therefore, if necessary, to revise it. In more recent years, reflection on action was recognized to constitute an important tool for a great range of professionals including teachers to grow as practitioners (Schön, 1987). Thinking is but one part of a profession, and thinking about one's thinking is but part of learning from one's own profession. That is, when I re-entered high school teaching in 1989 after getting my doctoral degree, it was clear to me that writing about what one has done during a learning task also should lead to what some others call *meta-learning* or second-order learning.

Although I am not certain today when precisely I began asking students to write about what they had learned, it likely has been at the same time when I introduced them to vee mapping. There were a number of contexts in which I asked students to do vee maps, which also include concept maps, to report the investigations that they did in my science classes (Figure 2.2.); as part of the assignment I asked them to reflect on their learning—the prompting questions under the CLAIMS include "What did I learn?" "How can this knowledge be used?" "Why did those results occur?" and "What do the results mean?" As Figure 2.2 shows, the students—Novak and Gowin (1984) also propose this vee mapping strategy for doing the research that graduate students conduct to get a master's or doctoral degree—are asked to make explicit what they know prior to investigating some phenomenon, in the same way that I suggest here that the teacher-researcher records what he or she thinks prior to a study. The vee map asks inquirers to structure their existing concepts into a CONCEPT MAP. After designing some investigation and gathering materials to serve as data sources, articulated under the headline EVENTS, the researcher processes and interprets the data sources, that is, conducts a DATA ANALYSIS. Ultimately, then, researchers state the claims and reflect about what knowledge they gained over and above what they had started out with as articulated on the left-hand side of the vee map. Readers should note that this process also underlies the praxis of doing teacher-research as I am articulating it throughout this book.

PLANNING AND REPORTING MY INVESTIGATION
FOCUS QUESTION
What do we want to find out?
KNOWING   DOING
KEY WORDS   CLAIMS
What words and phrases   interplay   What do your observations
do we currently know?   mean?
CONCEPT MAP   DATA ANALYSIS
How are our ideas about the   What did I observe and
topic related?   measure?
EVENTS
What did we do to answer
our focus question?

In part I was interested in students' reflections as a teacher-researcher—I would have been even if I was not conducting more formal studies—because it was important to me to find out more about students' experiences when they were learning about learning. They were using these learning-to-learn tools; and how they related to these tools was an important and little known topic not only to me but also to the educational community more broadly. The reflections and essays concerning the learning-to-learn tools became sources for my teacher-researcher investigations. The responses in the CLAIMS section always were rather brief, and I wanted to get students to think about learning more deeply, extensively, and reflectively.

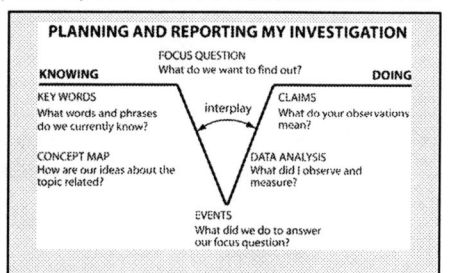

Vee Maps have been designed as tools to monitor how we learn from experience. The logic underlying the teacher-research I describe is consistent with the way an investigation unfolds according to the epistemological vee: beginning with a FOCUS QUESTION, moving to the identification of existing knowledge, designing the investigation (EVENTS), analyzing the materials collected, and constructing claims.

It is in this context that I asked students, as their teacher, to reflect and providing them with points toward a grade for completing these. These reflective essays also became data for my work as a teacher-researcher, allowing me to find out both how to improve both the vee and concept mapping exercises and the writing of reflections following specific learning events. The following is an excerpt from one of the ten reflections that Juliana submitted after mapping the concepts of a unit on the reflection and refraction of light. (Juliana had underlined some words.)

Concept Mapping Reflection
Juliana

The concept map is a very useful tool, when one is using it to unravel pieces of information from a larger, more general topic. It is made to give the student an opportunity to bring together a variety of topics and put them together, in a certain order of importance until there is one main subject heading. For example, in the subject of lenses, lenses are the main subject heading. Below this, may be a sub-topic such as <u>converging</u>, and <u>diverging</u>. The purpose of <u>converging</u> and <u>diverging</u> is to show different types of <u>lenses</u>, thereby creating hierarchy.

For the average student, physics can become a swirl of names, facts, formula and theories. The concept map is a purifier of confusing themes. It helps students when they are learning physics concepts, because it breaks everything down and lays it out in the open. It provides the student with an opportunity to reconstruct the chapter independently.

On a personal level, concept mapping does help me to learn more easily. This is because, not only can I see the subjects on their own, but also I can see how everything is connected. When I work in a group, this provides for another opportunity; not only to learn, but to teach, as well.

Readers should notice that Juliana also articulated the concept map as "a very useful tool." Whereas I do not doubt the claims students made in their essays, I did not necessarily take what they wrote at face value. Especially in the course of developments described in chapter 5 on the situated use of discourse, I began to view the reflections as a whole and each sentence or claim therein as a form of social action; as any social action, this one made sense within the activity that it was intended to realize. The activity in which students currently engaged was schooling, and Juliana did not *just* reflect on her thinking but also work toward a grade that added to her grade point average at the end of the year. Thus, although I did not doubt her when she said that the concept map was a useful tool, I also did not inherently believe that Juliana actually thought it to be useful. In fact, it is entirely possible that when together with her peers she might have made statements to the opposite. But again, saying to a peer that she does not like concept mapping would have been a form of social action for the purposes of helping her peers see her as a "cool student" rather than as a "brownnoser." All I therefore work with are public expressions people produce and I understand these productions in terms of the particular contexts. In my context, what Juliana wrote has to be taken as a form of social action in a context where what she wrote was made available to a person who also was in an institutional position for assigning her grades. In a sense, therefore, I was both suspicious concerning the content of students' essays and I was not suspicious simultaneously. In the course of my research I learned that this form of *unsuspicious suspicion* is a good research strategy during the analytic part of the teacher-researcher project.

In part, these concerns arose because others asked me questions such as, "How do you know that what a student writes in an essay or says during an interview is what s/he *really* thinks?" This and similar questions pushed me to better understand discourse (process and content) and in particular it pushed me to rethink the way in which individuals are embedded in and concretely realize the possibilities of culture. There therefore was another reason for writing the last paragraph, and I return to the attendant issues in chapter 5, which is concerned with discourse analysis and discourse as a form of social action. What should be interesting to both the teacher and researcher component of the inquirer are the ways in which students, here Juliana, support their claims rather than the claims themselves. This is so because in supporting some statement or claim, students have to be convincing. And for this to be the case, they have to draw on what are known as *interpretive repertoires* (for more on these see chapter 5), forms of talking that are taken as unquestionable. It is only when something counts as a reason that it may serve to support other statements that are more tentative. For example, Juliana said that concept mapping helps "because it breaks everything down and lays it out in the open." When thought in terms of the earlier statement of "useful tool," which may have been said to please the teacher, the clause following the term "because" is a statement that provides a reason for making the claim that the tool is useful. Whereas claims potentially are contentious, the interpretive repertoires generally are shared and likely uncontested. As a strategy, therefore, it has helped me a lot both as teacher and researcher to look for the ways in which claims and statements are supported; that is, it is helpful to look for the interpretive repertoires research participants use rather than for the claims themselves. The latter are made to fit the situation and to pursue certain goals, the intentions of which generally are hidden; the former are used to convince the other person and therefore are shared by speaker and listener alike.

Essay

As a science teacher, I have been interested in the way students talk about the nature of science and scientific knowledge and in the relation this talk may have to their own learning and learning strategies. Even before conducting my teacher-researcher studies, I had noted that in discussions about knowledge generally and about scientific knowledge specifically students often had little to say in support of the arguments (claims) they made. I therefore began reading with them essays and book chapters concerning the nature of knowledge (i.e., essays on epistemology). To prepare students for a whole-class discussion, I asked them to write an essay concerning a topic related to some reading; or I asked them to write on a topic related to knowing more broadly. I did the same with respect to the different techniques and tasks that we used in class, for example, concept mapping, vee mapping, designing and conducting experiments, and so on. There was at least one summary essay in the later part of the course in which I asked students to write about different aspects of knowing and learning more broadly and about how the different task forms and learning techniques helped them in learning the subject matter of the course, here physics. The following is a typical reflection one student wrote concerning the question whether concept mapping helped her to learn.

> Does Concept Mapping Really Help Me?
> By: Sarah
>
> Concept mapping is an exercise that helps to develop many different educational skills, which can help in many different subject areas. Mainly we

CHAPTER 2

use concept mapping in physics, to structurally draw a map of all the concepts used in a certain unit. These concepts are linked together with three "key" ideas in mind, these ideas are:

1. hierarchy—a graded system of concepts that places the most important concepts which are usually quite general at the top of the concept map and the more specific and less important concepts at the bottom of the map.

2. cross links—these bring together two very different concepts that in the concept map are far away from one another.

3. simple links—these are just general links that bring together common and easily made concepts.

See the below diagram for an example of each of the following key ideas that are used when making a concept map.

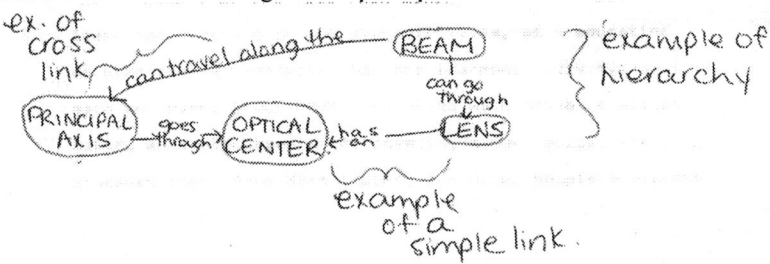

ex. of cross link — can travel along the — (BEAM) — *example of hierarchy*
can go through
(PRINCIPAL AXIS) — goes through — (OPTICAL CENTER) — has an — (LENS)

example of a simple link.

In my opinion, concept mapping is a very important exercise, which should be used whenever possible. It is an informative way of helping us, the students to learn the basic concepts of a certain subject. When making a concept map you and your group members must lawfully decide the best link that applies to each different concept. Most likely, each person in your group will have different ideas of what the "best" link should be, although together you all must sort through each link to find the one that your whole group decides on. To do this each group member must provide to the others a clear and concise summary of what their ideal link is, and must also be able to clarify any problems that the other group members have. . . .

[. . .]

[. . .] The reflections are an important part of concept mapping, which helps us to develop of memorization skills, although we must remember that memorization is not the only way to learn things. There are many other ways which help us learn, such as:

1. peer evaluations (ex. concept map links)

2. basic review of the facts (reflections)

3. step by step evaluations (concept mapping)

These help us to fully understand the ideas of each subject that we must learn, and understanding means learning, and learning means remembering.

As before, I decided to take particular claims—e.g., "concept mapping is a very important exercise"—with a grain of salt and am more concerned with the ways in which students supported such and other, similar claims. For example, of interest in this essay was Sarah's description of the tool itself, how concepts are related, and what she together with her peers did to negotiate the way in which concepts are related. Another interesting aspect can be found in the additional ways of learning that Sarah articulates for us. These ways also are useful to arrive at an understanding, and, because understanding means learning, useful to remember the subject matter.

Data Sources: Summary

By the end of the school year, I had collected a considerable amount of material that served me as a source for the data that I would construct in support of my claims developed from the materials themselves. These materials included:

1. 30 videotaped concept mapping sessions and their transcripts;
2. 30 concept maps from these videotaped sessions;
3. 100 concept maps from all other groups (10 sessions x 10 groups);
4. 460 reflections (46 students x 10 sessions); and
5. 46 essays on the nature of concept maps and learning.

As always, I transcribed each session within about 48 hours of having recorded it; in a few instances, because of one contingency or another, the transcription was delayed by a few days. Compared to the studies many other researchers conduct, the amount of material I collected may appear excessive. However, my point of view always has been that the more materials I have the more constraints there are on what I can claim because each new piece of material limits the stories that one can tell about how and what students know, learn, think, feel, and so on. This is not unlike in crime stories and real-life criminal cases. The more pieces of evidence there are the smaller the number of internally consistent narratives there are that link all pieces together. This is not to mean that there will not be contradictions that the researcher can bring out: I do so below in the section on *negative case analysis*. The amount of material in and from which patterns emerge therefore mediates what one can say in the sense that the more extensive the data sources are the more constraints there are for telling plausible stories. This is not a shortcoming

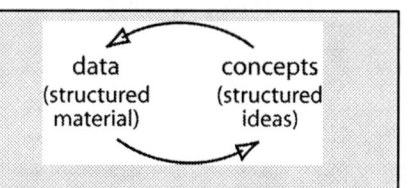

> data (structured material) ⇄ concepts (structured ideas)
>
> **Dialectics** Data and concepts (claims) stand in a mutually constitutive (dialectical) relationship. On the one hand, concepts allow us to see structures exemplified by the data; on the other hand, the concepts exist for the purpose of understanding the (material, social) world of which the materials that make the data are but a part. This chicken-and-egg situation lies at the origin of the trouble experienced by many newcomers to research when they are asked "to make sense of" the data source materials that they have collected.

but it is a strength of this form of research. If you have only four one-hour interviews with four different individuals you can tell many stories that are not contradicted by what your participants have said; if you have, as I did in some studies, 3,500 pages of typewritten materials, there are many fewer stories you can tell that summarize the contents of these materials into a coherent narrative.

ANALYZING STUDENT TEXTS

These materials I collected, here the student essays on concept mapping and learning, are not themselves data, because *data* are used in support of some claim. That is, what I include to support a claim that I make in a report, thesis, or article constitutes the data; it has been abstracted from and is constitutive of the database as whole. For example, I could make the following claim: *concept mapping helps students learn*. To turn this into a supported claim, I require some data. Thus, I could compare the physics achievement of students in a class that had used concept maps and those in another class that had not. I could then take the average grades of the two classes and compare them. If the average grade of the class that had done concept mapping is higher than the average grade of the other class, this difference in the two grades would be my data. The data sources, however, would have been the students' responses on the test on the basis of which I made the comparison. Thus, the *data* support a pattern that I have found in the set of materials collected, but the claim itself is based on the pattern. There is therefore an inner contradiction that claims and data presuppose each other: to make claims, we need to have patterns (data), but data only exist in respect to the claims that they support. That is, both the claims and the data that support them simultaneously emerge through analysis from the data source materials. This is a chicken-and-egg situation from which one cannot get out other than simply beginning the analysis and correcting oneself as the research process unfolds. To return to the crime story analogy: detectives such as Sherlock Holmes only know what is a piece of evidence when they have a plausible story of what happened, but a plausible story depends on the evidence. Does a cigarette butt tell us something about the crime or is it a coincident aspect on the crime scene? Is the position of a chair relevant to the story about how the person in the room died? Or is the position of the chair the result of an action unrelated to the events?

> **Data versus Data Sources** Interviews and their transcriptions, student essays, tests, and so on are *data sources*, from which you cull *data*, that is, excerpts *in support of some claim you make*.

These considerations should render evident the fact that in the absence of the plausible story that connects all the pieces (data), we rely on our auto/biographically developed dispositions for seeing the world in a particular way to structure the materials that we look at. This is precisely where the point about preconceptions and presuppositions addressed above becomes salient. Because we do not know what makes us see events or texts in a particular way, we need to be vigilant with respect to our own ways of understanding to better understand how what looks patterned to us is a function of our previous life experiences and the culture or cultures in which we are and of which have been a constitutive part. This point should become more salient and precise in the description of how to begin and conduct an analysis of texts.

In the first stage of the analysis concerning students' views of concept mapping, I enacted a procedure generally referred to as *open coding*. I repeatedly read all of the reflections and essays, highlighted what seemed to be important passages, and re-typed about one-third of these essays with a concurrent commentary (Figure 2.3). The figure shows how I used a highlighter to make certain parts of the text stand out. I also used a pencil to link parts of the text that appeared to be part of a theme. For example, the lower arrow links two circles, the upper one being around the words "lays it out" and the lower one around the verb "see." Although I had not thought about these descriptors, a brief moment of reflection reveals that both terms are related to visibility, the first of some entity (the concept map on the table) and the second one to the capacity to see. The upper arrow links two parts of the text in which the student appears to indicate some trouble. In the upper highlighted line and within the oval, the student used the verb "unravel"; in the lower circle, we find the term "swirl of names." Both these textual parts appear to point to something that is confusing, complicated, or complex. There is a swirl, and it needs unraveling. As I was reading the text for the first time, something made me notice this relationship, even though I did not know initially what it was. Upon reflection, I then was able to articulate the relationship in the way I am doing it in this text. That is, in this relation I have found what possibly is a theme: *Students find physics complex and concept mapping allows them to deal with the complexity*. We can think of this statement as a claim, which then allows me to check whether other students have made statements that confirm or, even more importantly, disconfirm this statement. The excerpt could then be used as a piece of data in support of the claim as stated.

In the next step of my analysis, I typed out the student essays into the first column of a table—at the time I could not easily transfer files between the Macintosh and DOS systems that were in use at the school so that only some files already existed electronically. Nowadays, it would be easier to do this research because I would ask students to submit their assignments electronically, as I already do with all of my students at the university. From the email or attached documents, I would be able to copy the texts directly into my own analytic files. As I typed out the text back then, I highlighted certain terms by using bold face (Figure 2.4), constituting a procedure that is similar to my highlighting on the originals (Figure 2.3).

In the second column (cell) of the table, I wrote interpretive text in my own words; in a sense, I wrote more global statements under which not only the piece of text to its left but also other pieces of text might fit. The figure also shows how in my interpretation I copied that sentence or part of the text that actually supported the statement. Thus, for example, I wrote a statement/claim "Justification leads to positive experience of Self because students experience themselves as knowers, as competent" and then added, immediately following in parentheses, the *data* that supports this claim "('you are proving to yourself that you do in fact know what you are talking about')." In this way I immediately had pieces of text

CHAPTER 2

> The concept map is a very useful tool, when one is using it to unravel pieces of information from a larger, more general topic. It is made to give the student an opportunity to bring together a variety of topics and put them together, in a certain order of importance until there is one main subject heading. For example, in the subject of lenses, lenses is the main subject heading. Below this, may be a sub-topic such as converging, and diverging. The purpose of converging and diverging is to show different types of lenses, thereby creating hierarchy.
>
> For the average student, physics can become a swirl of names, facts, formulas and theories. The concept map is a "purifier" of confusing themes. It helps students when they are learning physics concepts, because it breaks everything down and lays it out in the open. It provides the student with an opportunity to reconstruct the chapter independently.
>
> On a personal level, concept mapping does help me to learn more easily. This is because, not only can I see the subjects on their own, but I can see how everything is connected. When I work in a group, this provides for another opportunity; not only to learn, but to teach, as well.

Figure 2.3. Upon first reading, I highlight anything that strikes me, for whatever reason this might be, using different colors to distinguish between dimensions. I use lines to mark relations and note relationships to other student work.

that combined *claims* and the *data* that supported them should it turn out that this statement or claim was a pattern across students in the three classes. When necessary, I could even copy the text from this table into an article, report, or thesis.

Readers also should note that I rendered the term *confidence* in bold face letters; it, too, is followed by a supporting piece of text from the data source to the left. There are further terms and descriptors such as "aiding others" and "altruism." All of these—the fuller descriptions and the words—constitute *forms of noticing*. Whether they ultimately lead to something can be seen only once I have done several passes through the entire database. I learned an important lesson about noticing while watching eighth-grade students doing research on the environment: initially they saw little in the area they had selected for doing their research but ten weeks later they did not have enough time to study everything they noticed. The lesson is: the ability to notice things comes with familiarity of the relevant context

I found concept mapping beneficial also because when you have to justify your feelings, you are proving to yourself that you do in fact know what you are talking about. It gives you a chance to assure and reinforce yourself, along with **aiding** the other members to further understand and catch something which **they** may have personally **overlooked**. You are given the opportunity to **learn from other** people's mistakes. Also linked with the previously stated "learning from mistakes" is the fact that we are now able to view areas in which we had the most trouble, and then not make the same mistake again.	Justification leads to positive experience of Self because students experience themselves as knowers, as competent ("you are proving to yourself that you do in fact know what you are talking about"). Building **confidence** ("It gives you a chance to assure and reinforce yourself"), Aiding others (Altruism) Learning from mistakes, multiple perspectives, learning from others.

Figure 2.4. I copied or typed students' reflective essays into the left column of a table boldfacing words that point to themes that I thought were present. In the right column, I typed interpretive comments. (Stephanie)

or materials. Doing an analysis, therefore, also means becoming very familiar with your materials. I repeatedly went through the entire set for several reasons. First, the set was large so that I might have forgotten at the end what I noticed initially. Second, I began noticing aspects sometime during the reading stage that re-reading shows also to have existed in the already annotated parts where I had not seen (noticed) them. For example, Figure 2.3 shows about 9 lines from the bottom on the right side, I penciled in the name of another student. Quite evidently, I had noticed a similarity between *this* text and another one that I had come across.

Through this procedure emerged a first, tentative description of the students' views on concept mapping. I say *emerged* because the categories are based on pieces of data, but pieces of text were data only because they fit into the category. The verb "to emerge" is appropriate when we talk and write about processes in which the products are not determined but, in a chicken-and-egg like fashion, come to being at the same time.

Ultimately, my description of student views contained five main dimensions. First, the students showed a good understanding of concept maps, its structure, and why it is a good way of learning physics. Second, students identified in concept mapping a tool that provided them with extended opportunities to engage in talking science, in a sense, for helping them to establish a community of discourse. Third, the pupils extensively elaborated the reasons for how the rules that I had established to guide their discussions—i.e., to hold each other accountable for claims through justifications, explanations, and elaborations—helped them maintain the dynamics of student–student transactions. Fourth, students explained their views regarding the writing of reflections after a concept mapping experience. Finally,

CHAPTER 2

the view of two students who disliked collaborative concept mapping as a classroom task provided some evidence why this task might not have been beneficial to all students. This discussion served me to establish a *negative case* analysis (see below).

ASCERTAINING GENERALITY OF PARTICULAR VIEWS: MEMBER CHECKING

As I was analyzing students' reflections, I began to notice that students highlighted different types of experiences. That is, although I had identified five tentative themes, I had little idea how prevalent these themes were for *all* students who participated in the study. No single students wrote about all the dimensions that became salient to me in my reading. Thus, one student may have highlighted that she had learned from other students' mistakes, but other students did not mention mistakes and learning from them. I then thought that I should somehow check how prevalent this perspective was among students. That is, I needed to check the degree to which others agreed with her statement. I captured this in a research memo that I wrote as soon as I have had the idea:

> A questionnaire with Likert-type scale could be used to do the member check and to search for underlying structure using multi-dimensional scaling and hierarchical clustering. (03/15/92)

This memo alerted me to the fact that I should construct such an instrument and then ask all students to rate all statements. Based on the categories of responses I had identified, I selected 42 student statements about concept mapping that exemplified these categories (Figure 2.5). The statements, selected from the reflections and essays of the students, formed a survey on which the students indicated the level of their agreement with these phrases. The results of this survey not only represented another data source but also corresponded roughly to a *member check*: the students' answers to this questionnaire provided an indication to what degree certain views were *taken-as-shared* within the entire student body.

> **Memo Writing** It is a good strategy to write memos. Because I do not have my computer with me all of the time, or because I may not be able to use it when I have it with me, I keep a notebook. In this notebook, I even keep pieces of data sources I happen to stumble across, and write about everything that comes to my mind concerning the research I am currently doing and ideas I am having for other studies.

The figure also shows how I presented the response choices, as a scale where students could indicate the level of their agreement rather than in terms of numbers, which I did not need given that I was not interested in *measuring* some underlying psychological or sociological dimension. (If needed, the results of these questionnaires can be turned into scale scores simply by coding levels of agreement from 1 to 5 depending on which of the x's students circled.)

Member checking originally was a procedure used to test interpretations with the members of a stakeholder group and the single-most important technique for establishing the credibility of a study (Guba & Lincoln, 1989). Member checking

INVESTIGATING STUDENT VIEWS

Concept mappping questionnaire
Page 1

Name _____

Answer the following questions about concept mapping in physics by circling the "x" of your choice. The "x" in the middle means that you neither agree nor disagree. The two x's on the left indicate your degree of disagreement, while the right two x's indicate your degree of agreement.

1. The reflection after doing a group concept map helps me in understanding the importance of concept mapping and what I have learned.	Disagree...x....x....x....x....x....Agree
2. Reflecting about my concept mapping experience is too repetitive and I don't learn from it.	Disagree...x....x....x....x....x....Agree
3. Concept mapping is a good way of reviewing a chapter.	Disagree...x....x....x....x....x....Agree
4. Concept mapping helps to make sense of the many terms in a chapter, and to organize them into a meaningful whole.	Disagree...x....x....x....x....x....Agree
5. When I justify my ideas during concept mapping, I review how I understand it myself and thus I learn by rethinking what I already know.	Disagree...x....x....x....x....x....Agree
6. Sometimes when I try to justify my ideas during concept mapping, I find out that I didn't understand a concept completely.	Disagree...x....x....x....x....x....Agree
7. When someone explains his/her ideas during concept mapping, it helps me to learn something which I didn't know, or which I understood in a different way.	Disagree...x....x....x....x....x....Agree

Figure 2.5. Beginning of the 42-item survey in which students asked about the extent to which they agree with statements made by their peers.

serves a number of functions, including (a) verification of intentions for a person's acting, (b) opportunity to correct statements previously made, (c) opportunities for participants to offer additional information, (d) construction of summary information, (e) opportunities for stakeholders to correct interpretations, and (f) opportunities for participants to judge overall adequacy of a report concerning their views. In the context of the present investigation, I ended up doing member checking in a three-stage process: (a) in using a survey instrument I ascertained the prevalence of agreements with 42 descriptions of the learning environment; (b) by asking some members to read and comment on the first draft of my report I ascertained the adequacy of the report as a whole; and (c) in face-to-ace debriefings with the readers of the report I deepened my understanding of their readings, assessments, and positions. In the following, I describe my decision-making process and the type of data I obtained in each of these three stages.

Member Checking: Stage 1

In my situation, this first stage was more a way of finding out the degree to which individual statements reflected the realities of a larger proportion of my constituent group than an attempt to make claims about student views generally. I wanted to make sure that I knew the prevalence with which students supported a statement I made—e.g., "concept mapping allows students to build confidence." I therefore selected statements that reflected each of the five major categories (themes) and some of the subordinate themes that I had come up with in my initial analysis of their texts. From these statements I constructed a survey instrument providing a

CHAPTER 2

REFLECTIONS

Questions	SD	D	N	A	SA
1. The reflection after doing a group concept map helps me in understanding the importance of concept mapping and what I have learned.	16	9	22	31	22
2. Reflecting about my concept mapping experience is too repetitive and I don't learn from it.	16	22	11	27	24
38. Reflecting on concept mapping helps me to think about my own learning.	18	11	20	22	29
43. When I write reflections on the concept mapping experience, I can make suggestions for changing the activity.	0	4	22	31	42

Correlation Matrix for Variables: $X_1 \ldots X_4$

	Q1	Q2	Q38	Q43
Q1	1			
Q2	-.601	1		
Q38	.687	-.553	1	
Q43	.337	-.175	.484	1

Figure 2.6. Survey results after counting all student responses and calculating the percentage of all students who answered in each category. The correlation matrix allows the investigation of patterns in the student responses. (Research note entry 17/04/92)

five-point Likert scale to offer a limited number of response choices. I did not group the statements but, as this is the case for any of the measuring instruments used in education and psychology, randomly assigned them a place. Figure 2.5 shows the beginning of the resulting survey instrument handed out to all students in my junior year physics course.

Once the questionnaires were returned—there were $N = 45$ because several students were absent during the week that I distributed the questionnaires in class—I collated the responses and calculated the frequencies. Thus, rather than noting that 10 students strongly agreed with the first statement (Figure 2.6), I calculated the frequency, which turns out to be 22% ($10/45 = 0.222 = 22.2 / 100 = 22.2\% \leq 22\%$). The response frequencies for the group of questions relating to the reflections students wrote after each concept mapping exercise are provided in Figure 2.6. I learned that 16 percent of the students strongly disagreed with statement 1, "The reflection after doing a group concept map helps me in understanding the importance of concept mapping and what I have learned," whereas on the other end, 22 percent of the students strongly agreed with the same statement.

It should be evident immediately that the results from this survey were extremely helpful because now I had a much better understanding about the degree to which different aspects of concept mapping were prevalent in this student group *generally*. I was able to provide specific frequencies to specific views or patterns rather than having to be fuzzy about it and having to say/write "many students perceive" or "there were a few who thought." Counting how many students think one or the other way does not make a research project "quantitative," as I was not attempting to make inferences about similar students not involved in this study. But the precise frequencies gave me a better understanding of the degree of prevalence of views. (In one study of physics learning that I conducted with colleagues in Australia, I could show how teachers often misperceive what students think or how they perceive a classroom learning environment. All too often, we teachers have a tendency to say, "Lots of students say . . . ." or "Students are really interested in the topic," when in fact a study might turn out that only a few students say something or display such an interest.)

My interests went even further when I asked the question, "Are there patterns in the way students responded to the individual questions?" One way of answering this question is by calculating the correlations. For this purpose, I needed to code the responses as indicated above, from 1 for strongly disagree to 5, strongly agree. Back then I used *StatView*—a software package for my old Macintosh SE30 computer that my physics students also used in their experiments—to calculate the correlations between responses to the different items; nowadays even a spreadsheet such as Microsoft Excel can do the same calculations (see chapter 1). The resulting matrices, which present the pair-wise correlations between the answers to two questions (Figure 2.6), allowed me to deepen my understanding. For example, the matrix shows that the answers to the second statement were negatively correlated with the responses to the first statement. That is, students who agreed with the statement that concept mapping helped also tended to disagree—the relation is *negative!*—with the statement that the exercise is repetitive. A negative correlation of similar magnitude ($r = -.553$) existed between the second and the 38th statement, "Reflecting . . . helps me to think about my own learning."

Readers interested in making claims beyond their classrooms may ask, but what does each number in the matrix tell me? How large does it have to be so that it provides salient information? In this case, they want to make claims about students generally. Research termed *quantitative* uses levels of significance tests to establish the probability with which a correlation might have arise by chance in a group of students that actually only constitutes a sample of a larger student population, which in my case might be students studying physics in private schools. If a correlation arises by chance, it does not support the claim that two items are related because of some internal reason. A table with the critical values of the Pearson product moment correlations will help in answering this question (e.g., http://physics.mercer.edu/Younce/pearson.html). Thus, for example, for $N = 45$ individuals, the table will have this information:

N	Level of Significance for Two-Tailed test			
	.10	.05	.02	.01
45	.243	.288	.338	.372

This table tells us that when there are 45 students in the sample, as there have been in my study, then a correlation coefficient of $r = .243$ means that there is a 10 percent chance that the correlation has arisen by chance; when the correlation coefficient is $r = .288$ or larger, there is a chance of less than 5 percent that it has arisen by chance, and so on. Looking back at the matrix, we see that four values are larger than .372, which means, there is less than 1 percent probability that they have arisen by chance. There is one value of $r = .337$, which means, the probability that it has arisen by chance lies between 2 and 5 percent. There is one coefficient ($r = -.175$) with a value of less than the critical $r = .243$, which means, the probability that it has arisen by chance is more than 10 percent. The general rule in the social sciences is to accept errors with probabilities that are less than 5 percent. (Only in some instances, for example, when exploratory studies are done with a very small number of participants is the 10 percent error rate [sometimes] acceptable.) That is, in my study, the answers to any statements associated with a correlation coefficient with values greater than that for 5 percent—i.e., $r > |(+,-).288|$—can be considered to be related. The closer the value comes to 1, the more the responses are related and the less likely the relationship has arisen by chance. Again, these numbers are of interest to those who want to make claims that go beyond the actual population that they are dealing with, for example, my 45 students who responded to the questionnaire. (The values for r do not require a leading zero [i.e., .243 rather than 0.243] because the absolute value of the correlation coefficient always is less or equal to 1 [i.e., $|r| \leq 1$].)

Member Checking: Stage 2

In the first stage of my member-checking procedure, I had extracted from students' reflections statements that I thought reflected the entire breadth of comments made. Using the survey, I could then ascertain the extent and intensity to which some statement reflected the three classes as a whole. After I finished this analysis, I wrote a report. Because this report was *about student views* rather than my own views and interpretations of something, I thought it might be useful to engage in a second stage of member checking. At this stage, I would take my preliminary report, constructed on the basis of the data sources I had analyzed so far, and then ask about one quarter of the students to read and react to it.

Who would I invite? And why would there be about 25 percent of the students involved at this stage? Of course, I wanted a broad representation of the students who participated. Those who read the report with me should reflect the three physics classes as a whole; and I wanted to get the proportions right. One obvious representation was the inclusion of female students, as this was the first year of co-education at the school; also, I wanted to have students in the different achievement brackets; and finally I wanted to have at least one of the two students who had expressed themselves in strongly negative terms about the concept mapping exercises. Because I had 45 students, I thought that 10 to 12 respondents would suffice. I asked for volunteers and found nine, including two female students. I explicitly asked Richard whether he would participate, because, as I explained to him, it was important to me to have his voice represented to achieve my ultimate purpose, which was to improve the classroom environment to make it suitable for all students. He acceded to my request.

I provided the ten students with what might be considered the "findings" section of a report or research article. Although I had some tentative introduction and conclusion text, I did not consider it useful to include these parts in the materials I handed students, because, so I thought, they might be turned off should they experience the reading as difficult. Students were not the target audience for these other parts of my text, so that I omitted them from the materials I asked students to read. First, journals, theses, and reports require contextualization of some study in the literature. This contextualization occurs in the introductory section, which therefore includes many references and therefore are likely to be less readable by or of interest to most participants. The methods section, too, would be of little interest to my students, and I did not think that they could provide useful comments and the text would only weigh them down in their reading task. I still ended up with 10 pages of text (6,600 words) that I asked the ten students to read and comment on.

The findings were written using pseudonyms in the way I would also submit the text as part of an article to peer review. To be able to track the students' names—i.e., to make it possible for an audit to go from a report or article back to the original data—I created a file in which I captured the correspondence between the students' real names and their pseudonyms. In subsequent years at the university, I password protected such name correspondence files on my office computer so that I could ascertain *confidentiality*, which means that I would not divulge the identities of my research participants and that I had done everything to prevent others accessing this information. (This concept has to be distinguished from *anonymity*, which means that the fact of having participated in a research project is unknown to all but the participants. This is the case in anonymous questionnaires, for example.) For the text I had decided to use pseudonyms because I did not want students to be able to tie particular comments they were reading to a specific peer. My decision turned out to be the correct one, as some student readers felt that there were statements their peers had made that looked "jazzed up."

I prefaced my report, the beginning of which follows, by a paragraph that contextualized what I had done and what I wanted the student readers to do: making comments on the report, especially when and where I had misrepresented or omitted something. Directly after the explanatory paragraph, separated by an empty line, began the core part of my report. As the following excerpt shows, the report included claims that were subsequently supported by at least two excerpts from students' essays or reflections. The numerical information that I could glean from the survey results also appeared in my (author's) narrative.

> Please help me in reporting about student views of concept mapping. From your essays, reflections, and the questionnaire, I have compiled the following. Read it and mark places where you feel that I have not done justice to what you feel are student views. If I omitted something, please make a note and let me know. Thank you. (The names are all pseudonyms to protect the identity of the students involved.)
>
> Overall, the students held very positive views regarding concept mapping and the use of concept maps for learning. For example, nearly 90%

CHAPTER 2

thought that "concept mapping is a good way of reviewing a chapter," that "concept mapping helps to make sense of the terms in a chapter," or that "concept mapping helps to organize terms into a meaningful whole." None of the students disagreed with these statements. Gary and Ryan are but two of the many who thought highly of concept mapping:

> Gary: I think that [the] concept mapping activity during our physics course has given us a great deal of confidence in the subject. . . . It is a great way of learning. It is simple, easy, efficient, and a clever way to learn physics. It makes concepts clearer and much easier to understand.
> Ryan: The idea behind concept mapping is an excellent one and it is an excellent aid. Not only does it help to clarify confusion concerning those topics covered in the course, but also it tests the knowledge gained from the classes. Also, they serve as an excellent way of improving decision making skills as well as enhancing rational thought.

However, there were also a small number of students, two in particular, who expressed strong reservations to concept mapping. Yet, even these students found some positive aspects in the activity that helped them to learn physics. They commented:

> Richard: Concept mapping is a useful exercise in the long run, but I do not like creating them because it is so tedious and boring. . . . It has been said that the best education is when you make it, or experience it, but I'd have much rather have someone show me a concept map for me to take a look at.
> Mike: Concept mapping is a complete waste of time because it not only takes away one third of our class time but it also leaves the students in mass confusion due to the endless number of possibilities of the hierarchical organization of the concept map. . . . [Concept mapping] does to a certain degree benefit the student because he gets to hear other people's opinions and learns a certain bit about how their mind functions. It helps the student to see that there are other ways to approach the hierarchy and other structural aspects of the concept map.

Although such statements are helpful to a teacher for constructing a general impression of students' views regarding a teaching and learning strategy, a much finer grained analysis was necessary to draw and benefit from such a project. . . .

The opening of my report makes a statement about the generally positive reception of the concept mapping technique among my physics students, but also states explicitly that two of the 45 students "expressed strong reservations." In fact, these strong reservations to the generally supported claim of positive reception required attention, which it received later in the report in the form of a *negative case analysis* (see below).

In the introductory paragraph, I had invited students to read the report and "mark places" where they thought comments were appropriate. When I handed the report to the participants in this second stage of member checking, I suggested again that they should write comments on the paper immediately next to the piece of text that their comments pertained to.

About one week later, the ten students had returned the annotated reports. To make the annotations part of my database and available in electronic format, I transcribed them into a file named "students reactions." The following excerpts from the comments Liz made (the text in italics) exemplify the results of this second stage of member checking:

Liz's Remarks (Excerpt)
It is good that the teacher is there. Teacher should help only when asked by the students.
(Teacher = facilitator, guide, collaborator) *This may be beside the point.*
(p. 6: Explaining dynamics of interactions) *This is what is good about concept mapping.*
(5/6 girls, but she was one of the 5) *That's terrible.*
(To "everyone likes to shoot someone else down") *This is true.*
(Reflections) *Reflection may be more beneficial to teachers.*
(Reflections) *Beneficial, but not every concept map.*
(Rote learning vs. understanding) *Does it matter more that they learn or that they understand it? By rehashing the events of a concept mapping session, learning may be made a chore. To me, going through how I learned something is tedious and makes it less fun.*
(To Richard's remarks) *Hmm! Pretty cool. May be people would enjoy reflections if they loved physics.*
(To "Regurgitate") *It's much easier, but don't learn that much. Both would be most beneficial. Then we could compare the two concept maps.*

Readers should note that I had also transcribed the context within which the comment had occurred. I did this although I could always go back to the original printout that Liz and others had commented on to aid in my analysis. The contextual information, here rendered in parentheses, would make it easy for me to recall the referent for each comment. It also would make it easier to trace claims backward from the report or research article to the original source. To me, this constituted a crucial aspect of my work as a teacher-researcher, because in this way I made it possible for anyone to conduct an audit (even though this is not very likely to occur), and thereby opened my entire process of making sense. It was (and continues to be) a way of turning my interpretive process of sense making into objects (written artifacts), that is, I objectify the process and thereby render it objective.

I do no longer know what I expected, but I remember feeling that the comments were interesting but not yielding a lot. That is, I might have had some expectations but these were not at all articulated. Perhaps I had anticipated more extensive commenting. I do know that the time factor played a role, meaning that for students this task was extra work and likely received less attention than I would have liked; and also, these students as many of their peers generally did not like writing. (Those teachers who had been at the school for several decades said it was the "worst" cohort they had experienced ever in the sense that there was a particular reluctance to engage academically and many students did not appear motivated to learn, often did not submit assignments and homework, though they still wanted

CHAPTER 2

high grades. But using such information as part of an analysis would seem dangerous to me, as the analyst would use common sense and preconceptions to explain what really should be explained through careful analysis of the empirical materials.) Given that I wanted more commentary, I thought I might invite some of the students and get them to talk about what they had read. I thought that perhaps their talk might be more yielding than their written comments. So I instituted a third level of the member checking procedure: face-to-face debriefing sessions involving the readers and commentators on the report. Thus, I intended to invite all of the commentators in three groups of three or four; all students accepted the invitation and showed up for the interview/debriefing sessions.

Member Checking Stage 3: Debriefing Meeting

All of the students who had read and commented in written form also accepted to meet me for a brief period for debriefing their comments and for allowing additional comments. (We cannot ever know whether they had some hidden intentions or whether they would have participated if someone else had asked them and knowing that I would be unaware of their participation.) Especially, I invited students to talk about my report in ways that they might not want to put on paper. I had also noted that Richard, one of the two students who had been very critical throughout with respect to the usefulness of the concept mapping exercises, had not made extensive written comments. It was important for me to get him say more about the report generally and about the way in which he was presented in it particularly.

To capture the debriefing session, I used the video camera; it allowed me to subsequently transcribe these debriefing meetings and make the transcriptions part of the database. I did not want to work from memory, even if I had the time to work up any meeting notes into more comprehensive texts. I always felt that using the video camera made me more independent: I could record on any given day but did not have to write research notes on the same day. An ethnographic field note, on the other hand, would have to be written soon after the observed event. More so, there is a rule of thumb that ethnographic researchers should spend as much time writing as they have spent in the field observing. Given that I was a teacher in a school where I also had afternoon sports, extracurricular activities, and evening duties, there always existed the possibility that I would not be able to write field notes.

Video as Note-Taking Tool I tend to think of the camera as the modern-day ethnographer's note-taking tool. I am not concerned with shooting nice television-ready images but attempt to capture dialogue in particular so that I have access to what people have said precisely rather then to what I imprecisely recall them to have said. Using a camera in this mode means that I need to transcribe them as quickly as possible so that I have access to their contents rapidly.

The following excerpt from my transcript shows how the opening of the meetings typically unfolded. It is quite clear that writing reflections was a major concern to these students, David and Liz, who were among the high achievers in their cohort. The transcript also shows that the students did not shy

78

away from stronger language to characterize this aspect of their course: David describes the content of their reflection as "B-S." Of course, this open language itself reflects the rapport I had with students, being a teacher who was liked very well generally and who was known as open minded regarding critique and recommendations for change and improvement.

Excerpt from one of the Debriefing Meetings
Me: What do you think? Does it reflect what you think?
David: The majority of it, but the reflections.
Liz: Like we could do them every once in a while, but not every time.
Me: I have already decided that the students seem to learn, so next year if I was to do it, I would have may be three spread over the whole year.
Liz: Exactly, that would be much better. People just make up more and more elaborate stories.
David: Like a lot of time it is just B-S, the reflections...
Liz: Like people don't want to get a bad mark, like if you want to say I hated it.
David: I actually, a lot of times I write that I didn't learn much from this one.
Me: I know it is difficult, and I don't know if we can ever achieve that to give the students the sense that they can say what they want.
David: Yea.
Me: And not everyone will feel comfortable. But you see, there are negative cases.
David: I get that. I noticed a lot of things that were good, like how you learn, the justification and stuff, that is good, but I felt that a lot of it was overstated, in a lot of your cases, a lot of it sounds like the people wanted to jazz it up a little, to make it sound good.
Liz: Do they come from reflections?
Me: Yea.
Liz: Because it sounds like some people make an overstated case.

In this transcript both David and Liz articulated the sense that some of the statements made sounded like "people wanted to jazz it up" or "people make an overstated case." (Here, I attribute statements to individuals, though a little less than a year later I would explicitly write about the irreducibility of interviews to the opinions and knowledge of the individuals who participated. See also chapter 5 where I develop this and related issues more fully.) I did not feel that these comments invalidated the report but relativized the excerpts and, simultaneously, constituted particular views rather than general views—which I had attempted to capture in and with the survey. And again, these student comments needed to be understood in the context of the social activity, schooling, and one teacher's (my) effort to change the context in which students were asked to learn (scientific) language and to learn about topics that may not have been their primary interest. (For many local university programs, high school physics was an entrance requirement. Some students were taking the subject to keep their options open with respect to university entrance and program of choice.)

Some researchers might claim that using anonymous questionnaires and surveys would better represent "what students *really* think." But this is mistaken, because anonymous surveys simply constitute a different context, and their results need to be understood precisely relative to this different context. Thus, when filling out an anonymous questionnaire, students specifically and research participants generally are in a kind of situation where they do not have to account for their actions, that is, a specific response. More so, thinking always is a function of participation in concrete activity—the Russian philosopher Mikhail Bakhtin (1993) called it *participative thinking*. Knowing that you are not accountable for what you are doing (the answers you check, what you write) and that you cannot be held accountable for what you have done therefore mediates the ways in which respondents approach knowing and doing. Responding to anonymous questionnaires therefore is but another situation, implying different forms of participative thinking and different results, which are no more and no less mediated than any other form of data source that we collect as part of our teacher-researcher investigations. The relationship between the results obtained under different conditions cannot be presupposed but in my view ought to be an empirical question. At least, this is the position I take because it appears to make fewer assumptions than the claim that one result is truer than another or that the two should somehow be related *a priori*.

As part of these debriefing sessions, I was interested particularly in the conversation with Richard, one of the two students who expressed themselves very negatively about the concept mapping exercise, and perhaps even about physics. I already had included what these two students had written in the report in a section entitled *Negative Case Analysis*. My conversation with Richard was intended to help me gain a better understanding of his position, the reasons for his experiences, his descriptions of learning in the context of my physics class. It was intended to do justice to this particular view that another student and he stood for and to do everything I could to represent the two cases that seemed to go in a different direction than the remainder of students. I delve into these issues in the next section.

NEGATIVE CASE ANALYSIS

An important source for the construction of meaning in an interpretive study is the analysis of negative cases. *Negative case analysis* can be viewed as a process during which a claim or hypothesis is revised with hindsight (Lincoln & Guba, 1985). Thus, in the present case, my report began with the assertion "Overall, the students held very positive views regarding concept mapping and the use of concept maps for learning." I then provided evidence for the assertion in terms of characteristic student statement and the frequency with which students had agreed or strongly agreed on the survey: "For example, nearly 90% thought that 'concept mapping is a good way of reviewing a chapter,' that 'concept mapping helps to make sense of the terms in a chapter,' or that 'concept mapping helps to organize terms into a

INVESTIGATING STUDENT VIEWS

However, the annoying part about concept mapping us the creation and reflecting writing. It has been said that the best education is when you make it or experience it, but I'd much rather have someone show me a concept map for me to take a look at. Although I leave the classroom more intelligent, I do not feel a sense of accomplishment after creating a concept map. Doc always asks us to ask each other what we think about what meaning mean, so what's the point of the teacher? I still feel a little apprehensive about what other students feel about meaning, but they, like me, are probably wrong. To solve this problem, Doc comes around and offers suggestions about concept placement and meaning. It is often him who gets the group started and on a roll.	Doesn't like the discussion section

Doesn't like the reflection. The reflections received mixed reviews. Some think they are important, others feel that they are a "waste of time." Does this relate to the fact that they have to write at all, something they don't like, or is the activity implicitly problematic.

Apprehensive about asking others for their meaning.

Doc gets group started, offers suggestions for placement and meaning (placement and meaning cannot be separated, the placement has embedded in it part of the meaning through its relations and hierarchical arrangements.) |

Figure 2.7. I give special attention to the analysis of a negative case, that is, a case that contradicts the general pattern. Negative case analysis allows me not only gain better understanding but also make adjustments to meet the needs of individuals.

meaningful whole'." Now 90 percent is not the entire class so that there were exceptions to the claim "Students feel that concept mapping is a good way of reviewing a chapter." We can view this assertion as a claim or hypothesis that needs revision in the sense that not every participant agreed with the positive description. In fact, my use of the survey already provided me with an indication of the prevalence of agreements with different statements so that I did not have to say or write "students," "many students," or "all students." In my experience, reviewers of manuscripts submitted to journals tend to be suspicious of such statements, sometimes noting things like, "Surely not everyone is thinking like this."

The purpose of negative case analysis is to arrive at situations—in the ideal case—where all participants are accounted for in the results in one or another way. In the present situation, I wanted to understand better the ways in which students inclined positively articulated their experiences as much as I wanted to understand better those who were inclined negatively. Negative case analysis is precisely the means by which I could arrive at a better understanding of all those cases that did not fall under the main assertion.

I begin the construction of a negative case in the same way that I analyze other data. For example, I transcribed Richard's essay and reflections to make them available to commenting and highlighting (Figure 2.7). In the left column (cell) of the table, I entered the texts he produced. In the right column (cell) I typed my rearticulations, interpretative comments, and descriptive concepts. From the materials in the right-hand column (cell) I constructed descriptions and assertions, which

CHAPTER 2

I supported with materials from the writings of those students who were part of the negative case group. The following is the beginning of my negative case analysis in the report that had resulted from the process of negative case analysis that I had engaged in. It shows that here, too, assertions are supported with concrete case materials. Thus, I supported the assertion "In Richard's case the objection seemed to arise from a general malaise he felt in respect to school in general and to physics in particular" by providing an eight-line (100 word) excerpt from his writings.

> In the present study, the two students who held strong negative beliefs about concept mapping present the negative cases which bring a different perspective to this study. In Richard's case the objection seemed to arise from a general malaise he felt in respect to school in general and to physics in particular.
>
>> I despise . . . having to draw lines between concepts which I could frankly care less about. I have come to the conclusion that physics is not a subject which I enjoy, I am really not sure why I took it, probably university requirements. I'd much rather prefer a physics class where the class roams the streets and identifies physical properties and the laws of physics. This teaching method would be far more effective for me. However, it seems that this method of teaching was available to the Greeks and the aristocracy of nineteenth century England, Russia, and France. (Richard)
>
> He described his own analysis of the concept mapping activity as cynical because his "love for physics is somewhat less than passionate."

I particularly was interested in talking to Richard about his comments and reactions to the way in which I had represented what he had written and what he appeared to experience. To make it possible that he respond more freely, that is, out of earshot of his peers, I invited him to talk to me without others being present. After Richard had re-read the just quoted part of the report, he pointed out that his dislike for physics and his dislike of concept mapping were not linked. This part of our (recorded) conversation, as the following excerpt shows, took a broader perspective on his experience and did not limit itself to the responses concerning concept mapping and reflection exercises:

> Richard: I think, it sounds like because I didn't like physics, I didn't like anything that went on in it, so that just pushes me aside.
> I: Okay, this is important what you say. So you say, this is wrong or too strong?
> Richard: Oh no, I see how you can get that. It is not that I just don't like concept mapping because it's– I just don't think that concept mapping works for me. Sure physics is hard for me, but I don't know, I don't think that concept mapping is that much more interesting within any other subject.

Because I wanted to make sure that he knew he could make his comments as open as possible, I reiterated that what he said was important to me. I also wanted him to know that he could be open about what he thought about my comments. It shows that the way I had phrased my report "pushed him aside." He said that he could see how I came to interpret what he was writing; but he also acknowledged that physics was a difficult subject for him. Richard also felt that there was no linkage between his dislike of concept mapping and his mitigated feelings about the subject matter of physics.

In its entirety, the face-to-face conversation provided me with the understanding that for Richard, concept mapping and the physics course were just part of a, often-repressive system that forced him into certain modes of learning. As it did not fit him, he opted for a reception-learning paradigm and for getting by in the system he rejected. Thus, rather than trying to construct a concept map, he wanted the teacher to provide him with a map which he could then "regurgitate" on the tests and examinations. My analysis and conversations with both students in the negative case analysis category showed that despite their objections, both students found some positive value in using concept maps. Mike, for example, found concept mapping useful because it could help students to clarify the relationships between concepts. After constructing a map, he felt "infinitely wiser."

Once I had completed this conversation with Richard, I felt that I was in a much better position concerning an understanding of the ways in which students experienced concept mapping and the written reflections that went with the exercise. Without the debriefing conversation involving Richard, I would not have come to understanding how he had separated his appreciation of concept mapping from his experience of the subject matter. I also felt that Richard had been open, which had been mediated, not in the least, by the kind of rapport I had with students generally. For example, at about that time, students were learning about electricity and I had asked them to design their own set of exercises and projects. In contrast to all other students, who planned tasks that they could do in the laboratory, Richard had asked me whether he could do a library research project that focused on electricity in, and the functioning of, the brain. I acceded without subsequently controlling whether he actually was in the library. He told me at the end of the school year that he had appreciated a lot the trust I had placed in him in this instance. This comment about appreciation of the trust constitutes a bit of convergent evidence (i.e., data) that supported the kinds of analysis I was able to do in the context of the student views of collaborative concept mapping project. It should be evident immediately that we teacher-researchers are in ideal positions for gathering evidence not available to university-based researchers who are not based at the site in the same permanent way as we are.

The rapport teacher-researchers build with their participants is a particular issue in cases like this one, as Richard had things to say that were not positive with respect to the course he currently

Power Over is a big issue for institutional research ethics boards (IRBs). It also should be a big issue for teacher-researchers for at least two reasons. First, in the recruitment process, we want students to participate freely, not because they might think they will be rewarded for their participation in one or the other way. Second, as analysts of the data sources, we have to keep in mind our institutional relations with participants, because these relations mediate what is said and how it is said.

CHAPTER 2

took. At the same time, we were located differently from an institutional perspective, and he could have felt threatened by the fact that I would be responsible for assigning grades. This situation is known under the name of *power over*, whereby our respective institutional positions gave me greater resources for actions that affect him than he had resources for affecting me. Whereas this is an issue we teachers have to deal with on a day-to-day basis, institutional research ethics boards are particularly concerned with such situations, because they could lead some participants to act in certain ways *because of the relation and the possible reprisals, repercussions, and benefits* rather than because they want to act in this way. Participation in a research project has to be on the grounds of being well informed and out of free will—institutional ethics boards capture this in the language of *free and informed consent*. In the North-American context, it is only if teacher-researchers doing a study toward some degree can ascertain free and informed consent that their projects will be approved by the university-based research ethics boards.

In the teacher-researcher project described here, I had done everything I could imagine to come up with a manner of understanding the ways in which students experienced a particular feature of my teaching—concept mapping and the reflections associated with it. Because of the existing dependency relation between a teacher and his students, I was particularly concerned with deriving ways in which (a) students expressed themselves as freely as they wanted and (b) I interpreted what students expressed and how I represented these interpretations. In terms of research method, I took yet another step by including a high school student as a co-researcher, in a concurrent project designed to understand students' talk about the nature of knowledge, knowing, and their own learning: I collaborated with one of the students in collecting data and writing the research article that ensued. I report on that investigation in chapter 5.

TEACHER–STUDENT TRANSACTIONS:
INTRODUCTORY ANALYSES OF DISCOURSE

While I conducted the study concerning student views of concept mapping, I was interested in finding out how collaborative concept mapping in the way it unfolded in my classrooms provided the possibilities for new and different roles to teacher and students alike. I therefore also began to analyze the videotapes that I was collecting in the eleventh-grade physics course where I gathered the essays and reflections concerning students' views of concept mapping. I knew from years of working in schools that much of teaching was teacher-centered and teacher-controlled. The context provided by collaborative concept mapping, however, offered me many opportunities to interact with students in non-traditional ways. Thus, for example, during collaborative concept mapping I took on new roles: as coach, facilitator, or guide of learning. The metaphor of coaching implies a teacher who observes "students while they carry out a task and offering hints, scaffolding, feedback, modeling, reminders, and new tasks aimed at bringing [the students'] performance closer to expert performance" (Collins, Brown, & Newman, 1989, p.

481). It is inherent in the coach metaphor that the teacher rather than the student specifies learning goals: thus the goal directedness. The role of a facilitator implies teacher actions similar to the coach but without its directedness (or goal setting by the teacher) of constructing specific content or skills. The metaphor of the guide evokes the image of a more experienced learner who meanders the same paths as the students, but has traveled these paths more often. Implicit in all three metaphors is the constructivist assumption that learners are responsible for constructing their own knowledge but are assisted by one or more knowledgeable and more experienced person or persons. It is important in the present context to see teachers as co-learners, though their new knowledge is often of a different kind and degree.

I was interested in exploring these metaphors by providing descriptions of various ways in which a teacher as coach-facilitator-guide (CFG) can contribute to the ongoing student talk about science topics. At the same time, I thought that these descriptions would elaborate my understanding of the coach-facilitator-guide metaphor. I was thinking that through appropriate questioning as the teacher I could *elicit justifications, explanations, and elaborations*, processes that help the students in reflecting on their own knowledge. Second, I was thinking that although I was in the role of the teacher, I also could be in a position of a *primus inter pares* (first among equals), in which my contributions to a conversation were treated like those of any other (i.e., student) participant. Third, I thought that there are situations in which the students and I engage in the *collaborative construction* of new knowledge.

As I was reading through the transcripts, I had the strong impression—to be ascertained in, or contradicted by, the subsequent analysis—that through appropriate questioning, I, the teacher, elicited from the students (a) justifications for specific hierarchies or propositions, (b) explanations of statements which were sufficiently unclear, or (c) elaborations of partially verbalized concepts. All of these processes encouraged students to reflect on their current knowledge and in the course facilitated their integration of the various elements of knowledge that they had constructed in their previous activities. The following excerpt features me asking for clarification of the concept hierarchy. This excerpt therefore was a piece of data supporting my hunch, which I set up as a tentative claim (or assertion). (Consider the whole transcript to be a *data source*, the bit extracted in support of my hunch is a piece of *data*.)

> Teacher: How come you have inertia, mass, and acceleration that high up? And something like energy that far down?
> Damian: Well for a force, um (pause)
> Miles: Mass is
> Damian: Mass
> Rick: Acceleration
> Damian: Force needs mass and acceleration and a kind of force is weight, that's why they are together, that's why they are up. Acceleration causes, velocity over a period of time.

CHAPTER 2

---

a. **Bold**-faced, emphases in speech: "Like, considered **as**?"
b. Square brackets, "[. . .]", to add words that would facilitate the comprehension of the transcript: "It [light] consists of quanta."
c. Parentheses, "(. . .)", to indicate non-verbal cues and actions: (begins to draw sine waves)
d. <u>Underlining</u>, to mark overlapping speech:
   Don: Which is <u>measured</u>
   Max: <u>Which speed</u> is measured in Hertz
e. Comma, ",", and period, ".", to indicate breaks in the flow of speech.
f. Question mark, "?", if the context allowed the speech act to be interpreted as a question.

Figure 2.8. The first transcription scheme I used to transcribe the conversations that I used in the attempt to better understand teacher–student transactions.

The relative position of the terms inertia, mass, and acceleration with respect to energy is, of course, important. In a physicist's understanding, the concept of energy would be ranked as crucial because it is one of the central concepts that they use to assess many problem situations. To students, on the other hand, surface level concepts such as inertia, mass, and acceleration, seem to be more important. Thus, they will rank them further up in the hierarchy. My question can be interpreted as an attempt to raise the students' awareness of the all-inclusiveness of the energy concept. However, rather than telling them that energy was more important, I posed a question which encouraged the students to elaborate on their understanding of the topic. Although Damian began the formulation of a new proposition, it was through Miles' and Rick's input that the sentence came to be completed. Readers can see in this a first cut at an analysis of the kind I conducted to find out more about teacher–student transactions in the context provided by collaborative concept mapping.

At the time, I worked with rather simple transcription schemes (e.g., Figure 2.8). I did not have linguistic training or training in *discourse analysis* (see chapter 5) or *conversation analysis* (see chapter 6). In fact, in the very early stages of doing teacher-research, I did not even know about these fields and forms of analysis. It is not surprising that today I look at these initial attempts of mine as somewhat naïve. Today, as a supervisor of teacher-researchers and other graduate students, I direct my graduate students to get into more sophisticated kinds of analyses described in chapters 5 and 6. Figure 2.8 shows some of the transcription rules I used back then; more sophisticated schemes are provided in the later chapters.

I soon realized that this kind of analysis, where I began with metaphors and then looked at the data led to a reification of the metaphors and made me blind to a more critical analysis of the transactions in which I participated and the roles other participants and I played. I addressed the problems subsequently in a paper where I used two types of analyses, one beginning with and building on the metaphors I had used for teaching, the other from the perspective of *conversation analysis* (Roth, 1993a). This latter method of analysis focuses on how conversationalists achieve social situations in and through turn taking. The resulting analyses provided me with two different interpretations of teacher-student transactions in this classroom. The first showed a classroom from a global perspective in which the transactions between students and teacher became understandable in terms of the chosen metaphors and their constituent teacher actions, modeling, scaffolding, and fading. (Recall the warning I provide above about how human beings tend to reify their ways of understanding based on existing concepts and theories.) While in modeling the conversation was almost exclusively dominated by me, and after fading almost exclusively by the students, my present interest was with scaffolding, that is, with those transactions during which students and I contributed to about the same extent.

A potential problem with this kind of analysis is that my expectations were merely reified. That is, I came to realize that this kind of analysis lends itself to succumb to my ideology where, because I planned the curriculum according to some metaphor, I would find the metaphor everywhere I looked—much in the same way that to the proverbial person with the hammer as a sole tool tends to see the whole world full of nails. I had conceptualized my teaching in terms of cognitive apprenticeship, and there is ample evidence for me that I supported the use of the metaphor. But the danger was that I merely reified ways of understanding and perceiving rather than succeeded in looking at the situations in new ways, which might turn out to result in understandings that are inconsistent with my earlier understanding.

I came to realize the real dangers in working with metaphors. Whereas the use of metaphors may be beneficial in facilitating changes in teacher classroom actions—some researchers suggested that metaphors functioned like master switches—there exists the possibility that teachers merely appropriate forms of discourse without changing their basic beliefs, and with it their teaching behaviors once the metaphor has been legitimated as a desirable norm. If we, as classroom teachers doing research, are interested in changing our practices, we can find help in new conceptual tools that reject the use of *a priori* descriptions and frameworks, and seek understanding that emerges from the phenomena of interest. In this search for new understandings, even our descriptions should not be sacred and constrained by preconceptions of what descriptions ought to look like, but these descriptions should arise from the need of a best possible understanding of a particular phenomenon. Because of my interest in teacher–student transactions, I chose to take a close look at our conversations at the level of individual utterances to construct an understanding how all participants managed these. Such an understanding was exactly what my previous analysis based on metaphors could not provide.

The second analysis that I conducted highlighted several features of my discourse strategies when I interacted with the students: there were interruptions, expansion, and reflection questions, questions that problematized concepts, and repair sequences in a triadic transaction pattern. (In the triadic transactional pattern, the teacher *i*nitiates an exchange, a student *r*esponds, and the teacher *e*valuates what the student has said—so that this pattern has been denoted by the acronym I-R-E.) It may be possible to integrate these transactional patterns into the cognitive apprenticeship framework that I was using at the time, where they would be understood as providing fine structure to my scaffolding moves. However, there are some potential problems. In the apprenticeship metaphor, scaffolding is slowly faded out until students are independent. For some, this process may imply an almost linear transition from teacher control to student control of the problem. Yet the analysis I had done provided evidence that contradicted such a linear or nearly linear transformation in teacher–student transactions: my conversational moves were contingent on the students' discursive patterns. Thus, a group that worked largely independently and that constructed elaborated answers to occasional teacher questions that problematized some issue at one instance was engaged in an immediately following teacher-controlled repair sequence. A further problematic issue arose from the fact that some conversational moves could be understood both as a scaffolding device and as an instance of modeling scientific inquiry. Thus, I realized that the concepts of modeling, scaffolding, and fading were like analytic tools that were not sharp enough to do the job I intended them to.

From a methodic perspective, I knew I was onto something: my study was breaking new ground in science education research and teacher-researcher investigations. Much of existing research on teaching used metaphors and other *a priori* categories. My critical analysis showed how easy it was to reify these metaphors and categories, which thereby turn out to be inappropriate analytical tools. I was on my way to understanding the warnings Pierre Bourdieu (1992) provided to his readers even prior to having read them: the most dangerous enemy to a researcher are his or her own presuppositions (ideologies); these are dangerous because hidden from conscious deliberation. I began to suggest to others the use of transactional analysis that operated at a different level and is of a different logical type. I suggested that this double analysis had the potential to contribute much new knowledge to the community of practice consisting of teachers and researchers. Both forms of analysis provided teachers with analytical tools for improving their own practice, and for contributing to theoretical knowledge in our community. Simultaneously, I was working out the ways in which I could enact radical doubt with respect to my own preconceptions and ideologies.

I had begun my teacher-researcher investigations rather naïvely, without interest in writing research reports or journal articles. However, the more I was investigating the events in my own classrooms for the purpose of reporting it to other science educators, the more I was thinking about the methodical issues involved when teachers do research in their own classrooms. Among the most important issues were those that dealt with the charges of subjectivism that some educational researchers launched against those adhering to the constructivist paradigm. Readers may be able to see that in the course of the studies reported in chapters 1 and 2, my own resources for dealing with such charges evolved and developed. Whereas I had asked initially a university-based researcher to participate in my studies as a disinterested peer, the later studies on concept mapping were done without her involvement. In a sense, I had emancipated myself sensing that my research could hold its own even in the rather competitive world of publishing in academic journals.

CHAPTER 3

INVESTIGATING HOW STUDENTS LEARN IN AND THROUGH OPEN INQUIRY

The teacher-researcher study that figures as the background of this chapter 3—in the course of which I articulate some familiar aspects of issues dealt with in chapters 1 and 2 and many new issues—probably is the first of all my more formal teacher-researcher investigations. It emerged from a confluence of circumstances that could not have been predicted. The following account is intended to show the reader how entire programs of teacher-research can arise unpredictably from experiences and readings. In fact, such circumstances may lead others to become a teacher-researcher in the first place, just in the way it has happened to me.

During the summer of 1990, I was headed west from my high school to the University of Victoria to teach a five-week course of physics for elementary teachers, a course that was required in the process of upgrading their certification. I had promised the parents of a tenth-grade student from my school to tutor their son, who wanted to catch up about one year's worth of knowledge in chemistry, physics, and mathematics to be able to attend A-level science courses in a Scottish high school during the school year following the summer. I had made my promise under the condition that they and their son agreed to my tape-recording the tutoring sessions. I wanted to use these tapes to complete a chapter for a book on constructivism that Ken Tobin had invited me to contribute.

Although I subsequently used some of the tape transcripts on tutoring, I never went much farther because of other events in my life that led to a change in my life as teacher and researcher. During that summer in Victoria, I read *Laboratory Life* (Latour & Woolgar, 1986), *The Manufacture of Knowledge* (Knorr-Cetina, 1981), and *Cognition in Practice* (Lave, 1988). These three books had a tremendous impact on me since they fundamentally changed my thinking about knowing, learning, schooling, and research method. They focused me on issues of research and ultimately led me back to academia.

First, Jean Lave's study of mathematics in the everyday world and its comparison with school mathematics showed that there is very little transfer between what happens in schools and the mathematics people use to cope with everyday mathematical demands; and it showed that there is little if any correlation between how well someone does on school mathematics tasks and how well the person does, for example, in the supermarket (where there exhibited near perfect performance). I began to think about the differences between life in school, where everything a student does is decreed, and everyday life outside schools, where individuals have to look after themselves, frame situations as problematic in order to find out what is going on, and come up with solutions on their own. As a teacher, I wanted to address this issue by involving my students in experiences where they had control

CHAPTER 3

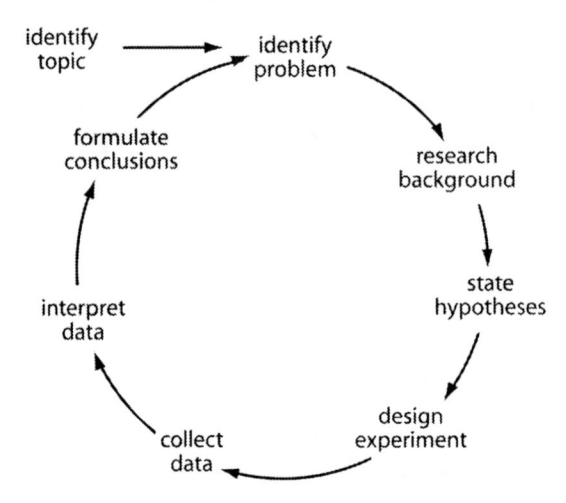

Figure 3.1. There continues to be a myth about the scientific method, which is supposed to follow a set of procedures arranged in a circular fashion.

over the goals of a task and over the means by which to achieve them. I wanted them to choose problems that did not necessarily have known solutions.

Both *Laboratory Life* and *The Manufacture of Knowledge* provided me with careful ethnographic description of what scientists really do rather than what they *say* or *write* that they are doing in the methods section of their research articles. It struck me like a big revelation. Although I had worked as a research physicist prior to becoming a teacher, I never had questioned the way in which students' textbooks and teacher guides depicted *the* scientific method as a set of recurrent practices often arranged in a circle: defining the problem, generating hypotheses, designing experiment, gathering data, interpreting data, writing conclusions, and perhaps generating new hypotheses (Figure 3.1). The same myth is often taught to graduate students in education, especially when they take research design and statistics courses. The two ethnographic reports I was reading showed that everyday scientific work in the laboratory has little likeliness with this image of method. (Similarly, the present book is intended to show that this idea of a scientific method is a myth but that our teacher-researcher investigations nevertheless can be rigorous endeavors that yield reliable knowledge as we continually interrogate ourselves critically about what we are doing and how we are doing it in the course of implementing a teacher-researcher investigation.)

As a result of my readings, I decided that I would let high school students develop their own research problems and experiments rather than telling them what to do and how to do it in the science (physics) laboratory. Until that moment, my students had done one independent research project during the year (e.g., as my records show for the 1989–90 school year). Now I wanted them to do independent research, that is, research where they specified the problems, design, data, and so on; I would assist them to achieve their goals rather than impose my own goals.

Allowing students to define the research problem they would answer by designing and conducting research also was to help me address another issue I had come across in the literature. (Although I was a high school teacher now, I continued reading journals that I deemed relevant to my job, including research journals [*Science Education*, the *Journal of Research in Science Teaching*, and *School Science and Mathematics*] and professional journals [*Science Teacher, Science & Children*, and *Science Scope*].) I had become aware of a movement whereby science students also were to learn *about* science and its nature. There was a second but unrelated movement in education and the learning sciences where researchers emphasized that students should learn in school the real stuff, do whatever scientists, mathematicians, or historians do. That is, followers of this movement in education recommended that school students engage in *authentic* science, mathematics, history, and so on. To me, this again meant that my students should be selecting or defining the research problems that they were interested in and then find answers through the design and realization of experiments. But what do students learn when they conduct open inquiry? How do they learn when they engage in open inquiry? These were important questions to me, as my students had begun to spend about 70 percent of their time on laboratory experiments and the remainder on other tasks.

At this point I had a problem concerning how to go about answering my questions. All three books had employed ethnographic research. But I have had training in statistical methods only, both as a physicist and as a social scientist. Should I use an ethnographic method? I knew there were a few (science) educators at the time who had begun using ethnographic methods, observing from the back of the class, taking notes about what was happening, and then augmenting their notes when they had returned home or to the university. In science education, one of the leaders of this method was Ken Tobin. Although I greatly admired what he was doing and how he did it, his method would not work for me. Because I was first a teacher, I knew that whatever method I used for documenting student engagement, practices, knowing, and learning needed to occur almost on its own. I knew I probably would have little time to think about and be concerned with recording field notes—there were too many demands on me during any one lesson, such as dealing with computer troubles, equipment failure, or student questions. Further, I could not imagine myself writing good and reliable notes in the evening after all the different lessons and after-school activities had ended. I also knew that my own perspective on events in a classroom was very different from the one a student would have working on a single project for the length of a period. My perspective on the classroom events would not give me much information about what any single student group experienced as they designed, experimented, collected data, interpreted results, and computer modeled the phenomena. It was at this point that I decided that videotaping students probably would provide me with an ongoing record of what students have done. At that time, videotaping classes for extended periods of time was rather new, and I was not aware of any work in the field of science education concerned, as I was, with studying learning processes as these unfolded in real time, in a moment-to-moment fashion, from inception to completion. What I was doing, therefore, emerged while I was doing it.

CHAPTER 3

EMERGENCE OF A RESEARCH STUDY

I knew that I wanted to look at the processes students engage in over the course of doing open inquiry; I wanted to understand how they developed their initial ideas, how they got from these initial ideas to designing an investigation, and how they arrived at the ultimate interpretation of their data. Teaching open inquiry appeared to me consistent with the statements that the then recent policy documents in science and mathematics education were making; but there was nothing available at the time that could have told me about how students were learning if they acted according to these newly minted policy documents. These documents included, for example, the following directions for learning contexts and learning outcomes that I duefully copied into my memos:

1. The use of real-world problems to motivate and apply theory.
2. The use of computer utilities to develop conceptual understanding.
3. Computer-based methods such as successive approximations and graphing utilities.
4. The connections among a problem situation, its model as a function in symbolic form, and the graph of that function.
5. Functions that are constructed as models of real-world problems.

These items were of particular interest to me—formerly a practicing physicist—because of the close integration of the subject matter physics with that of mathematics, statistics, and modeling. I knew that there was little if any research showing how students learn any of these subjects in the kind of learning environments I was in the process of setting up. My goal therefore was to find out about learning in ways that also should be of interest to others: first of all the other teachers in my school who did or wanted to teach through inquiry; second, it also should be of interest to others in the research community. But what should be the questions *focusing* my research? I could have just held or posed a camera recording students at work, but this would not allow me to make practical choices about what to record and how to record it. Here, another fortunate event mediated my choices.

During that same year, the journal *School Science and Mathematics* published an article entitled "Research on science laboratory activities: In pursuit of better questions and answers to improve learning" (Tobin, 1990). It centrally dealt with my interests, science laboratory activities and the improvement of learning. In it, the author articulated many at the time unanswered and unanswerable questions that required appropriate research studies. The author really had framed an *agenda* of studies to be conducted. From the questions he posed, I selected some of those that were most salient and relevant in my context and typed them up together with questions that arose in my own mind. In the course of the study, I wrote down more questions for the purpose of directing my attention during the process of building the data sources and, subsequently, for the purpose of directing my analyses (Table 3.1). In the course of doing teacher-research, I learned about the importance of writing questions, because these centrally oriented and mediated what I collected in terms of data sources and how I oriented my inquiries. I learned that

INVESTIGATING OPEN INQUIRY

Table 3.1. Before starting the investigation, I recorded several pages of questions that I might want to answer as part of the teacher-researcher study that I was about to begin.

- Is there evidence of framing and solving problems?
- How do students establish the focus of their research?
- How do students plan experiments?
- Are these plans turned into actions?
- Which part of the plans is turned into action?
- Are these plans executed?
- In which way are these plans realized?
- Are the goals within each group negotiated?
- How are the changes in goals negotiated during the implementation phase?
- What is the function of the teacher during the experiment? (In which part does the teacher ask guiding questions? When does the teacher tell? What sort of information is simply told versus elicited with questions?)
- What sort mof things seem students to learn during the planning, experimenting, analysis phases of experiment? How does this compare with the reports that they ultimately submitted?
- Indexicality of exchanges? Local ideosyncrasies?

the questions were more important than thinking about the method I would be using. In fact, the questions themselves were driving and determining the method I was using.

At the time, because it was my first teacher-researcher investigation, it was not too clear to me what I should collect in terms of data sources or how to plan my study. I thought that I wanted records of student investigations as complete as possible from the very first moment that they began discussing possible research topics to the moment that they handed in some final report. Still influenced by the quantitative research that I had conducted during my doctoral studies, I thought that I needed, to be convincing, a sufficient number of cases. I thought that I could get a substantial number by following one group or two in each of my three sections of introductory physics; and if I were to do follow students during several experiments, then I could build a substantial case about learning in this kind of learning environment within the first term of the school year while the curriculum entirely was devoted to the topic of motion.

On August 31, a few days prior to the beginning of the school year, I wrote a research memo that would become the driver for what I was going to do and looking for. The memo shows how what I had learned while doing the coursework for my doctoral degree about one particular curriculum developed in the 1960s and 1970s (SAPA) and the skills it emphasized had become salient to me (though I had forgotten about them during the three intervening years). I made a note about the hierarchy of the skills that these curricula presupposed and taught. I also noted the unwillingness of many of my teacher colleagues to teach through inquiry, a note that goes back to my reading of the previously mentioned Tobin article. Readers should also take note of the fact that I make reference in the memo to specific other studies that I was familiar with:

93

CHAPTER 3

> Traditional science teaching after 1960s have been teaching science process skills as independent skills with the understanding that they can be reassembled to a more complex skill of experimenting. This approach was the basis of the whole SAPA [Science: A Process Approach] curriculum. There were simple skills taught at the primary level such as observing, classifying, using numbers. And there were the integrated process skills such as identifying and controlling variables, hypothesizing, and experimenting.
>
> Problems with the curricula that tried to foster these skills were mostly identified in teachers' unwillingness towards experimentation.
>
> Isolated skills were taught with the assumption that they could be "concatenated" or "chained" (in Gagné's sense) to higher order skills. But traditional research practices have shown that all skills correlated highly and could ultimately be explained by one underlying factor common to both process skills and formal thinking skills (Roth, 1989; Baird & Borich, 1987; Tobin, 1984). Also, the hierarchy of the skills is in some trouble after Yap & Yeany (1988?) showed that those skills presumed to be subordinate appeared on the top of the hierarchy. (This part may have to be turned into a rather strong critique.) (August 31, 1990)

In the last paragraph of this memo I began articulating a critique, which was grounded in some work I had done while taking my last course during doctoral studies. My professor of statistical method, after I had proved by means of five different textbooks that he had erred on some point, invited me to strike out on my own, to learn some statistical technique, and to teach it to him. I chose to do a project, for which I used a relatively new statistical method to reanalyze some data on the hierarchy of "scientific process skills" that I had seen in the literature. My memo shows that I had become critical of this hierarchy, here based on the results of the study I had conducted in my statistics course, and which I subsequently published in a relevant journal (the reference to "Roth, 1989"). My research memo suitably entitled "teaching scientific process skills" contained many more critical comments with respect to scientific skills and scientific process as these were depicted in the junior and senior high school textbooks of the day. (Typing "the scientific method" into Google today will turn up many sites where the myths about scientific method continue to be perpetuated.)

While collecting the material evidence for this project—videotaping, collecting reports, writing personal research notes—I continued to note questions in my memo files as these became salient to me watching the research unfold. I wrote many of these notes on the computer, although I only was a beginning typist and although it would have been much faster for me to write these notes by hand into a field notebook. I still did so, depending on the moment and the availability of time and a computer, some of the questions were just jotted down on pieces of paper that I collected in a binder, whereas others I typed up; a printed version of the electronic memos was added to my binder for this project. Thus, well into the study, on November 18, I recorded the following set of questions:

- How do variables and questions crystallize? Initially? Finally?
- How do students make choices for a particular experiment?
- How do they decide which variables to study?
- Through what sort of negotiations do students come to a consensus?
- What sort of factors affect the decision making? Feasibility of study? Availability of materials? Negotiation of the tools to be used? (Kuhn, 1970; Brown, Collins, & Duguid, 1989) (November 18, 1990)

Here, the two references to the literature pertain to the nature of science, as described in *The Nature of Scientific Revolutions* (Kuhn, 1970) and one of several texts John Seely Brown and Allan Collins on the learning of *authentic* practices. Readers should note that the questions I was writing pertained to variables, which points us back to the work on process skills and the curricula designed to teach them.

In summary, I show in this section how my teacher-researcher research project was grounded in my previous readings and experiences. Although I did not know how the study was to unfold, not in the least because it was my first study of this kind, there was a context within which the study emerged. These prior readings and experiences mediated what I was interested in and how I looked at the classroom. Most importantly, readers should note that I had begun to question the common lore about science, scientific processes, and scientific (process) skills. That is, I had begun the kind of rupture that critical social research requires: rather than accepting to look at the events in my classroom through my existing traditional lenses, I began to distance myself from these lenses attempting to take a fresh look at students doing experiments in school science laboratories. Although I had been taught the myth about the existence of a scientific method and although I had taught the same myths previously, I began to rupture my way of seeing the world through this lens. In so doing, I began a conversion of my gaze, which ultimately allowed me to question my own presuppositions about how and what students learn in science classes, including my own.

It should be evident that my records, initially kept in the absence of any intent to do a formal (teacher-researcher) study, allowed me to become critical of my current ways of seeing and understanding. My notes now allow the reconstruction of the various experiences and readings from which the study ultimately emerged. These memos and notes allow me to locate the point in time when particular questions and foci emerged, at which instances during the research process I began to notice something or make connections between heretofore unconnected experiences and readings, and how these shaped my thinking at the time. In sum, therefore, these memos allow me to articulate the progressive nature of my subjectivity and the various influences that mediated my interests, my gaze, and my method.

COLLECTING DATA SOURCE MATERIALS ON OPEN INQUIRY

Having begun to think of my classroom as a workshop where members engage in whatever they need to expand their possibilities, it became clear that students would not stay in the same physical spot for the duration of an experiment, not in the least because each of these experiments extended over several lessons and lasted up to two weeks. This would constitute special constraints for the collection of data source materials, in particular would provide challenges for the videotaping. It turned out that in that year my school for the first time hired a laboratory assistant. I enlisted her to do some of the videotaping in exchange for preparing myself any laboratory materials required for my classes. Because she did not know my intentions other than the broad strokes of what I was interested in, ascertaining that she recorded what I wanted and needed and that would give me the kind of information I required for making sense and answering my research questions became an important aspect of the investigation. To provide readers with a sense of the work involved in collecting the data source materials and to provide the ground to discuss issues arising from this particular type of research on learning, I provide an ethnographic description of my classroom supported by materials that I collected: The following therefore is an example of the kind of ethnographic work you can do as a teacher-researcher to contextualize *any* type of study you may want to conduct.

Ethnography of Student Experiments

Over the course of a year, there were many experiments students could do and actually did that linked the curricular content with everyday life. All these experiments also permitted me to help students using and understanding the technology-based tools available in my classroom for bridging the gap between the real world and its representation in the form of mathematical symbols, a gap that is rarely bridged by school mathematics. Thus, in the course of their experiments, my students engaged in using a variety of technology-based tools including computer-based data collection, statistical software packages, mathematical modeling software, and handheld advanced calculators with statistical and graphical functions to produce graphs and mathematical formula that represented the phenomena that they studied. I intervened in students' data analyses, for example, when a new tool seemed to be appropriate, when students got stuck, or when there seemed to be an opportunity to develop a new way of doing something. However, any intervention was driven by the internal demands of student inquiries rather then by an external demand such as a curriculum-related agenda. Once one student group began employing a new computer or software tool, its use usually spread across the rest of the class very quickly.

Each research project arose from group discussions (Figure 3.2), during which the students negotiated an experiment based on their current interests and knowledge. In these discussions, they worked out some of the main questions they sought to answer in the project. I walked from group to group to be able to assist whenever students felt they wanted to bounce off some ideas they currently were discussing. Because of their interest in racing cars and the effect of drag on velocity, Matthew, Martin, Alex, and Andrew decided to find an answer to the question, "How does the velocity-time graph of an object dropping in a liquid?" Since these

INVESTIGATING OPEN INQUIRY

Figure 3.2. Each experiment arose from a discussion, often lasting for an entire school period, in which students clarified the phenomenon to be researched, some of the factors to be investigated, and details of the experimental set up.

students had done an experiment on the air track prior to that point, they decided using a set-up in which an object falling in a tall measuring cylinder had attached to it a ribbon with clear and black stripes (Figure 3.3). (An air track fundamentally exists of a metal pipe with many tiny holes. It is attached to a pump that forces air into the pipe, which then streams out through the tiny holes. When small carts are placed on the pipe, cushions of air are formed on which the carts "float" with negligible resistance. Students therefore could develop their own forms of resistance—objects of different shapes dropping in water—and determine their effect on the motion of objects.) The stripes triggered optical pulses in a photo sensor—off when the light was blocked by a black stripe, on when there was clear plastic. It is not surprising that these available tools mediated the selection of research questions, much in the way that Thomas Kuhn had shown in his *Structure of Scientific Revolutions*. An Apple-IIGS computer loaded with data collection and data processing software recorded the light pulses and calculated from it position, speed, and acceleration.

The data collected by the computer were plotted, given the characteristic distance from stripe to stripe, as distance-, velocity-, or acceleration-time graphs. Using the apparatus visible in Figure 3.3, Matthew, Martin, Alex, and Andrew obtained data similar to those plotted in Figure 3.4. Because the graphical analyses software packages on the Apple II were somewhat limited, the students also took their data and analyzed them using StatView II, a Macintosh statistical package with a wide variety of options, among them multiple linear and polynomial regressions. Over the course of the two years of physics, students learned to use this package for a variety of purposes, including those of other courses, such as mathematics.

CHAPTER 3

Prior to conducting each subsequent data collection run, the students interpreted their printouts to find out whether the run had produced the data they needed, whether adjustments needed to be made to the set up, and so on. In such instances, they sometimes called me to get some expert input (Figure 3.5). For example, these four students found that while plotting their data together with a larger range of the independent variable, the parabolas they expected did not describe the velocity of the objects well: The velocity graphs decreased after reaching a maximum, con-

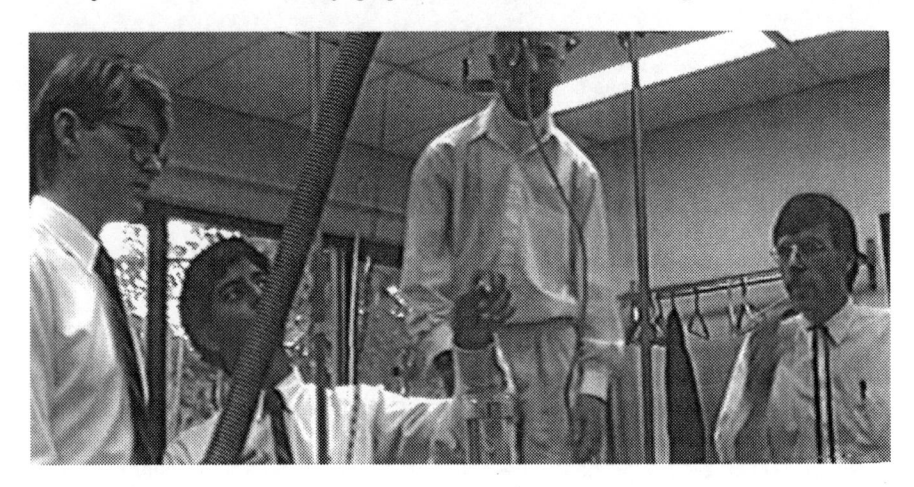

Figure 3.3. Martin, Alex, and Matthew (left to right) are setting up the experiment. I have stopped by to see how things were going, assisting students to reflect on what they were doing my asking questions and providing critical feedback.

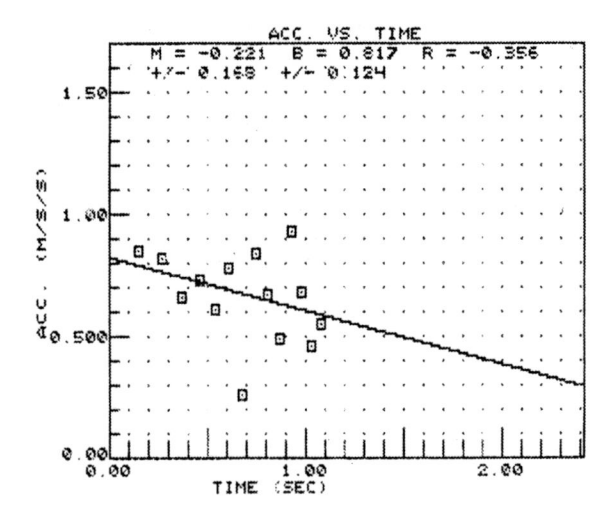

Figure 3.4. In their experiments, students produced numerical data and graphs, copies of which entered my database.

98

trary to the students' expectation that there should be a constant terminal velocity. When they approached me to seek help, I suggested an exploration of various mathematical functions with an advanced graphics calculator. Mark, Tom, and David began by exploring other polynomials and root-functions on their graphics calculators.

Upon my suggestions they also plotted exponential functions. The pupils found that exponential functions showed an asymptotic behavior for which they were looking, but with the negative x-axis as the asymptote. I suggested to the group exploring the reflection of the function at the y- and the x-axes to achieve a function that had the same general shape as their velocity-time graph. After some tinkering, the four arrived at a suitable mathematical function. Here I introduced some mathematical concepts that students had encountered in their eleventh-grade mathematics course. At this point the students were ready to use another tool that scientists often use, modeling software, which allowed them to run experiments without actually doing them (Figure 3.6). Here, physical phenomena could be modeled and simulated in microworlds that also allowed them to see what was happening in slow motion (see also chapter 6). They could then compare the results of their models with the results they obtained from the real experiment.

When the students used MathCAD to plot their data and a hypothesized function, they used equations I provided them with to calculate a measure of goodness-of-fit, which indicates the amount of variation in the data accounted for by the function. As the program did not calculate the parameters for a best fit, the students had to estimate the variables terminal velocity ($v_{terminal}$), initial velocity ($v_{initial}$), and a frictional parameter (k) to fit the function

$$v(t) = (v_{terminal} - v_{initial})*(1 - e^{-kt}) + v_{initial} \qquad (3.1)$$

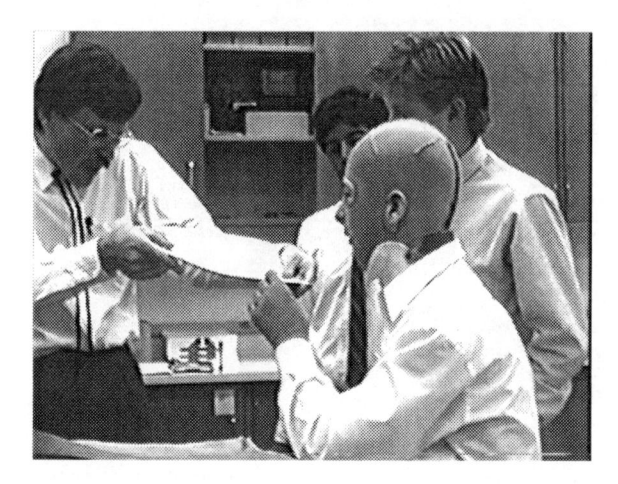

Figure 3.5. I am looking at the printout while assisting students in interpreting the results of one experimental run, here in the attempt to see whether the data are on a line or curve.

CHAPTER 3

to the data. After the first trial, the students used the goodness-of-fit index and visual inspection of the graph overlaying the data as feedback to determine the curve of best fit—the curve that yields the smallest sum of the squared distances between it and all the data points.

Before the students wrote up their lab, they modeled the motion of their object using the Interactive Physics modeling software available in my classroom (se chapter 6). The video offprints in Figure 3.6 show how they set up the experiment in the modeling environment; the offprint on the bottom left also shows me working with the students during this phase. By running simulations with different values for the free parameters, the four students could compare the results of the modeling program with their measured data. Observables such as the gravitational force of the object in the liquid were determined by the students and compared to the values in their simulation. After completing this part of their study, Matthew, Martin, Alex, and Andrew wrote a six-page typewritten report about their experi-

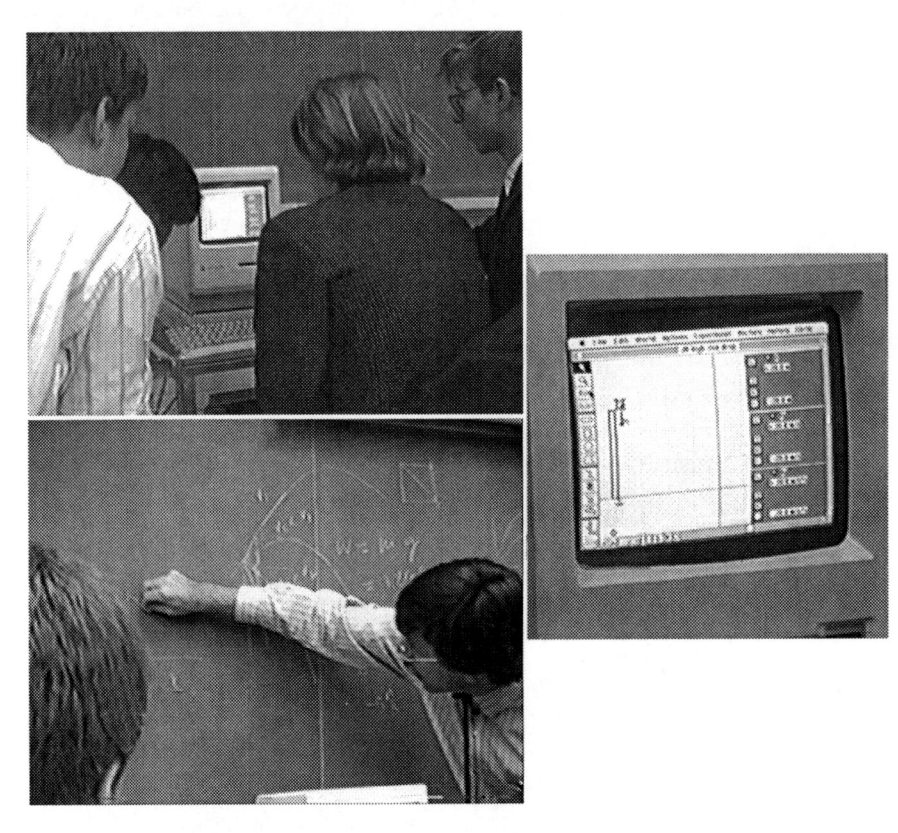

Figure 3.6. Three moments during the construction of a mathematical model for objects falling in air and in a liquid. Clockwise from top: Students from more than one group run and discuss the models; a close up of the model and computer interface; and I interact with students to bring together their experimental curves with those from the computer model.

100

ment, most of the space devoted to the data analysis, description, and interpretation of the results. All in all, it took the four a standard two weeks to complete this investigation and to submit their report (excerpts in Figure 3.7).

Seen from the students' point of view, they were in control of the activity from the beginning to the end. They generated a problem that did not exist for them before (ill-defined) and completely controlled the problem solving processes—characteristics of real-world, authentic problem solving contexts. As they proceeded, the four students described a physical phenomenon through graphs and mathematical functions making use of computers and calculators. When they faced a new problem—the velocity-time function showed a maximum rather than an asymptote—I suggested and initiated explorations on a graphics calculator.

This example shows how we, students and teacher, shared a common task; in and through this task, the students could learn and practice to speak the language of mathematical physics. Precisely this form of bringing a newcomer into full participation in a community of shared knowledge through face-to-face talk in the context of on-going work has been termed *cognitive apprenticeship* in the literature. Such participatory learning relies on the distinction between "experts" and "novices" in a physical and social context similar to that of real world, authentic practice. The context of the ongoing student inquiry context provided a backdrop against which conversation participants developed their shared interpretations.

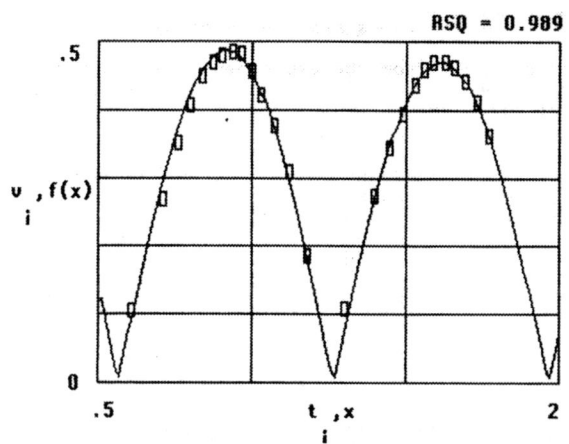

The maximum point on the velocity-time graph and any other maximum points on any other half cycle represent the cart's maximum velocity during the cycle's period. This point (crest) also represents the instant where both horizontal forces exerted by the springs acting on the cart are balanced. From this point on the cart's resistance to change its state of motion (inertia) propels it forward. After this point the spring on the left has expanded so much that it begins to force the cart to accelerate in the opposite direction; this is represented on the graph by the first negative slope.

Figure 3.7. In this excerpt from a laboratory report, a student has graphed his data and then plotted a mathematical function, the parameters of which he modified until he found the best fit, and then interpreted his curve.

When they were done, each student group submitted a report in which they accounted for what they had done in terms of the items available on the vee map (Figure 2.2): Existing knowledge, concept map, events (investigation), data and interpretation, and claims. Figure 3.7 features an excerpt from the data interpretation section of a laboratory report concerning an experiment in which the student investigated the damping an oscillating cart on the airtrack experiences because of friction. I kept copies of all the reports that the students in the three sections of junior year physics produced during this period. In addition, I kept copies of all reports several selected students did over the entire year.

From this description, readers probably can get a pretty good idea what was happening in my classroom. It is an ethnographic description enhanced with photographic images (really video offprints) and some of the materials students produced in the course of their investigations. Such descriptions are useful for those who have not been to our teacher-researcher classrooms, because they provide more extensive articulations of what a typical lesson looks like. In the literature, such articulations have come to be referred to as *thick descriptions*, following the conceptualizations proposed by the anthropologist Clifford Geertz (e.g., 1973). All teacher-researchers should consider writing such descriptions as part of their work, whether or not they actually use them in their theses, dissertations, reports, or publications. But I am certain that at least in theses and dissertations, such thick descriptions are highly appropriate because of their potential for providing a lot of the background knowledge required for understanding the phenomena of interest to the teacher-researcher investigation.

Monitoring the Research

Throughout the project, I kept memos with respect to research method. For example, on November 11 of the school year, I noted:

> Because of practical constraints, only one or two groups per class are taped. Also provided continuity.
>
> Lab reports, all, of all student groups; also longitudinal of 4 students over a period of 15 months into a grade 12 physics course.
>
> Written artifacts: notes, journals, have them submit labs in terms of vee and concept maps.
>
> As data are analyzed and interpreted, the purposes guiding new data collection strategies and at seeking convincing answers to emerging questions are to be noted. (See Exemplary Teachers, Tobin & Fraser) (November 11, 1990)

To aid me in monitoring the data source materials, I transcribed the videotapes as soon as possible after I recorded them. I usually did so in the evening after 8 P.M. and at night, sometimes until 3 A.M. in the morning. As part of the transcribing (on strategies see below), I also kept notes that would remind me to focus on certain issues during analysis. For example, on October 26, I wrote the following research note.

INVESTIGATING OPEN INQUIRY

> Videotape Oct 26, 1990
> AM 10:28
> MathCAD plot becomes "object" of conversation, is referred to:
>   tracing with finger
>   use of "indexical"
> T: "down a little the curve
>   [changes screen]
> S: "down a little more?
> T: "You want it [the curve] a bit up [shows with finger] and make it flatter [shows with hand]
>   Students take over

In this memo concerning the videotape shot on the same day, I entered the time at which the event happened (10:28 A.M.), which was also imprinted on the video frames, and described in sketchy terms what I found salient. Here it was the fact that the plot from the mathematical program had become an object of conversation. This object is material and therefore can be pointed to or followed (traced) with the finger. This aspect of the printout, tied to its material nature, was to become a major aspect of my research over the following years. In this memo, I also used a piece of transcript to show that the talk did not specify what the object, alerting me to the fact that those aspects of the setting that were perceptually available to the conversation participants did not require to be captured in words. In fact, it might have been taken as odd to describe what is perceptually available, because *it went without saying*.

As part of writing memos and keeping notes, I also recorded tentative hypotheses, which required careful testing in the data sources as a whole, especially when I would be writing a report—which turned out to be eight months after the videotaping was completed—i.e. during the summer holidays when I had lots of time at my hand. I recorded tentative hypotheses relative to the above stated scientific process skills on November 10 and 12, respectively, concerning an event that I had seen in the tape shot on October 17 in one of the classes:

> Use of paper maquettes to model objects under discussion. THINKING IN TERMS OF CONCRETES. *As soon as it becomes their experiment, students become inventive re setup, problems that occur* (a) taping pulley wheel to airtrack; (b) taped-stop for cart on track; (c) airtrack on top of shelves to increase # of points. (11/10/90)

> The design process involves all the skills: isolation of variables, hypothesizing, causal relationships, controlling other variables, and so on. Address "thought experiments" and students' reasoning in terms of concrete objects as mediators. (11/12/90)

The first of the two hypotheses is followed by three pieces of evidence that support it. The second hypothesis is simply stated, followed by a direction to look for particular issues in the data source materials, here the role of thought experiments and the role of objects as mediating resources in the design of experiments.

CHAPTER 3

The foregoing paragraphs should make it quite evident that it is worthwhile for teacher-researchers to frame tentative hypotheses, because these tend to focus our gaze to find contradictory or confirmatory evidence. Teacher-researchers should be suspicious, however, of lending too much credibility to confirmatory evidence because of the confirmatory bias that I already describe in chapter 2 in the context of metaphors. Human beings have a general tendency to see confirmatory evidence, because it fits what we currently think, rather than with contradictory evidence, because it is inconsistency with what we have learned and experienced. Nevertheless, it is through the disconfirmation of hypotheses that we can improve our understanding. Teacher-researcher investigations that actively seek contradictory evidence to research hypotheses are more credible than teacher-researcher investigations that confirm some concept or hypothesis.

Getting Help with Videotaping

The implications of doing a teacher-researcher investigation in a context where high school students pursue their own research may not immediately be apparent to outsiders. Some reflection, however, will probably allow us to understand at once that the situation is quite different than asking students to map some concepts, an exercise for which they have been provided with all the materials (paper snippets with concept words marked on them) and where they need nothing other than some space to move the paper snippets about and to transcribe the map they constructed onto a large paper sheet. In the latter situation, it is suitable to work with a fixed camera, which is set up and started prior to the lesson. Once students begin designing experiments, on the other hand, it cannot be known what equipment they are going to use, what—if anything—they need to build (e.g., some groups in my physics classes built cars from cardboard to investigate the influence of size and shape on friction and motion), and what kinds of resources they require (e.g., water, airtracks, computers, and stands). So the students likely are going to move about to access the resources. The construction of a complete videotaped record of students coming up with a topic, creating an experimental design, revising the design as part of the data collection, interpreting the results, and engaging in mathematical curve fitting and modeling would take the camera around the classroom (and sometimes even beyond). If I really wanted to have a video record, I needed to have someone follow the selected group of students. I personally did not have the time, as I knew from experience, because in open inquiry, as in my own research in a scientific laboratory, there was always something that breaks, goes wrong, or poses other problems to the high school students that required my attention.

The images of laboratory work presented here (Figures 3.2, 3.3, 3.5, & 3.6) should convince any reader of the necessity to have someone who takes the camera around to focus on the events *wherever* they may occur in the classroom. Furthermore, Figure 3.6 in particular shows that research in the context described here required an intelligent operator of the camera who knew how to capture that which is salient to the social actors in the situation. For example, the shot on the top left

(Figure 3.6) does not allow us to see what is on the computer monitor, yet at that time students were talking about the structures visible to them; the close-up shot, on the other hand, allows us to see the current display. More so, when I arrived at the physical location in the classroom where the group was working, the focal point was shifting again, now moving to the chalkboard behind the computer where I used chalk to provide students with some explanations. The diagrams on the chalkboard and the events on the computer were related; understanding the conversation students and I were having requires knowing what was perceptually present to all of us. Only an intelligently roaming, roving, focusing, and zooming camera is capable to record events suitably under such circumstances. What I was doing in the context of concept mapping would not have worked here. In the following, I describe several ways in which teacher-researchers can deal with such a problem.

It turned out that my school had hired a laboratory assistant normally assisting teachers in preparing lessons, and sometimes assisting teachers in supervising classes. As I had always done most if not all preparations myself, I thought of asking the laboratory assistant (Jane) to videotape in exchange for not involving her in my courses otherwise. She not only accepted but also found the task interesting and expected to learn from it—she was going to enroll in a teacher preparation course in the following year. Now, I know that not all schools have laboratory assistants who could help out, but there are other ways in which teacher-researchers can get help. In chapter 4, I describe how I collaborated with a colleague, where I did all recording in his classroom during my spare ("prep") periods. Other ways in which teacher-researchers may find assistance are students in the class—I did that once many years later in the case of a student who did not want to do research himself but was willing to produce a documentary showing his peers doing research. I also know about some teacher-researchers who enrolled the help of students in special programs, such as film- or arts-related courses, for doing a "documentary" and receiving credit for it in their course. Although I never did so, it is also possible for teacher-researchers to carry around an audiotape recorder, which can capture all teacher–student transactions in the course of a lesson. Audiotape, however, is not as good as the videotape because of the aforementioned indexicality of conversations, that is, the fact that humans do not normally articulate verbally what is there for everyone to see (i.e., whatever goes without saying).

To get someone else to record what is of interest in one's own research requires working with the person, watching tapes, and helping the person to understand what it is that needs to be shown. Thus, I repeatedly invited Jane to take a look at some videotape excerpts so that I could explain to her what I wanted. To remind myself, I wrote memos during my nightly analysis sessions such as "camera too close" and "don't move away from group" (10/22/90). Within the first of several student experiments recorded, Jane began to record precisely what I wanted. For example, as shown in Figure 3.6, Jane first recorded the students grouped around the computer, then zoomed in so that the current display on the computer monitor was captured, and, when I joined the group, she shifted the camera so that what I was writing and gesturing on the chalkboard became visible. In the same way, I

CHAPTER 3

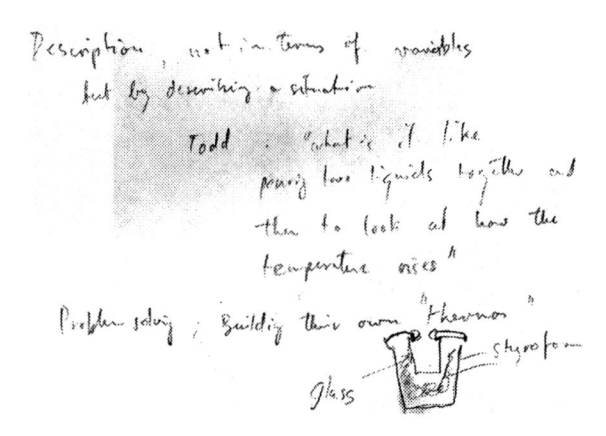

Figure 3.8. In this handwritten memo, I captured details of an event that might have been lost otherwise, but which supported the kinds of claims I was in the process of constructing.

worked in subsequent years with research assistants, who very quickly learned to shoot exactly what I wanted and needed for answering the research questions that I had articulated. In these situations, I was teaching again as part of my research so that I did not have the time to record.

It turned out that on some days, there was too much light coming through the windows so that we began closing the curtains and recording under the artificial ceiling lights. If we had not done this, the shot in Figure 3.3 would not have been possible as it was against the backlit window, which would have rendered all the figures and faces black.

Not everything gets to be on record, especially because I made the decision to have the camera follow one or two student groups in each class. (I still use this precept, as it allows me to construct detailed case studies of learning and change over time. However, as a university-based researcher using two or three cameras in a classroom, I can have a second camera follow one group through one project and then shift it to a second group, which allows me to get a broader perspective on learning in one and the same classroom. With a third camera recording, I can use it to roam and rove [e.g., Roth, 2005].) As a teacher-researcher, I write memos concerning remarkable events if time permits. Thus, for example, on November 22 I recorded an event on paper that the camera did not capture because it had been following another group. In this memo (Figure 3.8), I drew the situation that the students had constructed and which showed a moment of problem solving when they were building their own "thermos." I also recorded what one of the students, Todd, had been saying, "What is it like pouring two liquids together and then to look at how the temperature rises?" The event was significant in two ways. First, the student was not describing variables to be researched but rather described an event. (Much later I found that graduate students generally and teacher-researchers in particular describe what they want to do in the same way. Upon reflection, this is just how I got into doing teacher-research, as I was interested in finding out what

106

INVESTIGATING OPEN INQUIRY

and how students learned without knowing beforehand what I would have to look and look out for.) In the same vein, the first line of the text says "Description, not in terms of variables," which made the comment relevant in the context of my research questions concerning scientific process skills related to the identification and control of variables.

Second, once the students were conducting the experiment they had designed, it turned out that what we expected to occur did not. There was another trained physicist who had visited my laboratory. He, Todd, his teammates who was soon joined by others in the class, and I attempted to figure out why the expected changes in temperature could not be observed. As the other physicist and I were thinking aloud, students came to experience two trained scientists who did not have an answer and who were thinking aloud about how to solve the puzzling problem. In this way, my students were experiencing science in a way that they did not get to experience: two physicists wrestling with *real* problems and thereby exhibiting what they do in such cases. It was because I kept this note that details of the event did not get lost.

This episode should show readers how important it is to keep a research notebook even though one or more cameras might be used in the course of a teacher-researcher investigation. Any camera is as limited as a human being in what it is oriented to and what it focuses on. These notes that I was keeping in the course of my investigations provided many other pieces of data source material that I was subsequently able to use in my efforts of making sense about how students learn in the open inquiry learning environment I had created.

OFFPRINTS AND VIDEO-ETHNOGRAPHY

The ethnographic report provided above also shows an important aspect of teacher-research that comes with the use of video cameras. The images from the videotapes can be used to enhance the way in which a study is represented on paper. In the past, it was unusual to use (photographic) images in research reports. Personally I have experienced a situation where an editor made the publication of my manuscript contingent on the removal of the images provided, which nevertheless conveyed content that the text could not communicate. Thus, for example, together with my co-authors I had written about the way in which two teachers occupy the space in the classroom and how they mutually adjust their positions. As a consequence of working together for a while, therefore, new teachers became entrained in the rhythmic teaching performances of their lead teachers. Ultimately my three co-authors and I gave in and published that article without the images only to publish another parallel one with images in another journal.

There are some good reasons for using visual ethnographic materials: Photographs and other visuals provide information that cannot be made available in verbal form. This is so because the verbal and visual forms of expression are *one-sided* expressions of higher-order communicative units. Already from a material perspective, the sound that we hear as a word, the ink traces on paper that we read as a concept, and the ink plots that we see as a visual image are different. There is

107

little if anything alike between them. Humankind may have established conventions that allow us to go from one expressive medium to another, from word to image and vice versa, but all such translation comes with incompleteness and treason (Italians say, *traduttore traditore* [to translate is to commit treason]). Thus, a word cannot ever replace an image or a gesture. I therefore strongly advocate the use of multiple representational forms to articulate and present teacher-research.

> **Visuals and other Forms of Representations** Try to think about which means other than words there are for presenting the results of your investigations. Even capturing the situation of an interview by means of a line drawing may be important if, as is the case in science and mathematics, the participants use gestures to articulate themselves. Gestures are expressions in their own right and therefore should be rendered visually.

Another reason for using photographic and other visual materials is the richness of information that can be conveyed: folk wisdom tells us that one picture can be worth one thousand words. Therefore a lot can be communicated using film and photographic images. Words, on the other hand, may *interpret* a situation in ways that a corresponding image might not have done. For example, as soon as you gloss Figure 3.5 by writing "the teacher is estimating the straightness of the graph," you limit the ways in which the photograph can be seen. That is, the words already constitute a reduction of possibilities in making sense that the image itself does not constitute. First, you do not articulate in this gloss the constellation between teacher and students—which resembles one that you might see in everyday out-of-school life between a consultant and some development team. Second, by naming what the teacher does we reduce the possible alternatives for interpreting what other actions he might engage in. Thus, I might have been engaged in the practice of "let me look at it in another way," a strategy I use to look for different or alternative patterns.

Conversely, pictures may be inappropriate because the gratuitous detail available actually detracts from what you, the author, want to convey precisely because images can be interpreted in many different ways and possibly convey too much. A line drawing focusing on the most important aspects of a situation or a line drawing with certain elements shaded so that they stand out and are easily tracked by those reading a text may be more appropriate (see more on this below). That is, teacher-researchers have to make choices among the many different ways that are possible to articulate a situation. What the most appropriate form of representation is cannot be said beforehand but depends on the purposes of the report that the teacher-researcher prepares.

In the course of my research from the classroom, I have come to include visuals in an increasing manner to convey the events in a richer way than words alone can do. Images simply are irreducible to text, and the proper use of images allows teacher-researchers to provide a much a more complete account than if they were not using photographic and other visual forms. Even if I were to use photographs only during the analysis phase, I know that they would get me farther than if I did not use them. During conference presentations, the original video frequently does a much better job in communicating than text or offprints.

INVESTIGATING OPEN INQUIRY

The photographic materials used throughout this book derive from the videotapes that I had shot or had taken while doing teacher-researcher studies in my school. These tapes were in VHS format. Today, I use a digital camera for all of my studies: Once recorded, I transfer the video to the computer (iMovie on the Macintosh) and then export a version into QuickTime movie format. With the appropriate parameters, I can save a version at full pixel size but still amounting to about 2 Gb per one-hour tape; two hours of classroom video therefore fit onto one DVD. The QuickTime format has advantages over some other formats, for example, when you subsequently decide to work with the soundtrack (see the examples in chapter 6)—it can be extracted from a QuickTime movie but not from some other formats. It is also possible to quickly go to different places on the tape or, if you have the full version of QuickTime, to make clippings from the track or to splice together clips from different parts of the same lesson or from different lessons. This may turn out to be useful, as I saw on recent work done by one of my graduate students, who could thereby show the almost identical ways in which a teacher used hand gestures and body movements to communicate scientific concepts.

When I want to use individual images to add as a figure, to enter in a photographic transcript, or to write my first analytic comments, I simply do a screen shot of the video image on my monitor. If it is for analytic purposes, where I am unconcerned about the pixel density, I paste the image into my text-processing program (e.g., WORD). If I want to use an image for subsequent printing, I have to change its pixel density; I therefore import it into my image processing software (e.g., Photoshop). Because the screen shot will have a pixel density of 72 pixels per inch, but 300 pixels per inch are the minimum requirements for

Images and Pixel Density When you work with images you need to think about the ultimate use. If you use images for onscreen purposes only, no changes are required. But if you want the images to be printed, you need to convert from the 72 pixel per inch (ppi) density that you get in the screen mode to a minimum of 300 ppi that journal and book publishers require.

going to press, I have to change the density. Here is how I do it: let us assume the screenshot is 900 pixels wide and 600 pixels high. If you paste the screenshot into a Photoshop document, your ruler would indicate that you have an image 12.5 inches wide and 8.33 inches high. But to reach printing quality, your image cannot be but 900/300 = 3 inches wide. To make this conversion, I pull down the menu IMAGE and go to the item IMAGE SIZE. There, I change the pixel density from 72 to 300 and simultaneously decrease the width to 3 inches. As a result, the total number of pixels does not change.

Sometimes there is something on your tape that you do not wish to print. For example, on most of my VHS tapes, I have the date and time of recording. But I may not want to have this information on my images—it constitutes distracting information—in which case I remove it with the "smudge" and "clone" tools that Photoshop makes available. Thus, all of the videotape offprints used in this chapter had a date and time stamp, which I removed or rather painted over in Photoshop.

CHAPTER 3

A painting program also allows you to combine images to get a shot that covers more area than a single shot. Thus, Figure 3.3 is the result of combining two screenshots, one from before the camera had panned from left to right, where the second screenshot was taken. In this way, I was able to include myself, the teacher, in an image that originally only featured three students. In Figure 3.6, I created a new image by pasting three screenshots into the same image file.

Photograph versus Drawing Photographs show a lot of detail, much of which may actually detract your readers from the main features that are important to your argument. In this case, a drawing may be a more appropriate form of rendering the visual aspects of a situation.

But whereas I used the entire video shot for the two left images, I only used a partial screenshot for the images showing the computer screen. There are other ways of working with images as well. For example, in an article that I recently published, I overlaid four images simultaneously blending them. Because the background stayed constant, I was able to show how the hand of the person recorded moved in the course of the episode and therefore how it was used to highlight and communicate certain things.

For a variety of reasons, a drawing might be preferable over a photograph or a video offprint. Thus, if participants have not given consent to their photographs being made available in public or if you want something very specific to be seen, then it is advisable to generate a drawing. In Figure 3.9, I reproduced certain aspects of Figure 3.5 in the form of a line drawing in which the background was shaded grey to make the persons and their constellation stand out. I have used such drawings in many articles concerning the use of gestures in communication. In my early work, I used to take transparency sheets, tape them to the computer monitor, and then trace the main outlines. I subsequently scanned the drawing into the com-

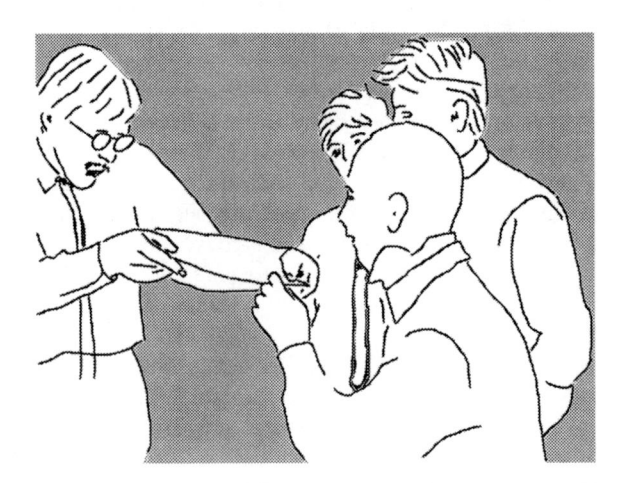

Figure 3.9. For a variety or reasons, a drawing may constitute the preferred representation. This image was prepared by creating a drawing layer on top of a video offprint; in this drawing layer, the main outlines of Figure 3.5 were traced.

110

puter where I continued processing the image in a drawing program. Nowadays, it is quite easy to create such a drawing rather quickly. First, you import the photograph or screenshot into the painting program (in my case, Photoshop). Then you make the pixel density conversion to 300 pixels per inch (ppi). Finally, you create a new layer, which should be on top of the photograph or screenshot. In this layer, you can now trace the main outlines of the relevant features to render only those elements that you need in your communication. Using this method, it only takes minutes to create an image such as the one depicted in Figure 3.9.

TRANSCRIBING

For as long as I have done interpretive research, that is, when I began as a teacher-researcher, I not only have written memos, kept copious field notes, and collected student artifacts in a continuous manner, but also have transcribed the recorded videotapes in an ongoing manner. Although some (academic) colleagues have suggested that transcribing everything was "the brute way" of going about research, history has borne me right in the sense that while transcribing I learned so many things that permitted me to follow up, change my teaching, add new data source collections, and so forth (see also chapter 4). In transcribing my tapes, I begin to attend to the detail of the social interactions that I might not have had I merely looked at the transcripts someone else produced. It also helps when you begin writing your analyses. The better you know your materials, the more you can make connections between the different parts of your study. So the time I put into transcribing my videotapes was an investment that always paid off and I gained in many ways. This should be evident even further in the following sections where I describe how I made sense, how I arrived at patterns, how I ascertained patterns, how I generalized from singular events to general phenomena, and so on. So my recommendation always has been, and continues to be, to transcribe videotaped lessons in full; and I continue to transcribe my own tapes to this day, though I have had up to twelve MA and doctoral students and postdoctoral fellows in my laboratory.

There is no one correct way to prepare a transcript; and the way a transcript ultimately features in a text will depend on its function and the particulars to be shown. That is, the transcripts (and images) you add to your text serve as data, that is, materials that precisely show the phenomena and support your claims and, ideally, contain nothing that might distract from your main message (provide readers with possibilities of alternative interpretations). Because I often do not know how the transcript is going to be used and what it is going to be used for, I begin with a "straight" transcript in which I am mostly concerned with capturing everything that has been said—to the extent that this is possible on a first go through—and, marking them off by double parentheses, I add some ("transcriber's") descriptions of what can be seen on the tape at the time. The transcript shows that some of the talk overlaps, though it does not indicate this overlap in precise term. Nor am I too concerned to have any or all the pauses. All I want at this stage is a verbal protocol that can be read quickly. For the analysis, I went back to the videotape rather than

CHAPTER 3

working from the transcript alone. I made sure to indicate where in the tape the episode occurred, by inscribing the time information or the VCR counter position in the transcript or in its header. This served me in rapidly finding the original source and was one of the strategies I used to create an audit trail—even if this information were not to be presented in the ultimate text made public (article, thesis). I always recommend carrying this information at least to the penultimate stage of the investigation and to the point just prior to making the investigation public. The following episode was recorded at the chalkboard near the computer (Figure 3.6).

> Episode OCT 22 1990, 11:11
> 1 Teacher: Look if you have minus five meter per second ((writes "-5 m/s")), this is obviously less than zero meters per second ((writes "0 m/s")) or less than plus ten meters per second ((writes "+10 m/s")).
> 2 Ceiran: But most [of the time it is the absolute value that is important.
> 3 Tim: [Yea that's zero ((gestures toward the chalkboard))
> 4 Teacher: Okay, the *speed* is different.
> 5 Tim: Yea.
> 6 Teacher: That's right, the speed is different ((points to -5 m/s)) you have more speed here ((points to 10 m/s)) than here ((points to -5 m/s)) than here ((points to 0 m/s)).

There are no inherent reasons why a transcript should look like this, however. For example, a teacher-researcher might be interested in separating what is available in visual and auditory form. In this way, readers would be able to more easily follow what has been said, unencumbered by the transcriber's comments. In such cases, I have used a tabular format of the following type, where I might mark the correspondence between text and action by means of underlining.

Episode OCT 22 1990, 11:11

Audio track	*Video track*
1 Teacher: Look if you have minus <u>five meter per second</u>, this is obviously less than <u>zero meter per second</u> or less than <u>plus ten meter per second</u>.	((writes "-5 m/s")) ((writes "0 m/s")) ((writes "+10 m/s"))
2 Ceiran: But most [of the time it is the absolute value that is important.	
3 Tim: [Yea that's zero	((gestures toward the chalkboard))
4 Teacher: Okay, the *speed* is different.	
5 Tim: Yea.	
6 Teacher: That's right, the speed is <u>different</u> you have more speed <u>here</u> than	((points to -5 m/s)) ((points to 10 m/s))

112

<u>here</u> than ((points to -5 m/s))
<u>here</u>. ((points to 0 m/s))

Teacher-researchers interested in the language their students and they use, without at the same time attending to the issue of other information in the room available to and used by the conversation participants may employ a transcript in this form. It is also of interest to those who investigate nonverbal aspects of communication because the listing of gestures in the right-hand column is precisely what these researchers want to feature. In this case, the words on the left-hand side constitute the ground against which the gestures become salient.

There is one important shortcoming to both transcripts—visual aspects of the setting are translated into words. The extent to which a visual aspect can be translated and represented verbally should be, in my view, an empirical issue rather than one of preconception and presupposition. Thus, in turn 3, we do not really know whether Tim gestures toward the chalkboard, the -5 m/s, the curves observable above my (the teacher's) current writing, and so forth. That is, whereas the gesture was more

> **Transcripts and Transcription** There is no one right way of transcribing a videotape or audiotape. The form a transcript takes should support the feature important in and to the analysis—consistent with Marshall McLuhan's (2005) dictum that the medium is the message. You may want to "play" with the way a transcript appears on the page to find out which one actually goes best with the claim you make. Choose visuals if your interpretation relies on aspects of communication that were not spoken.

or less undetermined or underdetermined, the verbal articulation attributes to it a sense that it may or may not have. But in any event, although the second transcript contains the same information, it is articulated and structured differently, and the teacher-researcher has to choose in which way his or her data should figure to support in the best way possible the claims made. As readers can ascertain, the second transcript makes some aspects of what has been said and what can be seen much more evident than the first one has done.

A teacher-researcher interested in the nonverbal aspects of communication, as I have become, may not be satisfied with the translation of visual aspects into words. This is particularly important when conversation participants talk about some phenomenon that is new to them, in which case—as I know from many studies that I conducted in the area—they are more likely to use gestures and point towards these phenomena should they be perceptually available. In this case, the use of photographs, offprints, or drawings to represent the situation becomes primordial. In the following transcript, I have added images that I first extracted as screenshots from the digitized videotape and subsequently processed in Photoshop to reach the pixel density required for the publication (including MA and doctoral theses) of the transcripts that I use as data in support of my claims.

It is self-evident that we cannot use every image from the video track; nor is it advisable to use too many images. The images we want to add to the transcript are those that are salient and help us to understand the relevant events. These are the crucial moments that photographs can assist in identifying. These moments should

CHAPTER 3

be chosen such that scanning the images from top to the bottom gives the reader an idea about the movement that has occurred between them; and it is precisely the movement and change in position that the sequence of photographs conveys.

Episode OCT 22 1990, 11:11

Audio track	*Video track*
1 Teacher: Look if you have minus <u>five meter per second</u>, this is obviously less than	
<u>zero meter per second</u> or less than <u>plus ten meter per second</u>.	((writes "0 m/s")) ((writes "+10 m/s"))
2 Ceiran: But most [of the time it is the absolute value that is important.	
3 Tim: [Yea that's zero	
4 Teacher: Okay, the *speed* is different.	
5 Tim: Yea.	
6 Teacher: That's right, the speed is <u>different</u> you have more speed <u>here</u> than	((points to -5 m/s)) 
<u>here</u> than <u>here</u>.	((points to -5 m/s)) ((points to 0 m/s))

Again, it is evident that there is different information available from this third transcript than from the second or first. However, because of the images, this transcript also takes more space on the page. Space does not matter so much in a thesis or in an online-only publication. But it does matter when the intended outlet is a print journal or book because here the editors and publishers are concerned with (costly) space and the limitations that are imposed upon them by their contracts. As the teacher-researcher, you therefore have to decide whether the photographs, off-prints, or screenshots are really necessary; and if they are, then your analysis needs

INVESTIGATING OPEN INQUIRY

to make this clear. That is, your analysis itself shows that it depends in crucial ways on the visual information that would not have been available otherwise. Whether you in fact want to use photographic images or drawings depends again on the purpose of the transcript and what precisely is to be shown to support the claims you make in your text. Thus, I show in chapter 6 under which conditions it might be more advisable to use diagrams and line drawings to make available visual information.

Although this third transcript already is much richer than the previous two, it does not contain information that might be of sufficient detail for teacher-researchers who are interested in studying the minute-to-minute organization of talk and the mutual constitution of events—such as this teacher–student transaction that may be glossed as *guidance* in the context of *cognitive apprenticeship*. Such a research interest requires transcripts that include precise timings of pauses within and between speaking turns, overlaps, and even prosody (speech intensity, pitch, utterance speed). I return to the production and interpretation of such transcripts in chapter 6.

ANALYZING VIDEOTAPES AND TRANSCRIPTS

My personal preference is to transcribe the videotapes as soon as possible after they have been recorded and produced. If I did not have the time—which I generally make available when I decide to do a teacher-researcher study—I would still watch the tape at least once, taking notes about the nature of the events and articulate interesting features in written form (Figure 3.10). In the memo displayed in the figure, I had made reference precisely to the episode transcribed in the previous

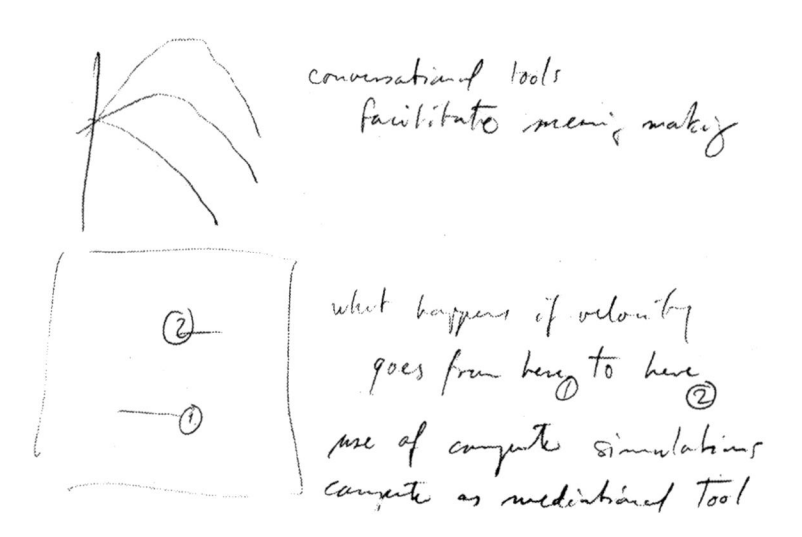

Figure 3.10. This is the earliest analytic note pertaining to the episode depicted in the transcript from the lesson on October 22.

section. I pointed out in this note the salient parts of the writings on the chalkboard and annotated the diagram of the curves with the text "conversational tools facilitate meaning making." The second aspect highlighted is the use of pointing (deictic) gestures in the course of uttering "goes from here② to here②," where the numbers refer to the points on the chalkboard that I had been pointing to in the process. Although this was my first teacher-researcher project, this aspect of communication—where gestures take an important and irreducible part—would become a main line of my research eight years later. Here again, readers note how much prior experiences and thinking become important to our thinking at subsequent points in time, which may be, in some instances, many years later. The third note pertains to the function of the computer: "use of computer simulations; computer as mediational tool." A little over a year later I would investigate as teacher-researcher what and how students learn when they use computer simulations; I investigated the role of computers in teacher–student–student transactions; and I analyzed the function of computers and computer simulations in structuring the situation (see chapter 6). This is but another example of how asking and answering questions by means of teacher-researcher studies leads to the production of new questions and new research.

I produced such notes and memos also when I transcribed, jotting down ideas and diagrams when it was easier and quicker than producing screenshots and typed text on the computer. They directed my subsequent analyses or allowed me to identify possible and interesting themes. Alternatively, either during the transcription or to begin an analysis, I made screenshots of "interesting" moments entered them in the left cell of a two-column table and then annotated them as seen in the following transcript. I did so well knowing that the interest is grounded in my own past experiences, which required historical analysis to prevent me from merely reifying received ideas. (Readers note that the images in this situation still have the time and date encoded in them, which I removed from other images in this book using Photoshop.)

Episode OCT 22, 11:11 A.M.

In this situation, I have joined a group of students who currently build a computer model in Interactive Physics to simulate the experiment that they have conducted. The students struggle with the interpretation, and the teacher seems to have noticed that the students make no distinction between speed and velocity. When I join the group, my assistance comes "just in time" and "as needed," which are two concepts familiar from a teaching–learning context denoted by *cognitive apprenticeship*. In this instance, the chalkboard behind the computer becomes a mediational tool, serving as a ground to the teacher–student transactions but also containing signs that serve as topics. At one point, Tim thrusts forward his right hand in which he holds a sheet of paper. What is he pointing to? Can we know as analysts? Do the participants know? Is not the purpose of the analysis what the participants note and what is salient to them? And if this is the case, then whatever the participants make available *is the phenomenon of interest. It is precisely in and through the utterances and other communicative forms that the participants make available and salient the sense of the situation.*

When there is something that can be pointed to, then it does not have to be verbally described. "It goes without saying," as the popular adage goes. Thus, not everything communicated is available in words; and in fact, words are subordinate to the communication in much the same way that everything else is made available in the situation. But words are privileged in such situations and by analysts. The structures on the chalkboard are resources or rather structures that are constitutive of the sense for these participants.

For each relevant and salient moment on the videotape, I write as much as I feel like or can before I move on in the video, clipping screenshots as I go along and writing comments. It is through this writing that my sense for patterns in the data sources comes to be sharpened; and the longer I do this, the more tends to become salient. That is, as mentioned before, writing is doing analysis and learning. The more of it we do, the more we become familiar with the materials; and the more familiar we are with our data source materials, the more we begin to notice. The more I write, the more I learn. When I use the term "writing," I mean something akin to "free writing," because initially it does not mean I am writing for someone else. What I want to do by writing is to generate ideas much as one does in brainstorming. Today, I recommend to my graduate students: "Write, write, and write." At this stage, interpretation is like free writing, whatever comes to mind. It is also part of the strategy by means of which I make available my own presuppositions for subsequent analysis. Once I have produced some text, I later can ask questions such as, "Why would I have described the situation in these words?" "What is it that makes me see the situation in *this* rather than some other way?" That is, it is important to first externalize and objectify oneself, which then provides resources for better analyzing and understanding one's own presuppositions.

At this stage, I also write first comments or interpretations. I generally enter such comments into the text clearly separating them by empty lines, using double or triple quotation marks, and the word comment: "(((COMMENT: . . .)))." Often, however, I simply copy the transcript fragment of interest into another file—which would have either "notes" or "analysis" as a file name and would have a version number—and begin to write comments and analyses. An example of such writing, which immediately follows the excerpt from the transcript and its associated im-

CHAPTER 3

age, is provided following the next excerpt. The memo shows how I am attempting to come to grips with my own actions, not by giving my version of it, but by analyzing the excerpt as any other researcher might have done, that is, without the privilege of accessing purported private thoughts.

Episode OCT 22, 11:11 A.M.

1   Teacher: Look if you have minus <u>five meter per second</u>, this is obviously less than <u>zero meter per second</u> or less than <u>plus ten meter per second</u>.   ((writes "0 m/s"))
   ((writes "+10 m/s"))

2   Ceiran: But most [of the time it is the absolute value that is important.

In this situation, the teacher begins by drawing students' attention to the chalkboard: "Look." Here, the chalkboard comes to be the focal point, for the teacher could have said "listen" if what is going to happen were presented verbally only. In uttering "look" the teacher not only articulates *that* students are to attend but also *how* they are to attend—by looking. It is as if the teacher already oriented to the use of the chalkboard although he has not had time to preplan what he is going to say or how this teachable moment is going to unfold. But in uttering "look" he already exhibits to us an orientation toward a shared perceptual space, the chalkboard, and he orients students to that same space. (This is the case although people in everyday life often say "look" when they mean listen. The ideology of seeing to express understanding ["I see"].)

As I talk, I am noting numbers in the order that they would appear on the graph, -5 m/s below 0 and +10 m/s. It is a way of pointing out that -5 is *below* 0 m/s, thereby highlighting the difference between velocity and speed (in which case 5 m/s would be larger than 0 m/s because it does not distinguish).

As soon as I write down the third number, Ceiran points out that the absolute value of the velocity—which is speed—is the factor of interest. The fact that he is going to say something that is somehow to be seen in contrast to what I have said is apparent with the first syllable uttered: "but." By uttering this contrastive connective, Ceiran, whether he has thought this out or not, alerts all of us present that something is forthcoming that needs to be heard as a contrast.

Indeed, whereas one might consider that I proposed a matter of fact, it turns out that in this situation, my statement comes to be contested. It is, from the perspective of the conversation, not a fact. And this not being a fact is available to use only after Ceiran has completed his turn. From the perspective of the conversation, a collective perspective, an utterance is a performance only; its function in the collective situation, whatever the intention of the speaker, is available only one turn later.

In this analysis, I articulate initial understandings of what is going on in the situation as captured on the videotape. I know that there were other events that went on in the classroom at the same time and that were not captured. I also know that events can be perceived in other ways as well. But I have to start my analysis somewhere, and therefore simply begin in an open and unstructured way and do this analysis as "free writing." In this way, I work myself through the videotape, stopping especially at those moments that are of interest to me at *that* moment in my research. It should be self-evident that I would pay particular heed to the events when there was a teacher if I were interested in teacher–student transactions and that I might go more rapidly through a tape when the teacher was not present. But this is not universally the situation, because some moment in the teacher–student transaction might mediate what happened later in student–student transactions. Thus, for example, I noted in several different studies that students were referring to something I had said previously while engaging them in a conversation. It turned out that students sometimes cited me later (i.e., in my absence) in support of claims that were not at all what I had intended to say at the earlier point in time. Yet when a student would refer to me as the source of some statement, others accepted his or her argument—unless, of course, the reference itself was contested such as when another student said, "but he didn't say this, I think he said. . . ."

Some readers may think that it takes a lot of time to go through the tapes in this manner. Personally, I do not set myself a specific amount of time for going through the videotapes but rather just analyze, sometimes for days, sometimes for weeks and sometimes even months. It turns out that eventually there are few if any new ideas, at which point I go back over what I have written thus far. I am then attuned to finding patterns in my own writing, which point both to structures in the data source materials—resources to support claims and assertions—and in my (developing) understanding—resources for establishing progressive subjectivity.

FROM CASE DESCRIPTIONS TO ASSERTIONS

As I work my way through the tapes and other materials collected, I begin to take note of patterns. Giving precise instructions on how to find patterns or what patterns to find is as impossible as writing a foolproof recipe, for there is nothing like a foolproof instruction. In fact, the whole idea of making something foolproof is inappropriate, because it attributes the irremediable gap between instruction (plan) and action to individuals rather than to the nature of the relation between plans and actions, which is inherently underdetermined. The impossibility to give such precise instructions arises from the fact that what we perceive is the outcome of the relationship between our (embodied) dispositions and the world that surrounds us. A perception therefore is the result of the coming together of the material world and our perceptual apparatus, which itself is a function of our prior experience.

CHAPTER 3

In the process of working through some tape or transcript, you will notice that some descriptive word arises, even though you may not be able to pinpoint from where it is coming. For example, while watching the tapes and also while interacting with students who are not videotaped, I noted the term "blind alley." Whereas in regular high school laboratory work, teachers make sure students are "on the right way" of getting the results that they are supposed to get, as a teacher I did not interfere with student investigations even when I thought that they may not get anywhere, that is, when I thought that they might be down a blind alley. Although as a teacher I acted in this way, the term "blind alley" actually emerged only when I leisurely watched the videotapes featuring students in their work. I was thinking that if blind alley were to be a concept that I use to describe particular situations then I needed to have descriptions of concrete cases that illustrated the concept at work. Thus, once this word became salient in my mind, I wrote first one, then another brief description in which I articulated a situation that the term was to denote. In the following memo, I refer to one group of students using the acronym CJP, which stands for the initial of the students' first names in alphabetical order. Readers may note that I refer to myself as "the teacher."

> *A "blind alley"*
> CJP suggested that because of the polar nature of water there should be an interaction between a magnetic field and the flow of water. They decided to measure the flow rates of water out of a burette when the whole assembly was placed in a magnetic field. To produce such a magnetic field, they shunted in tandem a total of ten electro magnets, five on each side of the apparatus. They then measured five times the flow rates with and five times without the magnetic field turned on. Although the mean flow rates differed by about one second, they intuitively concluded that the difference was not significant.
>
> When they came for help in finding a closure to this experiment, the teacher questioned them about the effect of both positive and negative charges in a magnetic field, which, when they were tied together, would cancel any effect. As conclusion for the experiment we admitted that with the strength of these magnets and the set-up they chose, an effect was not observed. As the students were already familiar with mean, standard deviation, and standard error, the teacher used the data collected in this experiment to introduce CJP to the statistical technique of determining whether a difference is significant. After school, CJP and the teacher built an experiment in which a stream of water was electrically charged with Van de Graaff generator. This stream showed an interaction with the magnetic field as the students would have expected.
>
> Comment by Matt: "Let's do one [experiment] where we know that it works." Similarly, those students and groups with innovative ideas are also concerned with experiments that will "work." Depending on the group, I let them go down the blind alley, especially if they seem to be able to cope with the uncertain situation of ambiguous results, or with the clear results of no observable effects. Some of the suggested experiments,

I don't know if and what results will be observed such as in the proposal of measuring the latent heat of fusion by submersing a sample of water in alcohol of -18 °C. The change in temperature of the alcohol, together with its specific heat and mass should have enabled students to measure the latent heat of fusion of the water. As a corollary, framing problems for which there are no suggested theoretical answers or theoretical answers beyond their conceptual preparation puts the students into a situation where they cannot hypothesize potential outcomes. Rather than trying wild guesses, students do without any hypotheses.

((This ties in with students' attitude to doing experiments to which the outcomes are not yet known by them, or readily available to them by looking it up in the textbook. Though in some cases, a proposed problem can be phrased in such a way that students do not immediately relate the question to the text and the equations therein. Such is the case with questions such as "What is the relationship between the distances of an object from the lens and the distance of its image from the same lens?" or "What is the relationship between the overall resistance in a parallel circuit and one of its components?"))

According to the findings of ethnographic work in scientific laboratories, "making the stuff work" is the prime concern for research scientists (Knorr, 1979; Knorr-Cetina, 1981; Latour & Woolgar, 1979). The research of scientists was found to be driven much less by epistemic concerns than by concerns for making it work, cost, simplicity, or feasibility under local circumstances (Knorr-Cetina, 1981). Thus, the tinkering associated with "making it work" is favored over the hypothesis-testing mode with which scientists had been associated with for such a long time.

Readers should note that the first case of a blind alley involving the group CJP is followed by another account of a blind alley involving the student Matt and his peers. This account also shows that as the teacher, I did not act in the same way with all groups, and would more likely let them go down a blind alley all the way if I thought they were "able to cope with the uncertain situation of ambiguous results." The second case study is followed by a commentary—which, as frequently in my notes, is enclosed in double (or more) parentheses. The commentary alerts me to make a link to a different topic, here, the way in which students related to the task when they know versus do not know that there are specific outcomes to an investigation. Finally, I relate the blind alley idea to something I had read, the ethnographies of the scientific laboratories, where researchers sometimes "make stuff work" rather than pursuing questions to which they do not know the outcome.

> **First Analyses and Free Writing** To get around the writer's cramp many novices at analysis experience, think of this part of your research as *free writing on the topic of the transcripts*. In this way, you are less likely to worry about the content. This content you can always revise. The most important issue is to get yourself to write as much as you can and to select from the writings once you better understand the phenomena at hand.

Blind alleys, of course, were not the only things I noted. Some of the other concepts I noted and then exemplified—when I worked myself in the subsequent stages of my analysis through my own prior writings—included *operationally defining*, *problem solving*, *formulating models*, *process skills as categories of analysis*, and *negotiating differences*. These were some of the other terms I used to denote collections of cases in subsequent stages of the analysis.

> **Estrangement, Objectification, and Self-Critique** In free-writing you externalize your thoughts, which become words on paper. As such, you turn something of yourself into a strange object: you both estrange and objectify yourself in the product of your writing. As something other than yourself, your writing can become the object of your own critique. In this way, you can enact self-critique mediated by your own writing that has become something external and foreign to you.

The entire text of the memo was the outcome of a writing process that I continue to characterize as "free writing." I am not afraid of writing, because I know that anything I write is open to correction, change, and analysis. When we look at the second paragraph in which I described what Matt and others have done, we see that I commented in a way that mixed my teacher and analyst roles. Today I would think that the two roles do not make good bedfellows. It decreases the value of an analysis if it is perfused with accounts of my intents, especially when these are not available to the participants. It helps us very little to understand a *social* situation in terms of the intentions of an *individual*, unless these intentions are made available to others present who can use them as resources in their own performances. Thus, today I would caution anyone using such writing other than in a research memo; if this occurred, I would ask the person to separate his or her personal experiences and thinking as a teacher and what they have available as analyst, which is the same that the students (e.g., CJP or Matt) would have available in the interactions. Only what can be seen and heard is available to participants and analysts alike, not what *might* go on in students' minds or my own.

The research memo also is interesting in the sense that it provides some evidence of the split that occurs when we are teachers and researchers simultaneously, such as captured in the term *teacher-researcher*. In some instances, I refer to myself as "the teacher." Writing about myself in this way allows me to distance myself and write as if I were to see myself from the outside, which I do in fact while watching the tape. It is a way of restricting my analysis to those aspects of a situation that are available to every other participant. As soon as I switch to the first person "I" (see second paragraph) I am in a danger zone where my researcher-I and my teacher-I may come to be confused. The confusion leads to thinking about intents that are not available to others in the situation and therefore cannot be used to explain *their* behavior. The danger also arises because as analyst I am looking at events that have occurred earlier, and my memory of theses events likely has changed, mediated by my understanding of what has happened between the two moments in time. As the teacher-researcher, it is easy to think in terms of what I-teacher wanted to do or what I wish I had done, and therefore, with intentions that are not available to others. By referring to what the teacher rather than the teacher-I does or has done, I-researcher provide an external description, something others would be able to see if they were to have access to the videotape.

Case descriptions subsequently provide me with resources to support claims, often stated in terms of assertions. Writing claims in the form of assertions may assist me in organizing what I ultimately write for the purpose of making it available to others. I began to write assertions after reading a few research articles in which the authors had presented their findings in terms of six or eight of them. Writing a claim in the form of a brief assertion assists me in organizing my understanding about what I have found and (hopefully) assists my readers in understanding the precise nature of your research. For example, following the construction of a number of cases similar to and including those of CJP and Matt, I wrote the following assertion that was in effect supported by my cases:

> *Assertion:* In some cases, "blind alleys," students framed research questions and planned experiments that did not lead to an expected result. I observed a remarkable flexibility to deal with problems that arose during the implementation of their plans in the context of the inquiry. These problems as well as their solutions and the necessary decision-making processes were characterized by their situated nature.

The first sentence of the assertion articulated the concept of blind alley. I then made a statement about how students coped in situations where they found themselves in a blind alley. Finally, I stated that the processes by means of which students made decisions were characterized by their contingent (i.e., context-dependent) nature. Each time I seemed to notice something as a pattern for which I had multiple cases, I wrote an assertion in italics and wrote or pasted my cases or case descriptions below. In some instances, I had to adapt my case description so that its features matched what I had written in my assertion. Thus, one analytic file I created consisted of seven pages of text, which presented cases to support the three assertions that I had written:

> *Assertion 1: The identification of pertinent variables in a particular context increases with the familiarity of the students in a specific physical and conceptual context.*
> *Assertion 2: The students used mediational devices of varying nature to negotiate meaning and to come to a shared understanding of context, variables, and the phenomena at hand.*
> *Assertion 3: During the experiment, the students framed problems in the context of the inquiry that they solved, resolved, or abandoned.*

Because assertions are brief, listing all those that I consider as going together and responding to a particular theme allowed me to get an overview of what I had found. I could then think about how to articulate the broader theme of which the assertions I collected together are constitutive parts. Thus, in the report on open inquiry that I ultimately published, the overall structure of my account of learning in my high school physics laboratory followed the structure of experimenting: planning, collecting data, analyzing data. The planning section was divided into three subsections concerned with (a) the framing of research questions, (b) the use of narratives for identifying interesting situations (rather than the identification of variables), and (c) the role of blind alleys in individual and collective learning. Here is how I presented what I would be reporting as findings; the paragraph in fact summarized the entire findings section and allowed my readers to envision how the three parts of my research report were connected.

> A major part of the students' planning sessions was taken up by their attempts in *framing research questions*. Framing questions is a critical part of any exploration because the research problem takes shape at this stage. In order to frame and negotiate their research questions, the students often resorted to *narrative descriptions* of interesting situations. The use of narrative descriptions to deal with complex situations is in stark contrast to the logico-mathematical mode of thought, which encourages the immediate isolation and testing of causally related variables. In some cases, the students framed a research question and planned an experiment in which they did not observe the expected effect. I termed such situations *blind alleys*.

Today I understand that such paragraphs are crucial in the writing of reports or articles, because they articulate overviews of what is to come and therefore provide the reader with a map for anticipating the findings I subsequently describe. More concrete assertions, such as the one about blind alleys, do the same, because they articulate why I was presenting a specific analysis and the data that support it. As an editor and reviewer of many different journals, I know that this principle of writing for the reader is one of the most violated. All too often authors immediately get into describing a case without telling readers why this case is important, what claims or assertions it supports, and so forth. Because the paragraph introduces and outlines the topic, I call such paragraphs *topical paragraphs*. Such paragraphs are important because they contextualize and articulate the contents of the section or subsection that follows. These topical paragraphs clearly and saliently structure your account, show how the different pieces are connected, and explain why you are writing your study in the way you are doing.

BUILDING A DETAILED CASE STUDY OF LEARNING IN ACTIVITY

One way of understanding what happens in a classroom is to summarize what appears to happen generally. Thus, in chapter 2 I show how teacher-researchers can arrive at making claims that cover the class or classes in their entirety. The assertions in the previous section, too, were supported by cases involving different students. Such analyses and findings allow us to understand what appears to have happened more broadly. The resulting assertions therefore represented more general phenomena. But they did not represent what it means to learn on the part of any specific individual, which required me to follow a student or student group over some time to see how in and through their actions they change, for example, in how about the processes of planning, executing, and interpreting experiments are interrelated. To get a better sense of learning at the level of the individual, I have repeatedly constructed detailed case studies in which I follow individual students or groups. Which student or students would we select to present a case? Why this rather than another student? What is it that we can learn *generally* by looking at the learning of one student (group) *particularly*? In what follows, I describe the decisions that led me to write a detailed case study of experimenting in my laboratory featuring Nico.

In the events described here, the students investigated non-uniformly accelerated motion (i.e., the speed of a moving cart changed in changing ways). Nico and his partner had completed an experiment in which they studied the motion of a cart on the airtrack that was suspended between two springs. As a result, they observed slightly damped oscillations as the cart moved from left to right and back but a little less far each time. They chose to study a realistic phenomenon, the motion of a cart pulled by a spring, and made all decisions with respect to the resources and materials to be used. Thus, they experienced themselves in control of their activities, interacting with their setting, generating problems in relation with the setting, and controlling problem solving processes. The photo gate, a cart, and the springs that Nico and his peers used in their experiment were part of the setting they controlled; the setting therefore was akin to what they were doing in the "real world" outside the school. So from this perspective, it was an interesting situation for investigating what a student learned and how he learned it.

Nico and his partner had collected motion data using a data collection program that permitted them to print out distance-time, velocity-time, and acceleration-time graphs and the corresponding data tables. I thought that studying him would be interesting because Nico has had difficulties covering most of his school subjects at the same rate as his peers and therefore took five years to complete high school rather than the four years it took his peers. He also has had difficulties interpreting the data he and his peer had collected and understanding his partner's explanations. One day, the occasion to study a student who tried to overcome his lack of understanding presented itself in a fortunate but unexpected manner. Nico had returned to the physics laboratory one afternoon after school bringing with him his data and graphs. He set up the apparatus, and repeatedly shifted between moving the cart slowly from one side to the other, running the experiment in real time, studying his data tables and graphs, and using the chalkboard as a scratch pad. As I was observing him from afar, it became clear to me that Nico was struggling to understand the experiment, and the relationship between the motion in real time and its representation in graphs and data tables. But he made a great effort in arriving at an understanding. In the course of the afternoon, he also ran a mathematical program, MathCAD, to fit a curve through his velocity-time data in order to find the functional relationship of velocity and time. He generated graphs of the derivative and the integral of the velocity-time function by applying the respective operators available in MathCAD. In sum, it was interesting to study what and how Nico learned because he had difficulties but was determined to understand. What would a student learn under such conditions? How would he go about learning?

CHAPTER 3

Throughout this afternoon, I watched Nico; when he asked me for help, I interacted with Nico only to leave him on his own when he appeared to be on confident about what he was doing. I kept copious notes of the event and my interactions with him.

A few days later, Nico submitted a laboratory report that contained distance-time, velocity-time, and acceleration-time graphs to which he had added (a) color to highlight specific data points, (b) labels to identify specific data points by their coordinates, (c) hand drawn lines, and (d) explanatory text. This text was typical for those submitted by students at this stage in the class. From this text, too, it was apparent that Nico had sought to understand the experiment, the data, and its implications. He made it very clear that he wanted to communicate this understanding to the reader of the report by making special provisions such as coloring important points of the graph which he discussed in the body of the text; by labeling these points with asterisks in the data table; by indicating his understanding of positive and negative motion; by indicating his choice of treating the air track as number line; and by using number pairs to refer to data in the graphs. It is likely that the effort of writing his report containing all this information itself was an important element in the understanding that arose from what he was doing that afternoon. These preparations showed that Nico used prior knowledge, even if it reached as far back as elementary school where he employed number lines to understand the direction of the basic arithmetic operations of addition and subtraction, or to middle school to understand the operations on negative numbers. In this manner, Nico's new mathematical understandings further developed through yet another consolidation and reification of actions on previously established mathematical symbol systems.

For all of these reasons, the particular student Nico was and because of the availability of data source materials made this ideal for constructing a case study. Although I had not known what the afternoon observations would lead me to, the experience and the report Nico subsequently submitted constituted ideal materials for constructing a case study of one student's struggle of coming to understand the relationship between an observable event, a cart attached on each side by springs moving back and forth, and the position-time, velocity-time, and acceleration-time graphs that the data-collecting computer displayed. As Nico described the motion of the cart, he made connections between several levels of conceptual abstractions. I noted four dimensions or levels of conceptual abstraction, which in fact became the main feature of my account: (a) the concrete objects and events with which he was dealing; (b) the description of motion in the form of data tables and graphs; (c) the mathematical symbolic framework; and (d) the explanatory, conceptual framework of the physical events.

Although I was interested in providing a detailed account of Nico's learning, I also wanted to have a more concise summary that would perhaps visually represent several hours of engagement and the learning that resulted. I wrote a summary paragraph, which also could have figured as the opening paragraph of a result section.

The complex of highly interrelated processes in which Michael was involved during this experiment is illustrated in Figure 5. From the real world data (RWD), the interfacing software generated data tables (T), and the graphs relating distance (GD), velocity (GV), and acceleration (GA) to time. Using the tables, Michael generated a new graph (VG) in MathCAD that he used to fit a function (F) to the data points. With this function, he produced the graph of the integral (IG) and derivative (DG) of the function (F). He matched these graphs with GD and GA. He placed the concrete objects and events of the interaction with the phenomena real world data into an explanatory conceptual framework (ECF), which itself was linked to the graphs (GD, GA) that he produced during the experiment. Using microcomputers allowed Michael to compress a lot of mathematical and physics experience into a short time. He was able to discover a rule (F) describing RWD. The rule in turn could be used to generate graphs that were themselves generated from RWD.

This paragraph can be understood as an assertion for the entire case study. In the way I ultimately wrote it up in a journal for science and mathematics teachers (Roth, 1993b), it followed as a summary the concrete case study that I had described in the article. Presented as a model, it is suitable to be tested in other cases of learning. If it were *transportable* and explained the learning of other students, the model or aspects of it would become generalizable.

After writing this summary, however, I felt that I could say more. I felt that I had provided sufficient evidence to articulate elements that had contributed to the learning event that I had observed and documented in the case. I felt that I could learn something *more generally*, no longer relevant and tied to the one case but to learning more broadly. I therefore wrote a paragraph in which I articulated a tentative explanation of the observed phenomenon.

Four sources appeared to contribute to the benefits of linking representations in multiple forms. First, the graphs can be thought of as helping to connect the data to a rule because previously learned knowledge from visual experience, knowledge about straightness, slope, curves can be applied to mathematical situations represented in the graph. Second, quantities such as distance, velocity, and acceleration can be thought of as playing a mediational role between the primary mathematical structure of (pure) number and the natural language. The experience of applied mathematics provided opportunities for building phenomenological mathematical entities that become palpable. Third, these entities were reified as objects through their link with the real world. In this system, the increasing number of referents supported the construction of meaning. Finally, the apparatus used, a relatively easily observed physical system that can be replayed in slow motion, played a major role in the construction of physics and mathematics knowledge.

CHAPTER 3

We can think of such a paragraph as "ratcheting up" from a case study. The question I had been asking myself was "Now that I know the particulars of this one case, what can I learn about learning more generally?" The summary and the broader statement may be considered as a research hypothesis driving the collection of specific artifacts and videotapes to seek evidence that both confirmed and disconfirmed the model embodied in the hypothesis as stated.

PRODUCTS: LEARNING OUTCOMES

From this study, I ended up writing five manuscripts focusing on different dimensions of what I learned conducting them. A first paper, "Bridging the gap between school and real life: Toward an integration of science, mathematics, and technology in the context of authentic practice" (Roth, 1992), was intended for a practitioner audience and described the kinds of studies my students designed, how I introduced them to mathematical and statistical modeling tools, and how they integrated mathematics, programming, and physics to solve authentic problems, generated by students according to their own interests. In the process of this work, the students were involved in the kind of activities that the then going reform documents had called for on the basis of research in cognitive science, science education, and mathematics education. I concluded with the hope that more governments, school boards, and teachers would feel the need for such an integration of real-life problems into school in the context of an interdisciplinary approach that includes the sciences, mathematics, and technology.

A second article, "Problem-centered learning or the integration of mathematics and science in a constructivist laboratory: A case study" (Roth, 1993b), featured in great detail the case study of Nico, the method for which I articulate in the previous section.

The intent of a third study, "The development of science process skills in authentic contexts" (Roth & Roychoudhury, 1993b), was to examine the development of integrated process skills in the context of open-inquiry laboratory sessions. Findings from the study indicated that students developed higher-order process skills through non-traditional laboratory experiences that provided the students with freedom to perform experiments of personal relevance in authentic contexts. Students learned to (a) identify and define pertinent variables, (b) interpret, transform, and analyze data, (c) plan and design an experiment, and (d) formulate hypotheses. Based on the findings of this study we suggested that process skills did not require being taught separately from and prior to student-designed experiments. We proposed that integrated process skills develop gradually and reach a high level of sophistication when experiments are performed in meaningful context.

The article that I now consider to be the most important, because my reading of Latour and Woolgar's book *Laboratory Life* had driven it, was "Experimenting in a constructivist high school physics laboratory" (Roth, 1994). (Its debt to the book is captured in the file name that the manuscript had on my computer: *Lablife*.) The study was intended to describe and understand students' experimenting and problem solving in an open-inquiry learning environment. In the article, I articulated students' remarkable ability and willingness to generate research questions and to design and develop apparatus for data collection. I suggested that in their efforts of framing research questions, students often used narrative explanations to explore and think about the phenomena to be studied; such narrative explanations contrasted the explicit statement of dependent, independent, and controlled variables in the way researchers had suggested experimentation to occur. I reported that in some cases, "blind alleys," students framed research questions and planned experiments that did not lead to an expected result and that one could observe a remarkable flexibility for dealing with problems that arose during the implementation of their plans in the context of the inquiry. These problems as well as their solutions and the necessary decision-making processes were characterized by their situated nature. I showed how students pursued meaningful learning during the interpretation of data and graphs to arrive at reasonable answers of their research questions. I concluded that students should be provided with rich learning environments in which they could learn to frame problems and solutions, design experiments, and investigate phenomena of their own interest and, in the process, develop complex problem solving skills.

A final article, "Interactional processes in a constructivist physics lab" (Roychoudhury & Roth, 1996), was designed to describe the processes by means of which students come to collaborate in the kind of learning environment I had created. My co-author (who had never seen the classroom and therefore had available only the materials I had collected and the transcripts I had prepared) and I described symmetric and asymmetric forms of interacting, adversarial modes and majority rules, and different forms of teacher–student transactions during the different stages of student experiments. We concluded that within-group transactions were multi-faceted and became inherently more complex during open-ended laboratory experiences that involve fewer structural (i.e., teacher-imposed) constraints than ordinary, highly structured laboratory tasks of the kind high school students normally do. Some of the high-achieving students remained passive in the transactional processes. It continued to be unclear, therefore, how these students constructed meaning from the group activities.

CHAPTER 4

COMBINGING QUANTITATIVE AND QUALITATIVE INFORMATION

Teacher-Researchers Collaborate Investigating a Community of Practice

In chapters 1 through 3, I write about teacher-research studies that I conducted entirely on my own. But I was not conducting on my own all teacher-research in my school at the time; rather, I conducted (and published) formal and informal teacher-researcher studies with almost every colleague in the science department that I headed at the time. First and foremost among these colleagues was G. Michael Bowen, who became my graduate student once I had taken a university position. The study we did in his eighth-grade science class especially during the curriculum unit on ecology constitutes the context for the present chapter; but Michael and I also explored together how to use concept mapping and vee mapping in the seventh- and eighth-grade science classes he taught. I also conducted teacher-research together with other colleagues. Thus, Tosh Macfarlane, John Nicholson, and I conducted a small study on a unit in tenth-grade science, where students learned about various aspects of heat, conduction, radiation, material properties, and so forth by designing and building their own solar energy panels, for which they calculated the efficiencies. These studies resembled the one on open inquiry that I conducted in my own classroom and provided considerable confirmation of what I observed there. Together with Guennadi Verechaka, I implemented concept mapping in his sixth-grade classroom showing that it was a good means for getting students in the elementary classrooms to use this learning-to-learn device. The results of these collaborations frequently were written up for publication in teacher- and praxis-oriented journals such as *Science Teacher* or *Science & Children*.

Some of the parents came to the school complaining that we science teachers were not teaching basic skills and concepts. I was asking my teachers to refer such parents to me, and also talked to the school administration about my goals for improving student interest, enrollment in the sciences, and an understanding of science as a career. As a teacher, I also had an open-door policy, allowing administrators and enrollment officers to bring any visitors to my laboratory to show them how students learn science. Nevertheless, I felt that we needed to show in more formal ways what and how students learned in our open-inquiry lessons; and I felt that we needed to provide some quantitative information as well. In the study that serves as the background to this chapter, I therefore investigated knowing and learning both through the interpretive analysis of videotapes and other data source materials and through the quantitative analysis of test results, outcomes on specially designed tasks, and the results of a learning environment scale on which students indicated how they viewed learning in the classes we offered and studied.

CHAPTER 4

This chapter, therefore, also is about how to integrate methods that might be considered to belong to very different research paradigms often denoted by the dichotomous terms *quantitative* and *qualitative* research. For a long time I have been a defender of multi-method research—certainly because of a combination of my background as a research physicist and statistician, on the one hand, and my extensive experience in doing interpretive research, on the other. Together with a statistician colleague, I recently articulated my perspective according to which it makes little sense to oppose so-called *quantitative* and *qualitative* approaches to educational research (Ercikan & Roth, 2006).

I had been hired by the administrators of my school not only to teach physics but also to bring about changes to the traditional, teacher- and textbook-centered approaches in science teaching at the school. Over a three-year period, through regular in-service, peer coaching, and self- and peer evaluation, five of the six science teachers came to use student- and activity-centered teaching in which making sense was emphasized over the memorization of scientific facts, definitions of concepts, and scientific theories. This new approach to teaching science had received the approval from (a) provincial supervisors of private schools who recommended site visits at my school to the science teachers of other private schools (although not publicly funded, they are supervised by the Ministry of Education making the school's diploma equivalent to those from public schools) and (b) an external evaluation team consisting of university professors of science from a nearby university.

Teacher-Researchers and Collaboration
There are many advantages to working with one or more other teachers to conduct research in one another's classes. For starters, it overcomes the isolation we teachers often experience. Second, there is someone else who can serve as a sounding board and with whom to discuss ideas. Third, sharing the onus of collecting data materials decreases the amount of work any single teacher has to do. Finally, if one of the teacher-researchers also wants to get a degree, then it is much easier to get the research project approved by the university research ethics board.

The collaborative studies we conducted emerged from a context that I had fostered in my function as the department head of science. Whereas the traditional evaluation system had the department head visit one or two lessons and then write a by-and-large laudatory report, I instituted a multilevel professional development effort part of which was accomplished, in some instances, through teacher-researcher investigations. At the first level, there was teacher self-evaluation, leading from the reflections teachers did to written reports in which they articulated strengths and weaknesses of their approach to teaching, their philosophy, and their praxis. Some teachers also used the departmental video camera to look at themselves teaching, through a third-person perspective so to speak, and thereby added another dimension to their self-reflections. The second stage consisted in observing someone else teaching and in writing a report, which was to benefit the teacher observed as well as the observing teacher, who, through writing, was encouraged to reflect on his or her own teaching as well. The third stage of the evaluation process consisted of several lessons taught together with one or more other teachers. (It was during this phase that one teacher told me that he could never teach in the way I did because it led to a messy classroom where everything is topsy-turvy and where there was too much noise.) These experiences provided the grounds for collaborative reflections on a joint and common experience, including the similarities and differences with respect to thinking about and practicing teaching. Finally, there was a formal observation by the department head (me), whose report was added to the portfolio each teacher was establishing.

Out of these collective teacher enhancement efforts, during which we also got to teach together, we developed our teacher-researcher collaborations the purpose of which generally was to better understand the learning of our students and the improvement of our techniques to facilitate student efforts at learning in a set of disciplines often considered to be difficult—the sciences.

Michael Bowen and I decided to conduct a study in his eighth-grade science class, where he guided students to progressively conduct independent research of their own. Once they began the ecology unit in the third and last term of the year, the students were well positioned for dealing with the open-ended nature of their science classes and with conducting research outside the school building where they had to work without a teacher standing next to them—though there was supervision as I outline below. The purpose of our teacher-directed inquiry was to better understand how middle-school level students learn in an open-inquiry setting in which the teacher and other adults oriented their interactions with the students according to an apprenticeship metaphor and its subsidiary metaphor of graduate student advisor. In this teacher-researcher study, we investigated (a) the shared concern for making sense and the changes in individual students' understandings often undetected by teachers; (b) the dynamics in groups of students that construct shared knowledge claims, negotiate differences in order to achieve a common course of action and how the dynamic affects the construction of individual knowledge; and (c) the acquisition of knowledge and laboratory skills at the classroom level. Most importantly for the learning science community, Michael and I combined very different kinds of data source materials and methods (statistical, interpretive) to provide detailed and generalizable descriptions of what learning goes on in the kind of innovative classroom learning environments that we provided.

CLASSROOM CONTEXT

I cannot emphasize how important it is for teacher-researchers to keep separate in their mind what they normally do and what students and they do for the express purposes of research. It is therefore important that teacher-researchers articulate what the curriculum consists in if there were no research conducted. This allows others—including thesis supervisors and members of human research ethics boards—to understand precisely the nature of your teaching and what events and artifacts it generates. The following is offered as an account of the way Michael Bowen and I were thinking about teaching and learning at the time and how it influenced our normal curriculum design.

CHAPTER 4

Our Guiding Metaphor

Because we both had trained as natural scientists—Michael had a master's degree in marine biology—thinking about teaching and learning in terms of cognitive apprenticeship made a lot of sense to us; we had learned much of what we knew by working with other scientists. We used the metaphor of cognitive apprenticeship to frame the conditions in which we wanted to introduce students to doing science and thereby provide a context to learn science by participation in authentic practice, that is, the ordinary daily practices of members of a field. Learning science can then be understood as *legitimate peripheral participation* in science such that a learning curriculum unfolds in opportunities for engagement in practice. Traditionally, legitimate peripheral participation in science begins at the level of graduate work. However, Michael and I saw no reasons for this process not to start much earlier in elementary and secondary school. Ever since I had started teaching, I wanted my students to experience the same joys of learning science that came for me only with the work on my Master's thesis in physics. The notion of apprenticeship implies a culture of sharing and learning among apprentices. Apprentices not only learn most from their peers, but, where the circulation of knowledge is possible, the latter spreads rapidly and effectively. (Whether it does in school science classrooms actually became an important research question for me several years later and as a consequence of what Michael and I were finding in the study reported here.) The metaphor of cognitive apprenticeship also implies patterns of transactions between teachers and learners. Depending on the situation, the teacher may model expertise-in-use, coach the students or scaffold their initial attempts in a new skill on a need-to-know or just-in-time basis, or serve as an advisor in the students' independent projects.

By using the metaphor of apprenticeship we did not mean to focus on the strongly asymmetric master-apprentice relation that can be observed in some trade apprenticeships. When we used the term apprenticeship to think about learning in schools, the term did not reproduce for us the economical and sociopolitical dependencies of craft apprentices, who frequently are at the mercy of their employers and masters. Rather, in our use, the metaphor included more of the relationship and dependencies that exist between university professors and their graduate students—which can but do not have to be highly asymmetrical. More so, even experienced professors learn from their graduate students and postdoctoral fellows. Thus, to us apprenticeship was characterized by the opportunities for learning that are structured by work practices. In such a decentered view of apprenticeship, mastery resided not in the master but in the organization of the community including the core practitioners. Reconceptualizing learning and teaching in terms of transactions in a community of practice changes the classroom talk from that of information dissemination by an all-knowing institutionally legitimated teacher to one of a culture of learning structured by student independence and teacher as co-inquirer and co-learner. This view moved the focus of our analysis away from knowing and teaching as individual accomplishments and onto a community's intricate structuring of learning resources. This notion of learning implied to us participation in the establishment of the social norms, and led us to focus on the norms that determine what counts as a problem and as an acceptable solution. In everyday out-of-school communities, these norms are subject to negotiations and social construction. We thought that under conditions to be created, we could provide opportunities for any student–student negotiations, in part, to constitute the community's sense-making practices. Such negotiations would be encouraged when students engage themselves and each other in problematic situations in the course of an interesting inquiry arising out of student-framed problems.

Our framework for teaching and doing a teacher-researcher study can thus be summarized in these terms: Our classrooms constituted a community of practice structured in terms of a cognitive apprenticeship metaphor; specific resources and practices constitute such communities. Through their practices, communities add to and change available resources. A change in the available resources, in turn, changes the practices in which members engage. Learning in our school science classrooms then could be understood as a change in the practices and resources of communities. The purpose of our teacher-researcher study was to understand learning as a social phenomenon at three levels: the individual, the group, and the classroom (community).

The metaphors of *cognitive apprenticeship* and *graduate student advisor* by and large determined our teaching styles. We also believed in the notion that students learn best from projects, a notion upheld at the time by numerous educators and psychologists. In our classes from seventh to twelfth grades, we implemented open-inquiry as a teaching and learning method. For example, the eighth-grade students featured in this chapter learned about ecology by investigating the correlations between abiotic and biotic factors under the constraint that their reports had to be suitable for convincing their peers; tenth-grade students learned about heat and temperature while constructing efficient solar collectors of their own design under the constraint that they had to research each design feature; and the eleventh- and twelfth-grade students investigated complex motion phenomena of their own choice with the constraint that their analysis included mathematical models (e.g., mathematical functions) describing various aspects of the motion. Our teacher-research agenda across the science department addressed various aspects of learning in open-inquiry learning environments in order to improve both the implementation of open-inquiry as method and, more directly, our modes of interacting with the students.

The metaphors served us well in this study because we had some additional assistance from individuals who also were trained scientist. Our laboratory assistant that year was Guennadi Verechaka, who, having obtained a Master's degree, had been a research physicist in the Soviet Union prior to coming Canada, where his first job was at my school. The other person participating in our unit was Allan Clark, a former scientist with a PhD degree in some area of chemistry, who, in the process of getting a teaching degree, spent several months at our school as a teaching intern. He spent part of his stay participating in teaching and supervising Michael Bowen's class.

CHAPTER 4

Preparing the Unit

The preparation of students for the open-inquiry curriculum can be thought of at two levels. First and at a macro-level, there was a progressive change in the format of the eighth-grade science course. During the first trimester in which the curriculum prescribed physics concepts, the students answered teacher-framed research problems to which the experiments were also pre-designed. This approach is akin to classical science teaching through discovery. During the second trimester with a focus on chemistry concepts, the students designed their own experiments that permitted them to make knowledge claims to answer teacher-framed research questions. The third trimester was organized such that students both constructed their own research questions and the experiments to answer them. To begin this third semester, the teacher Michael Bowen gave the following instructions, which, because we video recorded every lesson, became part of our data source materials:

> One of the reasons why you will be working like a real biologist and will be doing real biology things, is because you are going out there and trying to figure [things] out by asking a specific set of questions each week and trying to pick questions that'll allow you to figure out what the relationships are. That's exactly what a real biologist does. A real biologist—which I have [been] so I can speak from experience—a real biologist walks out into the field, into a stream or into a pond and looks around and starts to ask him or herself a whole series of questions. They ask, why do I find fish in that part of the stream and not in that part of the stream? And there [are] lots of different answers to that. Maybe the temperature is different and the fish like staying in different temperatures. So as a biologist I would go out in the area with a thermometer and find the different areas in which those fish were found and I'd stick the thermometer in the water and I'd see if there is a relationship between where the fish were found and the temperature of the water. I could go out there and I could ask myself, maybe it has to do with food? So I could capture some of the fish, figure out what it is they eat and then sample the area of the water in which they're found, to find if there is food there. Maybe it has to do with the amount of current? Maybe some fish don't like fast currents? Maybe you find a relationship with the speed of currents? Now the odds are that it is not any single one of those things but it might be a whole pile of them, it might be a combination of the temperature, where the food was found, how fast the stream was flowing, whether there was sediment in the stream or not, what kind of plants were there, what kind of other fish were around. Here is a whole pile of things that might be influencing why that species of fish was in that part of the creek.
>
> Well, you're gonna go out there as biologists and look at land and ask yourself similar questions. Why is this species of plant growing in this part of my land? And why don't I find it over here and measure the tree heights? Is there a reason why the trees are higher in this half than they are over here? And you'll go out there and you'll try to get a big picture

about what is going on. Working as a biologist and just looking at one simple little question and one simple little answer doesn't really tell you the truth about the big picture. But going out there and asking a series of questions that build on each other and taking these questions and putting them together to try out what the big picture is, that is exactly what a biologist does. And that is what I expect you to do as an assignment this term.

After this introduction, and an additional warning that misbehavior could lead to the cancellation of the project—after all, students did their research along a 1.5-kilometer stretch at the wooded outskirts of our 50-acre campus—the students proceeded to their field sites and began their research projects. Each student pair negotiated any other clarification with Michael while he made his rounds from student group to student group; or sometimes they negotiated relevant issues with one of the other adults present. Michael always emphasized the fact that the students' work was of the same kind as that of scientists, and he interacted with the students according to the metaphors we had chosen, that is, he acted as if his students were young scientists working on an independent project. In fact, my interviews conducted toward the end of the unit showed that the students distinguished their own research from that of scientists only in terms of the scope, the amount of time spent in the field, and in the complexity of the questions asked.

The Lessons

The study took place during the third term of the academic year lasting from the last week of March to the first week of June. At this time, the students were engaged in a ten-week ecological study of the campus. Ordinarily there were three 60-minute periods per week, but one period was often lost to assemblies, long weekends, and field trips for other subjects. For most of the activities, the students worked in pairs with self-selected partners. Occasionally, to share their findings with other students, we asked them to form groups of three with individuals other than their regular partners. Michael encouraged students throughout the unit to take responsibility for their learning, arrange for additional fieldwork after school or during the lunch hour, and consult with their peers, himself, or the advisors.

In this unit students studied the interrelations between abiotic and biotic features in a small plot of land called an "ecozone," about 35 m^2 in size. They were awarded the general location of these plots by a draw, but they determined the exact location and size themselves. The intent of the unit was to have the students develop (a) an understanding of the complexity of biological systems and how they change, (b) an understanding of the inter-relationships between biotic and abiotic components of an ecosystem, (c) their ability to formulate and investigate research problems on their own, and (d) their ability to analyze and report on their findings to the teacher and their peers.

After an introductory activity in which they derived and used their own schemes to classify the 50-acre campus (Figure 4.1), students used their own focus ques-

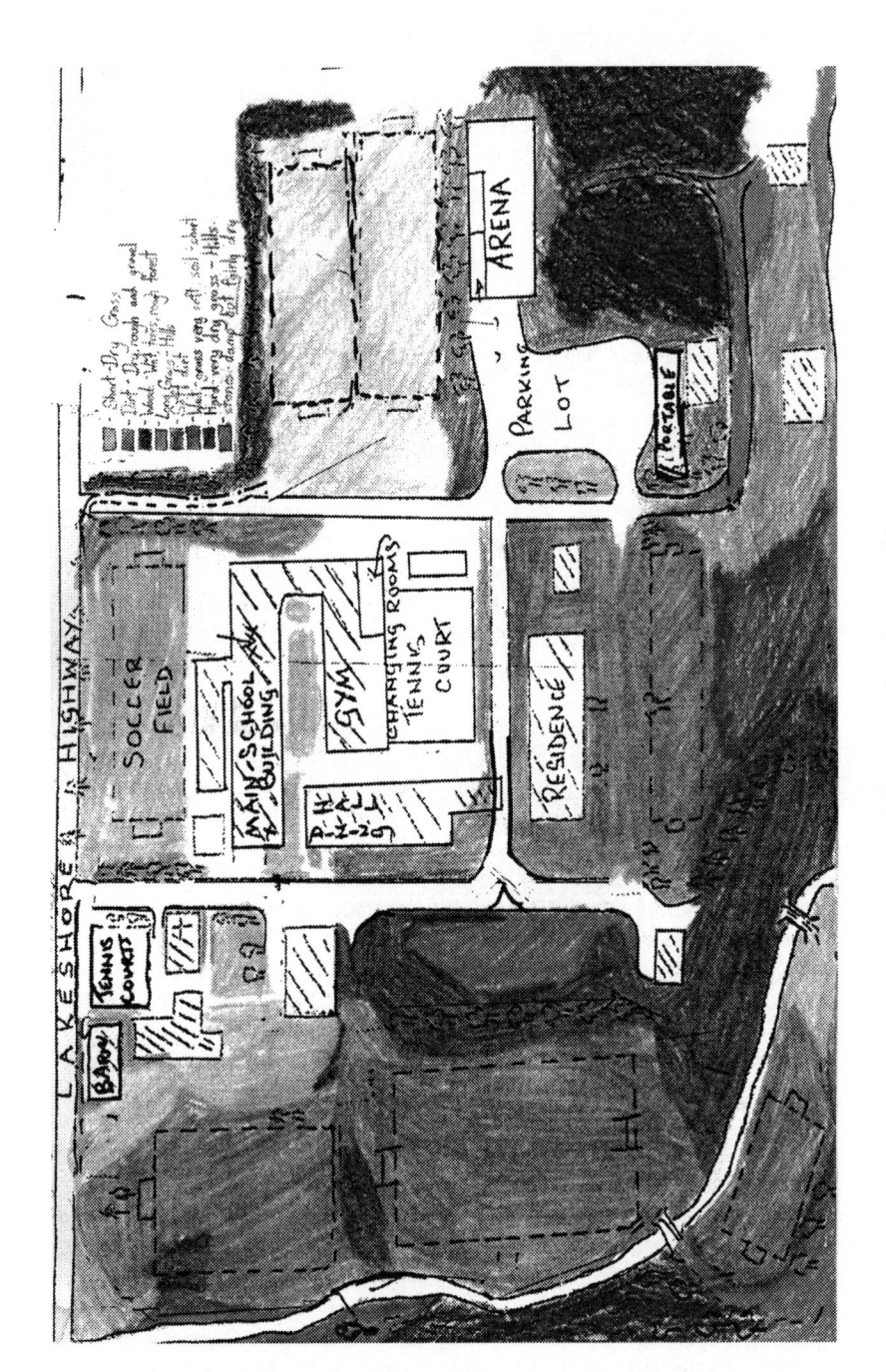

4.1. This map contains one student group's classification of the campus into ecozones.

QUANTITATIVE AND QUALITATIVE

Figure 4.2. A day of field research: a. signing out equipment; b. getting research question approved; c. running to the field site; d. collecting data; e. the teacher arrives; and f. the teacher interacts with the students

tions for studying the relationships of biotic and abiotic factors in their ecozones. The students kept field notebooks where they recorded focus questions, weather information, data from their investigations, background research notes, and new (concept) words with their definitions. For each investigation we scheduled two one-hour class periods in the field and one period in the classroom during which the students completed their reports, interacted with other students, constructed new focus questions, and did background research. In addition to field research and

CHAPTER 4

classroom work periods, we scheduled (a) several periods during which students exchanged their findings with two individuals from other research pairs and (b) one period for a slide show on the ecology of the Canadian Arctic.

To complete their investigations, the students had available varied resources including trowels, soil corers, soil thermometers, soil moisture meters and pH meters, testing kits for different soil nutrients, hygrometers, light meters, rubber loops for random sampling, meter sticks, and other small items. There were also extensive written resources including field guides on identifying anything from trees to insects to birds nests and a resource file with dichotomous keys, methods suggestions and background information culled from a variety of books and magazines. In a typical field period, students would spent 5 to 10 minutes preparing their tools and instruments, consult with the (teacher-) advisors, get their focus question approved where the approval was to make sure that the complexity of the students' research designs was increasing over time (Figures 4.2.a, b). Then they would walk to their field site (Figure 4.2.c), collect their data (Figure 4.2.d), do field research (40 minutes), and return their equipment and receive closing comments and instructions from their teacher. During the time in the field, Michael visited each group to discuss measurement issues, data recording and reporting, research methods, and any other problems identified by students (Figures 4.2.e, f).

The students worked mostly unsupervised in research sites that were dispersed along a stretch of about 1,500 meters in a semi-circle around the classroom buildings (see Figure 4.1). During any single lesson in the field Michael visited each research site once, which gave him about five minutes per group. Because of the physical setting of the campus, a second supervising person could keep an eye on about half of the class. In spite of the relative freedom in this organization of the class, most students could be seen working in their sites: we observed little if any behavior that would raise doubts concerning our approach. This work was also evident from students' field notes, which we periodically inspected at the end of a classroom period. While it would be difficult to ascertain the amount of time students actually spent on their field work assignments in general, because it is impossible to get into the mind of students, we could ascertain that there were fewer than a total of two to four minutes (out of 40–50 minutes in the field) of off-science talk by any given videotaped group.

A Typical Day

In interpretive research, it is assumed that the context plays an important role in understanding phenomena. Therefore, teacher-researchers, as other researchers, are held to provide *thick descriptions* of the context so that the phenomena at the core of the investigations can be properly understood. One of the ways in which teacher-researchers can achieve such contextualization is by means of a narrative that accounts for a *typical day* of some *typical members* of the culture. If the study were concerned with decision-making and administration, the description of a typical day might be that of the principal (head) or vice-principal (assistant head). But if the study were about teacher burnout, then the narrative of a typical day would be that of a teacher. In the present study, Michael Bowen and I wanted to understand knowing and learning in the special learning environment that we were setting up. Our narrative of a typical day therefore follows two students through one science lesson. Here, I also make use of photographic materials in Figure 4.2 to construct such a narrative.

It is 8:45 A.M. on a Wednesday morning. The students all arrive late from chapel service, but immediately go to work. Erica and Dilraj go to the cart in the front of the laboratory to get a bag, a thermometer, a moisture meter, and the only soil corer available for the whole class. On a 3" by 5" index card they mark the equipment they have taken (Figure 4.2.a) and return it to the teacher. Before they can leave the classroom for their field site, they have to check their focus question with the teaching intern (Figure 4.2.b). The question they had decided upon had arisen in the course of their inquiry and had been noted in their field notebook. Today, the two begin an investigation through which they want to find out whether there are any relationships between the density of worms (annelids) and the independent variables of soil depth, moisture and temperature. Michael Bowen has asked them how they would determine worm density. Erica has explained that they would count the number of worms in each one-centimeter section of a core sample. Michael is satisfied with this answer, and they can proceed to their field site. It takes Erica and Dilraj about five minutes to get to their site, one of the farthest from the lab (bottom left corner of Figure 4.1). When they arrive, they begin to collect data immediately. As usual, they achieve agreement about who is to do what almost instantly and without talking about it. On this day, Elizabeth will determine the soil moisture and temperature at several locations in their eco-zone, while Dilraj will take core samples at the same places. Both record the measurements in their field notebooks (Figure 4.2.d). They also prepare a drawing in which they record the distribution of plants in their field site (Figure 4.3).

Michael Bowen arrives on the bicycle that he uses to be able to visit all ten groups spread along the perimeter of the campus; he first talks to Dilraj, who eagerly tells him about their latest findings (Figure 4.2.e). Michael then advances to Erica, who talks to him about their research; he assists her in understanding their data collection strategy designed to create maximum variation with respect to the independent variable (Figure 4.2.f). Michael Bowen then leaves after about four to five minutes.

Erica finishes with her data collection before Dilraj, who is counting the worms in the different sections of each core sample. Because she already has an idea for another investigation, she begins to measure the number and size of buds on several branches that she marks for future reference. Time seems to fly, and Dilraj has to remind Erica that they have to return to the lab for a debriefing with the teacher. Because she did not complete her collection of the new data sources, Erica, who has another

CHAPTER 4

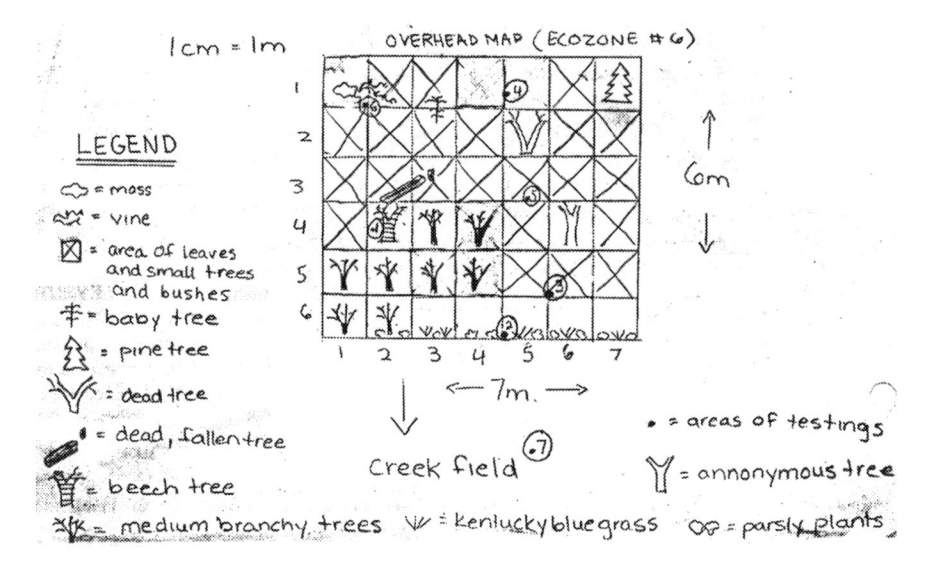

Figure 4.3. An excerpt from the field notebook Erica and Dilraj kept to record in the field.

commitment, asks Dilraj on the way back to the lab if he could return and complete the measurements after school.

When they get back to the lab, they sign in their equipment. Almost with the bell, the teacher questions them whether they had done okay. Nodding their heads they hurriedly leave the lab to go to their next class. A week later, they submit an extensive six-page report in which they answer the research question "How do temperature, light, and soil depth affect where annelids (worms) live?" They use a table to report the values of 5 variables for each of 7 measurement locations at their research site (Figure 4.4).

COLLECTING MATERIAL SOURCES

For logistic reasons, I predominantly videotaped one of Michael's two sections, but occasionally I also taped the other. In addition to videotapes, we sometimes audio-recorded all of Michael Bowen's interactions with students as he made his rounds in the field; and we audio-recorded the interviews with 14 students. When we used the audiotape, Michael put a small recorder into his vest pocket and we attached a microphone to it. So that he did not have to worry about turning on the recorder when he arrived at a new group, we decided to let it run for the course of the lesson, although this yielded some long pauses in the sound track while he was traveling between groups. Concerning the interviews with the students, I left the 15-minute sessions with each student or student group unstructured. I wanted the students to talk about what they found relevant about this learning environment that differed so much from what they experienced in their other courses. Thus I encour-

QUANTITATIVE AND QUALITATIVE

aged the students to talk about the open-inquiry learning environment, their interactions with peers, and about their learning. I conducted interviews with students from both of Michael's sections in order to understand their views of the open-inquiry teaching-learning environment and to clarify our on-going understanding about their comprehension of ecology and research method.

Besides video- and audiotapes, our data sources included (a) the transcripts of all taped materials, (b) students' field notebooks (e.g., Figure 4.3), laboratory reports (see excerpt in Figure 4.4), special assignments (e.g., a review of some literature), and examinations, (c) the researchers' field and reflective notes, and (d) miscellaneous documents such as the students' grade record for the three reporting periods of the year and the two scheduled examinations, the provincial curriculum guidelines, the teacher's course outlines, and the students' resource materials. We extended our collection of data sources to include word problems that we specially designed to test *in situ* emerging hypotheses about students' learning, and examination results from both eighth-grade classes that Michael was teaching (see later in the text).

The third section of eighth-grade science, which was taught by another teacher (Sheila Kuipers), was included in the collection of data sources only when we assigned the word problems. We drew on this third eighth-grade class because we

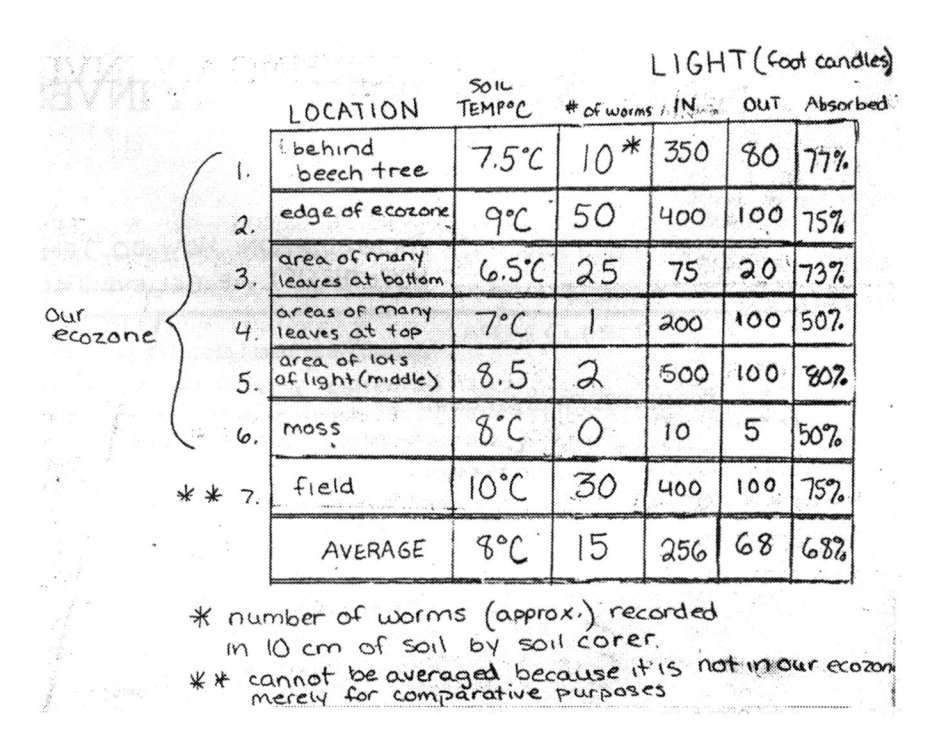

	LOCATION	SOIL TEMP°C	# of worms	LIGHT (foot candles) IN	OUT	Absorbed
1.	behind beech tree	7.5°C	10*	350	80	77%
2.	edge of ecozone	9°C	50	400	100	75%
3.	area of many leaves at bottom	6.5°C	25	75	20	73%
4.	areas of many leaves at top	7°C	1	200	100	50%
5.	area of lots of light (middle)	8.5	2	500	100	80%
6.	moss	8°C	0	10	5	50%
**7.	field	10°C	30	400	100	75%
	AVERAGE	8°C	15	256	68	68%

(rows 1–6 bracketed as "our ecozone")

* number of worms (approx.) recorded in 10 cm of soil by soil corer.
** cannot be averaged because it is not in our ecozone merely for comparative purposes

Figure 4.4. Some data Erica and Dilraj generated as part of their project on the distribution of worms in their field site in relation to temperature and light.

CHAPTER 4

were interested in conducting a statistical test; adding this other class provided us with a control group and a larger N. We did this because the result of a statistical test depends on the number of units (in our case student groups completing a test); and the N also affects the *power* of the statistical tests.

Videotaping

Our main data sources were the video-recordings of students at work in the classroom and out in the field. To be less intrusive, I carried the camera under the arm directing it at "interesting" events, people, or objects of conversation. Here "interesting" is meant to indicate something that requires the attention of the teacher-researcher, for it is related to our own prior experiences and therefore has to be investigated as an ideology. Why would I find one thing or event interesting rather than another? Why, as a researcher, do I direct the camera in one direction zooming in a particular way rather than directing it elsewhere and zooming out? To get a handle on one's decisions, a teacher-researcher has to engage in a careful note-taking schedule, which allows the tracking of unconscious selections and conscious choices. In my own situation, for example, reading ethnographic studies of scientific laboratories mediated what I was looking for and looking at: for example, mathematical representations such as calculations, graphs, statistics, maps (Figure 4.3), tables with measurements (Figure 4.4), and so forth. These are denoted, in the literature on the history, philosophy, and social studies of science by the term *inscriptions*, because they always appear on paper, computer monitors, or are inscribed in some other way (chalkboard, even ephemeral drawings in the air). Because the evolution of science was hinged on the emergence of visual and mathematical means of representing and communicating, the presence of anything other than language caught my attention. An important way of studying science—as well as mathematics, technology, and other subjects—consists in following the inscriptions, their translations, accumulations, transformations, and so forth (Latour, 1987). It therefore comes as little surprise that Michael and I collected anything and everything that looked like an inscription.

For much of this research in Michael Bowen's eighth-grade science unit, I used the camera in a *note-taking mode* pointing it where, as an ethnographer, I would have directed my gaze. In this mode, the camera is not more objective than the ethnographer; rather, it has to be considered as a tool that has the same purpose and subjectivity that the ethnographer's eye, pencil, and notebook. However, the camera does have at least one advantage over the ethnographer and his or her notebook: It allowed me to re-view and re-live what I had experienced in the setting. It also provided me with access to the precise words that had been spoken, which I made available to analysis by transcribing the conversations. I also could share these tapes with Michael Bowen, who thereby got to see the events precisely in the way they occurred from the angle they were recorded.

The offprints in Figure 4.2 may appear chaotic, but in fact reflect the mode in which I used the camera. In some instances, I was running behind the students whenever they were running leaving the camera on in the course of the sometimes tumultuous ups and downs in the field. I was not too concerned with achieving TV quality but wanted to be responsive to the situation capturing as much as I could of anything being said. This is even more important to me than the question of "nice" picture quality or "nice" shots. Thus, if it turned out that I cut off a part of a head or the feet because I did not always look through the ocular or at the monitor, then this was not tragic to me. If, on the other hand, the sound were to fail, this would be more tragic, as the sense-making efforts of the people on the video would have been lost. Thus, there was little that I could do with video footage where the microphone had failed for one or the other reason; but it mattered relatively little when the image was blurred as long as the sound could be recovered. In the present situation, much of the uneven footage I ultimately obtained derives from the fact that I held the camera under the arm in order to be less intrusive and still have what I need to do the kinds of analyses I planned to do. In part, the uneven footage also derived from the fact that we were walking a lot and I left the camera in the recording mode to capture what the students such as Erica and Dilraj were saying while walking to their research site. Nowadays digital cameras have monitors that can be turned in many directions, which provides researchers a better control of the recorded image than I had with my VHS camera that only had an ocular. Some digital cameras also have image stabilizers, which aids in getting more viable pictures than I could get with the VHS camera.

An important issue of any form of research is the selection of individuals and events to be recorded. Our decisions concerning who would be recorded were driven by the following criteria. We wanted to accumulate data source materials that (a) documented *practices* and *resources* (conversations, tool-use, manipulative skills, and objects-talked-about), (b) showed the same students continuously during one lesson and also over longer periods, and (c) represented a broad range of student abilities, interests, and attitudes. On the basis of these criteria and local contingencies (mostly in the form of absences), we decided on a daily basis who and what to record. Sharing this responsibility made this selection easier for us and allowed us to choose students on explicit rather than implicit grounds. Thus, I ended up video taping Erica and Dilraj repeatedly and therefore accumulated records suitable for making claims about what the two learned over the course of the unit. Similarly, I videotaped Mike and James over the entirety of two of their investigations, again yielding detailed data source materials to make claims about learning processes in this classroom that extended over longer periods of time.

During this study, I was absent twice for conferences and therefore could not do the videotaping. My laboratory assistant Guennadi Verechaka, with whom I had looked at some of the video footage to show him what and how to record, did the videotaping on those two days.

As with other teacher-researcher studies specifically and all studies generally, I transcribed the videotapes immediately after recording them with a maximum of 48 hours delay. The maximum delays came about, for example, when I had been away or because I had a many other things to do. There are many colleagues both teacher-researchers and university professors who think that I exaggerate by transcribing so quickly and so much. It turns out, however, this study in particular

CHAPTER 4

shows that I have been able to collect data source materials in a way few others have been able to do because my method allowed me to be responsive to questions that arose while watching and transcribing the lessons. Below I describe more extensively several situations in which the immediate transcriptions had become an invaluable practice and resource. Most often I just do a quick transcription, being not too worried about spending a lot of time to get every single word—which I can always try to recover when I want to do a close analysis and when I have more time at my hand—every overlap or every pause.

Interviews

Interviews are a standard part of many research projects. However, as teacher-researchers conducting studies in our own classrooms involving our students, we certainly end up having students talk in a double context: students (a) are in an interview situation and (b) are interviewed by the teacher of the course that they are taking at the moment. Whatever the interview protocol yields has to be seen through the lens of this double framing. Thus, we cannot expect students to tell us "what is on their minds" independently from the activity that they concretely realize in and through their talking. Thus, during whole-class conversations, they concretely realize *this* conversation, this class, and their and others' *schooling* in general. During interviews, they talk not only *about* some topic, such as about different dimensions of the classroom—e.g., the degree of autonomy or the connections a course allows to make with out-of-school life—but also and even more so, their talk *constitutes the interview itself.* That is, in talking about something they also contribute to producing the interview as a social activity sui generis. But it is the fact that the teacher has a double role that complicates the issues, because students might be led to think that by participating in one activity, research, they should expect favors in another, schooling. Here the teacher-researcher collaboration involving Michael Bowen and me came as an advantage: the person not teaching a course was able to conduct interviews more easily because he (in this I) is not giving the grades. Students still may talk to me presuming that the teachers (Michael and I) share the information—even though, in the present instance, I promised students to keep our interview confidential and to withhold any of the information from Michael Bowen prior to the end of the school year.

In the final week of the course, then, I invited ten eighth-grade students for interviews about the science unit they were in the process of completing. I chose ten because this constituted nearly one half of the class in which I had done most of the videotaping. I considered this number to be sufficient to get a good representation of student talk on the topic of the learning environment in this specially designed ecology unit. My intent was to get a little more information about how they experienced the learning environment but in a manner that was more open than the instrument (see next subsection) that we had used. Also, I wanted students to experience the interviews more like informal conversations than like formal interviews that implemented and followed a strict protocol—although I had in mind to cover the four dimensions that also were on the constructivist learning environment scale that we used as part of this research project. That is, I conducted open-ended interviews in such a way that students could talk about the course in their terms rather than in terms of the language used on the questionnaire. If I had been conducting research on the perception of classroom learning environments, I might have asked students to talk me through their answers that they provided on the instrument (see below), something that I was to do a few years later during a study in Australia. In the present study with Michael Bowen, however, I was interested primarily in knowing and learning that results in a course where students could frame their own research questions, design their investigations, and write reports that would convince their peers and the teacher alike. As this is an unfamiliar learning environment to most students, I wanted them to be able to choose their language and terms for articulating their experiences.

I conducted most of the interviews with pairs of students because I always felt that in this way students could be asked to respond to each other's comments. This allowed me to step back and talk (ask) less and I was able to get more student talk. Also, some students talk less when they find themselves in a one-on-one situation with a teacher-researcher than when they are in class. However, because students came on their own time for the interviews, often during their spare periods, I interviewed two students individually who could not make other arrangements. (This, too, I learned to be a requirement for doing teacher-research: flexibility to adapt maximally to the unforeseeable contingencies that will inevitably emerge in the course of a teacher-researcher investigation.)

All interviews were videotaped. For most of my research, I have videotaped interviews and I always tended to prefer this form of recording to audiotaping. Sometimes being able to see the face of a speaker allows me to lip read and therefore catch words that otherwise might be impossible to hear. Only if there is no other possibility—when participants prefer audiotape to videotape—do I use the former.

In interviewing, I attempt to get interviewees to talk about the issues at hand, keeping my own talk as much as possible to a minimum. I attempt to have my talk take up less than 20 percent of the transcript, giving the remainder to the participant. I do not know where these numbers come from, but it may have been something a colleague once told me to be a good rule of thumb. In some instances, I had a person talk up to 95 percent of the time, whereas in other instances I have to do a lot of encouraging to get the participant to talk. In my selection of interview participants, therefore, I attempt to invite individuals who not only are able to express themselves but also are willing to talk in a situation that is unfamiliar to most everyday folk. The following is an excerpt from one of the interviews that I conducted with one of the eighth-grade students named Shawn, which exemplifies the kinds of data that can be generated in such situations.

I: What I wanted to know about that science: did you like the third term science you did or did you like the other terms better in class?
Shawn: I liked the third term better, because you got independence by working outside.
I: So you like that when you can investigate in your own way?

CHAPTER 4

Shawn: Yea, I like that better, it is more independent and like, Mr. Bowen still sort of tells you if the vee maps are right or wrong but you have your own way of doing the investigations, it is totally up to yourself.

I: So in your case, I noticed you have a grade report, your marks did go up.

Shawn: Yea, I got like a B, a B plus, an A minus, and then an A on the last lab report. So there was an (improvement?).

I: And also from the first term?

Shawn: The first term, yea. First term I got seventy-two, the second term I got eighty-four.

I: So you like that when you get to think about your own ideas?

Shawn: I like that better, because it is more a challenge, and it is more enjoyable then having someone always on your head do this do this.

[...]

I: Do you understand, do you try to understand what [others] do?

Shawn: Like by writing notes and all that?

I: Well not necessarily notes but just by talking with them?

Shawn: Yea, because then you pick up like if he found out like, then I won't have to go if it is a two-part investigative question, like if he had already one question that was related to one of my questions, I wouldn't have to do the second part. I know if we had a similar area, because Mike was just down from our area, like behind the arena. Like he had the same claims that we did so by talking with him I found out a little bit more so then that made my lab that much easier.

I: What about, what would you like so that it becomes even more interesting?

Shawn: Like this term was good, but last term in the chemistry, it was more like Mr. Bowen gave us the question, so it was still like, it was still independent research, but we had like four or five questions so then I was really rushed for time, I felt because we couldn't put in our very best effort, because we had like six questions and in a matter of a term and they were like so hard they would take, we only had like four periods and that's three periods a week and six times three is eighteen or like six weeks sort of and the term is only eight weeks, so we were a little pressed for time.

In interviewing I tried and still try to get the respondents to talk much more than I do, because the intent of an interview is to get information from the other person rather than from myself. This is especially the case because the assumption underlying this form of interviewing is that what the interviewee says can be taken as a reflection of his or her thinking or attitude or beliefs independent of the interview situation itself. In the sample excerpt provided, I spoke 108 words compared to 348 words that Shawn uttered. This means that Shawn talked a little more than three times as much as I did. My target today is to slant the distribution even more toward the research participant than I did when I interviewed Shawn, which was at the very beginning of my career as a teacher-researcher specifically and as an interpretive researcher more generally.

> **How Much Did You Talk?** A quick way of finding out the distribution of talk is to create a copy of your transcript, then use your word processor to sort by paragraphs, which will get your and the respondent's talk separated. Then do a word count on each of the two sections.

A good strategy for getting better at interviewing is to do practice runs or to engage in a cycle of reflection and interview protocol improvement—which I ask the students in my graduate research methods and design courses. For example, if you have never interviewed before, it would be good to have available some possible questions to get the interview process back on track should you get stuck—even though you ultimately might want to encourage (life) narratives. A second good strategy is to have a "cheat sheet" containing sentence stems or individual words designed to get another person to talk more about a topic. Having a cheat sheet possibly would have allowed me to encourage Shawn to increase the amount of his talk and to prevent me from asking question after question. For example, in subsequent research projects I found these three terms helpful: elaborate, explain, justify. Thus, I might ask a person, "Can you elaborate on . . .?" "How did you justify . . . to yourself [others]?" or "Would you mind explaining to me . . .?" Quick looks at my cheat sheet during the interview then allowed me to generate much more and much more deep-going data from the interviewee without adding a lot of talk on my part.

After the first interview and prior to conducting the next one, transcribe the tape in its entirety. Then ask yourself questions such as "What is the relative amount of talk?" "Did I get the information I wanted?" and "Did I probe in depth?" Then ask yourself questions that seek to improve the interview protocol: "What do I need to ask to get the information required by my study?" and "How can I get the respondent to talk at greater length?" Once you have done this, arrange for another interview and then go through the same cycle of transcription and reflection. You will note that you are getting better at interviewing rather quickly. If you were to do all interviews without transcribing and reflecting, you might find yourself at the end not having the information you need for the study you designed and intended to conduct.

Constructivist Learning Environment Scale

Michael Bowen and I also administered the *Constructivist Learning Environment Scale* (CLES), designed to measure the extent to which students perceive their learning environments as consistent with a constructivist epistemology (Taylor & Fraser, 1991). The instrument consists of four subscales that are intended to assess important aspects of a constructivist learning environment. The *Autonomy* scale is intended to measure the degree to which students exercised control over their learning activities. A typical item reads, "In this class, I decide how much time to spend on an activity." The *Prior Knowledge* scale is intended to measure students' perceptions of the opportunities for meaningful integration of knowledge in the classroom ("In this class, I think about interesting real life problems"). The *Negotiation* scale was designed to measure students' perceptions of the opportunities to interact, negotiate meaning and build consensus ("In this class, I talk with other students about the most sensible way of solving problems"). The *Student-Centeredness* scale was designed to measure students' perceptions of teacher expectations for different aspects of their learning ("In this class, the teacher expects me to remember things I learned in past lessons"). Because of the way the items on the latter scale were formulated, we renamed it, for some purposes, *Teacher Expectation* scale. A high score on teacher expectations then precisely is the reverse of student-centeredness.

In contrast to the survey instrument used in chapter 2, which I had constructed to assess the prevalence of certain student statements, the present instrument was designed to *measure* perceptions for the purpose of correlating them to other measures. The issue was to assess the prevalence of agreement rather than the measurement of something. When social scientists generally and teacher-researchers in particular use such measurement instruments, they need to know how reliable the instrument is in measuring what it was intended to measure. A variety of indicators for reliability are possible. Frequently, researchers use the construct of *internal consistency*, which means, the degree to which the different questions that make a sub-scale correlate with each other. When the correlations between the different items are high, this is an indication that each item consistently measures the underlying psychological (or sociological) construct. Other measures of reliability are possible, including how consistent the instrument is when used again with the same individuals after some interval; in this case, we are dealing with *test-retest* reliability. In our situation, Michael and I decided to go with the measure the instrument designers themselves had used, internal consistency. This measure often is referred to as *Cronbach alpha (χ)*.

Generalizing and Generalizability If you want to generalize the results of your teaching beyond your classroom—to other classrooms in your school, to classrooms like your own elsewhere in the city, state (province), or country, then you have to use reliable measures and statistical means.

Whereas Taylor and Fraser (1991) had reported alpha reliabilities between $\chi = .69$ and $\chi = .85$ for these subscales, they ranged from .52 to .72 in our eighth-grade sample. In leading psychology journals, any reliability coefficient below $\chi = 0.80$ is considered too low as a rule of thumb, because, when an instrument is not very reliable, what then *is it measuring*? That is, we considered the values of the instrument in our study as being too low (although we were aware that others would and did regularly use measures that are not so reliable). Michael and I therefore took them only as indicators rather than as good measures. They could give us but some ballpark idea about student perceptions that they were supposed to measure. This is another reason why it was so important to me to conduct the interviews, as I was more than a little suspicious concerning the goodness of the information we were getting by using the instrument.

PERCEPTIONS AND ACHIEVEMENT

A search of the literature provided evidence that numerous research programs have shown that student perceptions of classroom environments are significantly related to cognitive learning outcomes. Better achievement was particularly shown in classes perceived as having greater goal direction and less disorganization and friction. Michael Bowen and I knew of studies that focused specifically on science, significant simple, multiple, and canonical correlations were found between cognitive outcome and students' perception of classroom environments. More specifically, the students' perception of order, organization, and task orientation were positively related to designing experiments, drawing conclusions, and making generalizations while the perception of innovation correlated negatively with the same outcome variables. Because the learning environment in this study differed considerably from that which students experienced previously or in their other courses, we were interested in their perceptions of the classroom environment and how these perceptions related to their grades. Our idea was to reproduce some of the statistics in our own classes, requiring us to collect the relevant data source materials.

Information about students' views regarding their classroom environment was obtained in three ways: (a) by administering the CLES with its four subscales; (b) by talking with students as we accompanied them to their field sites and in the classroom setting; and (c) by formally interviewing students. As an integral aspect of our studies, we wanted to represent what students had learned, how well they did on examination questions pertinent to the ecology fieldwork they had done, and we wanted to see whether there were any relationships to the measures—however problematic their low reliability—of their perceptions of the classroom learning environment. At the time we did our study—as perhaps again today—many educators and policy makers were interested in quantitative measures. We therefore decided to report some quantitative analyses of the relationship between perceptions of the learning environment and achievement followed by qualitative analyses; and we wanted to integrate these measures in our interpretive analyses that answered the questions that we had posed for directing our study in the first place. We also decided to present five vignettes featuring students who (a) appeared extensively in our analyses of learning and (b) were representative of the class in terms of their perceptions and achievement. Each vignette was established by *triangulation* from the three data sources, the multiple achievement measures, and our interpretations about learning as evidenced in the videotapes. We decided to present the five students' achievement in terms of the quartile ranges using both of Michael Bowen's classes because, so we thought, the larger number of students would give us a better estimate of where these students were with respect to their achievement. Using statistics, we thought that we would be able to tell other educators what kind of relationships *they* might be able to expect in their context between students' perceptions of the classroom environment and their achievement. That is, we wanted to be in a position of generalizing from our context to other contexts that are similar in many or most respects so that students can be understood as belonging to the same population.

Quantitative Analysis

The correlations between students' perceptions of the classroom environment (as measured by CLES) and the achievement measures (teacher evaluation of the unit test and the items on the final exam concerning the unit) are presented in Table 4.1.

CHAPTER 4

What we actually had done was re-define one of the variables from Student-centeredness to *Teacher Expectation* simply by scoring in the reverse; that is, whatever was a 5 we scored 1, the score that would have been 4, we scored 2, and finally the undecided (intermediate) responses retained their score of 3. The table shows that student achievement significantly correlated with three of the four classroom environment measures, *Prior Knowledge, Autonomy*, and *Teacher Expectations*. Each number in the table shows the correlation between the variables that form the row and column, respectively. Thus, for example, the first cell (top left), shows the correlation between the measure of Prior Knowledge and students' perceptions of the degree to which their classroom fosters negotiations: $r = .36$. The asterisk denotes that $p < .05$, which means that the probability that this correlation has arisen by chance is less than 5 percent. In the same way, readers quickly can find how the size of the correlations between all pairs of variables and the associated probabilities. Such a table generally is referred to as *correlation matrix*.

One of the ways in which a collection of measurements can be used is as predictors of achievement. If there is only one variable to be used, we have a situation of a simple regression. In such a situation, researchers would report the correlation coefficient and the probability associated with it (see chapter 1). When there are more variables, then multiple regression analysis is one of the ways in which the collection of variables can be used to see how much of the variation in the achievement measures is measured by a set of independent variables. (If you wanted to use such an analysis, a statistician could help you set up the study.) In our case, the four environment variables together predicted 29% of the variance in the achievement. This information usually is reported in terms of the squared valued of a single correlation using a capital R to show that the correlations involves multiple more than two variables: $R^2 = .29, p < .01$. Here we reported the probability associated with this analysis because we wanted to give an indication what researchers who were to repeat our study in a similar group of students with similar instructions should expect as results. The *p*-value suggests that there is a probability of less than 1 percent ($p < 0.1$) that the $R^2 = .29$ had arisen by chance; or in other words, there is less than 1 percent chance that we are wrong in saying that the four perception scales have a statistically significant predictive quality. Even

Table 4.1. Correlations between perceptions and achievement

	Prior Knowl-edge	Autonomy	Teacher Expecta-tions	Term Mark	Unit Test	Exam (Biology Section)
Negotiation	.36*	.37*	.32*	-.01	.16	.16
Prior Knowledge		.57***	.46**	.28	.42**	.09
Autonomy			.26	.45**	.48***	.42**
Teacher Expecta-tions				.32*	.30*	.11
Term Mark					.82***	.41**
Unit Test						.45**

* p < .05, ** p < .01, *** p < .001
Note: All probabilities are 2-tailed.

though the probability was small, there still was a chance that we were wrong in saying that there was a correlation. Another important point that needs to be kept in mind is that *statistical significance* does not mean *educational significance*. This is so because increasing the number of participants in a study increases the power of detecting even small differences. But small differences may not have any relevance to teaching at all. Thus, even though a correlation may be statistically significant, it may not be educationally significant. For example, with a sufficiently large number of participants, a variance of $R^2 = .10$ or less becomes statistically significant, though it may have no educational significance—such as the case in chapter 1 where the difference between valid links in concept maps rose by about one point.

Michael and I also looked a little closer into the individual scales. This additional looks revealed that only the *Autonomy* scale was significantly related to student achievement as measured by the section of the final exam directly related to the unit, which in fact can be considered as a *delayed posttest*. The total variance explained by the classroom environment variables was 21 percent ($R^2 = .21$, $p = .06$). This means that there was a 6 percent probability that we would have been wrong saying that the classroom environment scales predicted achievement; this probability for being wrong is, in most instances, too high to be acceptable.

We then looked at the relationships between individual scales and achievement. Because of the extent to which we encouraged both student autonomy and student–student transactions, significant correlations of these variables to learning outcomes might have been expected. The results in Table 4.1 suggest that there are no relationships between achievement, on the one hand, and the extent to which students perceived opportunities to interact, negotiate meaning, and build consensus. On the other hand, the extent to which students exercised control over their learning activities related significantly both to immediate and delayed achievement measures.

Now, as suggested, these results have to be taken with a grain of salt because the learning environment sub-scales did not have very good values for internal consistency. There was a possibility therefore that they were rather inaccurate, somewhat like a bathroom scale that shows different values each time you step on, off, and on again. Nevertheless, the reviewers and readers of the journal in which we ultimately published our study found this information helpful in assessing the outcome of our teaching in this classroom.

Qualitative Analyses

As indicated in the section on data collection, we attempted to gather information across a broad spectrum of students over the course of the investigation. The quantitative variables, especially because of their low reliability measures, provided us with tentative information only. We therefore decided to provide some more detailed, comparative information on individual students representing different student types. In one report from our work, we presented five vignettes featuring students who were representative of the spectrum on several dimensions related to learning and who appeared extensively in our data analysis. Such vignettes provide

CHAPTER 4

Table 4.2. Achievement levels of five students in the study

	Achievement (quartile)					
	Chemistry (2nd term)	Biology (3rd term)	Biology unit test	Exam (biology subtest)	Science (year end)	All subjects (year end)
Erica	1	1	1	1	1	1
Michael	3	4	4	2	3	3
James	3	2	2	1	3	2
Mike	1	2	1	1	1	2
Shawn	3	2	2	2	3	4

Note 1. $N = 43$. The two classes included were those taught by GMB.
Note 2. 1 = 75–99 percentile; 2 = 50–74 percentile, 3 = 25–49 percentile, 4 = 0–24 percentile.

substantial background information that contextualizes the real concern of a study, which in our case concerned knowing and learning in an open-inquiry learning environment. The question that naturally posed itself to us is related to the selection of the students that are to figure in the vignettes. Ultimately, the criterion for any selection has to be representativeness. We selected five students because they represented (a) each of the four inter-quartile ranges of their total grade point average (GPA) at the end of the school year, (b) various combinations of inter-quartile ranges on the different achievement measures in science (Table 4.2), and (c) the broad range of attitudes in the eighth-grade classes towards the learning environment. I established the quartile range as follows. I took all the grades achieved in the class and ordered them from the highest to the lowest. Then I made a dividing line between the bottom half and the top half of the grades. Each of the two sections I divided into half again. The result is that I had four ranges of scores. Each of these ranges represented a quartile.

One of the ways in which we had seen instruments such as CLES being used in classroom research was in the form of a diagram that compared the students of interest. Thus, we constructed a graph in which the scale scores of each of the five students were plotted; our graph is featured in Figure 4.5. Because a line connects the scale measures for each student, we obtained something like a *profile*. In the selection of students, we plotted a number of students and then selected the five based on the differences in their profiles. For example, the student Michael has a profile that represents an extreme with respect to the class average (the horizontal dotted line at the zero mark). We then presented some qualitative information together with the general and specific achievement levels. We used a figure such as Figure 4.5 to show each student's score on the four CLES subscales as measured by a standardized distance from the class means. The standard deviation (SD) is a common measure for differences from the mean when a distribution is Gaussian (looks like the "bell curve"). In this instance, about 68 percent of the scores fall within ± 1 SD of the mean and about 95 percent of all scores fall within ±2 SD.

Using representations such as Figure 4.5 allows us to see some interesting patterns. For example, Mike, a high achieving student, did not perceive the learning environment as student-centered as he wished it to be and felt pressured by very

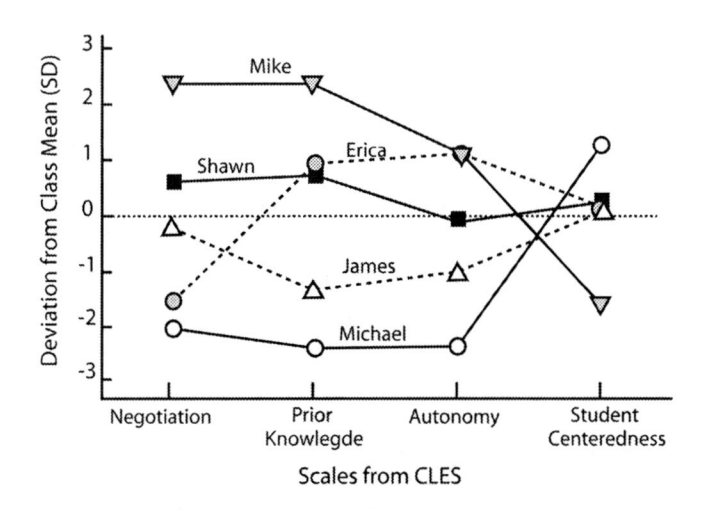

Figure 4.5. The scale scores on CLES for each of five individuals typifying a different kind of student; the graph together with Table 4.2 was intended to help readers situate the qualitative vignettes.

high teacher expectations. On the other hand, Michael, a generally poorly performing student in all of his subjects, perceived a high level of student-centeredness—or, expressed in the reverse, in this class he perceived there to be a lower level of teacher expectations than most of his peers—even though he scored in the opposite direction on all other scales. This information, though it is numerical, is not "quantitative" in the way the term quantitative frequently is used. When researchers use the term *quantitative* they refer to studies designed to infer patterns about large groups of individuals (e.g., all grade 8 students in Canada) based on a small, necessarily representative sample of may be 200 students. Numerical summaries as the one available in Figure 4.5 do not lent themselves to such inferences. To avoid the confusion between using numbers and attempting to make high-level inferences to large population groups, a colleague and I proposed to distinguish research not according to the use of numbers but according to the degree to which researchers want to make generalizations (e.g., Ercikan & Roth, 2006).

To give our readers an idea or perhaps a feel for the different individuals involved, what they told us during the interviews, and how well they did we constructed narrative vignettes. One of these narratives featured the student Michael, in many respects the kind of student teachers do not like in their classes. We added information from our observations and what he had told me during the interviews I had conducted with him. Here is what we wrote.

> Michael was well known as a troublemaker even by those who did not teach him. During the year, several teachers had referred him repeatedly to the administrator responsible for discipline. He often had difficulties meeting deadlines with his assignments, and found support from his parents for not doing his homework. When he received attention (as being at the focus

of our investigation during interviews and video-taping sessions), he engaged in tasks and was productive. On the other hand, when our research did not focus on him, we could often see Michael from afar engaging in activities not related to the course (climbing a tree, or lying on his back staring into the sky). Correspondingly, Michael—whose GPA ranks him in the third quartile—found himself in the bottom quartile on two of the three science achievement measures for this unit. This was down from his achievement in the chemistry unit where it had been possible to more closely supervise him. He did much better on the exam. On three of the four scales of CLES, he scored approximately 2 standard deviations below the class average (Figure 4.5).

Consistent with his score on the *Negotiation* subscale, he indicated during the interviews that there were not enough opportunities for engaging in discussions, collaboration, and exchange of ideas with others, especially with larger groups of students ("It is harder when you have small groups, [and] it gets very confusing when you have to work with the same person. . . . But when you are in a large group, everybody gets in"). When he worked in a large group, he often liked to receive credit for the main ideas, or for the collaborative achievements. On the other hand, he willingly shared credit with his research partner ("He is a good partner. We both do the same amount of work and we both brought in our ideas"). Because he knew much about and was interested in animals, he would have liked to focus his research on them but felt that he had no opportunities for doing so, a response which was consistent with his perception of not having enough time to think, few opportunities to connect his learning to past knowledge, or connecting the experience to real life problems (*Prior Knowledge* scale). He thought that he did not have enough autonomy and would have liked to have a greater decision-making power regarding several aspects of his investigations. On the other hand, he requested a greater presence of the teacher as he engaged in his research ("there wasn't enough attention").

By providing five of these accounts together with the information about their relative standing in class with respect to general and specific achievement levels and with respect to their responses on the constructivist learning environment scale we hoped to convey to our readers a sense of how students experienced themselves in this course that was very different from what might be considered normal for science courses. If success in the peer review process is a valid measure, then we were able to convey this sense because our research was published in a well-known journal focusing on cognition and instruction (Roth & Bowen, 1995). Citing from the formal interviews and from the informal conversations captured on tape while recording students in the field, we were able to put a little flesh to the students, who often are represented in research reports as disembodied and lifeless learning machines that operate like rational computers.

GENERATING AND TESTING HYPOTHESES EXPERIMENTALLY

The rapid transcription of videotapes and preliminar analysis of tapes, transcripts, and other artifacts collected allows researchers to generate hypotheses that can be tested within the period of collecting data sources. That is, it is much better to begin the analysis of the data source materials as soon as possible rather than to wait until everything one initially has planned is collected. In this way, the collection of materials as data sources can be orchestrated in a way that is responsive to the unfolding understanding teacher-researchers develop concerning the phenomena of interest. If you do not begin the analysis immediately, you may end up finding yourself in a situation where you wished you had collected certain materials but no longer can because, for example, the school year has ended. (This is particularly an issue if, as in my situation, institutional research ethics boards [IRBs] impose on teacher-researchers a waiting period—usually till the school year has ended—before they can access their data source materials.) If on the other hand you had transcribed video immediately and had begun the analysis, you could have collected further materials in a much more targeted way. In some instances, the domain of interest may become expanded, as the preliminary analyses reveal new, previously non-salient dimensions into focus.

As a result of such responsiveness, teacher-researchers can generate and test hypotheses in an ongoing manner. With such hypothesis tests, new knowledge is generated that possibly has implications for teaching as well. Under certain circumstances, the generated hypotheses can be stated in a form that they are suitable to experiments designed according to principles of standard psychological methods. For example, in this study I generated hypotheses or wondered about how students *generally* would deal with a problem that I had seen one student group to wrestle with. I then designed an experiment to test the hypothesis. Here I describe how the hypotheses and questions emerged, how we designed the tests of the hypotheses or investigations to get answers to our questions, and how we subsequently analyzed these. As a result of this method, we generated knowledge that otherwise would not have been able to be produced. Responsiveness therefore is key to generative teacher-researcher investigations.

There may be, however, conditions that prevent teacher-researchers to be as responsive as I advocate it here. Thus, institutional research ethics boards may require a teacher-researcher to invoke the assistance of a third party in the data source collection to mediate between

> **Ecological Validity** A test is ecologically valid when its conditions are such that students have to use the same form of knowledge as the one they acquired during the learning situation. If students learn something by doing laboratory tasks and then are asked to do a written test, we have to wonder whether on the written test they have to use the same knowledge that they acquired in doing labs. Similarly, when students learned something by using computers or by means of group work but are tested with paper and pencil or individually, then we have to ask ourselves whether the test really assesses the competencies students acquired in the learning situation. We achieve ecological validity only when the competencies required being successful in the two situations (learning, testing) are the same.

CHAPTER 4

student participants and teacher-researchers. In this case, a teacher-researcher does not have access to the data sources until after he or she has ceased to be the teacher of the student participants. Such a condition favors an approach that Michael Bowen and I enacted in this study. Thus, although there was no IRB requiring Michael to refrain from accessing the data sources, I had promised students during the interviews that he would not have access until after the school year had ended. In this way, we mediated possible anxieties students might have had concerning the power-over situation in which they found themselves with Michael.

Throughout our investigation, special tests and investigations were formulated in the form of story problems that were *ecologically valid* (authentic) (a) in the sense that these problems were embedded in students' own work and (b) in that they led to further learning in the unit itself. Thus, students were not involved in doing *extra* work but in and through doing these special tasks learned more of the science specified in the curriculum and more about science as well. The two story problems I discuss here were called the "Lost Field Notebook" and "Plant Growth."

The Emergence of a Hypothesis and its Test

Throughout the data source collection phase and as part of our ongoing analysis of data source materials, I designed story problems to test emerging hypotheses. The *Lost Field Notebook* problem was developed to answer two questions: "To what extent do students use graphs in their fieldwork?" and "Is there a relationship between the number of data pairs and the type of inscription students used?" To answer these questions I thought about writing a story problem that somehow captured what students were already doing, namely ecological fieldwork, and ask students to solve the problem articulated in the story. (I learned only later that the question whether a story really poses a problem ought to be an empirical matter. All too often I found out that what teachers think constitutes a problem actually turns out to be a very different one to the students working on it, or may not be a problem at all.) I wanted to use the results to see whether the use of graphs somehow was related to the amount of data that there was to analyze. I used story problems because, at that time, I believed that mathematical problems embedded in stories about the students' own science experiences constituted *ecologically valid* testing situations; that is, the stories, because they described the eighth-grade students' experience, should engage the same mathematical practices as in the real situation (i.e., their normal everyday science lessons). The stories I wanted to write were to be motivated by actual events in these classrooms (a lost notebook or a difference of opinions about the meaning of data). To increase further the likelihood of correspondence between the stories and students' experience, I decided that the story problems also should include student-produced inscriptions to present data. In this way, the story problems should be as close as possible to the everyday experiences of the students in this course. Here I provide an account for how this part of our research came about.

QUANTITATIVE AND QUALITATIVE

On May 26, while going through the laboratory reports (vee maps) the eighth-grade students in Michael Bowen's two classes just had submitted, I wrote the following research note. In this note I summarized some impressions I had had about the maps some students had drawn of their research site and the amount of numerical and non-numerical information these maps contained. The map of one of these student groups (Figure 4.6) should take on special importance.

Scales
a. On the axis of coordinate systems, graphs (categories, interval)
b. Maps, scales of
   Scale drawing used by students, which are not scale drawings because they did not measure the area exactly, at least initially (Fab/Tim).
   Kieran/Brendan. Why are the scales not drawn accurately? What could he have communicated more had he drawn them accurately?
   Michael McT., his map (vee 3) also is not to scale (the distance to the lake, but shows location, direction of lake), but it expresses some funda-

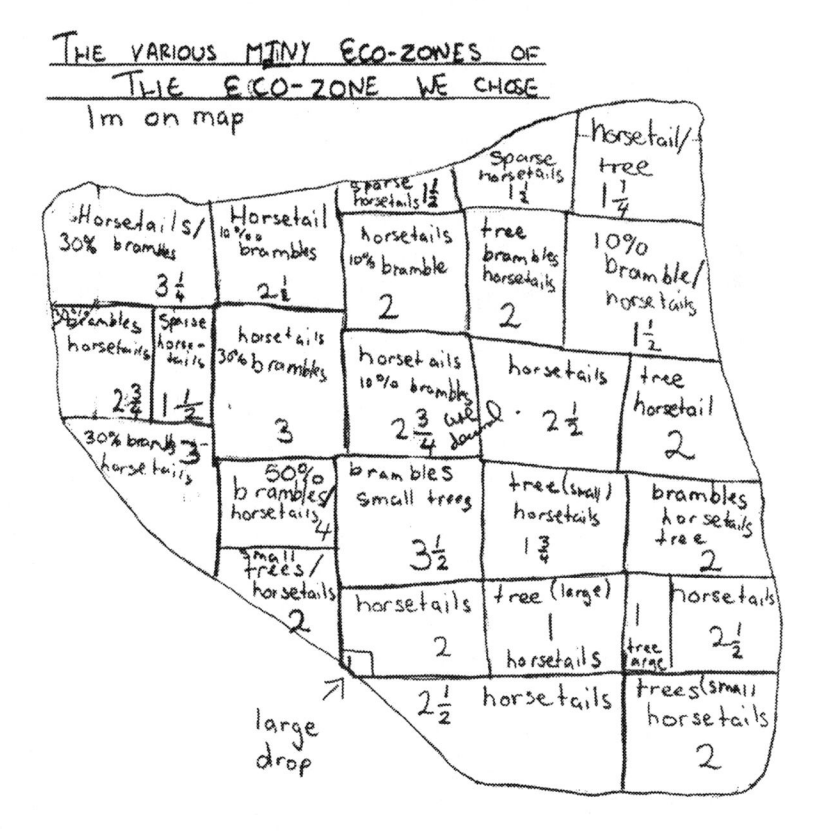

Figure 4.6. The map that one student group constructed became the template for a word problem Michael Bowen and I designed to test a research hypothesis.

159

mental relationships between the locations of the three sites.

The maps drawn by Gareth/K are quite elaborate (as those by Fab/Tim, Erica/Dilraj). Fab/Tim subdivided into 9/36 areas and counted plants, measured light. On the other hand, Shaun/Tim used their map (though they indicated the scale) only to give relative positions.

Mike/Jamie, Heintzeman/Dudek don't use graph or map. In their events, they indicated how they sampled, in each corner and the center of their three areas. Thus there was no need to draw a map. Similarly, they used only three areas that they compared, thus a chart was enough for them to generalize.

Pat/Adam, Grant/Haroun didn't use graph or chart, but simply drew the measurements into a drawing indicating the major features, but not to scale. Again, the task was at such a level that the two could generate their generalizations without the need of tables or graphs. The question is whether they would seek recourse to a graphing/tabling method if there were more data they had to cope with. (Should be tested by giving each class a task with a different amount of data on a chart, and the focus question.)

Mixture of category, interval axes for a line graph (Ho/Livingston, Ho/Moore, Manalo/Bara).

I think that it would be important here to generate more interactions among all of the students in terms of their individual accomplishments. In this way, they would establish community standards for all of them.

To begin with, this note is a good example of the kinds of research memos I was writing at the time. It constitutes a record of my first impressions immediately following an initial and preliminary analysis. It was generated on the same day that I collected this student work. Near the end of this note (in the penultimate paragraph concerning the maps and numbers), I had written an instruction to myself "Should be tested by giving each class a task with a different amount of data on a chart, and the focus question." Because I had written the instruction while the course was under way, it was possible to conduct a test right then and there. It is self-evident that we would not have been able to test it if this hypothesis had occurred to me during the summer holidays—especially given the fact that both Michael and I left the school at the end of that year. The test I am referring to pertained to the question whether students would more likely choose graphs as a representation of their data if "there were more data they had to cope with." On the next day, I wrote another research memo following a conversation I have had with Michael Bowen about the research hypothesis.

May 27, 1992
Conversation with MB. Negotiation/joint thinking about what to do with the area problem I took from Gareth. Should we give it home over the weekend? But then we don't see them actually doing it. Also, no more marked work after this Friday. How does the question have to be phrased

so that a graph is not suggested? Have another graph question from chemistry? But then the context of graphing is set. MB quite correctly mentions that the problem here is framed by the researcher rather than the student in the field. Also, students might chose just enough of sampling areas as they can handle. So the situation that they are presented with is not that they would have chosen on their own. But at a different level, we can get some sort of control in a real life classroom. It is exciting to think about changing teaching from this perspective. To talk it through with another person; then test hypotheses by making up a problem and see how students react to it.

In this memo, I made reference to the fact that we were considering how to test the hypothesis, in particular, how to go about testing it given that the school administration had instructed us not to give homework after that week because the students were beginning to study for the year-end examinations. We were also considering how to set up the problem so that students would not be primed to use a graph but that they would feel free to choose any method they considered best for solving the problem. We did not want to make the problem look in the way traditional word problems looked but somehow more similar to the kind of problems the students faced in the course doing their own research. That is, we wanted the test to involve a problem that would be *ecologically valid*, reflecting their processes and products in and of this ecology unit as a whole. I was therefore thinking about writing a word problem that squarely located the task in students' present work—the idea came to me that I could write a short narrative about a student from the class who had lost her field notebook. Because students recorded any emerging questions in their field notebooks as well as recorded their data in the field, it was plausible that if someone were to find a lost field notebook, they would have all the information necessary to do an analysis.

The *Lost Field Notebook* problem that I ultimately designed came in three forms, each with a different data set containing 5, 8, and 19 data pairs (Figure 4.7); the number of data pairs and the color of the sheet that students received and randomly assigned to student groups distinguished the forms. I chose this problem with the particular data pairs for three reasons. First, as discussed earlier, its apparent correspondence to a plausible experience seemed considerable. Second, the problem in its three forms is equivocal even for individuals much more experienced in research (e.g., graduate students). The consideration of various number pairs I had chosen made for interesting discussions if they were plotted: the data sets included "outliers" that made the interpretation equivocal. For example, considering some point as an outlier or using a curve rather than a straight line yielded a very different interpretation. The second data set with eight data points changed from a statistically nonsignificant to a significant relationship when one point was considered an outlier and dropped from consideration. The third data set (Figure 4.7) that I constructed was interesting because novices might consider the scatter of the plotted data points too large to support a relationship. This promised lots of discussions among students and, for us, an opportunity to study sense making over

CHAPTER 4

The lost field notebook

Elizabeth is a grade 8 student who is doing research on an ecozone. She wanted to find out whether there is a relationship between the density of brambles, a plant with a long narrow stem, and the amount of light these plants receive in different areas of her ecozone.

She subdivided her ecozone into smaller areas. In each area she measured the approximate coverage of the area (in %) by the brambles. For each area she also found the average amount of light, measured in foot candles (fc). She recorded her data in her field notebook in the form of a the map reproduced below.

Elizabeth lost her field notebook, and you found it. You wanted to know the patterns she had found, but besides the map there was no additional information. Based on the information provided,
1. what patterns, if any, do **you** see?
2. what claims would **you** make?
3. how would **you** support your claims?

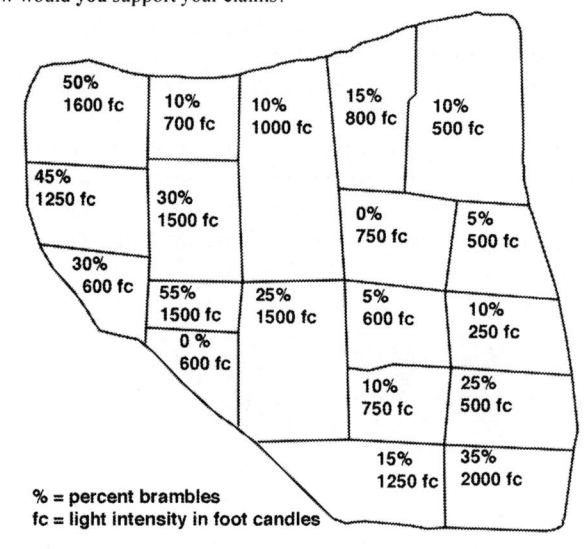

Figure 4.7. Based on the map in Figure 4.7, we constructed three versions for testing our research hypothesis that large data sets encourage students to use graphs.

and about those representations that students constructed in support of their arguments.

Third, from a didactic perspective, the Lost Field Notebook problem was interesting because it shared similarities (in the scatter) with data sets that Michael and I had encountered in our own work as practicing natural and social scientists. As such, this problem deviated from most traditional practices in mathematics education where students were provided with data sets or produce data sets that showed unequivocal functional relationships (e.g., all points are on the same line or curve). The present problem was consistent with the then current policy guidelines for the teaching of mathematics, which suggested that students deal with data from the real world. The different versions of the problem I designed were also used because I knew that many eighth-grade students would eventually take my junior- and senior-level physics courses in which experimental data were fitted with statistical or mathematical functions (see chapter 3).

We then randomly distributed the three forms in the three eighth-grade classes at the school, two taught by Michael Bowen and the third taught by a colleague, Sheila Kuipers, who always welcomed us in her classroom though we rarely made use of this offer lacking the time. In both of Michael Bowen's classes, I videotaped while students were completing the task; while Sheila was teaching her eighth-grade class, I also was teaching so that Michael Bowen took over to distribute and collect the students' answers to the Lost Field Notebook task.

My next field note shows that on June 1, on the very day we had handed out the different forms of the test in both of Michael Bowen's classes, we already generated new hypotheses and shared additional vignettes that would support what we called the "spreading hypothesis."

> *Spreading hypothesis*
> In 8D we observed the spreading of a practice—that of using graphs to summarize data sets—in the class, beginning with Fab's group, Erica's group, and then through the class. Several groups, Shawn e.g., did not take up on it that period. MB reported other instances of this in the chemistry section
>
> *Vignette*
> The task is to convincingly show that sugar does not disappear when put into solution (The intend of the problem is for students to use balances and the conversation of mass principle to show that the total mass before and after mixing is constant). The students begin by "mucking" around with taste, with trying to filter the solution, ((other methods they use?)). But all these solutions to the problem are not satisfactory enough, not convincing enough. Eventually one group begins to use a balance. More student groups, often without knowing why, begin using balances. Over a span of three school periods, the use of balances spread through the entire class ((were there exceptions?)).
>
> This spreading was not observed in 8C. Here, however, the only group that had prepared a graph was sitting partly hidden by equipment, far away from any other group. Gareth, from whose field research project the problem had been generated (he recognized the ecozone as his), had consulted with the teacher on how to represent the data and they had settled on an *x-y* graph. His partner in the field, however, did not use a graph to represent the data.
>
> We separated them intentionally so that they wouldn't work with their partners from the field to tease out transfer from field to classroom.

Although we had set out to test an hypothesis about the relationship between amount of data students collect and the use of certain mathematical representations (e.g., graphs), it turned out that recording and observing the students while doing

CHAPTER 4

the task we had assigned yielded yet another hypothesis. That is, the very fact that we videotaped and actively observed (ethnographically) led us to come to perceive a new type of phenomena that is of interest both to teachers, concerned with how one can use the sociality of a classroom to enhance individual learning, and to researchers, concerned with understanding how social practices come to be reproduced and spread in a learning community.

In this research memo, I was recording not only the new observations about how students were learning from one another but also similar types of observations that we had not actively attended to prior to the hypothesis. We therefore came to record these anecdotal observations of other moments long after they had occurred. It turned out that once we had written up this study, I would make this spreading hypothesis a major focus of my work—by then being a professor at a university doing research in an elementary school where I was also teaching science through student-centered design tasks. This study in our eighth-grade class thereby set me up to do more work—now as a researcher-teacher—to better understand how knowledgeable practices come to be adopted within a collectivity such as a science classroom with particular attention to the different knowledge dimensions that might be spreading—e.g., facts and artifacts, conceptual knowledge, and material practices.

The following excerpt from a research note on the following day (June 2) shows how I already had begun with my sense-making efforts to try to understand what had happened when we administered the Lost Field Notebook task. More so, because I had watched the videotape at night, I was able to follow up some of the questions I had with the eighth-grade students that I interviewed on June 2 concerning the learning environment. In particular, I made reference to the interview with Shawn, who, as my recording from the class showed (see above), explicitly had chosen not to use a graph to see whether there is a pattern in the data of the map (he had the task with eight data pairs). (Part of the interview with Shawn is reproduced on pages 147–148.)

> June 2, 1992
> Students don't see any need to use the graphs. From their perspective, in the case of a few numbers, a decision can be made. In the case of larger numbers of data pairs, a decision cannot be made, or no relationship exists. They abandon the problem, which wasn't theirs in the first place. It could be that they are using graphs only at the upper end of the zone of proximal development, with teacher assistance, at least at this point.
>
> This interacts with the spreading. If there is a "seed," then spreading might take over, and students use graphs without further assistance.
>
> Students were looking for alternate information to make a better pattern, to eradicate the discrepant cases with additional factors, information
>
> Interviews: Shawn
> Being thrown off by a few points not exactly on a best-fit line. Hypothesized, and being thrown off if a point didn't follow the pattern. He thought points needed to be exactly on a line. From this point of view it makes

QUANTITATIVE AND QUALITATIVE

sense that he didn't chose to do a graph because he already had counter evidence to his hypothesis.

Boundary: A pattern has to be connected to all of them. Line forms a pattern and the line has to follow exactly [the points]. (Shawn, interview)

Of course, the transcript of the interview contained more information. The point of the research memo was to highlight what could be found—the reference to the interview is a sufficient pointer that would allow me to look up the details. This research memo would allow me subsequently, when I was making several passes through the data sources and written research memos to go back to the original sources. The point for readers to retain is that it is more important that an aspect of the interview was conceptualized in terms of other events that had happened in this classroom. One can think in terms of a connection that I was able to make between two different sources of data, connections that constitute (and lead to new) learning on the part of the teacher-researcher.

In analyzing the responses student groups constructed following the task, I began by summarizing the approach each group had chosen; to do this part quickly, I used pencil, paper, and colored markers (Figure 4.8). I began by noting the names of the students, then the version of the problem they had worked with in terms of the color (blue, pink, golden), and then noted in a box how the students hand answered.

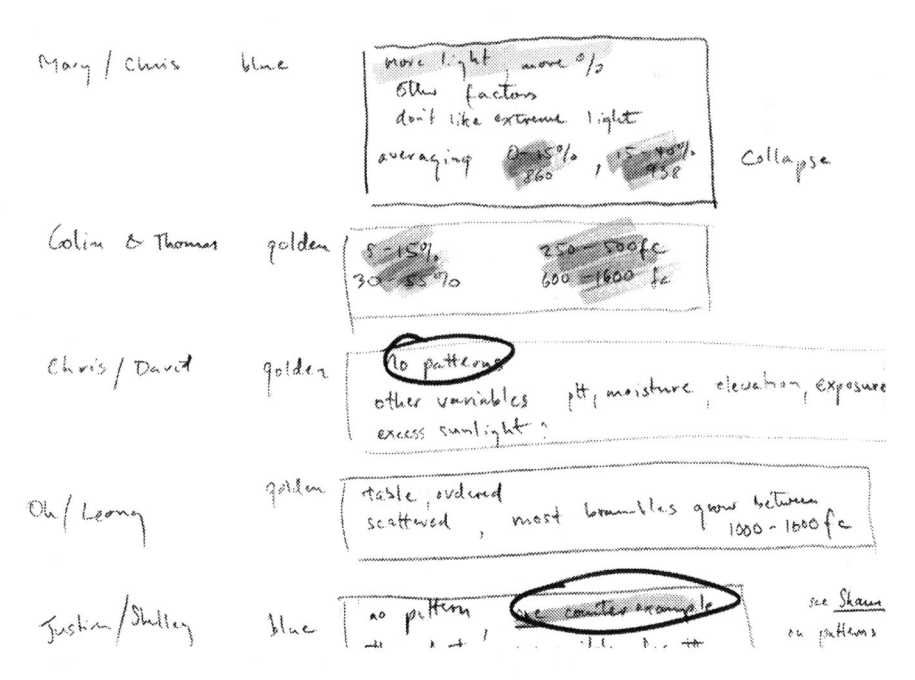

Figure 4.8. In this excerpt from my initial data analysis concerning the Lost Field Notebook task, one can see how different shading and circles are used as a means to identify patterns.

165

CHAPTER 4

Table 4.3. Distribution of solutions to "Lost Field Notebook" problem

	Frequency of Inscriptions Used (%)[1]				
	Mathematical				Verbal only
	Graph	Average	Ordered table	Pattern map	List
(n = 19 pairs)	37	11	11	16	0	42

Note 1: Some groups produced more than one representation.

Once I had done the summaries for all students in the three eighth-grade classes, I used different colors of markers and a pen to highlight or circle similar approaches. For example, the two circled items in Figure 4.8 both involve answers where students suggested that there are no patterns in the data set they were working on despite the fact that they had different versions. Other colors and even double-colored highlights are visible in the figure as different shades of grey.

Of the 19 groups (I excluded the group with the student who had originated the data set that I had used as template), 11 had used some form of mathematical inscription, whereas eight groups made only verbal presentations (Table 4.3). Among the mathematical inscriptions were seven graphed solutions, two tables with ordered values, two answers that resembled correlations between two dichotomous items (tetrachoric correlations), and three pattern maps (one group produced three inscriptions). Ten groups explicitly discussed variables other than light intensity that could have affected plant density and thus prevented a clear pattern from emerging from their data set. Seven groups suggested measurement or transcription errors as possible sources for the "irregularities" in the possibly existing pattern.

Because of the small number of groups involved, good statistical analyses were impossible. However, we attempted to get some idea whether this hypothesis about the differential use of mathematical forms was getting us anywhere. So we collapsed all the data into either mathematical or verbal-only responses; and we collapsed the numbers for the forms with five and eight data sets (thinking of it as "small data sets") to compare it against the responses to the form with 19 data pairs, which we considered to constitute a "large data set" (Figure 4.7).

Open Coding Use a highlighter to mark an answer that you see exhibits some pattern. When another student or group appears to exhibit the same pattern of reasoning or answering, then use the same color. Use different highlighter colors for different ideas. In the end, you will quickly see the distribution and frequency of ideas in the data you collected.

As a result, we had a two-by-two matrix with 7 and 3 mathematical representations for small and large data sets and 5 and 4 verbal only solutions for small and large data sets. This allowed us to do a tentative statistical test generally referred to as *chi-squared test* (χ^2), which revealed to us whether the distribution of responses across the small and large data sets was the same. The resulting test ($\chi^2(1) = 0.42$, $p = .51$) told me that I could not reject the null hypothesis of equal distributions; in other words, if we had said that there was a difference—e.g., more graphs for smaller than for larger data sets—there would have been more than 51 percent chance that we would have been wrong.

We conducted some more quantitative analyses. Thus, to find out if mathematics achievement would predict performance on the Lost Field Notebook task, a *discriminant analysis* was performed between groups who transformed the data into some other inscription versus those who did not. A discriminant analysis basically is a correlation where the independent variable is continuous (like a grade, an IQ measure) and the dependent variable is categorical (uses graph, does not use graph). Based on their mathematics term mark, a significant discriminant function was found that correctly classified 70 percent of the cases and accounted for 17.1 percent of the variance ($\chi^2(1) = 7.62$, $p < .01$). This analysis therefore told us that those groups with higher average mathematics achievement were more likely to transform the data into a graph, ordered data table, or pattern map; groups with lower average mathematics achievement were more likely to provide an answer based on inspection of the map alone. When contrasted with our earlier findings of no predictive quality of mathematics achievement on choice of inscription during field studies, this result added some support to the claim that, despite our contextualization efforts, the present task was more like a traditional mathematics textbook problem.

Plant Growth

One way that scientists can reduce the amount of data they collected is by calculating averages (means). On the basis of average grades schools are compared and school board policies are formed, and on the basis of average costs insurance rates differ according to color and make of car. Because of the importance of averages as inscriptions and data transformation techniques in the sciences, we were interested in their use by our students. Specifically, we wanted to know how students would deal with a situation in which they had to compare the growth rates of plants in two areas when the number of plants did not remain constant. This question had arisen from the investigation two students had conducted who seemingly could not resolve one of the issues that emerged fielding the process. As previously, this aspect of the study had become salient to me while transcribing and doing a preliminary analysis of the videotapes. Michael and I decided to design a word problem, which we again wanted to have *ecological validity*. Here is how the situation unfolded.

On May 16, I was looking at the transcript and the corresponding videotape that Guennadi had recorded for me on May 13 (Figure 4.9). I noted that James and Mike were having a problem with the fact that since their last visit to their field site, where they had recorded the size of the may-apple plants, there were two new plants. As they attempted to calculate the average size immediately, I watched them struggle how to deal with the additional plants, given that their average size had decreased. In my research notes I wrote "problem for Jamie" and then wrote down all the numbers that they were dealing with and talking about. On May 19, I constructed a task that began by simply articulating what I had seen on the video-

CHAPTER 4

Figure 4.9. Watching this video, featuring the data collecting James (left) and the data recording Mike (right), I noted that they struggled with the fact that against their expectations their average plant height had decreased because of several new plants.

tape (Figure 4.10). On May 21, I had recorded the following instruction to myself: "The issue with the growth in different areas if the number of plants changes. Use of a test to find out." This instruction had followed a longer note on mathematization and observations I was making on how James and Mike measured and recorded during their fieldwork. On the same day, I had a conversation with Michael Bowen about how to go about giving students the task. The outcome of the conversation was recorded in the following research note:

> May 21, 1992
> Negotiated with MB the use of the "average problem" in the class. Originally I wanted to have them do it in class so that I could videotape the students as they discussed the problem. However, MB's planning made it difficult to do the problem at that time, because he needs about 20 minutes for the sex role inventory [part of his own research in the pursuit of an MA in sociology], and he promised them 30 minutes to work on their latest vee map.
>
> We finally settled on giving the problem as homework, and then discussing it as a class during the first period next week. This is actually ideal, because we can then get to see how the class as a whole interacts to deal with different solutions (if there are any different ones).

In this research memo I articulated the contingencies that prevented me from recording students doing the task in the way we had done for the Lost Field Notebook task. During the evening of the same day, while transcribing the tape recorded May 21, I had made another note, this time handwritten: "Look at the average problem—appropriation of the problem by students but not in the way of the teacher."

Whereas I had to collect data source materials different from what I had wanted, we nevertheless gained good data allowing us to make some claims about how

QUANTITATIVE AND QUALITATIVE

Plant Growth
The following is a problem similar to that which some of your classmates faced when they were working in their ecozone. In your own group, try to solve the problem of this group.
   On Monday, Day 1 of your study you counted 3 may apples, a short plant with a single stalk, in each of your two test areas. The heights of each plants are recorded in Table 1. On Thursday, Day 4 of your study, you went to your ecozone again and found 3 may apples in Area 1, but 5 may apples in Area 2. The heights of each plant are recorded in Table 1. In Area 1 you have 400 foot candles of light, the pH level was 6.5. In Area 2 the level of light was 300 foot candles, the pH level was 6.8.

		Height of Plant	
Day	Plant #	Area 1	Area 2
1	1	17	19
1	2	20	22
1	3	23	16
2	1	18	20
2	2	21	23
2	3	24	17
2	4		5
2	5		12

Table 1

Answer the following questions
a.   How much growth do you observe? (Give a reason)
b.   In which area do you observe more growth? Why? (Give reasons for your answers)
c.   What is the average growth in each area? (Give a reasoned answer)
d.   From the information provided, what reasons for the growth patterns would you propose? Why?
e.   How could you test your hypotheses?

Figure 4.10. We observed students on videotape wrestling with the problem about how to figure out average growth if there are additional plants on the second field day.

students deal with the problem two of their own had faced in the field. When we analyzed the work students had done as a homework problem, we found that a fully mathematical approach was used by 38 percent of the students. That is, they had calculated the total growth of all plants in each zone to determine from it the average growth per plant (Solution A). Of these students, 38 percent also calculated the average growth per plant per day. A partially mathematical approach was used by 29 percent of the students. In their solutions, they first compared the growth rates of the existing plants (which were equal) and then reasoned that Area 2 showed more growth because of the added plants (Solution B). We did not further pursue the problem so that we were unable to show what these students would have done if the growth rates of existing plants had been different in the two areas. Nineteen percent of the students disregarded the new plants and indicated that the growth rates in the two areas were the same (Solution C). An equivalent approach would have focused on another dimension of growth, the total number of plants in each area, or the number of new plants. The remaining 14 percent of the students responded with answers that did not compare the growth rates. Steady growth rates in both areas, adding the heights at Day 1 and 2, and seeking other number patterns were some of the approaches these students used (Solution D).
   Before we asked students to do this problem, we conjectured that there might be a covariation between their mathematics grades and the levels at which they

mathematized the problem and its solution. In order to relate the students' approaches to their mathematical grades, we assigned 3 points for a fully mathematical approach, 2 points to the partially mathematical approach, 1 point for those solutions which disregarded the new plants, and 0 points for the other solutions. I decided on these scores on heuristic basis and to get some tentative idea. Other numbers (i.e., multiples of the scale) could have been chosen as well, including a nonlinear scale, though I did not have a good reason for choosing one. Based on the scale scores as assigned, there was no correlation between the students' mathematics grade and their solution on the problem ($r = .36$, $p > .05$). The covariation also was not statistically significant when we coded the solutions as correct or incorrect ($r = .42$, $p > .05$). To construct a better understanding, we studied in depth the learning of James as evidenced by our videotapes, interviews, and the written artifacts. Our case study revealed James' changing understanding and illustrated elements of all four solutions until he had developed a fully mathematical solution. We found that James' trajectory from initial understanding of the problem to his answers on the word problem was not a path from less to more mathematical but that his understanding varied with the context of the situation. But the classroom norm of using more and more abstract inscriptions encouraged James to move toward using that representation favored by the scientific community, although his initial solution had been legitimate and was not in need of change.

MAJOR DIMENSIONS OF LEARNING FROM THE STUDY

From this study, we published four major research articles. We were interested in publishing the findings, because we felt that if our work passed muster in the peer review process, we would have even stronger arguments in our school context where parents seemed to think that direct teaching (lecturing) of science and teaching "the basics" was the best way to prepare their sons and daughters for the future. (In fact, as shown in chapter 5, some of the older students adopted constructivism as their epistemology, and precisely for this reason wanted more direct teaching thinking that if open-inquiry allows different interpretations and understandings to emerge, then students also need to be told which answers will get them high scores on tests and examinations.) Once published in the scientific literature, we felt to have a much stronger card for continuing with and developing the kind teaching that we were doing in the science department.

In the article entitled "An investigation of problem solving in the context of a grade 8 open-inquiry science program" (Roth & Bowen, 1993), we documented and discussed the enormous work done by students in constructing research problems and resolving these problems through their engagement in independent field research. We showed how during this field research, many local problems emerged that students learned to resolve with their peers and the settings in a transactional manner. The students' framing of problems for research and their work processes in the field setting stood in sharp contrast with their work on teacher-constructed, contextual word problems. These differences led us to a critical analysis of traditional word problems. We found that the students' achievements in each of these situations emerged out of transactions (a) within a classroom community that encouraged independence, collaboration, and negotiation of meaning and (b) with the physical setting. Students' achievements and learning were meaningful because they were indexed to and situated in the setting of the students' experience.

Our second report entitled "Mathematization of experience in a grade 8 open-inquiry environment: An introduction to the representational practices of science" (Roth & Bowen, 1994) focused on the use of mathematical inscriptions and the development of the practices. We showed with extensive data from the unit that in the setting provided, students increasingly used mathematical representations such as graphs and data tables to support their claims in a convincing manner; the use of equations and percent calculations did not change over the course of the study. Inscriptions such as graphs, maps, averages, and mathematical equations were not only useful in themselves, but also as conscription devices (see chapter 2) in the construction of which students were able to engage each other in the collaborative construction of meaning. That is, the very nature of these inscriptions as material entities tended to provide a way for students to focus on common issues and thereby assist them in making sense. We also demonstrated that the use of inscriptions as conscription devices illustrates how the use and understanding of inscriptions changes over time. (Readers can see how the idea of inscriptions and conscription devices became central in my thinking across studies, to a large extent mediated by the attention these received in the social studies of science, a discipline where I also was and continue to be a member of the major international organization [Society for the Social Studies of Science, 4S].) Understanding graphs, tables, and other mathematical forms as inscription and conscription devices focuses on the social aspects of knowing, which has important implications for our teacher-researchers' conceptualization of learning and the organization of our science classrooms.

In our third paper, "Knowing and interacting: A study of culture, practices, and resources in a grade 8 open-inquiry science classroom guided by a cognitive apprenticeship metaphor" (Roth & Bowen, 1995), we analyzed the processes of knowing and interacting in this open-inquiry learning environment. We particularly highlighted the fact that it was planned and implemented by teachers (Michael Bowen and I) who used the metaphor *cognitive apprenticeship* as a referent for guiding their teaching. Based on detailed analyses of students' conversations, we documented the construction of and changes in eighth-grade students' understandings as they engaged in inquiries for which they planned focus questions, designed data collection procedures, and interpreted the findings. Through their interactions, the students also arrived at private meanings which they did not report in their findings and which are often overlooked by teachers who use static end-of-unit tests to measure student learning. We showed that in conducting their inquiries, students successfully negotiated courses of actions and established group structures through which they organized their transactions. Formal and informal transactions between students and research groups facilitated the formation of networks that contributed to the quick diffusion of knowledge necessary in the construction of a community of practice.

CHAPTER 4

On my own and already at the university, I wrote a fourth major research article entitled "Where is the context in contextual word problems?: Mathematical practices and products in Grade 8 students' answers to story problems" (Roth, 1996b). In this study I reported an investigation about how students approach contextual word/story problems such as the ones featured in this chapter (Lost Field Notebook, Plant Growth). I showed that problems in school mathematics do not become contextual by embedding them in more descriptions of story situations. Rather, the materials I had collected together with Michael Bowen supported the contention that a problem is contextualized if the mathematical practices in which students engage are integrated in a larger array of meaningful practices. I described how we had observed students in two types of situations: (a) open-inquiry field studies that included the production of convincing representations (inscriptions) to support findings and (b) word problems with stories and student-produced data based on these field studies. Through my analyses of students' mathematical practices I was able to show that word problems did not become more contextual through the narratives that depicted students doing field work, although the story situations were very familiar to the students (describing an aspect of their own activities) and although the inscription used as a template for presenting information had been produced by one of the students. Students' inscription-oriented practices in word-problem situations contrasted with those they employed during fieldwork. In a way, therefore, I also provided some evidence for the contention that the sciences constitute a suitable school subject in the context of which students can develop mathematical competencies. This solidified what I was learning through teacher-researcher investigations in my own physics classrooms, where students developed tremendous mathematical competencies that subsequently allowed them to do very well in their mathematics courses, where the curriculum covered the material and concepts from a mathematical perspective only after the students already were familiar with these.

QUANTITATIVE AND QUALITATIVE

A major advantage of our study was that we did not allow ourselves to fall into the trap of polarizing our work into a dichotomy of the quantitative versus qualitative. Rather, throughout the study we were driven by our questions and by a desire to better understand how students learned in this very unusual learning environment, what they appropriated in terms of scientific concepts and process as well as about science, and how their learning related to achievement and perceptions. We also had political goals: we wanted to construct evidence supporting our claims that the students not only learned but also, and more importantly, that they learned more than they were supposed to according to the provincial statements of required learning outcomes. In fact, we subsequently showed that on the data interpretation tasks our student groups outperformed new science teachers near graduation all of whom already had obtained bachelors or masters degrees in science. The difference between the number of eighth-grade student groups and the number of university students who used some mathematical representations rather than just verbal (vernacular) explanations for the presence or absence of patterns on the Lost Field Notebook task was statistically significant. However, we did not interpret these results to mean that our eighth-grade students were more intelligent or higher achievers than the future teachers. Rather, we suggested that our eighth-grade students had learned in an environment that encouraged them to make arguments and to use mathematical representations (graphs, statistics, ordered tables) for better supporting their claims than if they simply had used words.

In the pursuit of answers to our questions, we used those research methods that we deemed to be best suited. For example, we used statistics when we wanted to show how grades were related to the measures from the learning environment scale (CLES); we also used statistics to show how the use of mathematical representations in response to the Plant Growth problem was correlated with the students' grades. The statistics allowed us to support arguments that went beyond the particular classrooms in which we conducted the study. Thus, we were able to say something like "students taught in this manner learn more biology and mathematical methods than those taught in a different way" rather than merely saying that *our* students knew more than the students in some other class. In our case, we made claims that were general, concerning the entire population of students taught in the manner we did; in the second case, our claims would have been limited to *these* students. On the other hand, we used interpretive analyses for making sense of the processes we observed in our videotaped materials and used forms of analysis inspired by discourse and conversation analysis to interpret what students were saying, how they argued, and how they achieved consensus.

The ultimate point is not whether one uses this or that method to conduct a teacher-researcher project; rather, the point is to find yourself an interesting research question the answer to pursue which promises to be useful for one or the other purpose you might have. In our work, Michael and I wanted to improve our classroom learning environments, and the kind of qualitative studies we did allowed us to answer questions about how to improve what we were doing. But the statistical studies allowed us to make and support claims related to issues that the school and parents were concerned about: achievement and how it related to what we were doing in our science classes. The quantitative analyses also made our findings more convincing to the community of researchers concerned with science and mathematics learning. Such researchers are not so much interested in the question whether a *particular* school has increased achievement scores but in questions such as whether particular approaches to teaching science increase achievement scores *generally*. The statistical findings gave more weight to what we were saying in our discussions with school and parents because we had supported claims about learning generally—by extrapolating from our students to students of this kind generally using appropriate statistical methods that also reveal the degree to which the extrapolation is likely to be erroneous—rather than about the specific learning of a small group of students.

Some researchers make the claim that one's interests drive the research method. There are said to be three types of interests: *technical*, *practical*, and *emancipatory* (Habermas, 1971). The kinds of knowledge corresponding to these interests are

CHAPTER 4

instrumental (causal explanatory), *practical* (understanding), and *emancipatory* (reflective), respectively. The research methods associated with them are grounded in the positivistic sciences (empirical-analytic), interpretive (hermeneutic) sciences, and critical social sciences (critical theory), respectively. In the educational research literature, these distinctions sometimes are used to argue that the third form of knowledge (emancipatory), theories, and methods is better for teachers or truer to their interests and concerns. However, my writing of this chapter was driven among others by the intent to show how two teachers engaged in a variety of problems using a variety of methods to pursue a variety of interests and needs employ the methods necessary to answer interests rather than employ a method because this is all they have available. None of these methods inherently is better than the others; they simply are useful in pursuing questions that have different aims although the same individuals have asked them. Ultimately, all these methods—i.e., empirical-quantitative, interpretive-hermeneutic, and critical-reflective—allowed us to expand our room to maneuver, the possibilities for actions we had, and therefore, our agency with respect to parents, school administrators, and students. The statistical methods were part of an arsenal of methods that we (the science teachers in my department) used for emancipatory purposes.

TEACHER-RESEARCHER COLLABORATIONS

Throughout this teacher-researcher study, Michael Bowen and I closely worked together. Michael did a lot of the planning for the unit, checking with me on the need to design specific lessons. For example, one night I recorded a note to the effect that learning in the eighth-grade class might be enhanced if students had opportunities to discuss their work with individuals from different groups, especially if the task was set up such that they had to defend the research question, their approach to answering it, and their results. On the next day, I discussed this with Michael, who then set aside time during a subsequent lesson for students to do precisely that. He divided the class into groups of four and asked the students to discuss their research designs and findings. I recorded the gist of our conversations in research notes that were saved as dated files on my computer (where they are available to this day) and I also printed them out so that Michael could subsequently comment on them.

I took much of the responsibility for generating the videotapes and transcriptions, interviewing, and also for photocopying student-produced notebooks, laboratory reports, field notebooks, and so on. I also kept meeting notes and other materials that set up the audit trail for this teacher-researcher investigation. Every now and then, Michael came to my office to see parts of a videotape so that we could discuss what was happening. He also read through the transcripts and my research notes, annotating as he went along, and pasting sticky notes on the top of the pages with commentaries, theoretical concepts, and directions for what to do next (Figure 4.11). He frequently provided additional observations that supported the cases I was using in support of some concept. I already mentioned the situation where he had supplemented my text concerning the "spreading hypothesis" with another

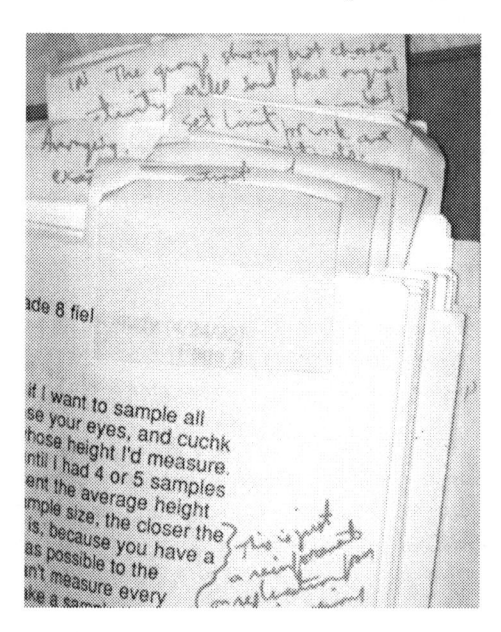

Figure 4.11. My teacher-researcher collaborator annotated the transcriptions, field notes, theoretical memos, and initial analyses and added sticky notes with his commentaries, theoretical concepts, and instructions for next steps.

case. Similarly, he annotated my handwritten research note "The tools provided become boundaries (limitations). Though sometimes used creatively" (May 26) by pointing to a particular case he had observed—Dilraj had used a soil corer for sampling worm density to find whether there was a correlation with depth ("Such as soil corer for sampling for worm density."). His note ended with the entry "Divergent thinking?," which in fact constituted a theoretical concept that he advanced as a possible candidate for explaining the creative use of tools and representations that I was remarking on the same page in the research memo folder.

Conducting the teacher-researcher study collaboratively allowed us (Michael and I) to deal with the numerous problems that emerge in such an effort; we were also able to separate teaching from some of the dimensions of research in the way institutional research ethics boards want them to be separated—though at the time, no such board regulated what we were doing and although at the time, even at the universities, the conditions were much less stringent for getting a teacher-researcher study approved. For example, we clearly separated grading, for which Michael Bowen was responsible, from research analysis, for which I took the responsibility during the school year. I took full responsibility for collecting most of the materials, such as the interviews about the learning environment, which I made available to Michael only once the school year had ended.

Although we discussed the structure of any tasks that students were asked to complete—doing a word problem, discussing their findings—Michael Bowen took responsibility for organizing the two sections of his science course. I was always present as a visitor, though I engaged with students, asking them questions about their inquiries and responded to their queries when they felt they needed advice.

The presence of a laboratory assistant, Guennadi Verechaka, and the teaching intern, Allan Clark, made it possible for Michael to teach the unit where students were spread over a distance of 1.5 kilometers and frequently out of sight of each other. Some teachers may feel that these are special conditions, and they are right. But I have taught seventh-grade classes doing outside research far from the school and any habitations with over 20 students from poverty-stricken areas and never have had problems. But this additional help was definitely an asset in the collection of the data source materials because we knew that there always was a backup when needed to do the videotaping or to get assistance with the photocopying of the artifacts students had produced.

Readers easily can imagine that there was another benefit arising from doing a collaborative teacher-researcher investigation: It allowed us to overcome the isolation that teachers often face. Because we made wise use of our time and enacted a division of labor appropriate for our context, we came to work together extensively concerning central issues of learning and teaching science. I am not attempting to argue that the way in which we enacted a collaborative teacher-researcher investigation constitutes *the* (only) method. Rather, I think that each context has its own constraints and possibilities that resident teachers are the best to harness for their purposes. I am certain that in such a collaborative project sufficient materials can be generated to support the writing of two or three theses and even dissertations. Viewed in this way, teacher-research becomes a central means to professional development that ought to be our own concern rather than that of others who impose it upon us.

CHAPTER 5

ANALYZING DISCOURSE

Text and Speech, Content and Interactions

In the course of the two-year period from 1988 to 1990, my thinking and teaching radically changed. First, I encountered (radical) constructivism with its main contention that knowledge is not out there but that there is only knowledge that the individual constructs in and for him- or herself. In other words, radical constructivists hold that there is no information getting into the individual from the environment but that any knowledge always is constructed inside. All we can ever know is whether this knowledge fits our behavior in the world rather than whether it is true. Knowledge is good when it allows a person to successfully predict situations; we cannot ever test this knowledge for its truth-value, that is, whether its structures are identical (isomorphic) to the structures of the world outside. At the time I encountered constructivism, I was going through an upheaval precisely because I had used lectures sparsely in my teaching career and instead allowed students to learn science by doing laboratory experiments or to learn mathematics through their own explorations. But if there are no patterns in nature that one can see and learn in investigations, then I had been barking up the wrong (pedagogical) tree in all my teaching to that point.

The second major revelation came to me during the summer of 1990, while reading ethnographic research studies reporting on the way science really is done (see chapter 3). Largely conducted from a social studies of science perspective, this research suggested that science and scientific knowledge are *social* constructions. That is to say, what ultimately comes to be accepted as scientific knowledge is the outcome of processes within (scientific) *communities*, including the processes by which claims are hardened through the successive removal of modifiers (e.g., going from the tentative "*I think* DNA has a double-helix structure" to the affirmative "DNA *has* a double-helix structure") and the replication of experiments in other laboratories around the world. These reports also showed that scientific research is contingent, which means that even the same researchers cannot necessarily make an experiment work under all circumstances or after moving into a different laboratory. The results of these ethnographic studies therefore undermined the very claim of natural scientists that the knowledge they construct is universal and factual.

Whereas these ethnographic studies changed my understanding of the nature of science, they also gave me hope again in the use of laboratory experiences as a way of introducing middle and high school students to science and even in the approach that they can in fact learn (at least some) scientific concepts through their own engagement in independent research projects. Once I dropped the idea that

CHAPTER 5

students can get the accepted scientific facts and concepts directly from their experiments and once I had moved to thinking about the negotiation of differences in perceptions and ideas, then there were new opportunities for open-inquiry science learning environments: All I had to do was get students into groups so that they could collaboratively conduct investigations, which differed from group to group. By setting up transaction opportunities within my classrooms concerning the purposes for conducting investigations, differences in their results when they conduct the same investigation, the usefulness of research questions and the solidity of the results, then students could gain an understanding not only of relevant and salient scientific concepts but also of science as process. Much of this would occur through interactions in small-group discussions and whole-class sessions, so that students would have the opportunity to engage in the social construction of knowledge, which they could then appropriate for themselves. Or so I reasoned at the time.

I realized however that high school students, by the time they ended up in my junior- and senior-level physics courses, will have had considerable experiences with schooling, most of which would have been in terms of the knowledge transfer metaphor. To allow them to reflect on scientific knowledge generally and their knowing and learning specifically, students needed—so I thought—opportunities for thinking about and talking through issues concerning the nature of knowledge. I therefore decided to plan regular whole-class discussions about the nature of science, scientific knowledge, and learning; and to provide my students with something to talk *about*, I would choose selected readings that provided different perspectives on knowing and knowledgeability than those perspectives and ideologies that they have come to be familiar with.

The question I asked myself at the time was whether my curriculum innovations would make any difference. Would students start to think differently about the nature of science and scientific knowledge when they (a) conducted open-ended laboratory experiments and (b) engaged in the discussion of texts that presented knowledge as socially constructed? Over the 1990–1991 Christmas holidays, while thinking about what I would be doing during the following term (March through May), I decided to conduct a small-scale study where I would ask my eleventh-grade students to respond to some items concerning the nature of scientific knowledge. I also thought that it would be good to have my students write an open-ended essay on the topic of knowing and learning and then interview a few of them so I would get more detailed information about their thinking. I thought that this then would give me some idea where they were with respect to their thinking concerning science and scientific knowledge after about six months in my physics course. As Christmas fell in the middle of our second school term, I decided to do this study at the beginning of the third and final term of the school year.

I did this small-scale investigation in the course of March and April 1991, and, in the course of the subsequent summer holidays, I analyzed the data. I found that a large number of students still thought about knowledge in a traditional way. But I also realized that I could develop this small-scale study into something larger, especially given the fact that some of these students would take my senior-level physics course. This would provide me with an opportunity to extend the study and see whether spending two years in my alternatively taught physics course would somehow mediate how students were talking and thinking about science and knowledge. During the summer of 1991, at the end of July, I wrote a memo to myself:

> IN HOW FAR ARE THESE LABS A REFLECTION OF "REAL" SCIENCE? An answer should be given in terms of the findings of current sociology of knowledge. Although there are accomplishments in terms of older conceptualizations such as the process skills, though from a new and critical perspective, these may not be the most advantageous to understanding the processes in these labs.
>
> SHOULD WE TEACH SUCH AS TO PROVIDE CONTEXTS OF REAL SCIENCE AS CURRENTLY UNDERSTOOD BY EPISTEMOLOGY, HISTORY OF SCIENCE, AND SOCIOLOGY OF KNOWLEDGE? What are the implications for content? What are the implications for standardized curricula? This would mean that we distance ourselves from older conceptions that tried to teach for example the "processes of science" separately (SAPA) from content, or current practice of focusing almost exclusively on content. These older approaches are in contradiction with current understanding of science and the construction of knowledge (its epistemology). Constructivism does favor different foci of instruction than those of the old paradigm. Cognitive apprenticeship is compatible with the constructivist paradigm, and provides for situations where students can be enculturated into the practices of real science. This enculturation gives a direction and does not permit complete openness or a willy-nilly of divergent activities. Ultimately the question is if we want a normative curriculum (or curriculum guidelines), or one that is sufficiently open to local interpretations of responsible and responsive practitioners.
>
> DO SCIENTISTS PERCEIVE SCIENCE IN AN OBJECTIVIST FASHION? If then, what are the implications of that on instruction? Compared to the conception of social scientists, historians, and epistemologists? (Notes 7/31/1991)

Readers should note that at the time I had many questions concerning the role that the students' laboratory investigations might have in their development of ideas about science and knowledge. My questions also related to the relationship between doing open inquiry and the learning of specific content. My memo specifically made reference to one science curriculum, *Science—A Process Approach* (SAPA), which had been designed to allow elementary students to develop the process skills said to be typical of "real science." My memo made reference to constructivism, the epistemology that I had become familiar with, and cognitive apprenticeship as a metaphor for learning to think in scientific ways. This metaphor should become a major resource for me for thinking about science education at the time: I wanted students to go through experiences where they faced situations similar to scientists, and where, when they struggled, I could interact with

CHAPTER 5

them as I would if I were a professor training graduate students. As seen in chapter 1 and especially in chapter 4, my colleagues and I made extensive use of this metaphor for thinking about our science curriculum and for the way in which we taught, that is, engaged in conversations with our students.

The thoughts articulated in the preceding paragraphs would guide me in setting up even more discussions and opportunities for students to reflect on the nature of science and scientific knowledge and they would guide me in collecting sufficient data source materials to be able to make claims about the development of students' thoughts over a period of time that by far exceeded the normal length of studies in the field—generally no more than a few weeks and often only representing students' ideas at a single point in time. I had already done some analyses of the initial data source materials collected, which I ended up presenting at conferences in 1992 and subsequently publishing in pertinent research journals.

It turned out that in the process of analyzing and then extending the study into a second year, I came to read a sociological analysis of scientists' talk about their research: *Opening Pandora's Box: A Sociological Analysis of Scientists' Discourse* (Gilbert & Mulkay, 1984). This book led me to find out about a second book, *Discourse and Social Psychology: Beyond Attitudes and Behaviour* (Potter & Wetherell, 1987). The two books radically changed how I was thinking about knowing, perhaps even more radically than the books on the social construction of knowledge that I had read during the summer of 1990. In fact, the two books came to lay the foundation for my interest in linguistics and discourse studies. All of sudden I realized that human beings generally and researchers specifically never have access to the minds of other people: All that we ever have are our respective actions and talk. As children, these actions and talk provide us with resources for developing our own ways of acting and talking without that we ever have direct access to the minds (knowledge) of adults, who nevertheless are said to bequeath their culture to the subsequent generations. Similarly, teachers and teacher-researchers specifically and social scientists more generally never have access to the minds of the students they teach or of the individuals they research—*talk* is all that they ever have access to. Why not stick with talk and theorize it, as well as theorize learning in terms of talk and the way it changes as a consequence of participating in everyday situations both in and out of schools?

Today, the changes I was undergoing can be seen at multiple levels—the references I used in the first two articles on students' talk about the nature of science and scientific knowledge following the small-scale studies substantially differed from the references I used in subsequent articles that analyzed the data source materials that I collected over the entire two-year period. Also, the tenor of the article titles changed: initially they included the term "students' views" and later contained terms such as "students' discourse." The change was not just cosmetic, for discourse is a resource that we all have available and that inherently is a social tool, a resource, and a terrain so that everything said inherently is presumed intelligible. No longer is the analysis of text and speech concerned with the individual mind but with the ways speech (language) communities make available resources to their members for expressing themselves about certain topics. Thus, any individual no longer is viewed in and for itself, but as a member of a speech community who concretely realizes the possibilities for talking (about) certain topics using the resources language provides to the collective. In a sense, therefore, at issue no longer are the particular individuals participating in a conversation but language itself, which can be understood as realizing itself in and through the conversationalists.

A second development occurred in the course of analyzing my materials from the study I ultimately conducted. Initially I had thought about discourse as a medium that I could analyze as a phenomenon in itself. I later came to realize that analyzing text outside the societal situation in and for which it is employed makes little sense, for the texts are not merely *about* something but rather constitute (produce) the very situation *in* which it occurs. For example, an interview does not just get persons talking about what they think in the process of which they use language as a (neutral) mediational means; it is not just a container in which interviewer and interviewee find themselves. Rather, language is a means for *making the interview independently from what it may be about*. That is, once we begin to think about talk (a) as being *about* some topic and (b) as a means for *making the interview context* in the process of talking about some topic, then the way in which we analyze interviews and their transcript has to change.

In this chapter, I describe how I collected the data source materials and how the ways in which I analyzed them changed over the course of a few years while my understanding of the nature of discourse changed. I also touch on how students might become part of a research project: In this study, one of my students (Todd Alexander) became so interested that he asked me to be involved as a student-researcher and full member of our two-person research team. Todd then conducted some of the interviews and analyzed the data source materials with me. He also collaborated presenting our results at an ethnography conference in a novel format—we used a re-enacted, improvised conversation to present our findings—and co-authored an article with me, which eventually also was included in an anthology of innovative methods for doing science education research.

ASPECTS OF THE CURRICULUM AND SOURCES OF DATA

In this as in all other studies, I made clear distinctions between tasks required by the normal curriculum and, if any, tasks required for the sole purpose of research. In addition to their normal experimental and textbook-related tasks, I wanted students to read selected material relating to epistemology. I thought that without reflecting about knowing and learning and thereby learning about learning, students would not get from their school experiences what they ought to know. (In writing the previous sentence, I am thinking of the diction "what every schoolboy should know," which was also used as a chapter title by Gregory Bateson, one of the authors that my students were reading.) To me, education goes beyond schooling, and as a teacher I am interested in fostering the former and I am critical in the ways the latter gets realized—likely one of the reasons why there was no love lost between numerous school administrators overly concerned with rules and myself,

CHAPTER 5

(perhaps overly) concerned with providing students with the resources and context for educating themselves, growing, and developing as human beings. The students reflected on these readings in written essays that were followed up by whole-class discussions.

Readings

The epistemology-related materials read by my students during their junior year included selected chapters from Gregory Bateson's (1980) *Mind and Nature: A Necessary Unity* and David Suzuki's (1989) *Inventing the Future: Reflections on Science, Technology, and Nature*. Both authors differ in their approach to the nature of scientific knowledge from the regular fare to which students normally are indoctrinated in school science. The nature of the authors' stance to knowing is best expressed in the following quote from one of the readings:

> Epistemology is always *personal*. The point of the probe is always in the heart of the explorer: What is *my* answer to the question of the nature of knowing? I surrender to the belief that my knowing is a small part of a wider integrated knowing that knits the entire biosphere or creation. (Bateson, 1980, p. 93, emphases in the original)

David Suzuki is a well-known Canadian geneticist who had become a journalist and now is a recognized protector of the environment who has come to value the position of Canadian First Nations tribes concerning environment and environmental issues. He, too, stands for a personal view of knowing, which is part of a wider biosphere.

Students who enrolled in senior physics read, as an integral part of their program, chapters 1 through 11 from *Inventing Reality: Physics as Language* by Bruce Gregory (1990), the associate director of the Harvard Smithsonian Institute of Astrophysics. I made the decision to leave out the remaining five chapters because these appeared to me more difficult for high school students than the first two-thirds of the book. As a teacher, I felt that the views of physics expressed in this book provided an interesting contrast to the students' textbook and that therefore quite interesting discussions might arise. Furthermore, in the course of the two years, the students had covered many of the physical phenomena that Gregory used to support his contention that physics is more like a *language game* rather than a representation of the world as it really is. I chose this book because it was consistent with my own position at the time, a social constructivist understanding of the field as developed in the social studies of science. It thus appeared to be a useful but alternative companion to the students' textbook that articulated a traditional view of scientific

---

Epistemology literally is the science (Gr. εεεε [logos]) of knowledge (Gr. εεæεεμε [episteme]). How we think about knowing and learning, our epistemology, shapes what we teacher-researchers do in our classrooms. This, in turn, shapes the kind of data source materials we collect and how we look at what and how students learn, how we interact with them, and the role language plays in our transactions.

knowledge. (Students all by themselves came to characterize their physics textbooks as written in the same authoritative style as the Christian Bible, which one has to take as is or reject. Students in my class repeatedly talked about having to take physics on faith in the same way that one has to take the contents of the Bible, Koran, or any other doctrinaire text on faith.) In the opening statement of the preface, the author outlines his program and sets the tone for the remainder of the book:

> Physics has been so immensely successful that it is difficult to avoid the conviction that what physicists have done over the past 300 years is to slowly draw back the veil that stands between us and the world as it really is—that physics, and every science, is the discovery of a ready-made world. As powerful as this metaphor is, it is useful to keep in mind that it *is* a metaphor, and that there are other ways of looking at physics and at science in general. (Gregory, 1990, p. v, italics in the original)

The author further explains that the book (a) tells a story of how physicists invented and improved languages to talk about, describe, and theorize the world; and he (b) explores the relationship between language and the world—where "language" includes all forms of scientific representations such as mathematics, diagrams, and words. In his narrative of how physics-related languages were invented, developed, and discarded, Gregory only touches on highlights rather than delving into historical details and caveats. Following a number of language philosophers in the American pragmatist tradition (e.g., John Dewey, Richard Rorty), Gregory portrays the relationship between language and world as socially constructed; the choice between competing ways of using language is always made on pragmatic grounds.

Student Writing

Writing constitutes an essential learning process and radically differs from talking, as can be gauged from the fact that oral cultures are very different from writing cultures when it comes to thinking and reasoning (Ong, 1982). It is for this reason that I believe writing to constitute an important element of learning to think like scientists—though I also believe that educational researchers do not yet know enough about the relationship between talking (science, mathematics, history, etc.) and writing (science, mathematics, history, etc.) and how the two can be used together in classrooms to foster student learning. Nevertheless, for me the science teacher, writing about the nature of science, scientific knowledge, and learning constitutes an important element for allowing students to become aware and self-conscious. In my course, I had two different kinds of writing assignments: structured writing, essays, and reflections.

Structured Writing One of the ways in which I engaged students to think about the nature of science and scientific knowledge was by means of a structured assignment in which they were asked to respond to five statements by indicating their

CHAPTER 5

level of agreement: "agree," "disagree," or "other." That is, this task initially forced students to make a choice. The assignment as presented to students is presented in Figure 5.1. Checking one of the answer possibilities would have been too easy, because it does not necessitate thinking. Therefore, following the opening part of the assignment, I asked students to justify and explain each of their answers in a three- to five-sentence statement. To better understand students' epistemological commitments, I had chosen statements that portrayed various aspects of the nature of scientific knowledge and the nature of its origin from either an objectivist or a constructivist position. In this way, I hoped to engage them in thinking about issues that to me are central to being an educated citizen.

Open-ended Essays As a teacher, I wanted students to come prepared to the five class discussions about pairs of chapters from *Inventing Reality*. Also, I believed that it is in articulating one's thoughts in writing that very different forms of understanding evolve. Finally, in whole-class discussions, there were always some students who talked more than others; a few even may have remained silent for the entirety of a discussion. More so, it is a mere game of numbers that there is too little time for anyone student to express himself (these were all-boys classes) extensively during one lesson. Thus, when I asked students to read something, I also asked them to write some reflections or an essay on the topic of the reading. These essays constituted regular assignments in my courses and the students received credit for them. Concerning *Inventing Reality*, students completed five reflective essays, each followed by a class discussion.

After completing the book, students studied the units on the wave and particle nature of light and matter as part of their regular curriculum content. This topic also featured prevalently in *Inventing Reality* so that students obtained a different perspective on the same topic through their work with the physics textbook. To engage them in further thinking, I therefore assigned an essay in which students were asked to reflect on the nature of light on the basis of their (a) reading of *In-*

Name _____

Circle whether you agree, disagree, or have another opinion on each of the following statements.

1. Scientific knowledge is artificial and does not show nature as it really is.   Agree Disagree Other
2. Scientific knowledge more and more approximates truth.   Agree Disagree Other
3. Science, like art, religion, commerce, warfare, and even sleep, is based on presuppositions.   Agree Disagree Other
4. Scientific laws and theories exist independent of human existence. Scientists merely discover them.   Agree Disagree Other
5. The social environment of a scientist will not influence the content of the knowledge he or she proposes.   Agree Disagree Other

All the above statements concerned science and scientific knowledge. In the space provided below, provide an explanation for your answers to the above questions

Figure 5.1. Questionnaire used to solicit specific answers, which students subsequently defended by writing supportive statements.

venting Reality and (b) experiences relative to the textbook. So that readers obtain a sense for the nature of these essays as data sources, I provide here an excerpt from one of the essays written after the students had read chapters 7 and 8. These essays became an integral part of my data source materials, which I subsequently used as part of the analysis of students' discourses on the nature of science, scientific knowledge, and theories of learning.

> I find myself questioning what is "truth" through out these chapters. The idea that there is a common set of underlying facts that mold the universe and its occurrences becomes a more difficult concept to grasp as new ideas are put forth by man and the old ideas, "truths" are left by the wayside. I still disagree with the idea that all knowledge is relative and believe in an absolute set of laws which governs nature. Yet Bohr's comment that "the laws of physics are our laws and not natures," on the surface seems to contradict with my view however I find that it is in agreement with it.
>
> Heisenberg's uncertainty principal which states that the position of an electron can be determined as accurately as desired with the cost of knowing less and less about its movement as we determine its position more accurately, creates dubious truths. This principle leads us to the ultimate conclusion that "position and motion do not seem to be properties of the subatomic world" but instead "seem to be our way of talking about the subatomic world." From these statements I realize that truth has always been for man, laws or facts that can be related to their perception of the world. The only truth we are able to get out of the subatomic world is that which we can derive from our own perception of it, it is impossible for us to understand and therefore relate to a world that is beyond our perception. This idea is difficult to grasp, we cannot perceive a world where position and motion are absent because these are qualities which we perceive. If we were bees and thus had the ability to see within the ultraviolet spectrum, then we could not understand a human world which was void of this perception. From these examples we realize that truth for us as humans is that which we can perceive, combined with what we don't perceive transformed into the terms of our perception, i.e., ultraviolet spectrum, light which we do not see however detectable form of energy causing skin cancer, subatomic world one which exists with the absence of our notion of position and motion. (Preston, Essay 4)

Whole-Class Discussions

To me, as a science teacher, whole-class discussions are an important way of learning. In the course of my own experiences of learning in everyday life, I have come to realize that learning something is less a matter of getting stuff into my head and more something of coming to participate in the knowledgeable ways of a culture together with other members. That is, the way we have come to think about learning, preparing ourselves for examinations, is not a good paradigm for how human

CHAPTER 5

beings learn. Rather, becoming good at something in everyday situations is a much better paradigm for thinking about learning. For example, as part of my research, I did a five-year study on knowing and learning in fish hatcheries. To better understand what it means to knowledgeably feed fish, I fed fish; to know what it means to extract fish eggs from does and milt from the males, I participated in extracting eggs and milt; at the hatchery, we subsequently mixed the eggs and milt in buckets so that the former would be fertilized. It was in and through participating in the life of a fish hatchery that I became knowledgeable about hatching and raising fish; and I simultaneously became knowledgeable about talking with fish culturists about the things that are integral part of their everyday life in the fish hatchery.

With respect to schooling, I began to think at the time about knowing and learning in terms of communities of practice. An important part in which individuals in any community learn is by having conversations with other members. To get my students to talk, I was increasingly organizing opportunities for them to talk—discussing contradictory outcomes of experiments (chapter 3), talking over and about concept maps (chapters 1 and 2), and, here, talking about the ideas in books and selected chapters. As a matter of course—in part because I wanted to improve their ability to discuss and argue—I videotaped or audiotaped the discussions and subsequently transcribed them for analysis. These transcripts became an integral part of my data source materials. To give readers a better sense of the nature of the data source materials that I had available for subsequent analysis, I present here a brief excerpt from the discussion following chapters 9 and 10 of *Inventing Reality*.

Todd:	I think he is going a little nuts when he says that we can change the past and the future (???)
Peter:	The universe?
Todd:	May be relative to our session things happen outside of what we perceive if we like it or not, but we can't change if we think about, about actually what happens.
Michael:	Yea, we can't change what actually happened but we change what we tell everyone that happened, like when you look after the revolution, like they totally changed the history they didn't change what happened, but the language . . .
Teacher:	There is an analogy in the, the historians of science, as Michael just said, the history books are re-written, science textbooks are *re*written over and over and over again.
Peter:	Well like Fermi, when he was shooting neutrons at uranium stuff, he really has seen fission but he didn't realize it, he thought that something else was going on, he didn't realize what was going one, because nuclear fission . . .

It should be evident immediately that the nature of this kind of data source is very different than, for example, the essays, which one might more likely or easily attribute to be the result of an individual thinking for himself about his idea. (Because language always is the language of the other, which comes from the other, and is for the other, even this idea of an essay as the emanation of a true self can be

ANALYZING DISCOURSE

questioned.) Such conversations are different from an essay because each turn at talk is occasioned by the previous turn or turns and itself occasions the next and subsequent turns. That is, what any individual says is not independent from what others say who have previously spoken and who take a turn at talk subsequently. In a way, the collective brings about the conversation and it constrains what any individual *can* say. But at the same time, the conversation only exists because individuals *do* express themselves—though always presupposing that what they say is intelligible and therefore already a possibility both in terms of form and content of talk.

DATA SOURCES

As teacher-researchers, we need to clearly separate what we normally do in our classrooms and what is particular to the research we conduct; this is especially important when we have to apply to a university-based institutional research ethics board for permission to conduct a teacher-researcher investigation. University-based institutional research ethics boards want to know precisely what types of tasks students have to engage in *for the purposes of the research*, because these constitute work over and above what students normally are required to do in the course where the investigation takes place. In the case of the research described in this chapter, the students did their readings, write structured responses, write essays, and participate in small-group and whole-class discussions. This participation and the artifacts collected in the process did not constitute additional work—though I still made it a point to ask students for permission to use them in my teacher-researcher investigations. Thus all of the curriculum elements described in the previous section were integral aspects of the course. Any permission sought would be the use of these materials for the purposes of conducting research and for participation to be recorded. Therefore, there would be an issue in whole-class sessions if a student were to not agree to participation. In this case, you might have to organize group discussions involving some of the students, grouping together those individuals who gave their consent, and put all those students who have not given consent to participation into another group. But *all* students would have to participate in these discussions because they would be part of the regular classroom structure.

> **Special Tasks** In an ethics application to an institutional research ethics board, I would write something like this: "In addition to the regular classroom activities, those students participating in the research would be asked to complete the following tasks. . . ." This statement would be followed by a description of the additional tasks and an approximate indication of the amount of time these tasks would require of the students involved.

As part of my research, I collected other materials as well; but these materials were specifically for the purpose of research. If I were to write an application for ethics approval, the acquisition of these materials would be described as requiring extra time from the students—e.g., staying after school to participate in an interview as I have done in the context of the study in chapter 4 or to do a concept map as described in chapter 1. Only students who explicitly signed consent can be asked to complete these tasks. Make sure your institutional research ethics board is clear about these distinctive parts of your research. Also be sure to specify how you organize your classroom such that only those students would be recorded who have given explicit consent to participate.

As in the research described in chapter 4, I used the *Constructivist Learning Environment Scale* (CLES) to provide me with a measure of how students perceived the classroom along four different dimensions. This, too, was a task that students did over and above their normal classroom work. If the task was administered during class time, students who decided not to participate would have to some other specified task, a description of which institutional research ethics boards normally require. In this instance, the reliabilities for the different subscales—as measured by Cronbach alpha, a standard index of internal consistency (see chapter 3)—ranged from $\rfloor$ = .75 to $\rfloor$ = .85 for the different dimensions; these measures turned out to be similar to those that had been reported in other studies and by the designers of the CLES. Compared to Michael Bowen and my study in the eighth-grade ecology unit, the present measures were much more suitable for making predictions in quantitative and experimental research.

I also interviewed students—some of them repeatedly over the two school years—concerning the nature of science, scientific knowledge, and learning. These interviews, too, constituted an *extracurricular* aspect of this teacher-researcher investigation. During the first year, I interviewed students (a) to clarify their written answers to the five questions and to points that they had raised in the essays on knowing and learning physics and (b) to follow up on their answers to the CLES. I felt these interview questions about the CLES to be necessary after realizing that different students were providing the same answers to an item for very different reasons. (In fact, a few years and a few more uses of the instrument later, I wrote a rather critical article concerning the usefulness of this and other instruments in teacher-research [Roth, 2000].) At the time I decided to interview as many students as necessary, that is, until I felt that the information they provided me with largely became redundant. Again, this required me to transcribe the interviews as quickly as possible so that I could gain some clear understanding about the nature of the interviews. After I had interviewed 11 of the 46 junior-level students, which I selected to get maximum variation in views about the nature of knowledge, there was little if any new information I could get. I therefore terminated the interview process.

During the second year, I interviewed all 23 students enrolled in the senior-level physics course at least once (one of the 23 had not attended the junior-year course, as he had become a student only to complete his final year); three students were interviewed twice to follow up on religious and ethical dimensions in students' discourse. Each interview was kept flexible, but we (Todd Alexander, the student who became a co-investigator, and I) asked students to talk more about the five statements (to which they had reacted earlier in writing), contents of their essays, and CLES items. I also attempted to elicit students' reactions to seemingly contradictory statements in their writings and talk and to elicit further talk about the nature of knowledge and truth. Here an excerpt with a student, who wanted to become an engineer; I interviewed him repeatedly because he was a very religious person, and I wanted to know how he would talk about the sometimes conflicting claims in the two domains of science and religion, for example, on the topics of genetic engineering, abortion, and the contrast between evolution theory and creation—about 28 percent of the words are mine, whereas John uttered the remaining 72 percent of the text.

MR:		Okay, you write about labs, physics is like a language, it can be difficult, what's the difficult part in physics, what . . .
John:		Um, okay well, I think the, there is so many formulas, and so many concepts to learn that I think, memorizing all those, and that's only part of the difficulties, and I think also like problem solving can be difficult, in dealing with the um extensive math problems.
MR:		But is that what a scientist does, a physicists . . .
John:		He does, in the end, the analysis to analyze his results, of his observations, but I think a scientist creates his own math.
MR:		So what, you said it is difficult to translate, what is the, what is difficult to translate into common knowledge?
John:		Probably, just scientists, some scientist's concepts, like in physics, Sir Isaac Newton, or Einstein his was complex, he was a genius, not everyone is a genius, I mean, also I feel chemistry is, for me it's easier to learn . . .
MR:		Why?
John:		I don't know, it feels that its a simpler topic, so it's easier to teach and explain, and physics is much more difficult and complex.

Over the course of the two years, the interviews lasted anywhere between 25 and 75 minutes. I always transcribed them as rapidly as time would allow me, usually within 48 hours of the interview.

One of the students, Todd Alexander, approached me one day saying that he was very interested in what I was researching and he asked me whether he could participate as a researcher. I was more than happy about these events, because Todd was able to gain understandings in his formal and informal discussions with peers focusing on how they were thinking about the issues we discussed in class. Sometimes he engaged in some of the member checking procedures, when we wanted to find out whether what we were writing corresponded to what Todd's peers had attempted to express. Over the two years Todd and I developed a close relationship and met up to three times per week. We kept personal notes and journal entries, which became part of the data sources. In our conversations we talked about epistemology, literature, poetry, cosmology, religion, and philosophy. In addition to these artifacts, we included in our database articles written by scientists who published these in *Zygon* (a name derived from the Greek word for "yoke"), an interdisciplinary journal with the mission to bridge science and religion. We

CHAPTER 5

used these journal articles to test the applicability of our *grounded theory* of interpretive repertoires beyond high school students (see below).

RESEARCH PLAN

In the first year of what turned out to become a two-year investigation, I just wanted to find out about students' epistemologies, perhaps hoping that my students might have views on the nature of science and scientific knowledge that differed from those reported in the literature because of the different kind of physics course I offered them. I conducted what I considered to be a small-scale, pilot study, more out of interest to accompany the studies of real interest to me, that is, knowing and learning in open-inquiry learning environments. I had already conducted a study on these students learning in open-inquiry environments (see chapter 3) and now was interested whether doing open inquiry mediated how these students thought about the nature of scientific knowledge and the nature of science.

When I did my initial analysis during the summer following the collection of the data source materials, I was surprised by the results, which to a great extent where unexpected. Consistent with the common length of many educational research studies—many lasting no longer than six weeks—I had naively assumed that my students might have developed ways of talking about the nature of science and scientific knowledge consistent with the constructivist metaphor underlying my approach. As this was not the case, I began to be intrigued. Although the students talked about experiencing the uncertainties of scientific research first hand, most of them expressed views that attributed to scientific knowledge indubitable truth and that considered science to be a surefire process for getting at these truths. This made me wonder whether there would be changes observable if the students were asked again in the course of a second year of physics. The resulting research was not planned other than that I had some general ideas about what I wanted to do in my double role as a teacher-researcher. My research actually emerged as I went along and as I became increasingly interested in the phenomena at my hand. Thus, two months into the beginning of the second school year and already in the course of reading *Inventing Reality*, I wrote the following research memo in which I captured the "strategies" for what I should do to complete my teacher-researcher project, which I called "The Epistemology Project."

> *Strategies for Epistemology Project*
> o Do units light as a wave and light as a quantum phenomenon.
> o 5 weeks in winter semester.
> o Questionnaire on the nature of scientific knowledge. Answer in typewritten paragraphs
> o Essay, towards mid-February (due around February 20 [1992] for entry into the winter-term mark which counts towards university entrance mark). On the nature of physics knowledge and the consequences for physics instruction at the high school level. Identify pertinent features of physics knowledge. What is the best way to study it? What are poor ways of studying it?

- o See if I can find more questions on the nature of scientific knowledge/the nature of my own knowledge. What do I have to do to truly understand?
- o Constructivist learning environment survey/ICEQ
- o Interviews (Todd, John, Thomas)
  The interviews should be conducted in such a way to test the ICEQ/CLES results at the same time.
- o Some sort of category sort of teaching strategies. What sort of teaching do I like most. Possible categories: lecture, lab, demonstration, problem solving, self-directed projects, portfolios. Who is responsible if you want to become a good pianist, hockey player, cricket player, etc.? How do you become a good pianist, hockey player, cricket player, etc.? Who is responsible if you want to become good at physics? How do become good at physics? How would you like to see the teacher teach? (November 11, 1991)

By keeping research memos such as the preceding one, teacher-researchers working within an interpretive paradigm can establish a record of their evolving research design and the ideas they are having in the process. Important thoughts and decision-making criteria ought to be noted in research memos so that someone else could backtrack the entire research project and all of its different parts to the varying points of origin. This is a different approach than the one taken in experimental studies that determine cause–effect relationships. In the latter type of research frequently characterized by the adjective "quantitative" (on the problematic nature of using the polarizing terms quantitative–qualitative see Ercikan and Roth, 2006), all design decisions have to be made beforehand. No changes can be introduced in the course of the study—though ideas about this have changed with the appearance of *design experiments*, which are studies that bring together interpretive and experimental approaches in the way Michael Bowen and I have done in the studies featured in chapter 4. If researchers were to change their design in the course of an experimental study, then they would not longer be able to attribute changes to the one or more underlying causes that are the real foci of the experimental study.

DISCOURSE ANALYSIS AS ANALYSIS OF CONTENT

When I began this teacher-researcher study approximately in January 1991, I did not have in mind something that would eventually extend over two school years. Perhaps somewhat naively, I was thinking that having spent about six months in my alternative physics course, where students were designing and conducting their own experiments and where they were discussing alternative views on the nature of science and scientific knowledge would bring about changes in the way they were thinking. I wanted to find out and therefore planned a "little" study for the purpose of checking whether my students would express views closer to constructivism than the students who participated in other studies at the time. When it turned out from my analysis that many students defended positions that researchers

CHAPTER 5

called "objectivist" and "realist," I saw an opportunity to extend this study into a second year. This, I thought, should provide me with some idea about the long-term effects of an alternative course with quite unusual readings on the way in which students articulated views on the nature of science, scientific knowledge, and their own learning. In fact, in the course of that year I realized that doing teacher-researcher studies put me in an ideal position for conducting research on learning over periods that went far beyond those that characterize most educational research studies. I wrote the following research note:

> Strength of this research—it shows/provides exemplar of teacher as researcher & change as consequence of research.

To the present day, I continue to think that way, for teachers are in positions where they can record evidence of student knowing and learning over long periods of time, evidence that allows us, the research community, to create theories and understandings that go far beyond of what we know today.

When I started this study, I was still thinking about knowledge and views as being particular to individuals—consistent with the going constructivist paradigm. Actually, I found myself struggling with the question of the relation between individual knowing and collective knowing. On the one hand, the investigations in the social studies of science had convinced me that knowledge is constructed collectively within communities of practice; on the other hand, I did not quite understand how individuals appropriated this socially constructed knowledge. I was conflicted by the fact that schools placed emphasis on individual knowledge but that the going epistemology highlighted its social nature. "How," I asked myself, "could these two seemingly incompatible views be brought together in the context of a system that places primacy on the individual?" Pursuing my teacher-researcher studies was one of the ways in which I wanted to find out more about the relation between individual and collective. So I designed the study as one in which I pursued "students' views" largely independent from the question of how language and culture might mediate the texts students produced in writing and the language we used when we talked in the class or during interviews about salient topics. This understanding also shaped the kinds of analyses I conducted: I was mostly interested in the content of what students said and my research was geared toward understanding what these views were and how these were distributed among the students that attended my courses.

Not surprisingly, I began my analysis during the first year by collating the responses students had provided to the structured questions. As it often happened, I did it the "quick and dirty way," taking a sheet of paper, drawing a pencil grid, labeling one dimension from 1 to 5 for the five questions and the other dimension with the three answer choices; I then used a simple recording procedure to note the responses from the 36 questionnaires I had received by that day (Figure 5.2). To get a better idea about patterns, I calculated the percentage of responses in each cell and marked those that were consistent with a positivist view ("pos"). To report these results in some more detail, I constructed a table in which I presented the prompting statements and then listed sample answers that identified response sub-

ANALYZING DISCOURSE

Figure 5.2. Most of my analyses begin with quick pencil jottings, usually on dated sheets of paper in my early work, later recorded in my research notebook where I keep all sketches for new ideas.

types and provided counts for these subtypes (Figure 5.3). In this way, I was making saliently available not only the frequencies of responses, as seen in the first of the two tables, but also a more variegated picture of what students actually said when explaining their answer choices.

Somewhat surprising to me at *that* moment was the fact that three cells marked "pos[itivism]" had percentages in the same range (1D, 2A, 4A) but two other cells supposedly consistent with positivism had low answer frequencies (3D, 5A). I asked myself, "How could it be that students were responding consistent with positivism on some questions but apparently respond in contradictory ways on two other questions?" At the time, I became a bit suspicious about the usefulness of the questionnaire to elicit answers in a consistent way. I gained a better understanding only subsequently while reading *Opening Pandora's Box* (Gilbert & Mulkay, 1984), a book-length report in which sociologists analyzed scientists' talk about science, scientific knowledge, and scientific method. It turned out that these scientists responded similarly to my students and in fact had developed ways of making their contradictory answers—some making them look like positivists (science leads to truth), others making them look like constructivists (science is affected by society and therefore often not true)—sound plausible. I further elaborate on this in the next section where I articulate the theoretical concepts of *discursive repertoires* and *discursive devices*.

I then engaged in the second type of analysis: Not unlike the method described in chapter 1, I read through all written materials, highlighted what looked interesting—without knowing off-hand why it looked interesting to me, which I knew I could make available to my consciousness only by radically breaking with my own

193

CHAPTER 5

The Nature of Scientific Knowledge: Content Analysis

Question	Answer categories	Frequency
1. Scientific knowledge is artificial and does not show nature as it really is.	Science is not artificial but based on facts (O)	18
	Science consists both of artificial (false) and correct (true) knowledge (O)	6
	Science is the **only** correct vision of nature (O)	4
	Science is only partial view of nature (I)	3
	There are multiple world views and science is just one of them, not more and not less correct (R)	5
2. Scientific knowledge more and more approximates truth.	It is only a matter of time until scientific knowledge is the truth (O)	21
	Science not only approximates but in fact is truth (O)	4
	Because of different rates of progress in its branches, science approximates truth in some areas but not in others (O)	4
	Truth is relative and absolute truth does not exist (R)	7

Figure 5.3. Part of the table used to represent the frequency of specific answer categories

ideology—and made notes and comments. From this first analysis while re-reading the memos after a first pass through the data source materials had been completed emerged some common themes. For example, in their writings, students often referred to the differences between learning in laboratories and learning from books; or they referred to the usefulness of learning while collaborating with others. I used these "themes" as tentative topics and began to use them to entitle blank pages.

In my next step, I then copied excerpts from the written or transcribed materials onto the sheets. Following each copied excerpt, I wrote a code that included the student's ID—I had assigned an ID and kept a WORD file with names, pseudonyms, and IDs—and the (consecutively numbered) page in the materials from the student in whose writing I had found the statement. The following are but a few of the hundreds of statements that I had copied in this way on numerous sheets, each entitled with the name of my tentative "theme." Readers note in the following excerpt that my student and source code was on the far right, which allowed me to easily find it however long the excerpted text was. At that stage, all my work first was done in pencil-and-paper and subsequently was transcribed into an electronic format. The fact that I was only a beginning typist—using two fingers searching for keys in a hawk-like fashion—certainly was a crucial moment that mediated this approach. Today I type most of these initial analyses and record in paper-and-pencil format only those things that I need to do very quickly in order not to forget them come to be recorded by hand in my field notebook. This allows me to return to those issues that I am currently busy with.

> The raw information gleaned from a lab must first be examined and its true meaning be discerned (9.4)

ANALYZING DISCOURSE

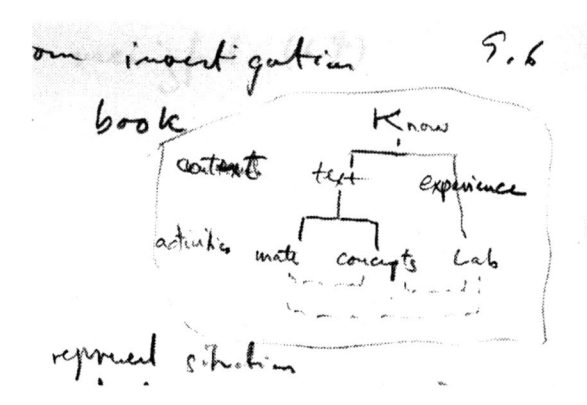

Figure 5.4. Right within a list of excerpts under the heading of "learning through experimentation," I had drawn a small concept map concerning some of the key ideas that emerged for me during the analysis. It is the first appearance in my notes, the growth point of an idea for presenting the results of this study.

Two major groups: knowledge is procured from investigation and passively "discovered" through book (9.6)
I learn most in labs (10.2)
When running labs, I most often find the concepts represent situation, represents the practical world (11.5) in real life (11.5)
I experience most of concepts in lab first, thereby simplifying problems most people have when they try to read from book; "when learning I look at the practical side" (11.3)

While writing out these comments, I had some ideas about how the different aspects of students' writings and talk connected. Perhaps it was because I was doing concept mapping with them and because I was doing studies of concept mapping that I ended up drawing a tiny concept map on one of these sheets, among the excerpts and right in the middle of the list transcribed above (Figure 5.4). The figure shows the abbreviations for the word "knowledge" and includes the terms "text," "experience," "math," "concepts," and "lab." Little did I know on the day I made this diagram that it would be the seed to an idea, the representation of my results in the form of a concept map, which was to grow, increasingly becoming more elaborate, and to be restructured as I went along. This concept map was going to become my grounded theory, which summarized in a succinct way the data source materials I had collected.

A few days after this first map, I drew a more elaborate map using a drawing software package for my Macintosh computer (Figure 5.5). Readers clearly see that the map already was more encompassing than the earlier one, including more terms; and it also was different in its structure. For example, the word "Text," which initially was near the top of the diagram (Figure 5.4) was at the very bottom of the hierarchy in the second iteration of the map (Figure 5.5). More so, the terms "Experience" and "Lab" had moved one hierarchical level lower than they had

195

CHAPTER 5

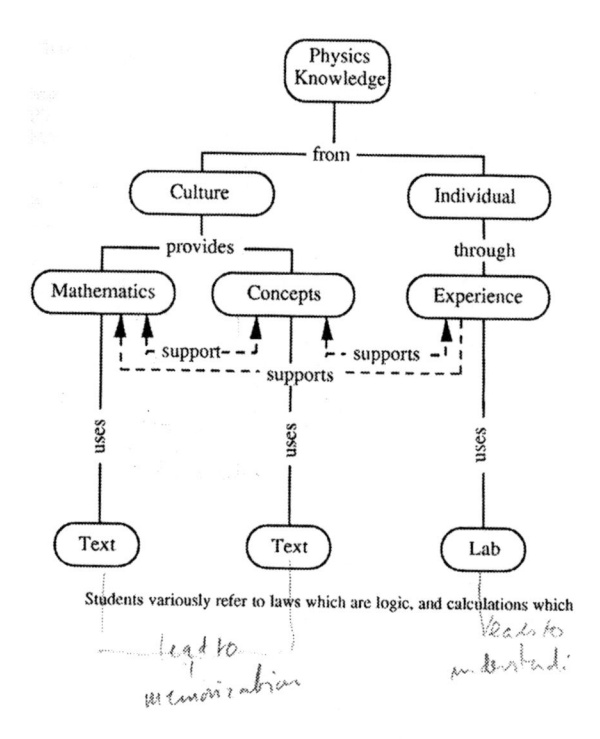

Figure 5.5. As I went along, I drew the concept using a graphic program and added more concepts, first by hand, and then on the computer.

been initially. Finally, I had used linking terms to show how the different concepts related to one another. That is, the theory I was in the process of building emerged, grew, and increasingly became a suitable description of the content that the students had expressed in the different situations that they were asked to write or talk about the attendant issues.

    This second figure only constituted an intermediary one, as the pencil notes on the bottom suggest. It was a work-in-progress, a way of learning through organizing and writing. My reading and reflecting on the student-produced data source materials had made it apparent that memorization and understanding actually were related to different parts of the course. Thus, students tended to write and talk about memorization in the context of working with texts but tended to write and talk about understanding when the topic were the laboratory investigations they conducted. This led me to make the penciled notes "lead to memorization" and "leads to understanding" in Figure 5.5. A subsequent version of the evolving map contained both these terms and the link "leads to" (Figure 5.6).

    Figure 5.6 provides further indication to how my understanding, as expressed in the map, continued to evolve. Here, the map has to be understood not only as an expression of my understanding but also as a constitutive element of this understanding. That is, as I tried to express myself in the form of the concept map, my

196

ANALYZING DISCOURSE

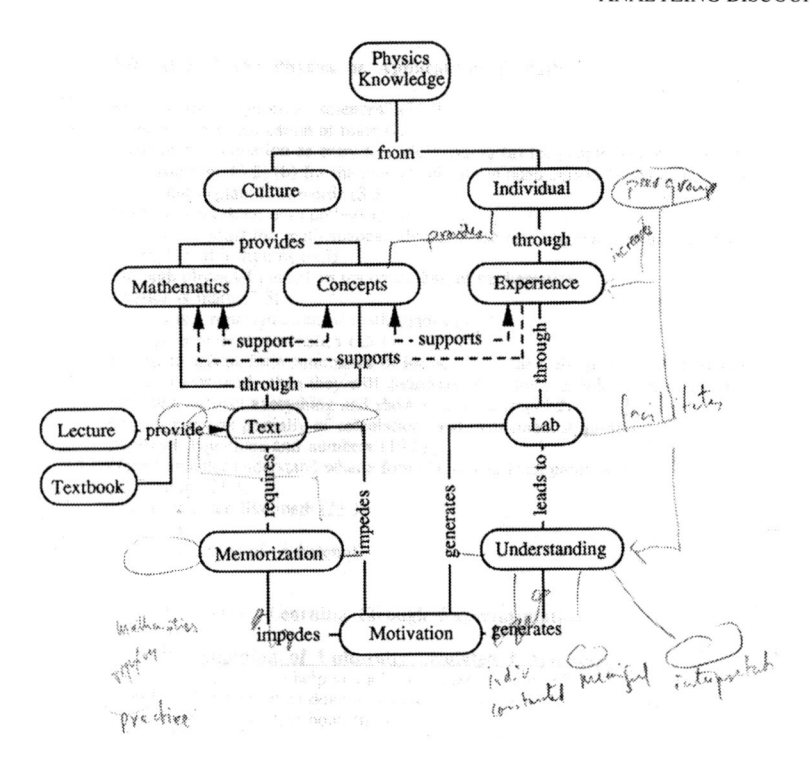

Figure 5.6. As I near the end of passing through the materials, the map neared what comes to be its final shape.

understanding changed, and the changing understanding came to be expressed in the next iteration of the concept map. Even though Figure 5.6 was already more elaborate than the previous iterations, there were more additions penciled in and one link had been crossed out (between "Understanding" and "motivation").

By now it should be evident to the reader that this unfolding nature of my understanding and the processes that lead to it are virtually unteachable in explicit form. My understanding had arisen as a product of my intense engagement with the materials at hand. Both the process and the product were mediated by my past experiences, the competencies I had developed at the time, and my then current interests. How does one teach how to conduct an analysis of data source materials if the analytic process can be learned only in the analytic process itself? This sounds like a chicken-and-egg situation: to do analysis one has to learn analysis, but to learn doing analysis one has to do analysis. Perhaps the best instruction I can give to novice analysts is this: attempt to articulate and express yourself in written or graphic form and *write* rather than ponder explanations. It is precisely in this effort of externalizing yourself such that others can (potentially) see what you see and understand what you understand that your own knowledge of and about the phenomena under investigation comes to unfold and develop.

197

CHAPTER 5

There actually is some reasonable explanation why learning through interpretation unfolds in this manner. Participating in the world gives us a practical understanding. This practical understanding precedes, envelops, and concludes any explanation that we might evolve for our practical understanding. Think, for example, about walking. You walk long before you have verbal means to express yourself to describe the process of walking; and it might take years of studying science prior to being able to provide a scientific account for our ability of walking. Or take another case: grammar. We learn to speak correctly even without knowing formal grammar. In fact, to know formal grammar requires that we know grammar implicitly, because without the implicit knowledge we would not be able to analyze sentences for their grammatical structure let alone distinguish their different parts or distinguish well-formed sentences from ill-formed sentences.

The upshot of all of this is that explanation, which we construct through our interpretive effort, always requires practical understanding of the materials we want to explain. Thus, if I want to find structures in students' writing and talk about the nature of science, I need to engage with their texts to such an extent that they become thoroughly familiar to me. This familiarity constitutes a resource for doing the analyses—we cannot really analyze something that we are not deeply familiar with. This familiarity makes explanation possible. But to arrive at explanations, I have to try to explain; and it is in these attempts at expressing myself that I evolve forms of expression, as seen in the way my own understanding (the concept map featuring the emerging themes) evolved in the course of reiterated production of a concept map that came to stand for the entire database.

Grounded Theory

What I describe in the previous section is a form of method generally denoted by the term *grounded theory* (Corbin & Strauss, 1990). It works like this. Once researchers have generated a set of categories, there are two avenues to be taken toward their refinement. On the one hand, the categories identified may be rather general, summarizing many textual excerpts. In this case, it may be advantageous to find out whether it is possible to construct subcategories that distinguish between groups of texts. On the other hand, when our work has resulted in many categories, it is advantageous to group them and thereby constitute new, higher-order concepts. Ultimately, we want to arrive at a system of concepts that summarize the different texts in the data source materials. That is, the concepts we create are not independent but stand in some sort of relationship. The entire set of concepts, such as depicted in Figure 5.6, constitutes a *grounded theory*, that is, a theory of, and therefore a theory *grounded in,* the evidentiary materials. Although mere textual renderings of a grounded theory are possible, the creation of a visual way of representing such a theory has the advantage that it is easier to apprehend and comprehend what the researcher has done, to make the outcome an object of our reflection, to objectify it (Strauss, 1987).

Other ways of presenting a grounded theory would be by means of an ordered table with major and minor entries. I have found graphical ways of representing grounded theories an important tool not only for exhibiting to others the results of my research but also for better understanding my materials and my own understanding. Sometimes I evolve such graphical means and then, when I have arrived at a good way of describing and articulating what is presented in the figure, I no longer need the graphical means as a form of communication. However, I know from experience that as long as I cannot represent my results in some brief form—in a table, diagram—I do not really understand what is going on in my materials.

> **Representing Research** It is a good strategy to represent your research (findings) in different ways. For example, a *grounded theory* provides a succinct summary of a rather large data set. Individual *cases* provide detailed information in how general ideas are connected within specific individuals.

Once I have arrived at some clean graphical representation, however, I may use the representation (table, diagram) only as a guide while I am writing the article or report but may not need to actually display it because my text has become so clear that it can stand on its own. However, if I were to use a figure, I know it would not be able to stand on its own. No figure can stand by itself: It has to be accompanied and explicated by a text. This text has two functions: (a) it provides a *description* of the graphic (e.g., Figure 5.6) and (b) it *instructs* the reader how to read the figure. That is, I never think that my description (reading) of a figure is superfluous because the results are already presented in the diagram—it would be the same for any excerpt from my data source materials. Rather, descriptive and explanatory text always is important because it simultaneously constitutes a pedagogy, instructions on how to read and therefore on how to understand the figure.

Writing a Case

Grounded theory, because it summarizes heaps of information in a diagram, table, or brief text, actively has to disattend to many singular aspects of the data source materials. Thus, to be able to present Figure 5.6 as a theory describing what I had collected, I had to disattend to a lot that can be found in the nearly 1,500 pages of data source materials. Whereas there are positive aspects about this—I can tell someone else very quickly what the gist of my research is—it also comes to abstract from the real everyday experience of the participants who contributed the materials. The grounded theory literally is abstract, because it has been abstracted *from* a considerably sized body of materials. To provide my audiences with a sense of how the grounded theory relates to an individual participant, I construct cases.

In my use, a case not only articulates an individual (Paul) in concrete detail but also provides a sense in which the case relates to the theory. In the following, I provide a description of the views on the nature of science, scientific knowledge, and learning, which I constructed from the materials gathered through his writings and from the interview that I had conducted with him. To get a sense about how his case relates to my grounded theory, I highlighted during the analysis all those paths in my final concept map that also could be found in the materials Paul provided (Figure 5.7). I do forewarn the reader: in its detail, even this written case is an ab-

CHAPTER 5

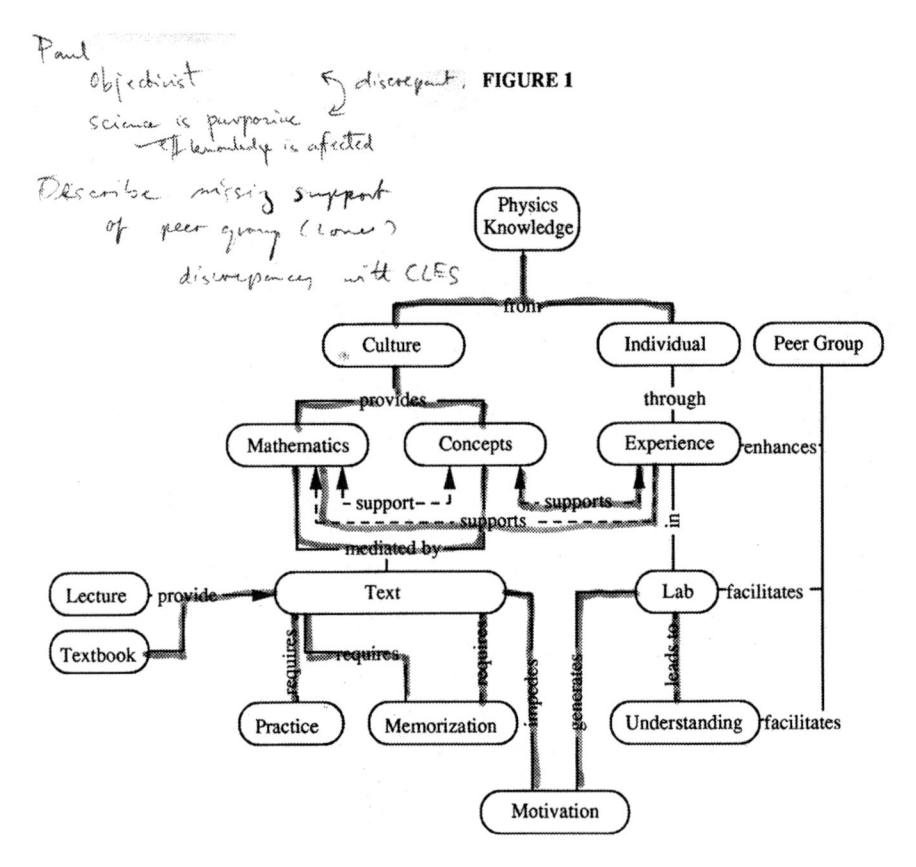

Handwritten annotations:
- Paul
- objectivist → discrepant. **FIGURE 1**
- Science is purposive
- — If knowledge is affected
- Describe missing support of peer group (alone?)
- discrepancy with CLES

[Concept map diagram with nodes: Physics Knowledge, Culture, Individual, Peer Group, Mathematics, Concepts, Experience, Lecture, Textbook, Text, Lab, Practice, Memorization, Understanding, Motivation, connected by labeled relations: from, provides, through, enhances, support, supports, mediated by, provide, requires, impedes, generates, leads to, facilitates]

Figure 5.7. I used the map representing the ideas of all students to trace out what students appearing in my case study have said.

straction from Paul's lived experiences. The written case would be an abstraction even if it were extended into a book-length manuscript; and it would be an abstraction even if it were written as an auto/biography. No narrative whatsoever can claim to have bridged the gap between life and its subsequent articulation in whatever medium this might be (film, photo, text, painting).

> At the time of the study, Paul ranked at about 70th percentile in his eleventh grade in overall academic standing (about 0.5 *SD* above the mean). In physics, his mark was only marginally below the course mean (-0.1 *SD*).
> Paul clearly holds an objectivist view of nature, science, and knowledge, but his views differ from those of Ferdinand. He indicated that science is very precise, exact, and rigid, with no margins of error, it does not show nature as it really is. Yet there are aspects of nature which scientific knowledge, that is formulae and diagrams, cannot explain. But the aspects described by formulae and diagrams are not left up to interpretation, such

as the facts of history and English, but they are the truth, "The right answer is the right answer!" Alternate interpretations or different descriptions of the same reality are "very scary" to him. It is scary to know that there are no laws, if nothing is constant. Paul holds that scientific laws and theories go hand in hand with human existence. In his view, the scientific endeavor is driven by a scientist's commitment to man's benefit, the betterment of society and its ailments. Because of the needs of society, and the scientists need to conform, society has a definite impact on the knowledge which scientists search for in nature. In some cases, society dictates scientists, through its institutions, what it wants them to look for. Thus, in scientific endeavor there is a purpose directed towards society.

Initially, Paul had thought that sciences are linear, unidimensional, focused on mathematical representation, and problems. He had believed that sciences were taught using the textbook and teacher as reference. Both of these sources are correct, because this was the only way for him to get an A. During the year of the study, Paul encountered a different sort of course in physics. It is multi-dimensional, developing mathematical, experiential, social, and writing skills. Physics to him took on a much broader perspective. Consistent with his view on scientific knowledge, teacher's notes and textbook are responsible to pass on the "correct" knowledge in the form of texts. These aspects, mathematical and conceptual have to be memorized as soon as they become abstract. Paul professes that only those things that you can actually see can be understood "If I can't see it, it doesn't exist to me," which leads to his memorization. But there is also personal component to physics knowing and learning. This knowledge is acquired through experience in everyday life and in the laboratory. Through experiencing, particularly seeing, Paul feels that he can gain an understanding. Experience supports his effort to understand the ideas of physics. Although he values his experiences, he views experiential knowledge as "learning about how the world works"; this working of the world is a real concern to Paul.

The mathematical aspect of physics is frightening to Paul. He feels that he has always had some difficulties in mathematics, gets confused and panics when he sees word problems. When graphs are to be interpreted in the laboratory, he relies on his teammate. Equations and formulae have something unreal to them, something that is not tangible. It would be similar with some of the concepts or phenomena. When he does not see them, he has problems seeing them for real. Because to him the textbook is merely a source for mathematical problems, he has aversions to working with it. Seeing the objects and events under study, however, helps him in his learning:

> They say p equals v times this, you know, and then its really like it seems like almost imaginary . . . I can't picture it, it is not tangible . . . When we were doing the wave or electricity, the current goes through there. I can't really imagine current going through a wire and stuff like this . . . it doesn't seem real. . . .

CHAPTER 5

> When you set [the experiment] up, you can actually visualize there is something to look at and you can see.

Seeing things helps Paul to get a sense of security. Paul receives similar comfort when teachers, parents, or the society at large tell him the norms for his behavior so that he can do it right. Paul's positive attitude towards sciences is congruent with these security needs. As long as the sciences are presented such that "the right answers" can be given, Paul knows that he can do well.

The *Constructivist Learning Environment Scale* indicates that Paul scored above the class mean on three of the four scales. According to this information, one would argue that he clearly has a constructivist orientation to the classroom environment. These results are contrary to our findings from the other data sources. Paul indicated that he did not like discussions or negotiations, and that he saw little benefit in group learning other than spending time with his friends. He preferred to learn on his own, and he consulted with others only when he felt he was in trouble.

Overall, the evidence seems to indicate that Paul is an objectivist, modified by the fact that knowledge being discovered because of scientists' purposive search for laws and theories for the betterment of human society. However, my investigation shows that matters are much more complex. Paul needs to conform to expectations, those of teachers, parents, and society. He does not want to look "dumb," always looks for the right answers. To him there is actually some comfort in a subject that is exact, precise, and rigid. He marvels at the scientific nature of the world and physics "teaches [him] about the world." Paul feels that he is "learning physics the 'right way' and the knowledge [he is] gaining is going to stay with [him] forever."

From this description, readers can get a better sense of how the different dimensions presented in Figure 5.7 are connected within one and the same person. A narrative provides a level of detail that allows readers to think of real persons, not the concrete student Paul that I have known, but more like a character within a plot, such as we find characters and plots throughout the belletristic literature and in the theater. By playing the two forms of description—grounded theory and case study—against one another, teacher-researchers achieve a double description that combines the general (overview) and the particular (specifics), the universal and the singular.

Readers should note that I used present tense as the grammatical mode in this case. I often prefer this tense to the past tense, for it makes the person more alive and present to the reader than the past tense. It is a narrative tense that human beings use in everyday situations where we talk about someone we know, whereas the past tense is a way to create temporal distance that also evokes physical and emotional distance.

The disadvantage of the kind of analysis exemplified in the case study of Paul is that it looks at the texts participants produced in writing and talking as if these were context independent. The analyses *presuppose* that identities and views are properties of persons; and they presuppose that these properties can be, depending on method, more or less faithfully expressed in texts by the research participants and recovered from texts by the analysts. As a teacher-researcher, while being plunged in the database, I began to doubt that this could be done, especially once my data source had grown to 3,500 page at the end of the second year. I noticed that students would use the same kind of arguments to support quite different claims, which may have been so far apart as being consistent with constructivism and realism, respectively. I also began to realize that interviews had their own momentum so that anything articulated in their course constrained what would be said subsequently. When I encountered sociology, discourse analysis, and discursive psychology I found some methodological answers to my emerging doubts.

MOVING TO DISCOURSE ANALYSIS

During the second school year (1991-92), while I was still collecting data source materials for the larger, extended study, my ideas about language, its uses and functions, were changing following the reading of *Opening Pandora's Box: A Sociological Analysis of Scientists' Discourse* (Gilbert & Mulkay, 1984), *Discourse and Social Psychology: Beyond Attitudes and Behavior* (Potter & Wetherell, 1987), and *Discursive Psychology* (Edwards & Potter, 1992). Reading these three books, I commenced thinking of language as an aspect of our world that we use in shaping not only the topics of conversations but also the conversational contexts themselves, and with it, the social situations. In addition, I began to think about the materiality of language itself, that is, the fact that it is dependent on the production of sound or other forms of matter. Language therefore is as material as other resources that we knowledgeably use in everyday life in the pursuit of our goals. To truly understand language, therefore, we need to understand both its resemblance to other material productions in human culture and its exceptionality. Pertaining to the former, I began to think of the conversations that I had with students while interviewing them about their views of science, scientific knowledge, and learning as products of the deployment of sound and language. This drastically changed my way of analyzing the texts my students were producing in written and spoken form.

Interpretative Repertoires and Discursive Devices

One of the first things I learned while reading these books and one of the first things I came to understand while analyzing the student-produced materials and interviews was that conversationalists draw on *interpretative repertoires* in support of the points or claims they make. That is, some of what human beings say in conversations is taken to be more tentative and therefore in need of supporting statements that supposedly are shared with the other interlocutors. A conversation frequently moves on only when a claim has been sufficiently supported; and the listener judges whether the support is sufficient. For example, one of my students said:

It is obvious that [scientific laws] exist in nature, and scientists discover them. In retort to this question, one could ask, 'Was there no gravity on earth before Newton clearly defined it?' Of course there was.

It occurred to me that one could split this statement into two parts. First, he made a claim "It is obvious that [scientific laws] exist in nature, and scientists discover them"; then he supported this claim by asking a rhetorical question that he answered immediately: "'Was there no gravity on earth before Newton clearly defined it?' Of course there was." I came to think that he was drawing on something that he knew intuitively or instinctively. But in using the rhetorical question–answer combination to support his point, he had to presuppose the shared nature of this intuition/instinct. That is, he had to presuppose that I, the interviewer—or rather, I as an Other generally—shared in this instinctive and intuitive experience. And precisely because and as long as he could take this interpretive repertoire as shared and uncontested, he could use it in support of a contested claim. Whether this presupposition is valid, of course, has to be borne out in the conversation. The shared and uncontested ways of talking I came to understand and use as *interpretative repertoires*. If I had contested the rhetorical answer, this would be a sign that he did not draw on a shared repertoire and he likely would have sought some other repertoire for defending his point.

In my first study of this new kind, which I conducted together with Todd Alexander, we were interested in understanding the discourse across two contexts, science and religion. I present more on this study in the next subsection. But this study set the context for subsequent analyses, which I conducted with an Australian colleague, Keith Lucas. Two years before Keith came to spend a brief sabbatical in my research group, and only months after I had left the high school, I wrote a research note in which the analyses with Keith came to be prefigured and conceptualized. This note therefore was an important element in the *audit trail* I established, which, in part, also constituted evidence for the *progressive subjectivity* at work with respect to my growing understanding of discourse and discourse analysis.

> *Process for the Epistemology II project*
> — provide sample transcript from classroom interaction
> — look at some trajectories, may be Todd, Matt, Craig, some of those who talk more than others. Pick up on how some of the ideas are formed, when they came out the first time, like in Todd's case about the language
> — analyze students' talk in terms of interpretive repertoire. The social, and the formal. The emotive (social) and the rational. Students/scientists are influenced in their emotive aspects which affects what they are saying
> — Need for clarity what exactly the EMOTIVE is
> — How are the repertoires changing? What is the change mechanism, is the repertoire the same? In terms of the boxes in the religion paper, it is the content of the box that is changing
>   science, knowledge IS

RATIONAL   Absolute, out there —> relative, construction, unavoidably social
EMOTIVE   Errors, social influences
The TWOD as a mediating device between the two
— Power of the talk, using images created to refer back to, conversation in part about conversation; using the image of the winding staircase returning on itself

This note allows us to understand how both research generally and teacher-research specifically begins with questions and uncertainties. The opening of my memo also included comments on the need for certain actions, for example, the reminder to myself concerning the need to clarify the *emotive* [repertoire]. In the note, I raised questions about change and change mechanisms, and a comment relating the work I wanted to conduct to the paper that I had just finished writing with my high school student Todd Alexander (see below). I stated a hypothesis about the nature of the changes—which I conceived of in terms of changes in the content of boxes in a diagram that summarized my research results (see also Figure 5.9 below).

When Keith arrived to work with me during his sabbatical, we immediately began our analysis using Gilbert and Mulkay's (1984) characterization of scientists' strategies to establish the factual nature of knowledge claims. We read that in their publications, scientists deploy an *empiricist* repertoire. Scientists' impersonal style, stylistic, grammatical, and lexical structural features contributed to the presentation of scientific knowledge as an expression of nature rather than the outcome of scientists' interpretive efforts. That is, scientists talked about their work as if they merely were the voices through which nature reveals itself. During informal talk, scientists frequently deployed a *contingent* repertoire, where scientists' actions no longer were depicted as generic responses to the realities of the natural world but as the activities and judgments of specific individuals who acted on the basis of their personal convictions, inclinations, and particular social positions. In this way, science and scientific knowledge through and through were marked by social and historical contingencies.

As we read the documents in the database that I had established as a teacher-researcher it became evident to us (Keith and I) that the empiricist and contingent repertoires were insufficient to account for the variation in my students' discourse. As part of this investigation, we therefore expanded Gilbert and Mulkay's framework to a total of nine interpretive repertoires. Keith and I actually split up the work, each taking about one half of the 3,500 pages of written text and transcriptions that I had accumulated. Because we worked in parallel, we first had to see whether he and I would come up with similar repertoires and then needed to have a good set of descriptions so that we could analyze the entire database with the confidence that we were counting frequencies, for example, in the same way. This was important because ultimately we wanted to test whether the frequency of student responses within and across repertoires changed and whether these changes were related to any changes in the claims students were making at the beginning and at the end of the two years in my physics courses. That is, because the analyses were to be statistical, we needed to provide our future readers with some confidence that our independent coding efforts reproducibly led to the same results: We wanted to have a high degree of *inter-coder reliability*. A sufficiently high level of inter-coder reliability exists, in my opinion, only when two or more coders agree in at least 90 or more percent of the cases to be classified (or, alternatively expressed, when $r > .90$). Thus, we wrote brief statements and used exemplary excerpts for each of the nine repertoires, such as for the historical repertoire, which we entered as a memo into our collection of research notes that served us as a reference while we analyzed independently.

> *Historical* The historical repertoire invokes specific incidents from the development of theoretical and applied science, technological advances, or revisions of scientific theories. Especially after students had read and discussed extensively about Newtonian mechanics and special relativity, students supported their claims by drawing on the historical repertoire.
>
>> Many of Newton's basic laws of motion work for a short time before breaking down. If one then considers friction the new, modified laws work even better, but not perfectly. By instituting Einstein's theory of relativity, the newer laws are even closer and appear to work perfectly. (Peter 5Q.920127)
>> [...]
>
> Similarly, frequent references were made to the development of wave and particle theories of light. Technological progress was used in two ways as a resource: first, to underscore that science was successful so that scientific knowledge must be true; second, to establish that technological progress also improved scientists' instruments and resulted in increased precision of measurement, bringing them "nearer to the truth."

Readers should note that in this memo we began the definition of the historical repertoire by providing a general description. We then concretized the description with several examples (only one is reproduced here for brevity sake), and completed articulating some of the variations that we observed. Our initial descriptions were tentative. We refined them in the course of working through the entire database and as we encountered cases that we could not easily classify, which gave rise to uncertainty about the nature of our classificatory system. Of course, we did not begin our analysis with a general description. Rather, as we read through the first 200 pages of our respective halves of the data set, we highlighted, annotated, and excerpted particular text samples. We grouped those that we thought belonged together. Then we articulated how the samples in the same group were similar and how they differed from other groups. Our general descriptions emerged from the attempts to describe what we saw as common within a category. We then began to seek for ways of identifying groups within categories, which allowed us to provide a more differentiated description for each category.

As part of our analysis, we began to notice how students drew on the same repertoire to make quite opposite claims. Thus, one of my research notes at the time read:

The same class experiment that was used by some as evidence that we cannot know whether scientific knowledge describes nature as it really is was used by Kevin to show the opposite.

> Because of experiments we can rightfully say that fields do exist. This can be easily seen if you pull a piece of paper over a magnet and placed some iron filings on the paper, the fields can easily be seen. (Kevin C2.911007)

Excerpt from class discussion

Mark: You can take a magnet put a sheet over it and pour iron filings on it, and you can actually see magnetic fields
James: Not necessarily
I: What do we see?
James: We see the iron filings
Todd: We see a pattern
James: We don't necessarily see the fields
Todd: It is obvious
James: You don't, it could be anything, it doesn't have to be necessarily, what we think. (SR1.2.911011)

Readers should take note again that at this stage of the analysis, I referenced all excerpts to the original source. Here, the excerpt from Kevin's file refers to the type of activity (C2) and the date on which he had handed this text to me (October 7, 1991), leading to the source code Kevin C2.911007. The transcript from the class discussion could be found in the materials from the Senior 1 (SR1) section of twelfth-grade physics, it was the second discussion, which had occurred October 11, 1991. This led me to code the source as SR1.2.911011. Any auditor would be able to find both sources, as all the tapes were labeled with the same source codes and as all the materials for each student were kept together. Even if this auditor never comes, the very idea of the research claims as being suitable and appropriate for conducting an audit is central to the credibility of the claims I have been making based on this research.

Initially I was thinking about these interpretative repertoires and discursive devices relative to my student population. Then, one day much later, I came to realize that for these devices to work, I (interviewer) had to have bought into these repertoires even though I was not conscious of it at the time. This idea arose when I realized that sometimes I was asking students to elaborate and even challenged them; at other times I (interviewer) moved on to a different topic. "Why," I asked myself on this day of realization, "would I challenge students sometimes but move on at other times?" Was it not that I moved on when I personally accepted the support for a claim? Whereas I, as interviewer, challenged the students concerning some point when I heard it as a claim (unsupported) I continued without challenging students in other instances. Therefore, something that operated as an interpretative repertoire functioned for me in the same way and even without my explicit understanding; these repertoires we (Keith and I) identified therefore were characteristic not only of the student population but also of the culture in which I (teacher-researcher, social scientist) was a constitutive member. As I was working through these ideas, I came to realize that I had just identified a way of getting at

CHAPTER 5

my own predispositions and ideologies, which could be found in the interpretive repertoires that students and I shared. That is, by analyzing those moments where I challenged students during the interviews and compared them during those other moments where I went on, I could get a better understanding of my own tacit presuppositions about the nature of knowledge and science.

Sometimes, my students—as the scientists in *Opening Pandora's Box*—came to contradict themselves within a few minutes of an interview. For example, my students and the scientists might claim in one instant that scientific knowledge is the truth but only minutes later they argued that there were social influences and other contingencies that lead to scientific studies that report falsehoods rather than truths. In both instances (students, scientists), the interviewees would say something like "but eventually, the truth will come out" or "even if it is not right immediately, science will get it right eventually." Because of the consistent way in which this argument was deployed, it has come to be called the "Truth-Will-Out Device" or TWOD. That is, TWOD is a discursive strategy to get around the contradiction scientists articulated that their reports may contain truths or (sometimes) falsehoods; but the TWOD suggests that in the latter case, the truth will come out eventually. The same discursive device allowed my students to claim simultaneously that scientific knowledge is the truth and that there are instances where reported scientific facts are false—i.e., artifacts—because of this or that contingency that emerges in the context of the actual research.

An important lesson teacher-researchers can draw from this is that creative ways of seeing one's data sources come from concurrently reading books and research articles (in my case the three books on discourse analysis, discursive psychology, and scientists' discourse) such that our new understandings can be tested in the concrete materials; and by attempting to test our understandings in the materials, we teacher-researchers come to modify our understanding of what we have read. Learning precisely derives from the gap between the different readings, where the teacher-researcher attempts to bring into alignment texts of very different order. That is, as you attempt to analyze your transcripts of interviews and classroom dialogues, it would be advantageous to also read research articles and books pertaining to the attendant matters. It is in the tension between the two different media—the published research and your own data source materials—that creative ideas might emerge concerning the analysis of what you have collected.

Keith Lucas and I wanted to see whether there were changes between the first and second year in the claims students made about the constitution of the world as determined by science (ontology), the nature of scientific knowledge (epistemology), and the role of individual and societal contingencies (psychology, sociology) in knowledge production. We therefore decided on a set of codes (a number) for the nine repertoires (recorded in a document). We then proceeded to establish tables in which we entered in abbreviated form the nature of student discourse in terms of repertoires and devices across the three categories. Figure 5.8 features an excerpt from one of these tables. Thus, for example, the table shows that in the first year, Roger claimed scientific knowledge to be relative and used the interpretive repertoire that we had given the code 3a in its support. In the second year, Roger

		Before	*After*
Roger	Ontology	KN relative [3b]	Makes no sense of talking about world a priori [2, 5]
	Epistemology	Impossible to know nature as it really is, FIT [3a]	language game [2, 3a, 3b, 4, 5, 6]
	Psychology	PK is limiting [5] Contingent	PK [2, 3a, 3b]
	Sociology	[3a, 3b, 5, 8]	Contingent
Tom	Ontology	Nature is a priori [2]	Nature's a prior [2, -5, 6]
	Epistemology	SK is truth (nature) [4?, 6, -10]	SK is math model [3a, 4, -5, 6, 7, 8b]
	Psychology	No presupps [-3a, 4], YES at cutting edge, TWOD []	No presupps [2, -10], YES at cutting edge, FIT [4, 7]
	Sociology	Contingent [2, 3a, 8a]	Contingent [2, 3a, 7, 8a, 9]

Figure 5.8. Excerpt from the table used to record the result of our analysis of interpretative repertoires (numbers) and discursive devices over the two-year period of the study.

stated that it made no sense to talk about the world as existing a priori and he used the two interpretive repertoires that we had given the codes "2" and "5." We conducted these analyses for each of the three dimensions that we were interested in, ontology (the nature of the universe), epistemology (students' theories of how scientists in particular and we human beings more generally know and learn), and psychology and sociology (the societal and personal factors that come into play when scientists or students do research and that affect their knowledge claims).

These tables then allowed us to establish a number of frequencies. For example, we established a transition matrix that clearly shows the frequencies of students who made particular claims and how these frequencies changed from the first to the second year (Figure 5.9). Thus, three of the students who made statements consistent with realism during Year 1 of the study also were consistent with realism during Year 2 (top left cell). On the other hand, 13 students who had made realist claims during Year 1 made constructivist claims during Year 2 (top right cell). The figure also shows that one student changed from a constructivist claim to a realist claim, whereas five students made claims consistent with constructivism during both years of the study. For each of the three dimensions in which we were interested in—ontology, epistemology, and psychology/sociology of scientific knowledge—Keith and I established such a transition matrix.

Our primary interest, however, was not the nature of the claims students made and how these claims changed in the course of the two years. Rather we were interested in the interpretive resources they used to substantiate and support their constructivist or realist positions. Again, the information available from tables such as the one shown in Figure 5.8 provided us with the resources to establish the frequencies with which students were drawing on the various repertoires that they drew on during the first and second years of the collection of the data source materials. From the comparison we learned that all interpretive repertoires were present in both years and that students had developed rich ways for supporting their claims. However, there were no differences in the relative frequencies with which students were drawing on the different resources available. That is, the students

CHAPTER 5

	YEAR 2 realist	YEAR 2 constructivist
YEAR 1 realist	3	13
YEAR 1 constructivist	1	5

Figure 5.9. This transition matrix shows the frequencies of students who made claims consistent with realism and constructivism during Year 1 and 2 of the study. It therefore also exhibits the number of students who changed from the first to the second year.

who had changed their positions generally drew on the same type of interpretive resources as before; but during the second year, each student had a more extensive library of such interpretive resources, a fact that can be seen from the larger number of codes in the last column of the table (Figure 5.8).

Scientific and Religious Discourses

The first study in which I came to use my new approach to thinking and analyzing data was in an article concerning the relationship of religion and science. In part, the interest was sparked because a number of students had invoked religion in their talk about science and it became apparent to me that for some students the two discourses were compatible whereas for others they were distinct domains that had nothing to do with each other; and for a third type of student, the two were in conflict. At that time, I was reading an article in the *Journal of Research in Science Teaching* (JRST) in which the authors made the claim that religious students also were less capable in science. My own observations did not confirm this but suggested a differentiated approach. Analyzing the discourse and using the interpretive repertoires approach appeared to be an interesting alternative to that published research study.

Todd Alexander had begun to work with me, and together we conducted the analysis of all those materials that referred to religion. Todd was a good student but by far the best in his grade level. Today, he is a medical doctor, specialist for infant nephrology, completing a PhD in microbiology. Whether his participation in our research is an expression of some innate ability or whether his participation mediated his interest in research cannot be answered. Important then was that Todd, too, disagreed with the tenor that the published article took, which he had read in its entirety. Todd was both deeply religious and very interested and successful in science. But his social constructivist position allowed him to understand truth and institutions as constructed—his personal religious experience was the only place where social construction was not applicable, as he thought of it as a singular experience that inherently cannot be shared. We also interviewed several students explicitly on the topic of science and religion. We constructed detailed case studies, one featuring him the others featuring two other students: in one case study, the student kept the two domains apart and in the other case study, the student despaired in the apparent conflict that existed between science and religion.

At the time, I was reading every issue of the *Journal of Research in Science Teaching* from its front to back cover. I therefore knew that in this discipline our approach was a new way of thinking about interviews, knowledge, and beliefs. I also knew that in the US, where the journal and the organization that publishes it are based, religion was (and still is) a touchy issue. This situation contrasted our own, where Todd as all other students at the school had, among others, enrolled in a course entitled "World Religions," which tenth-grade students irrespective of their religious affiliation completed. (In our school, all major world religions were represented [Jewish, Christian, Islamic, Hindu, Buddhist] together with some of their variants [e.g., there were Roman Catholic, Anglican, Baptist, and Reformist Christians].) On the one hand, in the US every politician can lay claim to the Christian God, asks the deity to bless America, and support their politics (on marriage, abortion) with references to religion. On the other hand, religion in school is highly contested—although in many other countries or parts thereof, such as some Canadian provinces or German *Länder* (states), it is a regular school subject. Nevertheless, Todd and I pursued in our effort to write a paper—and in the course of doing so learn about discourse, interpretive (discursive) repertoires, and discursive devices—concerning scientific and religious discourses of high school physics students.

Through our analysis, we (Todd and I) found out that when we asked participants to talk about controversial issues (evolution versus creation, abortion, euthanasia) they drew on two realms for answers, science and religion. When we asked participants to characterize the knowledge claims made by the authorities in the two realms, they pointed us to two types of warrants, *rational* and *subjective*. The former repertoire was introduced to account for students' arguments that certain scientific and religious knowledge claims are rationally warranted. The subjective dimension was introduced to account for students' claims that there are social and personal influences that make scientific and religious knowledge claims less than reliable. Realms and dimensions span a grid that leads to four repertoires for each individual. We decided to represent this grid in visual form (Figure 5.10). Each cell took one of two values for the kind of knowledge claims made, *absolute* or *socially constructed*. To mediate conflicting statements that arise from two discourse repertoires—such as "scientific knowledge is true" (quadrant A) and "society influences scientists' knowledge claims" (quadrant C)—some individuals had available mediating devices that they used to account for contradictory claims. Our students used two such devices. The *truth-will-out-device* (TWOD) mediated the conflict between rational and subjective claims within the science; the *incompatibility device* mediated the conflict between rational truth claims made in the realms of science as well as that of religion.

CHAPTER 5

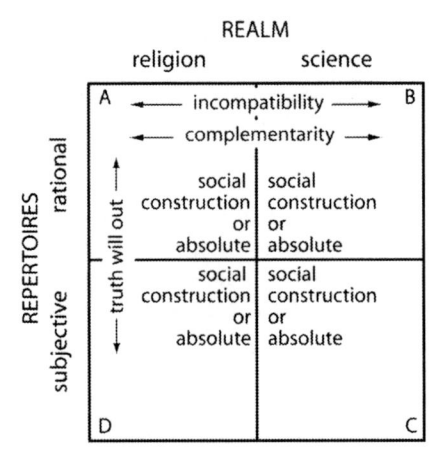

Figure 5.10. A grounded theory *for understanding the scientific and religious discourses suitable for both high school students and scientists publishing in* Zygon.

How or *why* we came up with this grid format to represent what is a grounded theory I no longer know, or perhaps better, I will not ever know. It is likely that because we were dealing with two domains and two types of repertoires, I might have actively looked for a way of representing the results in grid format where the two dimensions could be made to intersect. Then, in a way not unlike the grounded theory in the early part of the study (Figures 5.4–5.7) cycles of revision and redrawing led us to the end result. (Our unpublished versions no longer are available, as they were done in a drawing program no longer available, and which saved files in a format that cannot be converted into present day versions using one of the existing file converting software packages.)

To test the applicability of our framework, we analyzed four articles on the topic published in *Zygon: Journal of Religion & Science*, a journal dedicated for bridging the apparent gulf between the two domains (*zygon* is the Greek word for yoke). With this test, we in fact checked the degree to which our grounded theory could be generalized to other texts and contexts. Many authors who publish in Zygon are natural scientists writing on the topic of the relationship between the two domains. Todd and I found that all four authors wrote about scientific and religious knowledge claims in absolute terms. To mediate the potential conflict, two used the same device to maintain their adherence to conflicting knowledge claims arising from their work as scientists and practicing Christians. The analysis of published articles revealed that our model was not entirely sufficient to explain all forms of discourse that we had come across in our data source materials (interviews, articles). We felt that some scientists used one device not used by students for dealing with conflicting claims of science and religion: we created the *complementarity device* (Figure 5.10) to account for this form of talk. The complementarity device allows an individual to look at the object of inquiry (such as abortion or euthanasia) from two, mutually exclusive viewpoints and integrate these through a dialectical and hermeneutic process. However, we read in one article that this form of reasoning may not be available until people are in their late twenties or mid-thirties. It therefore was consistent with our own article that we did not observe the complementarity device in students' discourse.

Todd and I did not "discover" the structure represented in the diagram or the diagram itself *in* the data source materials. Rather, we had an evolving sense of there being different kinds of repertoires and different contexts (realms). We wanted to summarize our emerging understanding in some way; and as we attempted to represent our understanding graphically, we came to realize that we did not yet understand. Thus, the diagram and our understanding co-evolved until we arrived at the way in which we ultimately represented it in the manuscript.

Todd and I eventually decided that we wanted to represent more than the discursive devices. We also wanted to have parts of our paper in our personal voice. We did not want to write about ourselves in the third person but decided to use first-person voices to articulate our personal positions. Whereas the grounded theory and the case studies appeared in different articles on student views (see previous section), Todd and I integrated the two into one. Thus, in the paper that we ultimately published, we used both the authorial voice, where we wrote in the third person about the study, our methods, and our findings; and we used the first-person voice when each wrote about himself and articulated what he was standing for. The case studies featuring Todd, therefore, involved both voices. The authorial, third-person voice was used to present the context of the study, our everyday life at the school, and the analysis. We used a first-person voice to allow Todd to speak for himself about the different topics treated in the article. For both students who featured in the article, we presented versions of Figure 5.10 consistent with the case. Thus, for Todd, three of the four quadrants contained the term "social construction"; and there were none of the three devices because the discourses in different boxes were not contradictory. The fourth quadrant contained Todd's relation to his deity,

Grounded Theory The diagram in Figure 5.10 is a grounded theory in that it derived from and explains *all* the instances in our data source materials, including the articles. Whether it is a more general theory is an empirical question, for any expansion of the database might require an expansion of the theory, just as our inclusion of *Zygon* articles required an expansion of our initial theory.

which by definition is a singular relation and experience that *cannot be shared* (Derrida, 1995). For the second student, however, we required TWOD and had to mark "conflict" (between quadrants A and B), because he had no discursive device to mediate the inconsistencies and conflicting claims between the two domains. We did not draw on our written analysis and case of a third student (John) because of lack of space and because we did not think that the case added something that we could not express in any other form. The use of the two voices can be gleaned from the following excerpt from the methods section where we introduce the psychosocial setting of the study. (The journal ultimately did not implement our suggestion for using a different type or font. But in a dissertation or thesis, such a form of representation likely could be used without problems or resistance on the part of

CHAPTER 5

the supervising committee or university responsible for getting the text into the public domain.)

> *Science and Religion: Psychosocial Setting*
>
> The case studies are based on the interviews and essays of two students, Todd (as second author presents himself [changed type face]) and Brent.
>
> *(Todd:) Having been brought up in a household where science and religion were both part of daily life, it was easy for me to bring the two beliefs together. This co-existence of science and religion continued at our school where both chapel services and science are part of the daily experience. Thus, for me the notion of God became all encompassing including science and the knowledge constructed through its procedures. At the school, I liked very much and did well in all my subjects, including the sciences biology, chemistry, and physics. Besides sciences, I also took a keen interest in philosophy, poetry, and fine art all of which were part of my course work towards graduation. I was one of the chapel wardens, and member of the chapel choir. In my conversations with Michael, the senior author, I came to know that my discourse could be labeled "social constructivist." While this might be surprising, I do have a significant spiritual-religious life. These labels, however, like so many, do not express my specific discourse at the time of the study. (I will elaborate on science and religion below.) My contribution also presented us with a problem that we had to resolve as we wrote this article. I often felt tempted to change or add to my earlier written and spoken statements. Michael, on the other hand, felt that the article should be about high school students' discourse rather than a story of my changing discourse in the process of our inquiry. This is a different story that I would like to tell in another place. So we decided to present my views as we reconstructed them together from the essays, formal interviews, personal notes, and informal conversations at the time I attended Grade 12.*

Some readers may assume that a high school student (in transition to university) would contribute little to the writing of a study. With Todd, however, this was not the case. First, we had many conversations and spent much time looking at data source materials together. We discussed our mutual positions. Todd interviewed his student peers to clarify our (his, my) evolving understanding and returned to subsequent meetings with the materials he had gathered. Ultimately, I ended up writing a first draft. Todd reacted to this draft by writing a text almost as long as the text itself, adding, critiquing, and commenting, as appropriate, to the various parts of the manuscript. Todd also accompanied me to an ethnography conference where we presented the results of our work. Because we had worked dialogically, we planned and enacted our presentation as a recreation of the dialog situations from which our work had emerged. To allow spontaneity during the conference presentation, we did not fix the text we would use to present our work but merely used a general framework and then improvised an analysis session that simultaneously articulated method and results of our paper.

On Submitting Work for Publication or On Persistence

When we approached the completion of our article, I wrote to Ken Tobin, a mentor of mine, who had defended me that same year during a conference session when another science educator accused me of brainwashing my students.

> Here the draft of the manuscript about science and religion. In a couple of weeks or so, I have to take it up again and look at it. I will also get feedback from my co-author. I think it probably needs strengthening between the introduction, middle section, and conclusion. Also, I am not sure if the sections presenting the students' views are too long, and not enough interpretation. But I was torn with my other intention to let the students' voices come to the fore.
>
> I am sure that the direction which this paper takes is too far out for JRST although my outrage over Toni Lawson's articles was one of the driving forces to do the study at the moment when I realized my experience with, and the potential of, the material from the EPISTEMOLOGY study.
>
> I hope things are going fine at your end, and may be we both will have some time to deconstruct our own past thinking and actions to write a paper on the journey from "true knowledge in the mind" to "knowing and learning in the transactions with the (social and physical) world."

Here, I wrote to Ken my mentor rather than putting down my thoughts in a research memo. But the note had the same function as other notes I was writing on the topic of my ongoing research. It constituted a reflection on what I was doing, a way of becoming critical with respect to my own research method. The memo can be understood as a way of externalizing myself, in fact, externalizing an aspect (idea) of myself, making it foreign and strange. As external object, it then allowed me to confront it and become critical, now as potentially strange object that is the result of processes within me. As an externalization, the note also is an essential part of establishing an *audit trail*—available to any other person now that it was external to myself—that documented my (the teacher-researcher's) *progressive subjectivity*. That is, the memo objectified my thinking by turning the latter into an artifact, which can become an object of inquiry into my progressive understanding of student discourse. It documents, for example, the source for doing the study. Sending the article to Ken, who provided me with feedback, was also a way of interacting with a *disinterested peer*. By definition, the disinterested peer does not have a stake in a study, and perhaps is a complete outsider to the situation. Because of this, disinterested peers may see—to draw on the popular fish analogy—the water in which you swim. It allows teacher-researchers to establish a mediated relation with their situations, a first step in the *radical doubt* procedure by means of which we teacher-researchers attempt to come to grips with our personal ideologies. Disinterested peers can help us find other ways of looking at our materials, and through a changing perspective, of coming to understand better what we have (data source materials) and do (research method).

CHAPTER 5

Despite the ongoing reviews with disinterested peers, I knew that the article Todd and I had written was pushing the boundaries of the field of science education. If we had written just for ourselves, this would not have been an issue. But because we wanted to contribute to the scientific literature, what we would write also had to be consistent with the audience, its culture, its ways of thinking, and its interests. This is an important issue to keep in mind should you (reader) be interested in and pursuing the publication of your teacher-researcher investigation to an audience beyond your thesis or dissertation committee, or beyond your classroom and school. You cannot just write about what *you* are interested in; you publicly present or publish because you assume that there is a general interest. Whether such a general interest exists can be found out only by being in tune with the readership of the journal that you ultimately submit your work to.

> **Presenting, Writing, Audience** Should you be interested in presenting your work by means of public talks or by writing for journals, keep in mind that you are not just telling *your* story, but that in fact you are telling your story *for* an audience. You therefore have to tell your story not for itself but for what it can give to its intended audience. (Would you talk about your daily work in the same way were you to address a colleague and your children?)

That I was aware of the experimental and perhaps cutting-edge nature of what we (Todd and I) had done is evident in the following excerpt from a letter I wrote to Todd shortly after moving from the high school to the university.

> You need to know that this manuscript is experimental in several respects. First, as a former student of mine, you are contributing to the whole research process, including the writing. From a traditional perspective, this is a cause of concern because it reeks subjectivity. Second, as I am explaining in the design section, the use of two types of voices, an authorial and the personal, set apart in different type faces is new to the area of education. Third, the theoretical framework of "interpretive repertoires" is new to the area of education. So it might be problematic to get it published, and so the work needs to be as convincing as possible. I will have a colleague or two read it after you return the manuscript, and after I made the final changes. (September 24, 1992)

As it turned out, the manuscript and our study were challenging the field of science education and in the process, I also learned a little about the role of persistence—which is important when you are interested in getting your teacher-researcher investigations published. Although I was thinking that this work "was too far out for JRST," I did submit my work to that very journal. The editor at the time rejected the article because it was too contentious: four of the five professors asked to review the manuscript declined reviewing it, and the one person who did do a review rejected it. I am pretty certain that the reviewers mainly were American scholars concerned with the political aspects of our work. We faced similar issues with a second US-based journal in the field. After implementing major revisions for the third (an international) journal, our paper "The interaction of students' scientific and religious discourses: Two case studies" (Roth & Alexander, 1997) was published five years after we had completed our first draft (the delay in part being brought about by a publishing backlog).

Challenging the status quo comes with anxieties. For me, the anxieties about publishing increased once I had made the change to the university, where salary, salary increases, and decisions concerning tenure and promotion are based on performance. Performance, to a great extent, is measured in terms of the number and quality of publications a professor produces. I articulated these (new) anxieties in a letter to Todd, who was 18 years of age at the time, just after I had left the high school and started my new (university) position.

> To me to work on this is exciting but also a source of anxiety. My career depends on the amount and quality of what I publish. My salary increases, my promotion, and my tenure all depend on this. So when I spend so much time on a project, it really needs to work out. So I invest emotionally and professionally, it's more than a game. But I also like the risk, and I like to know that what I am working on is front line research, breaking new grounds, and so on—so much for my personal thoughts. (September 24, 1992)

To keep track of the different versions of a manuscript, I evolved a convention that has turned out to be useful also in my collaborations with others; I use the same convention to order my research notes and other materials. There are three parts to the file names in this convention: A name descriptive of the content of the study, a three-digit version number, and the extension indicating file type. For example, the manuscript I wrote with Todd began as "God&Devil100.doc," where the "doc" is the extension that Microsoft WORD uses to mark the files produced with it. While working with Todd on the manuscript, the version number increased to 101, 102, and so on until we were done. When we worked on the manuscript prior to submitting it to the second journal, the version numbers began with 200 and increased by one each time we saved a new version. The version that eventually got published was "God&Devil403.doc."

When working with a peer or colleague—at the school or university—using a version number always allows me to know who has the latest version. In this way, I have been able to avoid problems while collaborating on studies with others—while I was a teacher researcher, my fellow teachers included Michael Bowen and university-based researchers included Anita Roychoudhury—because we were able to catch those instances where we had not been aligned. We were able to avoid double work, which we would have had to spend in finding out the different developments papers take when multiple authors simultaneously work on a text. Today I use precisely the same convention when I pub-

> **File Names** Evolving a system for naming files allows you to locate them when you are searching for particular information, memos, articles, or article versions. As I work a lot with others, it has turned out to be paramount that I keep track of versions of a text—often manuscripts but sometimes also revised versions of transcripts when there are two or more collaborators working with the same materials, updating them when they are improved.

lish together with my graduate students, whether they are the first authors of an article or whether I take the major responsibility for writing a piece.

I follow the same convention with my research notes. To make sure that I do not lose written work should a crash occur, I regularly update the version number of the file I am working on—when I write and analyze a lot, the number changes repeatedly within the same day. Once there is a lot of text (especially when there are images), then I create the next note or memo file. Thus, the first file concerning a particular project will have the name "Notes1000.doc" and then change to "Notes1001.doc," and increases by 1 in the last digit each time I decide to change the version number. When I create a new file, its version number will begin with 2000 and then increase by 1 each time I decide to change. In the early days, I used the day in the name (e.g., "Notes93/0706.doc"); but I felt it did not work so well for me because I wanted to have the possibility of multiple files on the same day or have many days appear in the same file, using a separator to distinguish notes written on different days, but always dating each entry.

ON TOPICS, TOOLS, AND SITUATIONS

In the years following the work with Todd and Keith, my thinking about language evolved, and with it, the way in which I looked at and analyzed the texts that I had assembled as data source materials. I repeatedly returned to the materials I had collected as a teacher-researcher to articulate and develop my newly formed understandings. Consequently, the totality of my writings concerning this set of data source materials constitutes an interesting case how evolving theoretical understandings change the way in which we make sense of the same set of texts. In fact, this changing way of understanding is inherent in the nature of language that allows multiple ways of articulating the same sense (Ricœur, 2004), which never precisely is the same—otherwise we would not need to say something differently to allow others to understand (e.g., the use of dictionaries is based on the possibility to articulate and express the sense of a word differently than by using the word itself). In this section, I articulate my changing understanding and show how this leads to a different form of analysis of the same data source materials used in the previous sections.

In psychological approaches to understanding human beings, there is an implicit assumption that individuals not only are singular but also are independent of the culture of which they are constitutive part. The hidden assumption is that of culture as a box or container into which an individual enters. Novices are said to become "enculturated" or "acculturated," as if the culture stayed the same when a new person comes to participate in its characteristic and relevant activities. This view, however, is untenable, a fact that we can easily see in the limit cases where a culture or subculture is very small, consisting of a few individuals only. In those cases, what is possible within the culture is considerably mediated by the particular set of individuals constituting it. Returning to the issue of the independence of individual and collective, it is evident that what a person says necessarily is held to be subjective, totally the result of his or her thinking. Does it make sense to think of a person telling us her autobiography (identity) and of the autobiography as a singular phenomenon? What does an interview reveal in which the interviewee is asked to talk about his or her life? I learned an important lesson, though it took a while "to sink in," while teaching a course for teacher-researchers and other graduate students on research method only months after I had left my high school. As in all my courses, I have had set aside time in which the graduate students could develop ideas for a thesis topic and the associated research method. In this part of my course, the students began by articulating the context in which they were interested in and then stated a first research question, which subsequently came to be refined as other students and I asked questions that allowed the presenting person to reflect and rework the question until it was consistent with his or her interests.

> **Discourse as Resource** Discourse is used to constitute both the topic *and* the situation. But the situation is constituted collaboratively and in the transaction with other features of the setting. From this perspective, it is not legitimate to attribute a piece of transcript to the individuals who perform the utterances. Rather, an utterance is a feature of the situation as a whole.

During that course, one student told us about her life as a child of alcoholic parents, and pointed out that there existed books on the topics and a rising awareness in the culture about the special problems "adult children of alcoholics" were facing in their lives. She was interested in conducting a study in which she would interview other "adult children of alcoholics." In the course of the hour allotted to her design of a research study, other graduate students began to reflect on their own lives and started telling their autobiographies in new ways, from the perspective of being an "adult child of alcoholic parents." That is, the notion of being an adult child of (an) alcoholic parent(s) provided new discursive resources for telling their autobiographies; and, not surprisingly, others found the discourse *intelligible* and *plausible*: by the end of the course, almost one quarter of the students present not only had purchased books on the topic but also reconfigured their life narratives. That is, the life narrative of the first student accounting her life in terms of being the adult child of alcoholics was a cultural possibility that existed at the collective level, as shown in our comprehension of her story. Because it existed as a collective possibility, others, too, began to tell their life in terms of this plot where the children of alcoholic parents suffer in particular ways. That is, the auto/biography in terms of the concept of "adult children of alcoholics" was not so singular a story after all. If it were singular, it would be in the realm of that which could not be articulated (such as the religious experience, which inherently is beyond anything that can be shared [Derrida, 1995]).

Discourse as Tool

In much of educational research interviews are taken as direct pathways to knowledge, beliefs, motivations, and emotions, all of which are thought to reside in the heads of students were they might come into conflict, enhance or interfere with one another, and thereby change how students learn. However, against this view we

CHAPTER 5

can build another one that takes into account the fact that any interview presupposes a setup—an interviewer who asks questions and an interviewee who responds—and the use of language—an interview without some form of language is an oxymoron, in the modern use of the word. An interview is a situation to which participants orient, where they find themselves and language, and which constitutes a way of being, where some "I" bodily is confronted with some "You."

Discourse as resource The details of the situation, as understood by the participants, the language used, and the products of the transactions between interviewer and interviewee inherently constitute resources that structure the outcomes of the meeting—the interview text as recorded and transcribed and "I" becomes an "It," surrounded by a multitude of intelligible things that make a lifeworld. In the following, I show how my interviews with the high school students already presupposed narrative forms, characters, plots, and so on, all of which are to be thought of as resources that the students and I had available for constituting our topics. That is, we have these resources available in and as of the fact that we are members of the same society and culture. Characters and plots, for example, constitute discursive possibilities and therefore no longer are singular: they are *collective* possibilities. Discourse analysis therefore is a method suitable for disclosing those shared features of language that are relevant in the constitution of topics generally and auto/biographies particularly.

The following episode begins with my framing the topic of the conversation, the items of a survey to which students had responded by taking a position (agree, disagree, other) with respect to each of five statements (agree, disagree, other) and then explaining their choice. The first statement to be discussed was, "Scientific knowledge is artificial and does not show nature as it really is."

> Interviewer: I want to know from you what your ideas are about these five questions from the survey and if you change your view just let me know what sort of caused that change. Because I am going to a conference about the history and philosophy of science in science education and there are people who argue that what one should talk to students, you know, "Students should get an appreciation of these sorts of discussions." Why don't you tell me what you think about that first statement, "Scientific knowledge is artificial"?
>
> Preston: Well, first of all, I am a very religious person and that sort of rearranges my knowledge about science, how I think about different things. When I think back of all the things I have been taught such as how the Earth was made, how things are developing, it makes me think about what is true and what isn't, about what is real and what isn't, and sometimes the fact what I have heard in science and religion can be compared to each other.

In my framing, I accounted for the fact that I had invited the student (Preston) for an interview by stating a broader societal motive, a "conference about the history and philosophy in science education" where there are "people who argue that one should talk to students . . . about these sorts of discussions." The talk about conference and its topic constitutes a resource for making the interview intelligible and plausible. But inherently, it is presupposed to make the interview intelligible and plausible to the student, because it already is for me. That is—although I was not aware at the time—uttering such an opening only made sense (a) if I could presuppose the student to understand what a conference on the history and philosophy of science was or possibly might be and (b) if I presupposed the intelligibility of the fact that conference attendees were interested in students' appreciation of statements such as "Scientific knowledge is artificial and does not show nature as it really is." In this way, I was setting up the particular talk (action) in relation to a broader motive (interests of a science education community).

In the situation, Preston did not answer the question directly but rather produced a contextualizing frame. Although the original question was about science, the response has to be understood in the context of a narrative of an individual who also was (and perhaps still is) a religious person. The answer also was framed in terms of what he had heard in the past—memory work was being done here—and in terms of those things he has heard sometimes were addressed by both science and religion. Although the interview protocol had not foreseen questions about the relationship between science and religion, the topic, once it had emerged, came to be unfolded and carried by both participants. Importantly, in talking about himself as a "religious person," Preston presupposed the intelligibility of the term and of religiosity as a character trait. That is, in denoting himself as a "religious person," Preston had to presuppose that I (interviewer) could understand him as a kind or type of person. In his *singularity* as a person right in front of me, he also was a member of a *kind* of person. Discourse precisely is the tool that allows us to establish simultaneously who Preston is in his singularity and who he is as a general kind. Articulating himself as a religious person set up a frame within which I was supposed to understand what Preston was going to tell—though, because he had no opportunity to think about issues and rehearse them, the subsequent things he said were prefigured and made possible but not *determined* in this frame.

The very statement "I am a very religious person" is marked—for to make sense it implies a non-articulated horizon of others who are not so religious or are completely without religion. This, then, is one of the kinds of contrasts that have to be managed by the character

> **Collective Resource & Topic** Discourse always is a collective resource and topic, which inherently are presupposed to be *shared* rather than to be singular. It makes no sense to speak unless one can presume others already understand.

developed in the narrative, carried by both interviewee and interviewer. Thus, the interviewer will be seen to return to the contrast, requiring the responsive interviewee to articulate issues even if he had never pondered or discussed them.

Preston introduced the contrast that featured him as a source ("it makes me think") and recipient of agency ("the things I have been taught"). In fact, the phrase "it makes me think" already contained the dialectical tension between a person who was both agent and recipient of agency, subject of and contributor to life conditions. The character Preston developed in and through discourse also was subject to different messages ("all the things") that had to be evaluated in terms of their truth-value ("it makes me think about what is true and what isn't").

Through my analysis, I came to understand the central role discourse plays in the situated constitution of different versions of the world. Discourse inherently embodies possibilities for such versions. Each contingently produced version therefore is a concrete realization of a general possibility, and therefore is as much a collective (social, societal) as it is an individual (singular) phenomenon. Discourse provides a number of resources that speakers can draw on in support of the different versions of the social world they constitute; these resources also are possibilities available to everybody else within the same discourse community.

Sample analysis In the approach to discourse analysis that I articulate in this section, teacher-researchers have to ask themselves the question, "What is being done *in* and *with* discourse?" Here, I am using the preposition "in" to bring to the foreground the fact that discourse is something like a terrain or world. We find ourselves on this terrain and in this world; the geography of the terrain and the topology of the world provide resources for us to move about. For example, because Preston and I used the English language and because we were in a school with an Anglo-Saxon heritage and ethos, we were bound by the possibilities of the English language generally and the topic-specific discourses—some scholars denote topic or subject specific discourses by the capitalized term *Discourses*—available to us within this language and culture. I use the preposition "with," because discourse also is something like a tool that we use to configure the terrain and the topics of talk. In the following, I provide a brief sample discourse analysis that I might write if I were interested in showing how the identity of a person as a religious person is constituted *in* and *with* talk. I use the third person approach in articulating the account, which allows me to distance myself from myself and thereby allows me to be more critical and less prone to rationalizing my own discursive actions.

> At issue in the discursive constitution of identity is not merely one of telling beliefs or describing how and what one thinks; at issue in discourse is the person as a whole. "I am very religious" is a statement about a way of being in the world rather than about something that can be exclusively relegated to the (cognitive) mind. This becomes clear in the next interview episode, where Preston describes himself as a person who is "caught in the middle." The question of science and religion and the conflicting versions that they seem to provide about the origin is something that affects the person, that he has to deal with, that catches him in the middle where he has to make a decision.
>
> Interviewer: What do you do in cases when there is a conflict between what you, the bible, the church say and what scientists believe? Like, there is that big debate about creation versus big bang theory. How do you resolve a difficult issue like that?
>
> Preston: Well I am sort of caught in the middle, because I have grown up with religion. But I have also grown up with science. I guess I really can't determine what is right and what is wrong. If I were an atheist and not believing

in God at all, I would automatically go towards science. I would say, "Science is this, science is that," and then people say, "You know, science can actually provide the information about what is and what is not."

Interviewer: Do you just try not to think about that? Or is there something on and off about the differences?

Preston: It's something about which I think all the time.

Interviewer: But doesn't that of worry you?

Preston: It distorts me. It really troubles me a lot. Because if I think about science, I feel like I am drawn away from religion. That really worries me a lot, because I feel like I am being taken away from what I have been a part of, which is religion. If I go toward religion, I feel like I am not giving science a chance at all; and I can't see myself doing that because I am a person of morals.

Here, the interviewer asks Preston to provide an answer to the contrasting claims that (fundamentalist) Christians and scientists make about the origin of the universe—(spontaneous) creation versus big bang theory. In response, Preston articulated himself as a character that is caught in the middle between different versions of the world provided by the two systems, science and religion. This character finds it difficult to determine "what is right and what is wrong," which of the two versions to accept. He then develops a different plot, one in which the character was an atheist, who, because it implies a situation without conflict, "would automatically go towards science." For this person, there would be no conflict, there would only be science; and others in this plot would confirm, asserting that science actually provided the information about what is and what is not, an answer that is not available to him because the conflicting statements are made by different authorities (science, religion).

This text excerpt constitutes a beginning of an analysis for a chapter in which I focused on why Preston (or a person like him) would articulate as issues involving science and religion in the way he did. I wanted to argue that every (discursive) action not only produced something (an object, a sentence) but also produces the speaking subject; and I wanted to articulate a concern for the question of identity and the narrative elements used to articulate Self and (social) Other in lived experience and Self and lifeworld as mediated by knowledge. The former relation involves an experience of bodily presence, whereas the latter only has a past and no presence. Here is where I therefore could articulate the fundamental difference between science and religion: they constitute different modalities of time and being. Science is about objects, which consist in having been; religion is about thrownness, experience, and grace, all of which consist of being in the present. To this we may add a future-orientation, as apparent in revelation and being-toward death. For *me* (the teacher-

> **Orient Your Analysis** Give your analytic efforts a direction by framing some tentative hypotheses, which you might develop after an initial reading of your interview materials to get a sense of what they contain and are about. These hypotheses orient your search for patterns, especially those that disconfirm your hypotheses, allowing you to reframe them until they fit all the materials in your data sources.

CHAPTER 5

researcher and author) discourse analysis constitutes *the* method of choice for accomplishing these goals.

To do this kind of analysis, I work through one or more interviews in a line-by-line fashion—depending on the goal I set myself for this task. In fact, without an object or goal, we do not know what to do. Without a sense of what I am out to find, I cannot know whether what I am seeing is relevant or not—whether it, in fact, is a finding or just some clutter (noise). Every thought, as phenomenological philosophers have long pointed out, is interested and intentional. Without a particular interest or intention, there is no direction for our thoughts. Thus, I do not believe any analysis to be possible without some direction, interest, or intention. I am therefore rather suspicious about the recommendation some professors make when graduate students ask about how to go about to analyze the data, a recommendation that runs about like this: "Read the interviews and let the themes emerge." Because I do not believe that unmotivated looking reveals much at all, I begin my analyses and writing with some form of framing statement; and I do so knowing that in the end, I may be ending up somewhere different. But writing a framing statement is like writing a hypothesis for what I might possibly find; by doing the analysis, I then find out whether my hypothesis is in fact confirmed. For example, the forgoing sample analysis emerged after I had set myself the following context and argument.

Fundamentalist and scientific discourse: Beyond the war metaphors and rhetoric

Nowadays it is a common place not only that what we learn shapes our understanding but also that our understanding shapes how we perceive the materials from which we learn. Thus, students bring a range of understandings to school science, which constitute frames how they perceive curricular offerings. Traditionally, these shaping forces embodied in the form of common sense understandings about the world were considered as "misconceptions," "alternative frameworks," or "naive conceptions," when they were not consistent with standard science. While common sense notions of science have been studied quite well over the past two decades, other experiential sources that are potentially at odds with standard science are less charted. Thus, although scientific and the religious discourses of fundamentalist Christians often have been incommensurable at the institutional level, religious discourse has rarely been studied as a mediating element in science instruction.

The purpose of this chapter is twofold. First, I provide descriptions of (a) forms of religious and scientific discourse and (b) interaction of these different forms of discourse in the context of a two-year high school physics course. Second, I provide evidence from this classroom about how we can teach science such as to involve students in talking about knowledge more broadly, providing them with a context for developing their discursive resources.

Already the tentative title provides me with an orientation; the title provides a frame that allows me to orient myself toward the data source materials. In the first paragraph, I articulated the context of my analysis, whereas in the second paragraph, I outlined a purpose or plan. I turns out that I never got to the second part of this plan, but ended up delving in great detail into the processes by means of which we (Preston, I) constituted his "beliefs" using discourse as tool to shape the terrain of discourse. But writing the title and the two paragraphs definitely oriented and thereby predisposed me for doing this particular analysis. Because I think of all of my writing as being for myself initially, while keeping open the option of using some of it in the texts made available to others, I am not afraid of writing. I know I can clean up anything that initially is part of a memo text prior to providing someone else with access to what I have written.

Once I have such a frame, I begin open and unstructured writing (coding) in a first file with the word "notes" in its name. This unstructured writing includes anything that comes to my mind, excerpts from books and articles I read or remember having read, and selected excerpts from the transcriptions that I analyze. These initial notes then constitute resources that I can elaborate or use in subsequent memos and notes to myself until the chapter is completed some time down the road. I end up not using a lot of the text (my notes) produced. Rather, writing to me constitutes a form of learning; and most of the texts I produce are the results of writing processes by means of which I have come to understand. But the texts themselves are resources in the sense that I can use the cut-and-paste function of my word processor once I know more precisely what I want to argue and the points I want to (or can) make and cover. Thus, the following statements constitute the first text fragments I wrote when I started to do the analysis for the chapter on scientific and religious discourses.

> Even if we agree that languages are not representational means, they continue to be media of communication, tools in social transactions, ways of maintaining and further weaving and reweaving of the network of human relations that makes society. We think of human life as the always incomplete reweaving of such a web.
>
> Taking the stance of pragmatic philosophers (James, Wittgenstein, Rorty)
>
> If human being were the sum of their traits, they would be no more than machines, subject to the program inscribed in traits, memory, etc. But human beings are active molders of their situation, coparticipating in social interaction and thereby actively producing and reproducing themselves and society.
>
> Discursive descriptions are used to produce versions of self and other; these versions themselves are used to contribute to and stabilize current activities
>
> Motive espousal or attribution is itself a move in a moral universe (Edwards & Potter, 1992).
>
> Acquired habits and identifications

225

CHAPTER 5

> There is no self without the other; self and other emerge at the same time. Language is inherently both individual (private) and social: at the very moment someone utters a sentence, he or she expresses himself but also concretely realizes an expression that is possible at the general level.
>
> Character is acquired and maintained by means of language, which always comes with the self-other dialectic.
>
> Character leads us to narrative; the character has lasting disposition and traits.
>
> Narrative is never ethically neutral (Ricœur, 1990).
>
> We understand people not in terms of their attributes but in terms of how they behave in situations, where the goals of individual actions are related to the collective motives of activity.

Readers can see in these notes already some of the nuclei of the ideas that are beginning to be worked out in and emerge from the sample analysis provided earlier. For example, near the end of this excerpt from my memo, there are two lines with statements pertaining to character and narrative. These two lines became the nuclei for a substantial part of what the ultimate chapter came to be about. In fact, following up on the notion of *narrative* in the entry following those on character, I returned to some of the books by the French philosopher Paul Ricœur. In reading his work concerning *time* and *narrative*, I also came across some passages in which the philosopher writes about characters and plots. These readings then led to my subsequent elaboration of the ideas about characters and about how discourse is a means for constituting an individual as a singular phenomenon and a character at the same time.

WHAT I LEARNED AND HOW THIS CHANGED

The extensive nature of the data source materials and the changing nature of my own understanding of the essence and function of discourse led to a number of publications. After the initial articles, I revisited the materials in order to articulate my new understandings. Each time I was writing something, I learned; my articles do not so much represent what I know and communicate to others. Rather, in the process of writing, I have learned; and in the end, my learning process has left a text (article, chapter) as the product. Why might this continuous learning be the case? Why might I view the same set of data source materials in different ways in the course of my life? The philosopher Paul Ricœur (2004) may have the answer to these questions when he writes that understanding means translating. The meaning of this is immediately evident as soon as we open a dictionary, where a word is explicated in terms of other words from the same language. This explication in fact corresponds to a translation. Understanding therefore means translating. And representing what is contained in 3,500 pages of written materials in the form of a chapter or research article requires a translation, which is possible only when it goes hand in hand with understanding. Therefore, as my understanding of language unfolded, my translations changed; and with changing translations, my understanding of language also changed.

Viewing understanding, translating, and writing in this way allowed me to grow in a continuous manner; each time I wrote about the data source material, I could expect to learn and grow. In the following summary of my learning from this teacher-researcher project—or rather, what began as a teacher-researcher project and then grew into something much larger by far exceeding what most teacher-researchers might want to accomplish—I therefore present the studies in the order that I wrote them, which reflects my intellectual journey, rather than in the order they were published, which is mediated by the length of the review processes and publication queues of accepted article, which differ between journals and over the years.

The most substantial lesson for me, the teacher-researcher, were the implications that I was beginning to draw from viewing language in progressively new ways: Any idea of eradicating ideas, beliefs, misconceptions, or versions of the world has to falter, given that the linguistic possibilities always exist at the collective level in terms of the means and resources of articulating and expressing ideas. Even if students give in to pressures (e.g., to do well on tests) and repress using certain linguistic resources (e.g., talk in terms of "misconceptions"), teachers will not have succeeded in eradicating the ideas, beliefs, misconceptions, or versions of the world.

Discourse as Neutral Means for Accessing Mind

From the initial study, I co-authored two papers. The first, "Physics students' epistemologies and views about knowing and learning" (Roth & Roychoudhury, 1994) constituted a rather broad qualitative inquiry that provided a dynamic view of students' understanding of knowing and learning in high school physics. Our analyses revealed a spectrum of epistemological commitments commensurable with positions from objectivism to relativism, most of them with experientialist coloring. Even within individuals, these commitments could be at once commensurable and incommensurable with the same epistemological position. We also reported rather significant inter- and intra-individual differences with respect to the consequences of a specific epistemological stance to learning, the learning strategies employed, and the learning environment preferred. The purpose of the second study, "The nature of scientific knowledge, knowing, and learning: The perspectives of four students" (Roth & Roychoudhury, 1993), was to provide detailed descriptions of students' epistemological commitments and their concurrent views of knowing and learning physics. We provided four *case studies* that served as paradigmatic examples representative of the different types of views that our analyses had produced. The epistemologies we had identified ranged from objectivist to radical constructivist. In spite of these differences, there were aspects of the learning environment that all four students liked, though for different reasons. We concluded that the experiences in a constructivist learning environment are not enough to help students understand the tentative nature of scientific knowledge as long as their understanding is measured against the norms of canonical science. However, we realized that the wealth of student views provided a great potential for small- and large-group discussions about the nature of scientific knowledge, knowing, and learning. We concluded that there existed a great potential for students to learn about the nature of knowledge from each other.

Discourse as Means to Constitute Topics

While I was collecting data source materials during the second year of the study, my understanding of language was changing. I began to write the text for "The interaction of scientific and religious discourses" (Roth & Alexander, 1997) during the school year and had completed a draft in August of 1992. I already included the new references to discourse analysis and discursive psychology. Todd and I reported that although the discourses of science and religion often have been incommensurable at the institutional level (e.g., the evolution versus creation debate in the U.S. courts and media), religious discourse had rarely been studied as a potential interference with the learning of scientific discourse at the individual level. In the study we identified different interpretive repertoires on which pupils drew to talk in sometimes-contradictory ways about controversial issues (abortion, euthanasia, origins of humankind). We thought that these contradictions might interfere with students' science learning. We illustrated in detail two students' scientific and religious discourses.

Subsequently, I conducted together with Keith Lucas an analysis that covered the database in its entirety (3,500 pages) leading to an article entitled "From 'truth' to 'invented reality': A discourse analysis of high school physics students' talk about scientific knowledge" (Roth & Lucas, 1997). In this study, we particularly focused on the 23 students. We analyzed the entirety of their written and oral discourse about ontology, epistemology, and sociology of scientific knowledge collected over a 15-month period in the context of two consecutive, junior and senior level physics courses. I this study we showed that students drew on nine types of discursive resources (i.e., the intuitive, religious, rational, empiricist, historical, perceptual, representational, authoritative, and cultural repertoires) to support their ontological, epistemological, and sociological claims. Toward the end of the study, the range and number of supportive statements had increased. Simultaneously, few students changed their ontological and sociological claims, but a considerable number changed their epistemological claims. We used two case studies to illustrate the development of student discourse in the course of the study. The study also was interesting because it used a variety of advanced statistical techniques to show the presence of patterns and to provide measures for the probability of the findings to have arisen by chance.

In a companion article entitled "The nature of scientific knowledge and student learning: Two longitudinal case studies" (Lucas & Roth, 1996), we provided two extensive case studies to illustrate our understanding of how students' discourses changed over time. We described the changes in students' discourses concerning the nature of scientific knowledge and of the science teaching and learning process, which were not always complementary, with the aid of a model. We thought that the findings of this research should have direct relevance to the planning and implementation of science courses in which the development of understandings of the nature of science is an objective. Subsequently, I published an article entitled "The interaction of learning environment and student discourse about knowing, learning, and the nature of science: Two longitudinal case studies" (Roth, 1997), where I presented two further case studies to illustrate the interrelation of learning environment and student discourse about knowing, learning, and the nature of science. The students featured in the two case studies, Todd and Tom, though both were successful, actually represented opposites: the former enjoyed learning in this environment, whereas the latter considered himself on the receiving end in the learning process. He therefore wanted to have concrete directions for what and how to do in order to maximize his chances of being successful so that he could achieve the high grade point average required to enter the university and program of his choice.

Discourse as Terrain and as Means for Constituting Topic and Situation

When invited to contribute a chapter for a book on science and religion, I came to revisit the data source materials I assembled as a teacher-researcher. By that time, my position had substantially evolved. In "Fundamentalist and scientific discourse: Beyond the war metaphors and rhetoric" (Roth, in press), I took the position that language is not neutral but plays a constitutive role in the situated establishment of different versions of the world. Language inherently embodies possibilities for such versions. Each version that is contingently produced is a concrete realization of general possibility, and therefore is as much a social as an individual phenomenon. Language provides a number of resources that speakers can draw on in support of the different versions they constitute. These resources also are possibilities. The implications of my findings appear evident. Any idea of eradicating ideas, beliefs, misconceptions, or versions of the world has to falter, given that the possibilities exist at the collective level in terms of linguistic means and resources of expression. Even if a teacher succeeded in making one student change his or her ideas, the general possibilities of talking about nature in a certain way exist at the collective level. People in everyday life continue to talk in these ways. It would therefore not be surprising if the students, who responded on school tests in the way desired by the teacher, nevertheless would continue talk in ways incompatible with science in conversations outside school and therefore reproduce the possibility of talking in this way.

CHAPTER 6

ANALYZING CONVERSATIONS AND LEVELS OF ANALYSIS

Learning With Information Technology

Past research has described *metaphors* as powerful tools for understanding teacher actions and as tools for changing teachers' understandings of themselves—and with it their practice. For example, a teacher who thinks of himself as the captain of the ship will (attempt to) behave accordingly, giving orders, holding the reigns, and maintaining the control; a teacher who thinks of herself as a gardener and of students as her plants will orient differently to the transactions with them, for example, in terms of nourishing, helping, and protecting students. However, a limitation of metaphors is that they often have little fine structure—the different forms of action that a captain or a gardener engages in—so that they can incorporate a multitude of beliefs. That is, metaphors are open to multifarious interpretations. To direct a teacher's decision-making processes in more specific and constraint directions, metaphors need to have fine structures. Such fine structures develop only slowly, as failures (if events are constructed as such) occasion accommodation.

In my teaching at the time of working at Appleby College, I used the apprenticeship metaphor: I wanted students to learn by doing and talking physics in a context where I thought about myself as a graduate student supervisor or as an older scientist bringing new adepts into his field (e.g., chapters 2 & 4). However, once I realized the shortcoming associated with the use of metaphors and learned about conversation analysis, I knew I required this additional tool if I wanted to be able to deal with my own ideologies, that is, my tacit and unreflected ways of perceiving and acting in the world. In my first study using this method, I learned that *conversation analysis* provided for fine-grained descriptions of transactions (see chapter 2). These descriptions could be used to build up new metaphors. I thought that through an ongoing process of reflection on action (of which the article issuing from the study was an obvious example and outcome) enhanced by collaborative inquiry with peers and video-based data sources, I could elaborate and make compatible metaphors and fine structures of my teaching, such as specific forms of questioning. Such fine structures should not be developed in the form of lists of rules and prescriptions: in this form they would not be easily accessible to us, the teachers-in-action. Rather, these specific discursive action patterns should use the demonstrated power of metaphors to convey complex information in economical ways. Thus, discursive action patterns may be tied to a metaphor in such a way that they are available as soon as a teacher uses the metaphor as a referent during his or her reflection-in-action. Conversation analysis then provides for descriptions nec-

CHAPTER 6

essary to build and structure metaphors that help teachers to structure their ways of teaching in specific and desired ways.

In this chapter, I describe conversation analysis as a method for the analysis of transactions, both those of the student–student and teacher–student type. I provide this description in the context of a teacher-researcher investigation that I conducted after purchasing for my physics course a piece of modeling software that was intended for students to learn about a variety of motion phenomena. At the time, my school already had a computer laboratory, but students taking computer science courses used it extensively; and in a much less intense fashion other students of other course went there for typing out assignments. But it was in my physics laboratory, for which I had purchased a set of Apple II and Macintosh SE computers, that computing was an integral element of the course. (Many students also came to the physics laboratory during their study periods [7–11 P.M.] because they found the atmosphere there more conducive to working and learning.) My students already used the Apple II computers to collect data in their experiments (see chapter 3) and the Macintosh SE computers to analyze their data using statistical software. But it was after purchasing *Interactive Physics*—the modeling software—that I was thinking about conducting a teacher-researcher investigation for finding out how students were learning in a computer context and with computers. I was interested in better understanding, for example, the beginning phases of learning with a new tool, what students were doing as they were engaging with the computer software, and the resources they needed during the start-up time.

Everyone doing anything with computers at the time appeared to be gung-ho. I personally had been working with computers since tenth grade (i.e., for about 25 years], when I got around the administration of the local university—forbidding high school students to take courses—and had a computer science professor accept me to a course in the programming language ALGOL60 on a mainframe computer. Two years later, I took a computer science course in my high school, where we punched cards by hand with a stylus—I had felt like going back to the Stone Age. At the university level while doing my Master's degree in physics, I enrolled in another programming course, but then learned on my own to program in machine language and the computer language BASIC when I was confronted with the task of collecting data by running computer simulations on the collisions between protons traversing thin films of beryllium. In the 1980s, I became certified as a computer science teacher after taking additional courses in programming and in computer science teaching methods. This is to say that I was really onto and into computers. But I also was a bit skeptic with respect to what and how students learn while using computers, perhaps because I always had the sense it was not quite like what computer aficionados claimed it to be. Although I always had been a heavy computer user, I felt that many of those promoting them insufficiently knew what really was going on while students were working with them and, perhaps, how much more difficult it was to learn with and about computers than generally was assumed. But rather than just forming an opinion, I decided to conduct a study.

Figure 6.1 shows how the computer interface of *Interactive Physics* looked like when students ran some of the simple exercises that I had designed. There was a

ANALYZING CONVERSATIONS, LEVELS OF ANALYSIS

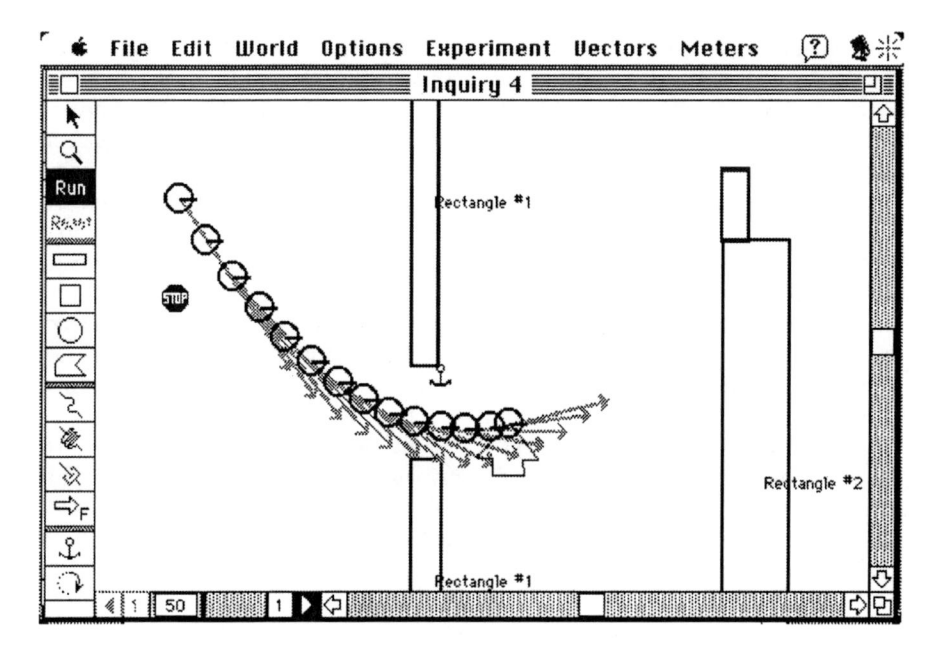

Figure 6.1. Interface of the computer modeling software Interactive Physics my students used to learn about linear motion and the relation between force and velocity.

circular object to which one singe-line arrow was attached (I had set it like this from the beginning), which had the label "v" near its tip. A second outline arrow, presently visible at the right-most take of the circular object, could be pointed and attached to the center of the circular entity. (That the arrow was attached or not attached was itself something students had to learn—for example, by finding out that an object moved with constant velocity without the arrow but accelerated when arrow moved with the object.) In this particular task situation (Figure 6.1), students were asked to figure out how the two arrows affected or were related to the motion of the circular object after the simulation had been started. They were asked this question in a context where they objective was to get the object through the hole in a wall and then kick the rectangular object of the tower it was standing on. (I had designed this task so that it was more like a game. That students learn more in a fun, game-like setting is one of the great presuppositions [perhaps ideology] in education and requires critical study and analysis.) This occurred after students had configured the direction and length of the two arrows, and after they hit the "Run" button on the top left of the interface (Figure 6.1). This set the simulation in motion and turned the cursor into a stop sign (see left half of the figure); pushing the mouse button made the simulation stop. The trajectory of the object was captured by means of a feature that looked like time-lapse photography. The replay feature (bottom left) allowed students to inspect individual states in the motion of the sphere.

233

CHAPTER 6

There had been another reason why doing a teacher-researcher investigation on learning with computers generally and learning with Interactive Physics particularly was a plausible thing to do for me in the 1991–92 school year. In April of 1991, I had attended the annual conference of the American Educational Research Association where I had seen a presentation related to learning physics with computers. The presenter, Jeremy Roschelle, had designed (as part of his dissertation work) a software program that had intentions similar to Interactive Physics. It, too, presented phenomenal objects and arrows standing for the force and velocity concepts. In his application, however, the phenomenal (moving object) and conceptual aspects (arrows) appeared in two different, side-by-side windows so that students were seeing, on the one side, a moving object, and on the other side, two arrows connected to each other. Also, in Jeremy's program, the force arrow was attached to the tip of the velocity arrow whereas in Interactive Physics, the force was attached to the center of the phenomenal body (the circular object in Figure 6.1). To me, it was an interesting question whether my students would be learning in a similar way as those in Jeremy's study and whether mine would have similar difficulties when working with the two media that embodied similar intentions (deep structure) but appeared quite differently on their surfaces. Also it was interesting to me to find out how students learned in my class as compared to the out-of-class situation in which Jeremy had done his research.

CURRICULUM CONTEXT

Interactive Physics is a computer-based Newtonian microworld in which users conduct experiments related to motion (with or without friction, pendulum, spring oscillators, or collisions). The microworld allows different representations of observable entities (measurable quantities). For example, force, velocity, or acceleration can be represented means of instruments such as strip chart recorders or digital and analog meters. I introduced the computer activities to my course precisely because Interactive Physics superposes conceptual representations of these quantities, vectors, and the objects creating hybrid objects that bridge phenomenal and conceptual worlds (Figure 6.1). Students therefore had concurrent access to phenomenal and conceptual presentations, which they do not have when they conducted real-world experiments (cf. chapter 3). By alternating between real-world and computer-based microworld tasks, I (as their teacher) had hoped to be able to assist students in developing a stable discourse about motion phenomena across situations.

All student activities in the present study included, at a minimum, one circular object. The object's velocity was always displayed as an arrow (i.e., a *vector* in physics lingo) and students could modify its initial value by highlighting the object, "grabbing" the tip of the vector, and manipulating its magnitude and direction. Students were instructed to find out more about the microworld, especially the meaning of the "arrows," that is, the vectors representing force and velocity. Although students concurrently conducted real-world experiments on motion in which they analyzed distance-time, velocity-time, and acceleration-time graphs

Figure 6.2. Four students huddle around the computer, three are close to the keyboard and monitor, the fourth student sits in "the second row" because of lack of space.

(see chapter 3), they were not told the scientific names of the "arrows." In part, I did this because as a teacher who believed in inquiry-based learning, I wanted to know whether students would eventually use the scientific names without being so instructed. Some of the activities I prepared displayed nothing more than the circular object (including its velocity) and a force. Others required students to manipulate the "arrows" (force and velocity) to hit a small rectangle and knock it off its pedestal (Figure 6.1).

At the time, my school had four computers in the physics laboratory; I also made my own Macintosh SE II computer—standing in my office next to the physics laboratory—available to students. My computer also came to be the station where I videotaped one group at a time (Figure 6.2). With only five computers but up to twenty students, I had three to four students per group working on the tasks. Whereas some may find this a shortcoming, I thought that this in fact provided opportunities for students to talk and argue science, which is precisely what I wanted. I did not want students to fiddle with the software on their own. It also turned out that collaborative group work was an excellent research strategy because the students made available all the problems in understanding available to one another thereby providing me with a protocol of their transactions and difficulties. That is, when they encountered trouble, they made available to each other their respective understanding of what was wrong and how to fix it. My videotapes and the associated transcripts of the talk therefore yielded a natural protocol of the reasoning my students engaged in while framing problems and solving the tasks—in the course of which they came to frame series of other problems as well.

It appears self-evident that what happened in this segment of my course could be understood independently of other aspects of the course, and even other aspects

CHAPTER 6

of this school. My course was premised on the assumption that learning means to achieve a certain level of competence in talking (and doing) physics. Thus, as shown throughout this book, I planned many activities that engaged students in conversations concerning the language of physics. In the process of talking about the language (e.g., the concepts), students learned to talk the language. The activities that involved them in talking physics included (a) open investigations of motion phenomena chosen by students according to their own interests (see chapter 3), (b) explorations of phenomena in a computer-based microworld (Interactive Physics), and (c) collaborative concept mapping with the main concept labels of a unit (see chapters 1 and 2). Students also were asked to read relevant chapters in one of the available textbooks on their own, and to complete six problems per week from a textbook of their choice. The open investigations of natural phenomena constituted the core of the curriculum, the microworld activities occurred once every other week interspersed, and the collaborative concept mapping took place about once a month. Microworld activities and concept mapping were contexts specifically designed for students to focus more on the conceptual aspects of the physics of motion than on the mechanical aspects of implementing practical research.

DATA SOURCES

As a teacher-researcher, I was interested in understanding how my students learned in the different activities I had designed because I had become suspicious of the common lores of teaching practice, which suggested or presupposed the learning benefits of this or that type of task. I prepared and started the camera equipment and microphone immediately prior to students' arrival in the class and stopped recording once students had left. Because of the nearly continuous presence of the camera in my classrooms over the 1990-92 period of teaching in the school, it was as if the camera did not even exist. It had faded into the background of the classroom.

Collecting Data Sources

In each of the three sections of my junior-year physics course where I used the computer program, one group of students was recorded. I selected the three groups so that students representative of the entire physics course in terms of achievement and gender would be included. I had scheduled four 60-minute classroom periods separated by two-week intervals for a total of ten hours of analyzable material. Figure 6.3 shows how the camera was set up behind the students so that what was on the computer monitor would be visible to me while analyzing the materials. Because the students were talking facing away from the camera, I placed a microphone right in front of them and connected it into the plug for an external device. In this way, I was able to see what students were talking about and could clearly hear their talk as well. It is evident that the zooming level of Figure 6.2 would not provide me with direct access to the display; I therefore zoomed in so that the

ANALYZING CONVERSATIONS, LEVELS OF ANALYSIS

Figure 6.3. I zoomed in sufficiently so that I could subsequently see what the monitor contents were that students talked about; this zooming level also provided me with clear access to their gestures and the objects they were pointing to.

monitor contents were clearly visible to me when I analyzed the recordings. Figure 6.3 shows what the videotapes actually revealed. In contrast to the concept mapping task, where I did not have access to the words on the snippets students moved around, the configuration in this situation allowed me direct access to what the students had in front of them. Although it was impossible to read the text, I knew what it was given that I knew the program and the task. Furthermore, I could always replay the same arrow-object configuration that I saw students working with, thereby getting the same displays that they were looking at. (I had heard of researchers who used a device that allowed them to feed the signal from the computer monitor together with the signal from the camera and produce a new display in which both the wide-angle and zoom perspectives were available simultaneously. I did not have the financial means available to purchase such equipment.)

The data source materials I collected for the purpose of the investigation into the computer activities exist in a larger context that also includes other data sources materials collected during the same school year with the same three classes (which allow inferences about the changes in collective practices). These data source materials include, for example, video records obtained during students' experimental work, during concept mapping activities, and during individual interviews about knowing and learning physics. Furthermore, hard

Natural Protocols Faced with one or the other form of trouble, students communicate to each other their understandings for the purpose of framing the problem and possible solutions. They do not have to articulate whatever they can take for granted as being shared understanding. In this way, the recording and transcript come to be natural protocols of problem posing and problem solving in a naturalistic setting, all the while leaving unarticulated whatever can be taken as shared.

CHAPTER 6

copies of the results of laboratory work and student reflections on knowing and learning in diverse physics activities also entered the database. For each group of three to four students, the additional database contextualizing the Interactive Physics study included the following. From each of the three sections, I obtained 15 reports of independently-conducted laboratory investigations, ten one-hour sessions of concept mapping, one exam and three tests per trimester, 13 essays on knowing and learning, and a series of semi-structured interviews focusing on physics knowledge and epistemology.

Analyzing Data Sources: General Framework

This study was designed to investigate the role the computer environment (software and hardware) played in students' conversations and sense-making activities. Because of the collaborative nature of the computer tasks, the students talked among each other about the mechanics of manipulating the microworld, over and about the images displayed on the computer screen, and about their theories relevant to the microworld. In this way, students made available to each other their understanding of problematic situations. Their conversations therefore provided me with *natural protocols* available for analysis in the form of video recordings and their transcripts. The analytic method was informed by interpretive approaches to understanding everyday work practices, human-machine interactions and conversational analysis. Two graduate students (Carolyn Woszczyna, Gilian Smith) participated in some of the analyses with me. When we did collaborative analysis, we viewed the videotapes and read the transcripts repeatedly in individual and in joint sessions. From our initial viewing and reading emerged first and tentative assertions. During viewing and reading, we attempted to find confirming and disconfirming evidence to establish the level of generality of each assertion. Through this process of *constant comparison*, we arrived at assertions and claims.

The analytical perspective taken in this study is depicted in Figure 6.4. I came up with this perspective by thinking in the following way. Students made available to each other actions and talk; and they had available the display for inspection and consideration. The same was available to me, the teacher, during our transactions; and it was available to the researcher(s) as well (see the box on Figure 6.4). I did not have available putative thoughts: Only the talk, gestures, and current state of the interface were available to other students, teacher (me), and researchers (me, graduate student assistants). I realized that *this* (talk, gesture, interface), therefore, was the stuff I had to theorize, because *this* was the only stuff I, the teacher, would ever come to face not something that might be going on in the singularity of their private thought. As a physicist I knew how the software oper-

Unit of Analysis To conduct good analyses, you need to know precisely what is your phenomenon, where its boundaries lie, what lies inside and what lies outside of the entity you attempt to understand. What exactly is your (smallest) unit of analysis? What is the smallest element or unit that you can understand independently and in its own terms? Is it the contents of the mind? Is it groups of students, the things in their setting, plus the talk they make available to each other?

238

ANALYZING CONVERSATIONS, LEVELS OF ANALYSIS

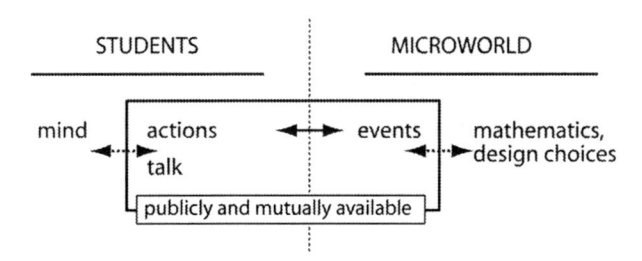

Figure 6.4. In analyzing the videotapes, my basic concern was to understand what students had and made available to each other in their talk and practical action. Neither students nor computer had available the frameworks (mind, mathematics) that underlay their actions.

ated and how it arrived at the displays; I also understood differently from students some of the feedback that the computer provided because I knew how such simulations work. I took a pragmatist approach to the analysis, which means that I produced descriptions of students' actions (verbal and practical) as explanations of meaning, that is, as indications of their knowing and learning. In these studies that I conducted concerning learning with computers, I also heeded the ethnomethodological advice to consider gestural, practical, and verbal action as rational and purposeful and therefore treated students' practices for constructing understanding as the identifying accomplishment of their learning. To reiterate, if students did something, I presumed it made sense to them to act and talk in their ways; if I did not understand, this was my rather than their problem. If actions appeared irrational or absurd I knew that my frames of reference were not yet appropriate for describing and explaining what was happening.

To direct my analyses, I was using—implicitly at first but, as soon as I thought about doing "a sociology of using computers in science classroom" (in fact, "Sociological" was the descriptive name of the manuscript file of one of the articles) it became explicit—a diagram to conceptualize the different levels at which my analyses were taking place (Figure 6.5). Thus, we can think of the computer as a device that constitutes a ground; part of the computer was the interface as a whole but only some aspects of which constituted the current topic of talk and these aspects, I thought, would be salient in individual and collective consciousness whereas other aspects would be nonsalient. For example, in the situation depicted in Figure 6.3, the students were focusing on the possible trajectory that they wanted the object to move along to make it through the hole in the wall and then hit the little rectangle on top of the pedestal to the right. But they did not attend to the buttons on the left-hand side of the screen; at this point of the transactions, these buttons therefore were nonsalient. I began by assuming that what is and what is not salient to students is subject to empirical analysis. I could not assume that because *I* see a certain button or a certain object students, too, were seeing it. In fact, numerous studies that I subsequently conducted showed that students did not see what teachers see precisely because observation is theory driven: we already need to know the concepts to see instances of them when confronted with relevant situations.

239

CHAPTER 6

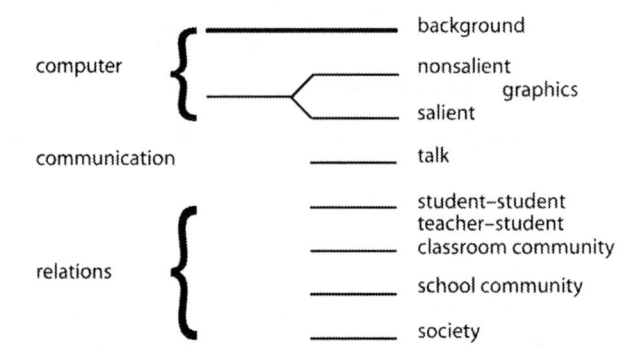

```
computer      ┌─── background
              ┤    nonsalient
              │         graphics
              └─── salient

communication ──── talk

              ┌─── student–student
              │    teacher–student
relations     ┤    classroom community
              │─── school community
              └─── society
```

Figure 6.5. For my analyses, I was thinking about the different levels and locations where I might find meaningful structure. What I will find and construct through analysis depends on where I zoom and focus.

Such considerations constitute an important aspect of teacher-researcher investigations, because they make us think about the unit of analysis. What precisely is the phenomenon we are studying? Where are the boundaries of this phenomenon? We have to ask such questions even in the case that we do not yet know the precise nature of the phenomenon because questioning leads us to doubt our own presuppositions and thereby make available our ideologies to critical thought and inspection.

SETTING EFFECTS

Having followed the literature on interactions and collaborations in the workplace, I was aware of particular effects that settings can have on ongoing activity. Such effects are still insufficiently addressed in educational research. However, my own studies revealed mediating effects of and transactions among representational artifacts, social configuration, and physical arrangements (a) on student participation during science conversations and (b) on the form and content of these conversations. As such, I was interested in searching for structure in cognitive engagement by zooming to bring into focus representational artifacts, social configurations, physical arrangements, and student interactions. That is, I thought that structure in the tasks (and therefore cognition) arises from structures at a more global consideration of "setting" salient to students and teacher—and reflexively, to me in my role of a-posteriori analyst. The questions I attempted to answer therefore included, "What is the role of computers in the coordination of the groups?," "How does group size afford/constrain the development of the ongoing activity?," or "How does the physical arrangement mediate participation?"

How does one go about finding answers to such questions? How do teacher-researchers investigate such questions in the context of computers, computing, and the Internet? I began considering my investigation in the following way. As a first step, I have to think about what it is that I analyze. That is, I have to think about the *unit of analysis*. If I presuppose individual human beings as the unit of analysis and everything else in their setting either as information or as tools that are at their service, then I end up having to make theories about what is in their brain cases, where the things and processes are to be found that essentially are at the origin of what they do. If, on the other hand, I considered individual human beings as part of the situation as a whole, I could begin studying transactions, which are not solely due to structures of the mind. (It took me another 10 years before encountering dialectical agency|structure theories in sociology that were suitable for understanding this mutually constitutive nature of individuals and settings.) As the very term *transaction* implies, the two or more entities involved in a process cannot be defined independently of each other. Thus, different individuals in a class may have different institutional roles, such as teacher and students, but at any one moment during class, who teaches and who studies (learns) is a question of empirical analysis because there are moments when teachers are students and students are teachers. More so, if I took communication as the unit of analysis (see Figure 6.5), then I could not reduce a conversation to the additive contributions of individuals.

If you experience difficulties wrapping your head around this framing, attempt thinking about it this way. If one person says something and the next person responds, then what the second person says is not entirely independent of what the first person has said. The second person's utterance has been *mediated* by the first. We can approach human-computer and human-human-computer (i.e., people talking in front of a computer *over* and *about* what is happening on the computer interface) transactions in the same way. Let us look at a brief exchange, which I, upon reading the initial rough transcript and upon seeing the video, identified as one in which trouble was occurring. The purpose of conducting the analysis was to find out what the trouble was, how it was framed, and how it came to be resolved. In the following, I show how I went about such an analysis and what such an analysis might reveal.

Similar to the process I describe in chapter 1, I transcribed the videotapes from this teacher-researcher investigation. In the present case, not all where transcribed immediately because of all the other studies I was conducting at the time (i.e., those described in chapters 2, 4, and 5); this transcription work was done during the year following my departure from Appleby College. Two students graduate students at my university, Carolyn Woszczyna and Gilian Smith, assisted me in transcribing; they then also participated in the analysis of the tapes, learning how to do it in the process, and they co-authored one of the articles based on these data sources. Later, I built up the transcriptions including pauses (or place-holding parentheses) and the overlaps between adjacent speakers. How much detail you put into a transcript really depends on what you want to do with it. If you are interested in the contents of speech only, then transcribing in the way I present it in chapter 5 is sufficient. If, on the other hand, you are interested in getting the moment-to-moment constitution of a learning situation, then you need a transcript that is more fine-grained. In Table 6.1, I present some of the conventions frequently employed, which have been developed on the basis of those conventions usually used in the area of conversation analysis (Paul ten Have [1999] provides a nice introduction to

CHAPTER 6

Table 6.1. Some transcription conventions I currently use for transcribing materials used in conversation analytic studies.

Transcription	Explanation
A: ⌋⌊m⌋ looking D: ⌋⌊h⌋	Brackets indicate the extent to which speech or actions overlap.
A: curves= D: =oh	Equal signs are used when there is no audible gap between two utterances next.
(0.56)	Pause measured in hundreds of a second are enclosed in single parentheses.
(.)	A dot in parentheses indicates a slight pause, less than 0.10 seconds long.
faster	Underline indicates emphasis or stress in delivery.
YEA	Capital letters are used when a syllable, word, or phrase is louder than the surrounding talk.
A: s:o::	When a sound is longer than normal, each colon indicates approximately 0.1 of a second of lengthening.
A: envi–	The n-dash marks a sudden stop in the utterance.
;.,?	Punctuation marks are used to capture characteristics of pitch toward the end of utterance rather than grammatical features: slightly falling, strongly falling, slightly rising, and strongly rising pitch, respectively
.hh::	A dot prefixed "h" denotes inbreath; without dot, exhalation.
(stay out?)	The question mark following items enclosed in single parentheses denotes an uncertain hearing.
((circles))	Double parentheses enclose transcriber comments.
<<p>or?>	<p> indicates low speech intensity for everything enclosed by outer brackets

this field) and have been further developed by a group of German linguists and conversation analysts interested in also focusing on the prosodic features of speech, that is, features as such pitch, pitch contours, speech intensity, and speech rates.

The transcript was entered in the left column of a two-column table. Into the right-hand column I entered video-offprints wherever I felt these were required to understand what was going on. (On this way of transcribing see chapter 3.) To answer the question about what is going on, one has to make some heuristic decisions taking the subsequent speaker's contribution about what the sense is that talk, gesture, and other nonverbal means current mark and highlight. It is in this part of transcribing at a fine-grained level that I usually located many of the interesting instances and moments of trouble. Once I located trouble, I made another heuristic decision about where the episode started and where it ended. The following constitutes such an episode: the software provided feedback and my sense was that the students did not (and could not) understand it in the way the designers had intended it. (The asterisk [*] indicates the moment at which the offprint was taken.)

ANALYZING CONVERSATIONS, LEVELS OF ANALYSIS

```
01  E:  * yea, leave it there ((G sets veloc-
            ity))
02  G:  okay, let us not go it too fast
03      ()
04  R:  no that's direction ((G has cursor
            on "run button")) make it go
05      ((G clicks run))


06      * o::h, my
07  E:  a little higher
08      ((quack from software))
09  G:  quack




10  R:  * you must reset you can't change
            it while you are in there
11      ((G clicks on the "OK" button))
12      just see what'll happen () when it ()
            run




13  R:  * () oh::
14  G:  OOHH
15  R:  ((object bounces back from left)) it
            comes back
16  G:  oh, baby
```

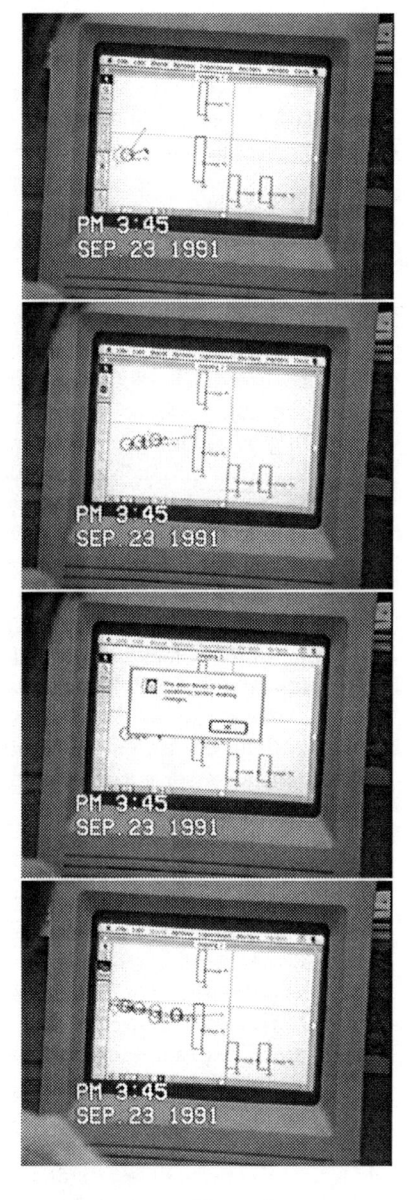

This way of transcribing gives readers a pretty good sense of how the conversation unfolded and what was on the monitor available to perception and therefore was taken by students as topic and ground. I now provide a first analysis of this transcript to exemplify how I go about finding out patterns in students' task engagement. Readers should note that this "analysis" consists in a close, word-by-word and line-by-line reading of the utterances and gestures while making a mini-

243

CHAPTER 6

mum number of presuppositions about what goes on *in* the students' minds and focusing instead on those features that are available to all participants, and therefore to the analysts and readers as well. To provide close readings is part of a phenomenological agenda that rejects explication, because of its reductionist and causalist tendencies, in favor of precise descriptions of phenomena at hand (e.g., Depraz, 2006). It is therefore not surprising that disciplines who have grown out of phenomenological pursuits, such as ethnomethodology and conversation analysis, prefer close readings of transcripts and observed (video-recorded, audiotaped) situations.

> The episode begins while students make a decision for the setting of the arrows, that is, while they prepare a specific investigation in this microworld. Elizabeth suggests to "leave it there" (turn 01) where, to know what the indexical terms "it" and "there" refer to, we need to know what they are looking at. Researchers often supply such information in square brackets, but such a procedure already constitutes an interpretation. By supplying the offprint, we could leave the moment in the way it was available to the conversation participants, which means, without verbal articulation; but I inserted the transcriber's comment, "G sets velocity," though we do not know whether *he* is conscious that the arrow in fact *is* velocity. Whatever Glen is changing at the moment—we can see the cursor on the tip of the velocity arrow and, something we can also see, he is in the process of moving in clockwise direction and shortening. Glen comments, "let's not go too fast," which, in the context of his shortening the velocity arrow could well mean that of the reference of his talk is this arrow and its function—set initial velocity and indicate the speed and direction of the object's motion.
>
> Ryan then provides a commentary, "no, that's direction" (turn 04). This "no" directly follows Glen's statement about not going too fast, so that Ryan's utterance can be heard as being about the arrow and as indicating direction rather than how fast the object goes in addition to the direction in which it moves. That is, we have an indication here of different forms of sense marked out. It is not clear whether they are aware of these different senses—the transcript does not show that it is at issue right now. My analyses of all transcripts though show that it is precisely such misunderstandings that create trouble in their learning. But this misunderstanding is not the one I am most interested in right now. Let us move on in the episode.
>
> Glen hits the run button, which leads to the start of the simulation. At the point displayed with turn 06, Ryan comments, "o::h my." We see that the velocity arrow has hit the wall; the drawn out "o::h my" may be an indication of perceived trouble. Elizabeth then comments, "a little higher" (turn 07). To understand this utterance, we have to go back in the history of their actions, still available to their retention: Glen had moved the velocity arrow in clockwise direction after the object had hit the wall *above* the hole; now it appears to hit the wall *below* the hole. In this context of

Glen's action, Elizabeth's comment marks out a particular form of sense: She instructs Glen to move the tip of the arrow higher than it is.

At this point, the software produces a sound, "quack," one of the noises that software engineers embed and activate whenever the users attempts doing something inconsistent with the intents of the software. Glen apes the computer, which displays a message. Ryan in part reading the message utters "you must reset, you can't change it while you are in there" (turn 10). This highlights an observation about the software generally that the arrows cannot be changed while a simulation runs or is stopped; the arrows can be changed only prior to a simulation. That is, the user has to click the reset button, which puts the entire simulation back to its origin, at which point the parameters velocity and force can be changed. Surprisingly, perhaps, Ryan then makes a suggestion: "just see what'll happen when it run" (turn 10). That is, although the computer had produced a "quack," indicating trouble, Ryan suggests going on although there was a warning message indicating that parameters could not be changed and although the object seemingly was going to hit the wall. When the simulation runs on, the object does hit the wall, bouncing off; and, again surprisingly, it appears to be bouncing off something on the left-hand side, too, though the world normally is unbounded at the edges defined by the monitor, which are merely horizons rather than boundaries.

Here, then, there is a moment of trouble. Glen has expressed wanting to change the parameters after the software stopped the simulation—the velocity was too high. But students acted incompatibly with respect to the software command and the decisions the designers had implemented. The quack indicates trouble, but Ryan asks Glen to continue the simulation and the latter does so without having changed the parameters.

This first level analysis provides us with a lot of useful information. It allows us to understand that the interface provides students with a context that facilitates their mutual orientation to each other and the joint problem. Through such mutual orientation to objects and talk, students coordinate their utterances and gestures with the microworld objects and events, allowing them to mark and make sense and to evolve common observation sentences of, and explanations for, the microworld phenomena. In this way, we can understand the present data as suggesting that the co-presence of physical and conceptual aspects on the interface also interferes with student interactions in two important ways. First, Interactive Physics frequently constituted a tool that was *unready-to-hand*. In contrast to a transparent tool that can be used without cognitive effort (which an individual does not attend to at all), a tool that is unready-to-hand draws the user's attention to itself, and thus away from the real problem to be solved. The notion "readiness-to-hand" draws attention to the fact that what is salient is different in the two ways of tool use—i.e., the tool does not afford the same kinds of activities that it affords to the teacher and other "experts." We learn from the close reading that although considered "user friendly," students find the interface to be complex requiring considerable time to learn. Second, we can learn from this close reading that when there

CHAPTER 6

were more than two students, the physical arrangement of people and computer organizes interactions in such a way that it curtails the mutual orientation of the students. (As in most schools, the computers in this study were on tables and against a wall to minimize accidents involving the various forms of wiring.)

The interface can be considered as a tool for exploring the microworld, and by means of this activity, to learn physics. However, along with similar studies of human-computer transaction, this study brought out that whereas tools constrain actions in some ways, they can also be interpreted in multiple ways and therefore do not embed unambiguous meanings. What and how entities are salient therefore is an empirical matter. But how can we get at the source of the trouble that is evident between turns 08 and 14? This requires detailed analysis, which can be aided by using a particular representational form that pulls out and exposes who makes available what to whom. That is, if we pull out what students make available to the computer and vice versa and what the students and computer have available to themselves but not for the other, we may be able to make some progress in better understanding the events. Such a representation was suggested to me while reading a book that analyzed human-computer interactions (Suchman, 1987). I use a tabular format to show the different levels involved in this analysis (Figure 6.6).

> **Don't Try Getting into People's Headspaces** In the analysis of conversations, the sounds (words), gestures, and body positions is all you have. You do not know what—if anything—is "behind" the publicly available. Participants may utter the same sentences and check the same boxes, for quite different reasons. It is therefore more parsimonious to analyze and theorize aspects of a situation that are available to any observer rather than attempting to get into people's headspaces. *What are the methods by means of which people identify and solve trouble?*

This tabular format is similar to the one I had used to analyze and represent the conversations over and about the concept maps (chapter 1). It represents both the temporal unfolding of the actions and transactions. It also separates out who does what and who/what has available which information. In the first column, I represented students' utterances, which they made available to each other, but which were not available to the software. In the second column, I entered the actions that students actually made available to the software, whereas in the third column I entered what the software made available to the students via the displays on the monitor, that is, the simulation and eventual feedback when there was trouble of some kind. In the fourth column, I entered design decisions that underlie the output but which were not available to the students and which required understanding the physics of motion, which students were in the process of learning.

This representation allows us to understand that students act upon what the computer makes available to them, in the way *they* rather than teachers or programmers perceived these structures, and not the underlying design decisions. In the same way, students acted and reacted upon what *they* made available to each other, not any intentions and private thoughts they might have had—if any. But in real-time behavior, there usually is no time out for thinking about what one is thinking and going to say. We simply talk and, in talking, exhibit thinking; in thinking aloud, we

People Action		Software Action	
Conversation	Also available to Software	Available to people and software	Internal
01 E: * yea, leave it there	((G sets velocity arrow))		((sets parameters consistent with position and length of arrows))
02 G: okay, let us not go it too fast			
03 ()			
04 R: no that's direction ((G has cursor on "run button")) okay, go	((hits run button))	((moving object))	((executes movement according to parameters))
05 * o::h, my			((velocity too large; stops motion; quack noise and panel with info to users))
06 E: a little higher			
07		((quack from software))	
08 G: quack			
09		((you must reset its initial conditions before making changes))	
10 R: * you must reset you can't change it while you are in there			
11	((G clicks on the "OK" button))		
12 R: just see what'll happen () when it () run		((running simulation))	((continues same simulation))
13 R: * () oh::			
14 G: OOHH			
15 R: it comes back		((object bounces back from left))	
16 G: oh, baby			

Figure 6.6. Human transaction participants make available to each other and the software different structures (information); the software also makes available certain structures but others are hidden from users unavoidably giving rise to problems in use and understanding.

provide all there is, there is no further thinking behind talking. The talk students produced, therefore, is to be understood and analyzed as thinking aloud or *participative thinking*.

The computer, on the other hand, did not make available the thinking underlying the messages, which nevertheless were produced deliberately because something was problematic. For example, in the present case, Glen attempted to modify the velocity although he had not reset the simulation. (Note that I use "attempted" as a descriptive term, for one can see Glen attempt to make modification; the term would not be legitimate if it was used in an explanatory mode, expressing something that cannot be seen.) Although the software had stopped the simulation, Ryan proposed going on and seeing what would happen when they did. There therefore was trouble and the students did not achieve resolving it in this instance. This form of analysis and the way I choose to represent the transcript allows me to come to grips with the source of the trouble, which was a product of the human-human and human-computer transactions.

CHAPTER 6

In such analyses, I am interested in finding out *how people deal with and resolve trouble*. I am interested in this not only because of the trouble qua trouble but because what people do in moments of trouble allows me to better understand what makes their everyday actions so efficient that these actions normally hide the work that underlies this efficiency. That is, trouble allows me to get at the "methods" "people" use, methods that normally are hidden from view and which need to be made visible so that we can see and understand them. There is an entire subdiscipline in sociology interested in such questions and doing research. The subdiscipline is called ethnomethodology precisely because it attempts to get at the *methods* ordinary people (*ethno-*) use to make everyday life—showing us that there is more to even the apparent simplest things we do, like queuing, beginning and ending meetings, and tutoring (e.g., Garfinkel, 2002). The books on the subject are not easy reads, but the following section should provide you with an intelligible introduction about how one can get into doing analyses that are consistent with the ethnomethodological program and its allied field of conversation analysis. To show how teacher-researchers can analyze videotapes to figure out the work involved in their classrooms (the work of teaching, the work of collaboration, the work of talking, the work of teaching, the work of tutoring), I produce in the following section another exemplary analysis together with a commentary on how I do it. I feature an episode from the same tapes from the Interactive Physics project where I, the teacher, approached the group and where, while engaging in a conversation about what they had done and found out, I got the sense that they did not understand something that was essential to the task that I had ask them to complete.

DOING TUTORING

To do the kinds of analyses exemplified in this section, I needed to prepare a transcript suitable for representing the moment-to-moment unfolding of events. To begin with, because "timing is everything," as the popular diction suggests, I needed to include in the transcript all the pauses within and between speaking turns and overlaps. Years ago, I measured the pauses using a stopwatch, and, after repeatedly playing the instant and measuring the pause, calculated an average. In this way, I found that I could get to ±0.1 seconds accuracy. I also listened repeatedly to overlapping speech in the attempt to distinguish, as accurately as possible, those parts of the utterances that were spoken simultaneously. But this was very time consuming and laborious and not as reliable as the kinds of transcriptions that I can produce today. Nowadays I digitize my video—even the ones used here, originally shot in VHS mode—and then export episodes from iMovie both into QuickTime (video) and aif (sound) formats. I then import the aif sound file into PRAAT (www.praat.org), a freely available software package for different platforms, including Macintosh, PC, and UNIX. Its interface provides me, among other options, with a display of the sound wave (Figure 6.7, top [black when in color]), speech intensity (continuous line [green when in color]), and pitch (interrupted line [blue when in color]). The PRAAT software allows me to highlight certain segments of the display, which, here, is the pause between the utterance "ah:m" and the word

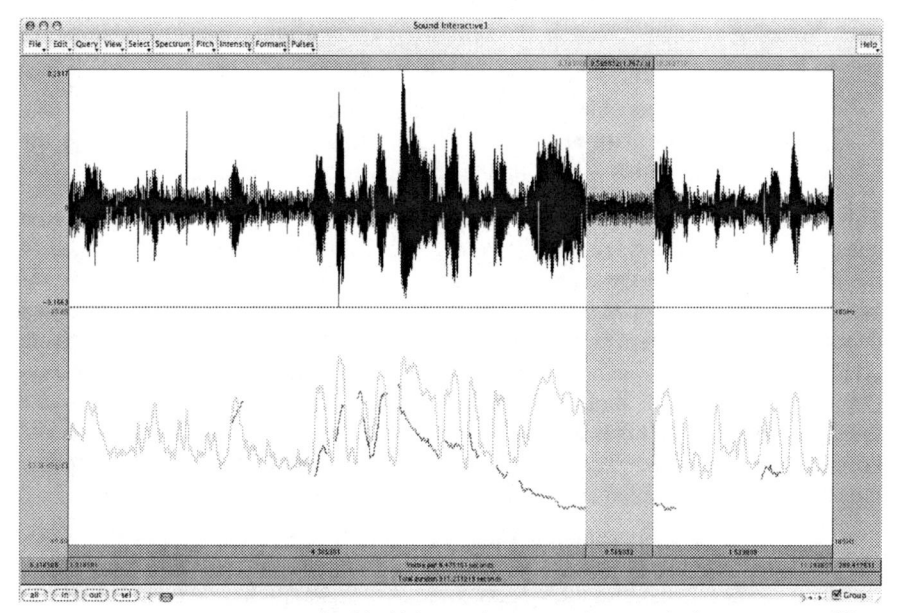

Figure 6.7. PRAAT display of turn 09 in the transcript; the text of turn 09 has been added in Photoshop for illustrative purposes.

"velocity" (turn 09); on the bottom of the display, I find the length of the highlighted area to be 0.565 seconds.

To produce the transcript on page 250–251, I used this software to listen to the soundtrack again to make sure all the words have been accurately transcribed. I also used the window technique from the left side to find precisely the spot where only one speaker speaks just prior to the second individual beginning his or her turn; similarly, by approaching the overlap from the right side, I find the moment where the second speaker speaks alone, that is, where the overlap has ended. It is in this way that I can find the overlap between two utterances with an accuracy that is closer than one phoneme, that is, for example, I can hear that an overlap begins or ends within the extended "ee" while a person pronounces "beach." To be able to mark the overlap in the transcript, I follow the convention to use an equal spacing (nonproportional, monospaced, or non-kerned) font, such as Courier, so that the square brackets that indicate the overlap will automatically line up because the computer keeps the spaces per letter constant. Also, I do not use the justify option in the word processor but for these transcripts leave the text in the left alignment mode (otherwise the program would pull the spaces until the text exactly fills the line from the left to the right edge). So let us take a look at one classroom episode, in which the teacher (I) approached a group of students involved in a task with Interactive Physics and then asked and answered a number of questions about what was happening there and how the participants made what might be glossed by the

CHAPTER 6

term "tutoring session." That is, I exemplify how we might get at the work involved in concretely realizing (i.e., *doing*) tutoring.

> As I was approaching, I uttered "well, what did you find out?" (turn 01). The question mark at the end of the utterance denotes the fact that the pitch of my voice was rising toward the end.

This piece of analytic text may lead us quickly to the conclusion that I had asked a question. But, when we take the conversation as the unit of analysis, we need to have confirmation that the utterance indeed is a question; and this can only be established when we look at a turn pair. Whether an utterance in fact is a question depends on the next turn. If a student were to utter, "eff off," evidently something other than a question was happening. To make the reason for such an argumentation more salient, think about all those situations when, for example, you *intended* to make a joke but the other person felt insulted, indicating to you that she is (feels) hurt. That is, in this case, the conversation would proceed on the basis that you had hurt the other person rather than made a joke.

> Glen then utters something that we might hear as complying with the implied request to provide an answer and talk about what they have found out; in uttering, he has a hard time pronouncing what may have been intended to be the word "arrow" saying instead "arreo" twice. (Watch how in this situation, the transcript does not follow standard English use of apostrophes [e.g., "ive" instead of "I've"], capitalization, and so on. The purpose is to render what can be heard, which already is a translation of sound patterns [there are no words in the air!].)

```
01   T:   ((Approaches students from neighboring classroom))
          well, what did you find out?
02   G:   the longer the arreo (0.26) the longer the arreo
          [an ive an      ] (("Grabs" the tip of the velocity
          vector, turns it from 3 to 9 o'clock.))
03   E:   [the longer the] BI:G arrow: is,
04   T:   the b[ig?]
05   E:        [the] higher the velo[city (.)]
06   G:                              [yea that]
07   E:   like this (0.30) its steepe:r.
08        (0.43)
09   T:   'whi 'which 'which on::e do you
          think shows you: ah:m (0.56)
          velocity. (.) you, you, you
          were talk[ing]
10   R:            [the] big arrow
11   E:   the bi[g arrow].
12   G:         [the (.)] big arrow.
13        (0.42)
14   T:   shows velocity? ((Glen moves «velocity» into new po-
          sition.))
15        (0.89)
```

250

ANALYZING CONVERSATIONS, LEVELS OF ANALYSIS

```
16   G:   <<p>or>
17        (0.15)
18   R:   OH, NO. cause it ^carries it to redirection.
19        (0.33)
20   T:   so so wh 'wHAT wh 'what does it <<dim>to carry some-
          thing>.
21        (1.02)
22   R:   well like if you have the
          (0.49) little arrow: (.) in
          on:e direction <<p>and the big
          arrow in another direction> the
          little arrow (0.40) or jus like
          the whole (0.61) trajectory
          will be able to go— will go the
          way that the big arrow is pointed <<pp>eventually>.
```

One of the first things you may note reading through this transcript is that everyday talk is not as rational as it appears when researchers write about concepts and ideas. When you look at everyday conversations, including those in classrooms, you realize that these are full of mumbles, stumbles, unfinished words and utterances, overlaps, and pauses. To go from such talk to "ideas" and "concepts," a lot of reduction and presuppositions are necessary. What evidence is there that the participants have finished ideas and use language to make them available to others? I would suggest there is very little evidence. To the contrary, there is a lot of evidence that ideas, if there are any, are in the process of unfolding and forming. The many restarts of "which" and "you" until I get my "question" out in turn 09 are indications that I am in the process of setting up rather than implementing a lesson. It is not quite clear what I have to do and there is no time out for doing reflecting-on-action.

But there are some consistent patterns that we can be identified in this transcript. One of these can be found in the turn pairs 01–02ff ("ff" is for "and following"), 04–05ff, 14–15ff, and 20–21ff. In each case, I (teacher) have a first turn in which interrogatives ("what," "which") are used or in which there is a rising pitch (inflection) toward the end of the utterance, which in our Anglo-Saxon culture therefore is heard as a question. In the subsequent turns, the "students" make statements that bear on what the prior interrogative or questioning utterance was about. That is, we find in all of these question-answer pairs or sequences. That is, in this situation, one person (I, the teacher) is using interrogatives and utterances with rising inflections toward the end, and the other three individuals produce statements that pertain to the same issue but with falling inflection at the end, heard in our culture as statements. In part, the work involved in *doing tutoring* is producing question-answer sequences. That is, my utterances are reified as questions and students' utterances as answers in the particular way that we contributed to *make* this situation what it was. This way of describing the situation allows, even at our descriptive level, for other possibilities in which the event could have developed. Already at the descriptive level, therefore, events no longer are *determined* by the institutional positions that the different participants in the situation occupy but the events

251

inherently come to be described and understood as the product of a collaborative effort to which all participants contribute, even those participants who do not say a single word. The situation is in part what it is *because* these individuals did not speak, and it would likely have been different if they had spoken. This way of analyzing therefore allows me to produce non-deterministic understandings of social life, which are closer to our everyday experience of the unpredictability of events in which we participate.

Now in the literature on teacher-student transactions, we can find research that points out a certain pattern in which teachers initiate, students respond, and teachers evaluate—leading to the term I-R-E for this type of sequence (e.g., Poole, 1994). We may ask if the teacher and students in this segment *achieve* I-R-E sequences or whether this tutoring session produces another transactional pattern. Here is how the analysis unfolds that provides an answer to the question. In turn 03, Elizabeth contributes to the conversation following my question about what they have found out by saying, "The longer the BI:G arrow: is." The comma at the end of turn 03 shows that her inflection was slightly going up, rather than down in the way it would be expected if it were the end of a statement. In turn 05, Elizabeth seemingly continues by making a statement about velocity, which may be heard as a restatement of the "longer the . . . arrow." However, the teacher (I) already has begun to take a turn, "the big?" (turn 04), where the rising inflection (pitch) toward the end marks the utterance as to the problematic nature of the word "big." Because this utterance raises the question about a word a student had said, it could also imply an unstated evaluation. That is, my contribution raised the possibility that there was something incorrect about what Elizabeth had been saying. However, her next turn could not yet have been in response to the teacher question, as there had not been sufficient time to reflect and she continued even while I was producing the sounds heard as the word "big."

In my next turn (turn 09), I produced the interrogative "which" with rising inflection (see the transcription sign prior to the word) so that the utterance could have been heard as a question although the inflection strongly fell toward the end (see also Figure 6.7). At issue in the turn is the question about which object showed us "velocity." All three responded, in their turns, indicating the "big arrow" as the one showing velocity. Now take a look at the video offprint provided in the transcript. There are two arrows while I was asking about the arrow that shows velocity. In this situation, the skinny arrow also is the shorter one, whereas the outline arrow also was the longer one. At this moment, the teacher (I) did not know what they had talked about prior to his (my) arrival. But when I analyzed those instances on the tape when the teacher (I) was not present, it became clear to me that the students used the adjective "big" alternatively for the outline arrow (which is "fatter") and for that arrow that was longer; but the students apparently were not aware that by using the same adjective they were referring to different objects. "The big arrow" could at once be the one denoting force and the one denoting velocity. Here, the situation was easier, as the force arrow was both "fatter" and longer than the velocity arrow so that my question does not come as a surprise. "Shows velocity?" (turn 14). Once again we find a situation where the teacher raised a question about a particular item, which also could be heard as questioning it, and therefore as implying an evaluation. As the analysis of the entire database shows, students were not aware of their different uses of the signifiers "big arrow" and "small arrow" so that it is not surprising that they were not even aware of misunderstanding each other.

In response, with a little delay, Ryan exclaims "OH NO," and then continues, "cause it carries it to redirection. Thus, my rising inflection in the utterance "shows velocity" was followed by an indication of surprise and a restatement on the part of Ryan. That is, here we do not have a question–answer sequence. Rather, there is an event that we might mark as a problematization-realization sequence. Something is problematized and has a realization as its effect. At this moment, Ryan made available to all those present that he just has realized something by means of the interjections OH and NO, uttered, as indicated in the capitalization, much louder than his previous and subsequent talk. It was Ryan's utterance that allowed us to understand the effect of the teacher's performance ("shows velocity?"). To understand this way of talking and writing about conversation, I provide a little background from speech act theory (Austin, 1962).

In *speech act theory*, on which the presently articulated form of conversation analysis builds, a turn pair is taken as the fundamental *unit of analysis*. That is, if the turn pair is the unit of analysis, we cannot analyze individual turns at talk on their own, as if these existed independently of all the other turns, but we always are forced to look at pairs of turns. This is so because in speech act theory, three components are ascribed to the act of speaking: the performance (locution), the intent (illocution), and the effect (perlocution). Whereas the first two parts would be consistent with traditional psychological treatment of verbal data, whereby speakers implement in their speech acts specific intents, the third part explodes the psychological analysis and forces us to do, if not a sociological analysis (as in ethnomethodology), at least one in which the conversation is taken to be an irreducible collective phenomenon. When people talk, they do not give off singular signs, but they talk with a language and about things that are inherently intelligible: it would make no sense to attempt engaging in a conversation if we could not assume (in implicit or explicit ways) that others understand what we are communicating and how we are communicating it. The effect of a communicative performance on the conversation is available only in the turn pair, for whether I have been joking, insulting, or hurting is available in and through the next performance. To return to the example of the utterance heard by the recipient as hurting her. The immediately following turns are intelligible only when we think of the effect the preceding turn has had, and this effect was available only in the utterance by the person who felt hurt.

But the issue is not quite so simple, because as we look at the transcribed episode, we see that a question–answer sequence may not be completed in two adjacent turns. Rather, the answer may be spread over a number of (student) turns. Or it might turn out that the answer is not the right one or an insufficient one so that a teacher might engage students in a repair sequence—finding out what a particular expression such as "the big arrow" denotes or assisting them in seeing an arrow in

CHAPTER 6

a different way "OH NO. it carries it to redirection." The expression *doing tutoring* precisely denotes and means that the participants collaborate in getting a situation (e.g., tutoring) realized *as* a specific situation (e.g., tutoring) rather than as something else (e.g., lecturing, exploring). Clearly, if one of the three students had responded by saying "eff off," the event would not have deserved the label "tutoring session." Some other event would have occurred, which analysts might explanatorily describe as "disruption of the lesson" or as "challenge to the teacher authority." Returning to the issue of tutoring, the teacher alone cannot bring about this event; students have to be complicit in realizing the transaction *as* tutoring, for otherwise some very different transactional form is realized. That is, part of the work done by talking is the bringing about of the situation itself as precisely that what it is in its recognizable form.

ANALYZING GESTURES

The two episodes I have featured so far both exhibit the use of indexical terms such as "this," "that," and even "the big one"; in all of these situations, the participants point us to some entity in their material setting that is available to all of them (which also can be words that are realized by means of sound or as text). But words are not the only way in which we can "point to" objects in our environment; hand gestures, head nods, and body orientations are other means conversationalists use to orient others to particular objects and phenomena. But, hand gestures do not only point but also may produce performances that are taken to stand for something that they resemble. Because such gestures have some likeness with the things and processes that they are used to make salient in the conversation, they are denoted by the term *iconic* gesture. Both pointing (deictic) and iconic gestures are prevalent in everyday conversation, so that to really understand classroom transactions, we need to study gestural productions in the same way we study and analyze sound productions (i.e., words).

When I report the analyses that involve gestures, I generally produce drawings that leave out what in all likelihood are irrelevant aspects of the situation and only feature those that are important in (analysis as process) and to (analysis as product) the analysis. Let us take a brief look at the end of the previous episode, where Ryan and the teacher enacted a question–response sequence. The teacher's (my) partially mangled, grammatically incomplete utterance appears to be asking for something ("what") intended "to carry something." Ryan produced a turn in which he talked about the little arrow and the big arrow being in different direction—this part was at very low speech volume as the transcription convention (<<p> . . .>) suggests—and about the fact that the trajectory ended up being in the direction of the big arrow. The question is whether there is any additional information that would have allowed the participants—and thereby analysts and readers—to figure out which one the little or big arrow is?

20 T: so so wh 'wHAT wh 'what does it <<dim>to carry something>.

```
21          (1.02)
22    R:    well like if you have the
            (0.49) little arrow: (.) in
            on:e direction <<p>and the big
            arrow in another direction> the
            little arrow (0.40) or jus like
            the whole (0.61) trajectory
            will be able to go— will go the
            way that the big arrow is pointed <<pp>eventually>.
```

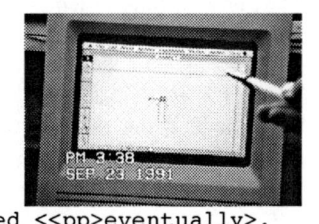

I suggest that such additional information is available in the gesture visible on the videotape. This gesture is important in the process of analyzing the excerpt and I decide, because I want to support my argument graphically, to render key moments in the gesture visually (Figure 6.8). The right image has been produced from the offprint shown in the transcript above, the left image from an offprint just preceding it. The gesture unfolds from right to left while Ryan is talking about the little arrow. Three aspects are important. First, the direction of the pen in Ryan's hand is nearly parallel to the velocity vector (simple arrow); second, the hand moves from right to left, which is the direction in which the object would take off if the simulation were to be started at that instance; and third, the pencil tip approximately is in the direction of the upper part of the configuration. The pointing gesture is hard to make out because of the position in which the single camera recorded it, so we cannot be certain that Ryan actually pointed toward the velocity arrow while saying "the little arrow." But the other two pieces of evidence support such a perception, for the pen is perceptually similar to the velocity vector (i.e., they stand in an *iconic* relationship) and the movement of the hand perceptually reproduces the beginning of the object's motion. To increase the plausibility of this reading, I would, of course, seek more information to confirm or disconfirm this initial analysis. My main point here is that a drawing of the gesture (Figure 6.8) can support me in the attempt to convince readers of my analysis. You may ask

Figure 6.8. For the analysis of gestures, I generally prepare drawings—through an overlay procedure in Photoshop—that present salient features only.

CHAPTER 6

now, how to make such drawings, and perhaps, how to make such drawings without spending too much time? Here is what I do.

By going back and forth in the digitized version of the video (either in QuickTime or in iMovie), I decide which positions reveal most with respect to the point to be made in the analysis. (In fact, I know from experience that as you attempt to make such a decision, you come to better understand what is happening in this instant.) I then use the screen grab feature to capture the current frame and paste it into my drawing program (Photoshop). In the present instance (Figure 6.8), I created space for a second image and then grabbed and pasted it next to the first one. I then create a new layer, which is the one where I do my drawings. Because the screen grab produces an image of 72 pixel-per-inch (ppi) density but journals and book publishers require a minimum of 300 ppi, I change the size of the image and pixel density concurrently but leave total pixel numbers constant. For example, if I grab an image that is 600 by 400 pixels. At 72 ppi, its dimensions will be 8.333 inches by 5.555 inches. When I change the settings to 300 ppi keeping the 600 by 400 pixels constant, I end up with an image that has a size of 2.00 inches by 1.33 inches. Once I have made this conversion, I take a paintbrush of about 8 pixels thickness and then follow the outlines of those features that I want to come out. Sometimes, as here, I use the "paint bucket" to fill in some of the background or some of the important features to make the latter stand out. I then save two copies of my work: the original Photoshop format, which allows me to make changes, if the need arises, and a JPG version, which I can import into my word processor. One way of doing a series of images quickly goes like this: If the background does not change, as when you work with a stationary camera, then you can create the background in one layer of your painting program, copy it, and then paste the background image side by side as often as you need. Then you produce the gestures for each image separately on top of the existing background.

DOING PHYSICS LESSONS, DOING SCHOOLING

In the previous sections, I show how to analyze the data when teacher-researchers attempt to get at some microstructures, such as students' deployment of gestures as part of communication with other students and with the teacher; and I show how to reveal structure in the communication with computers, which allows us to understand where misunderstandings come about between computer software and human users, each having only partial information available from the other. However, the kind of data I collected in this study—as indicated in the layers of Figure 6.5, also can serve to support analyses that take a more macro-perspective on teaching and learning. This is so because talk is employed not only to get the task completed but also to make the tutoring session the very tutoring session that it is. Thus, unless students and teacher collude, a tutoring session could not emerge; and they collude to achieve larger goals and motives as well. For example, a more immediate goal for us was to produce a physics lesson in a recognizable way, that is, students and teacher in the previous episodes had to collude to produce transactions so that a visitor—such as the many that have come to observe my classrooms—would recognize is the events as a physics lesson in progress rather than "a zoo," "a music lesson" (my students were allowed to have the radio on when appropriate), or just some after-school meeting where everybody does what he or she wants.

One of the ways in which readers may want to think about the phenomenon is as follows: By repeatedly achieving question–answer sequences until the students were correctly describing and explaining the events visible on the monitor, we (they and I) produced and reproduced a typical small-group or tutoring session. The tutoring session was part of a lesson, which, because we all colluded, itself was produced and reproduced as a recognizable physics lesson. Finally, by successfully completing the lesson, we also contributed to the production and reproduction of schooling.

The directionality of "causation" is not just from bottom up, as some readers of the ethnomethodological and conversation analytic literature appear to think. In fact, in our lives, we orient to the situations in which we find ourselves. Thus, I do not just go into a classroom and let things emerge; as a teacher I prepare tasks and think about the best ways in which the curriculum could be realized. Whether this actually happens is another question, for, as I show above, students and I have to collude to bring about question–answer turns, tutoring sessions, lessons, and schooling. This is so because I am only a constitutive moment of a lesson, which is to say, I am part of it without being in the situation to *determine* (cause) the events in their specific and concrete detail. I may be in a situation where I have greater influence on the events—because institutionally in a position where I have control over grades, can get students suspended, and have other means to get students penalized and punished—but I do not have *total* or even *partial* control. How various aspects of a lesson are produced and reproduced—control, the reproduction of teacher and student roles, or question–answer sequences—is something that we teacher-researchers can study by looking at the minute-to-minute details of the unfolding transactions.

Thinking about teaching in this way comes with great advantages both to my teaching—where I am aware of the precarious nature of an envisioned successful lesson—and in research—where I look for *empirical* evidence that allows me to support claims that in the *collaborative production* of a specific lesson (which could be a good or bad one) we actually *re*produced a successful lesson. Here, I understand successful in terms of student learning not in terms of noise, teacher control, or student obedience.

Let us return to the opening of the tutoring session. Here, the collusion is available in the way we mutually contributed to reproduce a question–answer sequence. In performing an utterance that can be heard as asking students what they have found out (turn 01), I am setting them up to achieve with me the desired sequence. By responding in the way they do, Glen (turn 02) and Elizabeth (turn 03) contribute to completing the question–answer sequence. The subsequent turns, in which I repeatedly query students about what they are saying, show that the answers initially provided apparently were not sufficient.

CHAPTER 6

```
01   T:   ((Approaches students from neighboring classroom))
          well, what did you find out?
02   G:   the longer the arreo (0.26) the longer the arreo
          [an ive an    ] (("Grabs" the tip of the velocity
          vector, turns it from 3 to 9 o'clock.))
03   E:   [the longer the] BI:G arrow: is,
```

At the end of the previous paragraph, readers may note that I do not write that the answers *were* insufficient to me. This, in fact, is not available to me, the analyst, to the students, or to other analysts watching the videotapes. Rather, in my analysis I show the function of subsequent turns, which, because it is an elaboration and differentiation of what has been said previously, contributes to leading students to a successful answer. That is, the phenomenon of a successful question–answer sequence, which was part of making the lesson as successful as it was, took place over a period of time and across several turns at talk.

The episode also shows how we reproduced the division of labor in a classroom: teachers ask questions and students respond. It could be otherwise, and there are student questions in regular classrooms. We teacher-researchers need to ask ourselves, however, what the structures of the resulting question–answer sequences are; and this we can find only through empirical analysis. For example, in some classes, we find frequent and repeated questions of the type "Am I right so far?" or "Is this what you want me to do?" and the teachers respond by saying, "Yes you are on the right track" or "No, you have to. . . ." In other classrooms, such as my own, students might ask "How and where can I get the liquid nitrogen I need for the experiment on superconductivity I designed?" and I might answer, "There is the telephone" or "Look up the term cryogenics in the yellow pages and call them up." Very different forms of lessons are realized in these examples. That is, the study of microlevel transactions allows us to get at the production and reproduction of *types* of lessons and therefore, at the production and reproduction of particular approaches to schooling (others might be more typical of those used in Waldorf, Yeshiva, Quranic, or Montessori schools).

For the purposes of analysis, therefore, I suggest not using concepts such as "power," "intelligence," or "good/bad student" to explain what is happening in the unfolding conversations such as the one that I provide here. Rather, it is a better and less presupposing approach to study *what people actually do* in conversations and with words, gestures, prosody, and so on. If you can show how power relations are produced and reproduced, then you actually know more about the processes by means of which differential institutional positions are used as resources to establish this type of relation. The most general take on this approach is to accept as evidence only what the interaction participants make available to one another. What is available to be used in communicative exchanges is then understood as *transactional resource*, deployed consciously, nonconsciously (e.g., pitch, speech volume, gesticulations), and unconsciously.

WHAT I LEARNED

During this school year, I had collected so many data source materials—second year of concept mapping (chapters 1 and 2), the study with Michael Bowen (chapter 4), the second year of the epistemology study (chapter 5), and the present materials concerning the learning with computers—that I did not get to the analysis until the month of June of the following year. At that time, I wrote a long paper in which I investigated a series of phenomena. When I was done, I asked Jeremy Roschelle to provide me with feedback. He did. The most salient advice was to break the paper into three parts, separately reporting the different aspects. As in other situation, because of delays in the review process and the differences in publication queue lengths with different journals, the publication order differed from the order in which I had completed the papers. The phenomena I investigated in the different articles occurred at different levels, as prefigured in my conception of the analysis (Table 6.2): extended time scale, macrostructure, unfolding activity, perceptual ontology, and physical setting.

The first article, "The co-evolution of situated language and physics knowing" (Roth, 1996a) focused on the evolutionary changes in students' language over and about animated objects and associated vector diagrams in a computer-based Newtonian microworld. I used the concepts of *emergence*, *convergence*, and *interpretive flexibility* as analytical notions to describe and explain changes in the students' discourse. In my analysis, I documented how new ways of talking emerged and illustrated how convergence of meaning within student groups and towards scientific meanings arose from the affordances provided by the interpretive flexibility of objects and events in the microworld, the conversations with the teacher (me), and the microworld as backdrop to student talk. I could show how in the students' learning processes the computer microworlds did not function as cultural tools that embedded unique meanings to be recoverable by students on their own. (This realization therefore was similar to the one I made about nature as open to interpretation so that students could not extract from it unequivocal structures through their own investigations.) Rather, these microworlds achieved their meaning in part through the teacher's situated practices.

With this article, I also learned another lesson about submitting papers for publication: Never take it for granted that an article is going to be published until you have a definite confirmation. I had submitted the article for publication in a special issue of a well-known journal of the learning sciences. The feedback was positive and I was asked to make minor revisions, which I did prior to resubmitting. I was sure that the article was or would be accepted because of the positive nature of the feedback and the hardly significant nature of the changes I had been asked to make. That is, I was sure that my article would be published as part of the special issue on learning with computers until one day I received notice from the special editor that my paper would not be included. Of course, I felt that my paper had been "un-accepted" so that buddies of the editor could get their (latte submitted?) paper published. I submitted the paper to the *Journal of Science Education and Technology*, where, following the normal review process, it was accepted *as is*. So

CHAPTER 6

Table 6.2. Depending on their zooming levels, teacher-researchers can learn about very different types of phenomena.

	Level	Description of Importance of Level
1.	Extended Time Scale	By focusing on the development over longer time scales, I showed how students develop a common set of signifiers within and across groups. That is, this analysis shows aspects of the individual and collective trajectories.
2.	Macro-structure	By focusing on physical arrangement, social configurations, and the nature of focal artifacts I showed how these interact to give rise to different participation and discourse patterns, and therefore to what we understand as macrostructure in cognitive activity.
3.	Unfolding Activity	By focusing on the unfolding activity, I showed how students co-constructed descriptions in real time and subject to the history and contingencies of the activity.
4.	Perceptual Ontology	By focusing on the perceptual ontologies of students and teacher, I showed (a) how the "same" screen events were perceived differently by students and teacher and (b) how the teacher's (my) interactions with students constrained their perceptions of the on-screen events.
5.	Physical Setting	By focusing on different parts of the physical setting, I showed how gestures interacted with the visual display, and how they may have foreboded understandings that verbal discourse revealed only much later. (Here, knowing is understood as distributed across body and setting.)

the second important lesson I learned was this: don't (ever) give up until you have published the work in some relevant journal.

My second paper allowed me to learn about teacher–student transactions. In "Affordances of computers in teacher-student interactions: The case of Interactive Physics" (Roth, 1995) I focused on the possibilities that the microworld offered to a teacher who engages his students in conversations about representations of phenomenal objects and conceptual entities that make the world. In the study, I showed how I, the teacher, used the context of Interactive Physics to identify students' ways of seeing and talking physics. The article showed how I then implemented a series of strategies to make forces "visible" to students, which they had not seen while working on their own. The data I provided illustrated that students' learning—which I conceptualized and articulated as *knowledgeably talking about relevant phenomena*—was not just in that computer context but that they learned about motion and transferred this learning to other settings. The conclusion focused on Interactive Physics as a tool that did not embed meaning as such but took on meaning as part of the specific (scientific) practices in the context of which it was used.

I did the third paper, "Affordances and constraints of computers in science education," (Roth, Woszczyna, & Smith, 1996), with two full-time Master's level students in educational and counseling psychology interested in gaining research experience and earning some money as research assistants. In this article, we squarely addressed the issue that had been a central concern of mine, namely the fact that throughout the 1970s and 80s, computers in science teaching were seen as a panacea for some of the many problems plaguing education. We argued that whereas considerable research had been done to determine cognitive achievements of students who interact with computers during their science learning, more basic questions had not yet been addressed. In that study, we therefore investigated how computers and Interactive Physics had contributed to student–student transactions and to student learning in my physics course. The interpretations we reported focused on the microworld as a *tool* that supported but also limited and delimited students' sense-making activities. We showed, first, that the computer-microworld had contributed in significant ways to the maintenance and coordination of students' physics talk. Second, we had learned that the computer environment (a) sometimes was *unready-to-hand* so that students spent more time learning the software rather than physics and (b) constrained and limited the transactions within groups. We concluded that whereas computer environments have some potential as learning tools, they also limited and delimited the transactions in significant ways rendering computers and software less than ideal for occasional—as compared to persistent—everyday classroom use.

In other articles I have used excerpts from these videotapes in a variety of studies concerning the function of gestures in computer-mediated conversations or in studies concerning the embodied nature of knowing. For example, I was able to show that students such as Glen correctly depicted the relations between velocity and force long before they could actually describe and explain in words. He used, for instance, the everyday word "push" in concert with the hand standing for the force arrow to say how this arrow was pushing the object and thereby changing the velocity. But he did not, in this explanation, use the words *velocity* and *force*—especially not in the way a scientist would use them.

Across the studies I published, I had learned much more than the individual and separate contributions to the scholarly literature. A few years later, invited to present a paper as part of a symposium on classroom research, I reflected on how the different things I learned connected up, and what the common theme was. In my paper "Situating cognition" (Roth, 2001), subsequently published as part of a special issue of *The Journal of the Learning Sciences* on research methods, I showed how researchers can, by using the metaphor of zooming and focusing, learn at quite different levels and about very different phenomena.

EPILOGUE

SO WHAT? WHAT? AND WHO FOR?

Criteria for Judging the Adequacy of Teacher-Research

In this book, I present different aspects of enacting teacher-researcher investigations in the context of the work that I have done and the materials I have collected while working full time as a physics teacher who also served as a department head of science. Not having a family allowed me to stay up until the wee hours of the morning; being in my thirties allowed me to do with little sleep. But the point here is not *how much* any individual teacher-researcher does or can do; rather, the point is to do well in what we decide to do. Most importantly, what we teacher-researchers learn should be useful in some way: contributing to making our classrooms better places for learning, contributing to the research literature on learning and teaching, improving the administrative processes in our schools, and so on. Although many teacher-researchers might be content with improving classrooms and schools, I believe that teacher-researchers generally are in an ideal position to contribute in legitimate ways to the research literature as well. In fact, they are in better situations than most university-based researchers, who often do not have sufficient time to collect materials over extended periods of time, to assemble good data source materials. For example, few researchers (usually doctoral students) collect data source materials consistently over the course of a year, which requires spending every day in the classroom of interest. Most educational research is conducted over shorter periods of time. More so, a many investigations simply use questionnaires or interviews, which do not allow researchers to get at the methods in which real students, teachers, principals, and support personnel produce and reproduce the system of schooling.

Here at the end of this handbook for perplexed practitioners, I elaborate on issues concerning the adequacy of teacher-research. What knowledge was generated? How trustworthy is the knowledge generated? Who was the knowledge generated for? Who benefited from the knowledge generated? What are the purposes the generated knowledge serves for? In response to these and similar questions, two main ways of establishing the adequacy of research and evaluation have been proposed: *trustworthiness* and *authenticity* (Guba & Lincoln, 1989). In the following, I discuss these two dimensions in the context of my own teacher-research studies featured throughout this book.

TRUSTWORTHINESS

Throughout this book I emphasize the different dimensions of credibility as procedures for establishing the trustworthiness of claims issuing from teacher-researcher investigations, especially when researchers are interested in sharing their findings with a broader audience (see chapters 1 and 2 in particular). In chapter 1 (the section "Quality and Audit" [p. 47ff]), I also underscore the importance of addressing *confirmability*, especially when I am interested in disseminating my findings and even in the context of doing a thesis, where a supervisor might ask me to take him or her through the process by means of which I got from the raw data to the final assertions. Here, I address two other concepts that denote processes intended to establish the trustworthiness of a teacher-researcher investigation: *transferability* and *dependability*.

Transferability

In experimental studies, which intend to make general claims representing large populations based on small samples, the concept of *generalizability* or *external validity* is important. This importance is immediately intelligible because of the way the research is set up: use a few participants from a target population and then make claims about all people in the target population. For example, researchers might be interested in the ways of which seventh-grade students in urban centers of Canada learn from a particular curriculum unit. The researchers then select a number of seventh-grade students from a few urban centers and test them before and after the unit and compare their achievement to an equally sized sample of seventh-grade students doing the curriculum unit in another way or not doing the unit at all. Although the researchers conducted the study with a limited sample, let us say 500 students, they want to make claims about learning if all seventh-grade in urban centers had gone through the unit. In the kind of teacher-researcher investigations I describe in this book, generalizability is not a useful concept—except for the empirical studies where Michael Bowen and I randomly distributed different tasks to the eighth-grade students in the sections (chapter 4). At best, one might ask a question about *transferability*, that is, about the extent to which what I learned studying my students is applicable to other students and classrooms in my school, my province (Ontario), my nation (Canada), or even the world beyond my immediate context (e.g., all industrialized nations).

The question now is to what extent I actually need transferability. As a teacher-researcher interested in improving the quality of teaching and learning in my classrooms, transferability is not an issue. It may become an issue if I studied one group of students, for example, my eleventh-grade physics students, and then asked the question about the extent to which what I learned also is applicable in my twelfth-grade physics courses. I personally take the position that transferability is not something that can be presupposed; rather, transferability should be an empirical issue. That is, the question whether what I learned in one classroom actually can be transferred to, and thereby informs, another classroom has to be answered in another teacher-researcher investigation. Two years after the studies in this book were completed, I came up with a method that I named *confirmatory ethnography*. Some chastised me for the method, but for me it captures what needs to be done—rather than conducting ethnographic research studies one after the other, I sug-

SO WHAT? WHAT AND WHO FOR?

gested that we need to see which of our findings and theoretical concepts are useful in another context. I felt that the variation in context constitutes a way of ascertaining the stability of my concepts and knowledge and gives me greater confidence in the usefulness of what I have learned from my teacher-researcher studies. If I had to engage in the same kind of research each time I have a new cohort, then the usefulness of teacher-research would be much more limited: the results of one study would not allow me to predict what happens in another context, for example, the next cohort of eleventh-grade physics students. Thus, whereas I do not have to be overly concerned with the transferability of theoretical concepts and empirical findings to other school contexts as a teacher-researcher, I have to be concerned with transferability at least in my own context, which may change from year to year and even may differ even within a school year (across grades, subject matter).

As a teacher-researcher aspiring to make my findings public, I have to be concerned to a greater extent about transferability. This greater concern is intelligible when we consider the question, "Why should another reader be interested in what I have found out?" Why should the European or African reader of an international journal on science education be interested in a study conducted in a Canadian private school for boys? It is evident that if the readers of my report or article cannot expect to learn something useful, that is, something that is relevant in and to their own situation, my text would be of little interest. In the limit case, if something is only of interest and relevance to me, why would or should someone else be interested reading about it? That is, in the case of writing for others I also have to take into account *their* interests, *their* situations, and the possibility that my findings and theoretical concepts are transferable to my readers' contexts.

Dependability

The dependability criterion parallels the criterion of *reliability* in conventional research. Reliability, for example, concerns the consistency with which a particular instrument measures some construct or surveys a population (see chapter 4). In the context of the teacher-researcher studies featured in this book, we might think of the survey used to find out the prevalence of certain student descriptions of their classroom learning environment (chapter 2). To what extent would I have gotten the same results had I administered the survey on a different day or during a different week? In this case, the question of reliability concerns the stability with which something is measured or surveyed over time—the researchers interested in this stability would establish test-retest reliability. Another form of establishing reliability is by means of internal consistency (see p. 150). Thus, in the context of my survey, researchers would be concerned with the extent to which the responses to those items that are deemed to belong to the same dimension are correlated.

In the context of interpretive research studies, investigators are not concerned with the traditional reliability concept—though they would have to be if they were to administer an instrument such as the *Constructivist Learning Environment Survey* that I discuss in chapters 2 and 4. Rather, they are concerned with the stability of the data over time. A threat to the stability of the data consists when you begin

265

to code or observe differently because you are tired, bored, exhausted, and so on. It therefore concerns those moments when your research method changes in unintended and unconscious ways rather than when you make an explicit and informed choice of changing the method. Thus, there is no threat to the dependability of your study if you consciously change hypotheses or coding schemes in the research process and because of unforeseen reasons.

The most important issue is not the change in your research process itself but the technique you use for recording and therefore making trackable your decisions, including the reasons for going this rather than that way. *Dependability audit* is the term used to denote the process by means of which you documented the logic of your research, decision-making processes, and other issues pertaining to research method.

There are six major categories of material that should be kept to establish an audit trail (Guba & Lincoln, 1985). These six categories include: (a) raw data source materials (field notes, artifacts, video); (b) products resulting from abstraction and analysis (summaries, quantitative information from surveys); (c) products resulting from the construction of data, synthesis (themes, definitions, concepts), and the final report (e.g., the one I submitted to the students for feedback); (d) notes concerning research process (my notes concerning procedures, design, strategies, questions); (e) records where intentions and dispositions have been captured including the kind of personal notes I have kept; and (f) information concerning the development of instruments, such as the survey I used in chapter 2. (In a several-page appendix, Guba and Lincoln [1985] provide an extended table featuring the different subcategories that they had gleaned from a dissertation completed in their institution.)

AUTHENTICITY CRITERIA

Throughout this book, I exhibit what I have done, why I have done it, and what teacher-researchers in general can do to ascertain the credibility of their studies. These criteria have been established to *parallel* those that in experimental research are used to ascertain the reliability of a study. These criteria, therefore, are at the level of method, which gives them a technicist ring that not all researchers are comfortable with. Such researchers seek to resolve their discomfort with a different set of participant-centered criteria including *fairness* and *ontological, educative, catalytic,* and *tactical authenticity*. These criteria are not equally applicable to all teacher-researcher studies because they had been developed for evaluators who come into a setting from the outside. In the following, I articulate those aspects of the authenticity criteria that are relevant to teacher-researchers.

The first authenticity criterion is *fairness*, which Guba and Lincoln use to refer to the extent to which different stakeholders have been invited to contribute to the sense-making process. When participants make different sense, these differences need to be brought to the table for discussion. The procedure I used to invite students to contribute to the study on student views of concept mapping (chapter 2) can be thought about in terms of fairness. What I ultimately reported was not just my understanding of what students had said. Rather, they had checked that what I said represented the situation in the way they could have talked about it. More so, involving the students who deviated from the norm and constructing a negative case study that was then checked and changed by one of the two students involved. Thus, I changed my report when Richard felt that what I had written made him look bad and put his views into an inappropriate light. Having him provide feedback to the written report and talking with him through the salient issues in an open interview situation allowed me to articulate *his* position in a way that *he* agreed with. The student views, as ultimately presented in the article I published, were not just figments of my imagination, but were in agreement with the ways in which students were thinking about them.

In teacher-researcher studies conceptualized according to the model of *participatory action research*, where two or more teachers are involved in evaluating aspects of schooling in their concrete situation, open negotiations may be required to achieve the goals that participants set themselves. Because my studies were concerned with better understanding events in my classroom and with the possible changes I might make to improve learning, negotiations were not required to the extent that they would be in other situations. For example, the purpose of my studies on student learning in open-inquiry environments would have gained little if students would have been involved because I was interested in what they *actually* did rather than in any hidden intentions they might have had; and what they actually did was available on the videotapes and in the products of their labor. Their intentions, however, might have been described differently with distance from the actual events.

The second criterion is *ontological authenticity*, which refers to the extent to which the participant's or participants' own understandings are improved, matured, expanded, and elaborated. Above all, for example, I wanted students to understand what the research was about and what I hoped to learn. It was an indicative event, therefore, when a group of students approached me one day in my office saying, "Doc, we think you love to learn." The students had understood what teaching and researching was about for me, and they had expressed this understanding in way that I thought to be the best compliment ever. More so, they had made this inference not based on what I was saying about myself but what they could see expressed in my actions. If the issue is evaluation, as in the case Guba and Lincoln discuss, then it is necessary for the outside researcher (evaluator) to ascertain that those who commissioned the report or who are part of the system to be evaluated do in fact learn in the evaluative process. In my own situation, students did gain both implicitly and explicitly from the research process. Thus, for example, when I saw my eleventh-grade students struggle with the process of reaching agreement during collaborative concept mapping, I told them about my observations. I then told them about the strategy I had come up with: ask (challenge) others to provide *elaborations*, *justifications*, and *explanations*. I then modeled the process in whole-class settings by playing the role of a student peer in a situation involving two or three students and a specially designed concept-mapping task. I also posted the three terms in large letters on the wall and, while making my rounds as students

EPILOGUE

were doing a mapping task, reminded them of the strategy. In this way, students and I were direct beneficiaries of the research I was conducting. More so, I explicitly told students that I learned about the problems that they were having through my analysis of the videotapes that they had experienced me taking.

The third criterion is *educative authenticity*, which denotes the extent to which individual participants in the research come to better understand and appreciate the thinking of others. As a teacher-researcher, I was not only interested in finding out about student knowing and learning processes but also in communicating what I found out. Guba and Lincoln list two techniques for ascertaining whether educative authenticity has been achieved. First, educative authenticity has been achieved when there is testimony of individual participants that they have grasped and understood what and how others think; such testimony often arises from negotiations and other forms of transactions that have come to be on record. My own conversations with students about the intentions for the research and what I was learning allowed them to better understand their own situations as learners and how it changed as part of the investigative process. It was to a great extent out of such conversations that Todd Alexander became my co-researcher and co-author (chapter 5). The second way of establishing educative authenticity exists in producing database entries that testify to the new and better understandings of research participants. First and foremost, I was researching my classroom and my changing understanding is amply recorded in the audit trail I have produced and, to a considerable extent, have provided evidence of in this book. There is ample confirmation available in my materials that students, too, have changed their understandings—as can be taken in their changing understanding of their own views on learning. Thus, for example, in the context of the study reported in chapter 5 Tom said that he had come to understand scientific knowledge as socially constructed but that he wanted to enter an engineering program and had to have high grades. He wanted to learn and know what he was supposed to know at university rather than construct knowledge—alone or with peers—that may not be consistent with the scientific canon. That is, Tom precisely understood what is at stake in learning and being accepted into a university program, and he therefore chose a particular strategy for achieving acceptance.

The fourth criterion is *catalytic authenticity*, which denotes the extent to which the research leads to and facilitates actions. Readers should immediately recognize that this has been the case throughout the studies featured in this book. As soon as I learned something, it led to changes in my classrooms: in the way I organized student groups, set up tasks, and provided resources for facilitating learning processes. Even though I ultimately came to report my research to a scholarly community, the primary beneficiaries were my school and my students. There was no gap between theory and practice; there was no outside researcher telling me/us what to do or how to change what we were doing; students, other teachers (e.g., Michael Bowen), and I acted upon our new understandings, often beginning the day after we had evolved them while watching and analyzing tapes and other data source materials.

SO WHAT? WHAT AND WHO FOR?

The fifth and final criterion is *tactical authenticity*, which denotes the degree to which the action possibilities of participants are expanded. All too often, teacher-researchers develop new understandings but are not in institutional positions to bring about the changes that they deem necessary. This was not the case in my situation, because I did implement the changes I wanted and felt to be necessary. But some teacher-researchers might find themselves in situations where others—e.g., principals or superintendents—also need to assist in bringing about change. In this case, I would recommend involving these stakeholders actively, not only in the implementation stage but also in the research. Whether a teacher-researcher project achieved tactical authenticity can be assessed in a variety of ways. First, there should be evidence in the form of testimonies, available as part of the audit trail. Second, there should be evidence of the participation of various stakeholder groups following the research, which probably requires a follow up study. Finally, participants should articulate some judgment about the research process and the extent to which their actional room to maneuver has expanded.

CODA

When I started my teacher-researcher investigations, I had no intention to pursue a university career. I was happily doing what I knew I am best at: teaching science and assisting the teachers in my department to become better at what they are doing. I therefore started my investigations without a sense that there were any stakes other than that I could only learn and benefit. My motto was: *Just do it!* Over the course of the two years that I enacted an intensive teacher-researcher agenda, I followed this motto; and it has served me well. I strongly believe that it might serve other teachers equally well. This entire book is about encouraging other teachers to enact teacher-researcher investigations and about providing some exemplary cases about what they might do and how they might do it. The most important aspect of my work clearly was the fact that I kept detailed records of what I was doing and thinking, which provided me with the means to investigate my own presuppositions and ideologies. The most important advice that I might be able to give, therefore, is to document as much as possible your own thinking and decision-making processes, because these documents allow you to learn from your learning. That is, you come to be aware of how you have changed, and, ideally, come to understand why you have changed (perhaps even without initially knowing that you have done so).

REFERENCES

Austin, J. (1962). *How to do things with words*. Cambridge, MA: Harvard University Press.
Bakhtin, M. M. (1993). *Toward a philosophy of the act*. Austin: University of Texas Press.
Bourdieu, P. (1992). The practice of reflexive sociology (The Paris workshop). In P. Bourdieu & L.J.D. Wacquant, *An invitation to reflexive sociology* (pp. 216–260). Chicago: University of Chicago Press.
Collins, A., Brown, J. S., & Newman, S. (1989). Cognitive apprenticeship: Teaching the crafts of reading, writing, and mathematics. In L. Resnick (Ed.), *Knowing, learning and instruction: Essays in honor of Robert Glaser* (pp. 453–494). Hillsdale, NJ: Lawrence Erlbaum Associates.
Corbin, J., & Strauss, A. (1990). Grounded theory research: Procedures, canons, and evaluative criteria. *Qualitative Sociology, 13*, 3–21.
Depraz, N. (2006). *Comprendre la phénoménologie. Une pratique conrète*. Paris: Armand Colin.
Derrida, J. (2005). *The gift of death* (D. Wills, Trans.). Chicago: University of Chicago Press.
Ercikan, K., & Roth, W.-M. (2006). What good is polarizing research into qualitative and quantitative? *Educational Researcher, 35*(5), 14–23.
Garfinkel, H. (2002). *Ethnomethodology's program: Working out Durkheim's aphorism*. Lanham, NY: Rowman & Littlefield.
Geertz, C. (1973). *The interpretation of cultures: Selected essays*. New York: Basic Books.
Gilbert, G. N., & Mulkay, M. (1984). *Opening Pandora's box: A sociological analysis of scientists' discourse*. Cambridge: Cambridge University Press.
Guba, E., & Lincoln, Y. (1989). *Fourth generation evaluation*. Beverly Hills, CA: Sage.
Habermas, J. (1971). *Knowledge and human interests*. Boston: Beacon.
Have, P. ten (1999). *Doing conversation analysis: A practical guide*. London: Sage.
Knorr-Cetina, K. D. (1981). *The manufacture of knowledge: An essay on the constructivist and contextual nature of science*. Oxford: Pergamon.
Latour, B. (1987). *Science in action: How to follow scientists and engineers through society*. Milton Keynes: Open University Press.
Latour, B., & Woolgar, S. (1986). *Laboratory life: The social construction of scientific facts*. Princeton, NJ: Princeton University Press.
Lave, J. (1988). *Cognition in practice: Mind, mathematics and culture in everyday life*. Cambridge: Cambridge University Press.
Lincoln, Y. S., & Guba, E. G. (1985). *Naturalistic inquiry*. Newbury Park, CA: Sage.
Lucas, K. B., & Roth, W.-M. (1996). The nature of scientific knowledge and student learning: Two longitudinal case studies. *Research in Science Education, 26*, 103–129.
McLuhan, M. (1995). *Understanding media: The extensions of man*. London: Routledge.
Novak, J. D., & Gowin, D. B. (1984). *Learning how to learn*. Cambridge: Cambridge University Press.
Ong, W. J. (1982). *Orality and literacy: The technologizing of the word*. New York: Routledge.
Poole, D. (1994). Routine testing practices and the linguistic construction of knowledge. *Cognition and Instruction, 12*, 125–150.
Potter, J., & Wetherell, M. (1987). *Discourse and social psychology: Beyond attitudes and behaviour*. London: Sage.
Ricœur, P. (2004). *Sur la traduction*. Paris: Bayard.
Roth, W.-M. (1992). Bridging the gap between school and real life: Toward an integration of science, mathematics, and technology in the context of authentic practice. *School Science and Mathematics, 92*, 307–317.

Roth, W.-M. (1993a). Metaphors and conversational analysis as tools in reflection on teaching practice: Two perspectives on teacher-student interactions in open-inquiry science. *Science Education, 77*, 351–373.

Roth, W.-M. (1993b). Problem-centered learning or the integration of mathematics and science in a constructivist laboratory: A case study. *School Science and Mathematics, 93*, 113–122.

Roth, W.-M. (1994). Experimenting in a constructivist high school physics laboratory. *Journal of Research in Science Teaching, 31*, 197–223.

Roth, W.-M. (1995). Affordances of computers in teacher-student interactions: The case of Interactive Physics™. *Journal of Research in Science Teaching, 32*, 329–347.

Roth, W.-M. (1996). The co-evolution of situated language and physics knowing. *Journal of Science Education and Technology, 5*, 171–191.

Roth, W.-M. (1996). Where is the context in contextual word problems?: Mathematical practices and products in Grade 8 students' answers to story problems. *Cognition and Instruction, 14*, 487–527.

Roth, W.-M. (1997). The interaction of learning environment and student discourse about knowing, learning, and the nature of science: Two longitudinal case studies. *International Journal of Educational Research, 27*, 311–320.

Roth, W.-M. (2000). Learning environments research, lifeworld analysis, and solidarity in practice. *Learning Environments Research, 2*, 225–247.

Roth, W.-M. (2001). Situating cognition. *The Journal of the Learning Sciences, 10*, 27–61.

Roth, W.-M. (2005). *Doing qualitative research: Praxis of method*. Rotterdam: SensePublishers.

Roth, W.-M. (in press). Fundamentalist and scientific discourse: Beyond the war metaphors and rhetoric. In L. Jones & M. Reiss (Eds.), *Teaching about scientific origins: Taking account of creationism* (pp. •••–•••). New York: Peter Lang.

Roth, W.-M., & Alexander, T. (1997). The interaction of students' scientific and religious discourses: Two case studies. *International Journal of Science Education, 19*, 125–146.

Roth, W.-M., & Bowen, G. M. (1993). An investigation of problem solving in the context of a grade 8 open-inquiry science program. *The Journal of the Learning Sciences, 3*, 165–204.

Roth, W.-M., & Bowen, G. M. (1994). Mathematization of experience in a grade 8 open-inquiry environment: An introduction to the representational practices of science. *Journal of Research in Science Teaching, 31*, 293–318.

Roth, W.-M., & Bowen, G. M. (1995). Knowing and interacting: A study of culture, practices, and resources in a grade 8 open-inquiry science classroom guided by a cognitive apprenticeship metaphor. *Cognition and Instruction, 13*, 73–128.

Roth, W.-M., & Lucas, K. B. (1997). From "truth" to "invented reality": A discourse analysis of high school physics students' talk about scientific knowledge. *Journal of Research in Science Teaching, 34*, 145–179.

Roth, W.-M., & Roychoudhury, A. (1992). The social construction of scientific concepts or the concept map as conscription device and tool for social thinking in high school science. *Science Education, 76*, 531–557.

Roth, W.-M., & Roychoudhury, A. (1993a). The concept map as a tool for the collaborative construction of knowledge: A microanalysis of high school physics students. *Journal of Research in Science Teaching, 30*, 503–534.

Roth, W.-M., & Roychoudhury, A. (1993b). The development of science process skills in authentic contexts. *Journal of Research in Science Teaching, 30*, 127–152.

Roth, W.-M., & Roychoudhury, A. (1993c). The nature of scientific knowledge, knowing, and learning: The perspectives of four students. *International Journal of Science Education, 15*, 27–44.

Roth, W.-M., & Roychoudhury, A. (1994). Physics students' epistemologies and views about knowing and learning. *Journal of Research in Science Teaching, 31*, 5–30.

Roth, W.-M., Woszczyna, C., & Smith, G. (1996). Affordances and constraints of computers in science education. *Journal of Research in Science Teaching, 33*, 995–1017.

Roychoudhury, A., & Roth, W.-M. (1996). Interactional processes in a constructivist physics lab. *International Journal of Science Education, 18*, 423–445.

REFERENCES

Schön, D. A. (1987). *Educating the reflective practitioner*. San Francisco: Jossey-Bass.
Strauss, A. L. (1987). *Qualitative analysis for social scientists*. New York: Cambridge University Press.
Suchman, L. A. (1987). *Plans and situated actions: The problem of human-machine communication*. Cambridge: Cambridge University Press.
Taylor, P. C., & Fraser, B. J. (1991, April). *CLES: An instrument for assessing constructivist learning environments*. Paper presented at the annual meeting of the National Association for Research in Science Teaching, Lake Geneva, Wisconsin.
Tobin, K. (1990). Research on science laboratory activities: In pursuit of better questions and answers to improve learning. *School Science and Mathematics, 90*, 403–418.

INDEX

A

Agency|structure, 241
Anonymity, xiii, 7, 75
Apprenticeship, 87, 88, 101, 115, 116, 133, 134, 135, 171, 179, 231
Assertion, xiii, xvi, 80, 81, 82, 85, 123, 127, 238
Audience, xi, 42, 75, 128, 216, 264
Audit trail, 112, 174, 204, 215, 266, 268, 269
Austin, J., 253

B

Bateson, G., 181, 182
Bourdieu, P., 56, 88

C

Camera, ix, 2, 3, 13, 17, 18, 20, 21, 22, 23, 78, 92, 104, 105, 106, 107, 109, 110, 132, 144, 236, 255, 256
Cause–effect, xiii, xiv, 3, 4, 191
Confidentiality, xiii, 7, 75
Confirmatory ethnography, xiii, 264
Consent: ongoing, 7
Constant comparison, 238
Contingency, 39, 88, 107, 123, 177, 205
Contradiction, xiv, xv, 66, 179, 208

D

Data sources, vii, ix, xiii, xvi, xvii, 4, 5, 8, 11, 15, 18, 20, 35, 57, 61, 65, 66, 74, 92, 93, 103, 117, 141, 143, 144, 151, 157, 158, 165, 185, 189, 202, 208, 231, 237, 241
Decision making, 35, 71, 76, 95, 123, 129, 140, 156, 191, 231, 266, 269
Dependability, xiv, 48, 264, 265, 266
Derrida, J., 213, 219
Description: thick, xiii, xv, xvi, xvii, 102, 140
Design experiments, 8, 9, 129, 191
Dialectic, 226
Disinterested peer, 50, 88, 215, 216

Doubt: radical, 57, 88, 215

E

Ecological validity, xiv, 19, 26, 167
Epistemology, xiv, xvi, 63, 149, 170, 179, 181, 182, 184, 189, 190, 192, 204, 208, 209, 215, 227, 228, 238, 259
Ethnomethodology, 239, 244, 248, 253, 257

F

Fieldwork, 137, 151, 158, 168, 172

G

Geertz, C., 102
Generalizability, xv, xvii, 127, 133, 264
Gesture, 108, 113, 238, 242, 254, 255
Grounded theory, xiii, xv, 190, 195, 198, 199, 202, 212, 213
Guba, E., 35, 47, 70, 80, 263, 266, 267, 268

H

Habermas, J., 173
Hypothesis testing, xiii, 38, 80, 103, 104, 128, 157, 158, 160, 161, 163, 164, 165, 166, 174, 205, 224

I

Ideology, xv, 87, 118, 144, 194, 233
Illocution, xvii, 253
Interaction analysis, xv
Interpretation, xvii, 31, 67, 92, 101, 102, 115, 116, 117, 129, 161, 172, 198, 200, 215, 244, 259, 279; sense-making, 135, 145, 164, 238, 261, 266
Interpretive repertoire, xiv, xv, 63, 190, 204, 205, 208, 209, 210, 216, 228
Intersubjectivity, 43
Intervention, 52, 53, 58, 96

275

DOING TEACHER-RESEARCH

Interview, xiv, xviii, 4, 7, 62, 78, 146, 147, 148, 149, 164, 165, 178, 181, 187, 188, 189, 199, 204, 207, 208, 219, 220, 221, 222, 223, 267

K

Knorr-Cetina, K., 89, 121
Knowledge, vii, viii, xiv, xvi, xvii, xviii, 1, 5, 7, 8, 10, 17, 18, 24, 25, 38, 40, 43, 45, 48, 49, 57, 60, 63, 76, 78, 79, 80, 84, 85, 88, 89, 90, 91, 96, 101, 102, 105, 107, 116, 126, 127, 131, 133, 134, 136, 141, 147, 149, 152, 154, 156, 157, 163, 164, 171, 173, 177, 178, 179, 180, 181, 182, 183, 185, 186, 188, 189, 190, 191, 192, 193, 195, 197, 198, 199, 200, 201, 202, 203, 204, 205, 206, 207, 208, 209, 211, 212, 214, 215, 219, 220, 221, 223, 224, 227, 228, 237, 239, 259, 261, 263, 265, 268, 269, 279

L

Laboratory experiment, xiii, 91, 177, 178
Latour, B., 89, 121, 128, 144
Lave, J., 89
Learning, viii, ix, 1, 2, 3, 10, 13, 17, 20, 23, 26, 28, 29, 30, 31, 34, 42, 43, 47, 48, 50, 51, 53, 55, 57, 58, 60, 61, 62, 63, 64, 65, 66, 69, 70, 71, 73, 75, 76, 77, 80, 83, 84, 89, 91, 92, 93, 95, 96, 101, 106, 107, 117, 123, 124, 125, 126, 127, 128, 129, 131, 133, 134, 135, 137, 141, 142, 143, 145, 146, 149, 150, 151, 153, 154, 156, 158, 164, 165, 170, 171, 172, 173, 174, 175, 176, 178, 179, 180, 181, 183, 185, 186, 188, 190, 191, 192, 194, 195, 196, 198, 199, 201, 202, 203, 208, 215, 225, 226, 227, 228, 231, 232, 234, 235, 236, 237, 239, 241, 244, 246, 256, 257, 259, 260, 261, 263, 264, 265, 267, 268, 269, 279
Learning environment, ix, 51, 53, 55, 73, 93, 131, 141, 143, 146, 147, 149, 151, 154, 227, 229, 272
Lifeworld, 220, 223
Lincoln, Y., 35, 47, 70, 80, 263, 266, 267, 268

M

Mediation, viii
Metaphor, 84, 85, 86, 87, 88, 104, 133, 134, 135, 137, 171, 178, 179, 183, 190, 224, 229, 231, 261

Microphone, 21, 22, 23, 142, 145, 236

N

Negative case analysis, xvi, 65, 70, 76, 79, 80, 81, 82, 83, 267

O

Observation, xv, xvii, 30, 48, 133, 239, 245
Offprint, 100, 110, 242, 244, 252, 255
Ontology, xiv, xvi, 208, 209, 228, 259

P

Perlocution, xvii, 253
Photograph, 108, 110
Photoshop, 109, 111, 113, 116, 256
Pitch, 115, 242, 248, 250, 251, 252, 258
Posttest, 153
Potter, J., 180, 203, 225
PRAAT, 248
Practice: collective, 237
Praxis, x, xvi, 61, 132, 279
Preference, 115
Progressive subjectivity, xvi, 35, 48, 119, 204, 215
Protocol: natural, 20, 235, 238
Psychology, 70, 72, 150, 157, 180, 203, 208, 209, 218, 228, 253, 260
Publication, ix, 5, 40, 107, 113, 114, 131, 212, 215, 216, 217, 218, 227, 259

Q

Questionnaire, xvii, 7, 70, 74, 75, 80, 147, 190, 193

R

Reflection on action, 60, 231
Reflection-in-action, 231
Reflexivity, xvii
Reliability, xiv, xvii, 150, 151, 153, 206, 265, 266
Repair, 87, 253
Researcher: university-based, vii, 50, 88, 106
Resources, x, 19, 23, 25, 26, 43, 53, 84, 88, 103, 104, 117, 119, 122, 123, 125, 134, 135, 140, 145, 171, 180, 182, 203, 209, 219, 220, 222, 224, 225, 227, 228, 229, 232, 258, 268
Ricœur, P., 218, 226

276

S

Sociology, 70, 150, 168, 179, 180, 203, 208, 209, 228, 239, 241, 248, 253
Speech act theory, xvii, 253
Statistics, viii, ix, xiv, xv, xvii, 3, 4, 90, 92, 94, 144, 151, 173, 279
Strauss, A., 198
Subjectivity, 48, 56, 95, 144, 216
Suchman, L., 246

T

Tobin, K., vii, ix, xi, 89, 91, 92, 93, 94, 102, 215, 279
Tracer, xvii, 24, 25, 29, 39, 41, 42
Transaction, 23, 31, 34, 49, 51, 53, 57, 69, 86, 87, 105, 115, 116, 119, 129, 134, 153, 171, 178, 215, 220, 225, 231, 232, 235, 238, 239, 240, 241, 246, 247, 252, 254, 256, 257, 258, 260, 261, 268
Transcription, xviii, 4, 5, 8, 11, 14, 22, 30, 31, 44, 65, 86, 102, 111, 116, 144, 145, 149, 157, 166, 167, 168, 241, 242, 243, 252, 254
Transferability, xv, xvii, 264, 265
Triangulation, xviii, 151
Trouble, 67, 94, 202, 235, 241, 242, 244, 245, 246, 247, 248

U

Unit of analysis, xvi, xviii, 23, 240, 241, 250, 253

V

Video recording, 21, 44, 238
Videotape, xv, 18, 19, 20, 30, 38, 54, 103, 105, 109, 111, 113, 117, 119, 123, 145, 147, 164, 167, 168, 174, 248, 255

W

Wittgenstein, L., 225

AUTHOR NOTE

Wolff-Michael Roth is Lansdowne Professor of Applied Cognitive Science at the University of Victoria, British Columbia, Canada. For most of the 1980–1992 period, he taught science, mathematics, and computer science at the middle and high school levels. At that time, he conducted many studies from a teacher-researcher perspective. From 1992 on, already working at the university, he taught science in British Columbia elementary schools at the fourth- through seventh-grade levels always associated with research on knowing and learning. More recently, he has conducted several ethnographic studies of scientific research, a variety of workplaces, and environmental activist movements. His research focuses on various aspects of scientific and mathematical cognition and communication from elementary school to professional practice, including, among others, studies of scientists, technicians, and environmentalists at their work sites. Although a trained statistician, his research questions now are framed such that they exclusively require forms of research practice that are classified as *qualitative* or *interpretive*.

After being responsible for the statistics courses during his four years at Simon Fraser University, he now teaches doctoral seminars and courses in interpretive analysis. In his courses, students learn to do research generally and the interpretation of data particularly by doing qualitative research—consistent with his belief that the competence to *talk about* a practice always follows the practical understanding of a practice in an embodied way, which is appropriate in and through the lived experience of praxis. It is by reflecting on experience that practical understanding is developed in an understanding way.

Wolff-Michael Roth publishes widely and in different disciplines, including linguistics, social studies of science, and different subfields in education (curriculum, mathematics education, science education). His recent books with SensePublishers include *Doing Qualitative Research: Praxis of Method* (2005), *Learning Science: A Singular Plural Perspective* (2006), and, with Ken Tobin, *Teaching to Learn: A View from the Classroom* (2006). He also edited *Auto/Biography and Auto/Ethnography: Praxis of Research Method* (2005) and, co-edited, with Ken Tobin, *The Culture of Science Education: A History in Person* (2007) and *Science, Learning, Identity: Sociocultural and Cultural-Historical Perspectives* (2007).

Further Reading:

Doing Educational Research: *A Handbook*
Kenneth Tobin, *The Graduate Center, CUNY, USA* and **Joe Kincheloe,** *McGill University, Montreal, Canada* (eds.)

Doing Educational Research explores a variety of important issues and methods in educational research. Contributors include some of the most important voices in educational research. In the handbook these scholars provide detailed insights into one dimension of the research process that engages both students as well as experienced researchers with key concepts and recent innovations in the domain. The editors and authors believe that there is a need for a handbook on educational research that is both practical as it introduces beginning scholars to the field and innovative as it pushes the boundaries of the conversation about educational research at this historical juncture.

In this collection the authors explore a variety of topics from methodologies such as ethnography, action research, hermeneutics, historiography, psychoanalysis, literary criticism to issues such as social theory, epistemology, and paradigms. The book addresses complex topics in an accessible and readable manner. The book will be very useful as a text in educational research at the graduate and the undergraduate level.

> September 2006, 480 pp
> paperback: ISBN:90-77874-48-8
> hardback: ISBN:90-77874-01-1
> SERIES: BOLD VISIONS IN EDUCATIONAL RESEARCH 1

Auto/Biography and Auto/Ethnography: *Praxis of Research Method*
W. -M. Roth, *University of Victoria, Canada* (ed.)

In a number of academic disciplines, auto/biography and auto/ethnography have become central means of critiquing of the ways in which research represents individuals and their cultures. The contributors to this volume explore, by means of examples, auto/biography and auto/ethnography as means for critical analysis and as tool kit for the different stakeholders in education.

The book was written to be used by upper undergraduate and graduate students taking courses in research design andd professors, who want to have a reference on design and methodology.

> July 2005, 448 pp
> paperback: ISBN:90-77874-04-6
> hardback: ISBN:90-77874-49-6
> SERIES: BOLD VISIONS IN EDUCATIONAL RESEARCH 2

Doing Qualitative Research: *Praxis of Method*
W. -M. Roth, *University of Victoria, Canada*

The author takes readers on a journey of a large number of issues in designing actual studies of knowing and learning in the classroom, exploring actual data, and putting readers face to face with problems that he actually or possibly encountered, and what he has done or possibly could have done. The reader subsequently sees the results of data collection in the different analyses provided. The book is organized around six major themes (sections), in the course of which it develops the practical problems an educational researcher might face in a large variety of settings.

The book was written to be used by upper undergraduate and graduate students taking courses in research design and professors who want to have a reference on design and methodology.

>August 2005, 508 pp
>**paperback:** ISBN:90-77874-05-4
>**hardback:** ISBN:90-77874-51-8
>SERIES: BOLD VISIONS IN EDUCATIONAL RESEARCH 3

Learning Science: *A Singular Plural Perspective*
W.-M. Roth, *University of Victoria, Canada*

How do you *intend* (to learn, know, see) something that you do not yet know? Given the theory-laden nature of perception, how do you *perceive* something in a science demonstration that requires knowing the very theory that you are to learn? In this book, the author provides answers to these and other (intractable) problems of learning in science. He uses both first-person, phenomenological methods, critically analyzing his own experiences of learning in unfamiliar situations *and* third-person, ethnographic methods, critically analyzing the learning of students involved in hands-on investigations concerning motion and static electricity.

This book, which employs the cognitive phenomenological method described in the recently published *Doing Qualitative Research: Praxis of Method* (See page 1 of this brochure), has been written for all those who are interested in learning science: undergraduate students preparing for a career in science teaching, graduate students interested in the problems of teaching and learning of science, and faculty members researching and teaching in science education.

>March 2006, 372 pp
>**paperback:** ISBN:90-77874-25-9
>**hardback:** ISBN:90-77874-26-7
>SERIES: NEW DIRECTIONS IN MATH AND SCIENCE EDUCATION 1

Teaching to Learn: *A View from the Field*
Kenneth Tobin, *The Graduate Center, CUNY, USA* and **W.-M. Roth,** *University of Victoria, Canada*

A recurrent trope in education is the gap that exists between theory, taught at the university, and praxis, what teachers do in classrooms. How might one bridge this inevitable gap if new teachers are asked to learn (to talk) about teaching rather than to teach? In response to this challenging question, the two authors of this book have developed coteaching and cogenerative dialoguing, two forms of praxis that allow very different stakeholders to teach and subsequently to reflect together about their teaching. The authors have developed these forms of praxis not by theorizing and then implementing them, but by working at the elbow of new and experienced teachers, students, supervisors, and department heads. Tobin and Roth describe the many ways coteaching and cogenerative dialogues are used to improve learning environments—dramatically improving teaching and learning across cultural borders defined by race, ethnicity, gender, and language. Teaching to Learn is written for science educators and teacher educators along the professional continuum: new and practicing teachers, graduate students, professors, researchers, curriculum developers, evaluation consultants, science supervisors, school administrators, and policy makers. Thick ethnographic descriptions and specific suggestions provide readers access to resources to get started and continue their journeys along a variety of professional trajectories.

July 2006, 282 pp
paperback: ISBN:90-77874-81-X
hardback: ISBN:90-77874-91-7
SERIES: NEW DIRECTIONS IN MATH. AND SCIENCE EDUCATION 4

For more information on these and our other titles go to
WWW.SENSEPUBLISHERS.COM